PAUL SITES

CONTROL AND CONSTRAINT
An Introduction to Sociology

MACMILLAN PUBLISHING CO., INC.

NEW YORK

COLLIER MACMILLAN PUBLISHERS

LONDON

This book is dedicated
to those sociologists who still believe
that a course in introductory sociology
should and can be a liberating experience
for their students

and

To Marvin Henricks, a teaching sociologist,
who contributed much to my own liberation

Macmillan Publishing Co., Inc.
866 Third Avenue, New York, New York 10022

Collier-Macmillan Canada, Ltd.

Library of Congress Cataloging in Publication Data

Sites, Paul, (date)
  Control and constraint.

  Includes bibliographical references and index.
  1. Sociology.   I. Title.
HM51.S585   301   74-7715
ISBN 0-02-411150-3

Printing: 1 2 3 4 5 6 7 8   Year: 5 6 7 8 9 0

P R E F A C E

It has been my experience as a teacher during the last fifteen years that the presentation in most introductory sociology texts is either eclectic—that is, a variety of theoretical frames of reference are used, with one contradicting the other—or functionalistic in point of view. The former approach is confusing to the new student of sociology; the latter fails to explain adequately the complexity of social life.

This text draws on the many ideas contained in the variety of schools of thought in contemporary sociology and weaves them into a consistent frame of reference integrated around the concepts of control and constraint. I believe this integrated approach will lessen the confusion for new students in sociology and at the same time give them a usable tool in their attempt to understand the social world and their place within it.

The frame of reference used in this text was developed in the author's *Control: The Basis of Social Order* (New York: Dunellen, 1973). I want to thank Mr. Eugene Nellen, President of the Dunellen Company, for his kind permission to use ideas contained in that work. Thanks also go to my many colleagues and students for their reviews, criticisms, and suggestions and particularly to James B. Skellenger, who prepared the Instructor's Manual. In addition, I want to express my gratitude to Kenneth J. Scott, Macmillan's sociology editor. Ken's insistence on quality and clarity, along with his willingness to take a risk with a unique theoretical frame of reference in an introductory text, places him among the very best. Finally, I want to publicly express my deep gratitude to my wife, who sacrificed companionship without complaint during the time the manuscript was in preparation.

P. S.

C O N T E N T S

INTRODUCTION

Commentators about human behavior from Aristotle onward have observed that people are social animals. They are born into a social group, derive their identities from it, live out their lives within its confines, and satisfy their needs through it. Only recently, however, have scholars systematically and deliberately examined what it means to be social animals with the tools and techniques of science. The scientific process of observation, inference, abstraction, and generalization was first used to explore the physical universe. Applied to people and their enterprises it has produced the social, or behavioral, sciences: economics, psychology, political science, anthropology, and sociology.

This book presents the leading ideas and findings of sociology within an organized and coherent framework. Several main themes dominate this framework and provide the structure for the book: the problem of social order and how it is established, maintained, and changed; the problem of individual meaning, which explores how people comprehend their own lives and relate to their environment; the problem of individual needs, which forces people to attempt control of their social and nonsocial environments through a variety of what we term *control strategies;* and the problem of *constraints,* which shapes and determines the kinds of social ordering that are possible. As yet, of course, these themes of social ordering, individual meaning, human needs, control strategies, and constraints are undeveloped and remain empty abstractions. The balance of this text is devoted to giving them body and life and to demonstrating how they enable us to organize and make sense out of a myriad of observations about people and society.

Many people incorrectly tend to take the social world for granted, as though it has some mystical life of its own. The social world is neither a mystical nor a static *entity.* It is in constant process. This process or change is not completely random. Under most conditions it is orderly and somewhat predictable, thereby making possible meaningful social interaction among people. This patterned process is the *process of social ordering..*

What are the elements that are involved in this process of social ordering? It will be shown that control strategies used by individuals and groups are the elements or basic units that structure social order and keep it dynamic over time. A *control strategy* is a behavior or activity used by individuals or groups in an attempt to exert control over other individuals or groups. If these attempts are successful, control has been achieved.

The ability to control the behavior of others derives from *power*, defined by the German sociologist Max Weber (1864–1920) as "the chance of a man or a number of men to realize their own will in common action even against the resistance of others who are participating in the action."* As Weber's definition implies, control is reciprocal. No person or group in interaction is completely powerless. People use various types of control strategies to control each other's behavior. *Because control is always reciprocal, it is this continuing reciprocity of control attempts that is the process of social ordering.* The use of control strategies has a *structuring* effect on social interaction and makes interaction roughly predictable.

The process of social ordering does not take place in a vacuum. It occurs under a variety of constraints. *Constraints* are produced by conditions not directly traceable to a specific individual or group in the immediate present (and, at times, they are not traceable at all), but they nevertheless affect the behavior of individuals and groups and thus the process of social ordering. Examples of constraints include geographic and climatic conditions; population growth, decline, and density; and the availability of natural resources. Individual and group control strategies are used within the framework set by these overarching constraints.

For example, the German sociologist Georg Simmel (1858–1918) pointed out how residents of modern cities receive continual high mental stimulation from a variety of sources, and therefore tend to take a matter-of-fact or blasé orientation in their interpersonal relations. If they took every person they met seriously, or responded to every novel situation with excitement or elation, social life would tend to break down. Thus, high population density in urban areas produces many different stimuli and places a constraint on individuals to take an impersonal attitude in their interaction with most others.

Another type of constraint occurs where natural resources are scarce. Individuals or groups act differently where different quantities of natural resources exist. Thus, oil shortages now and in the future

*H. H. Gerth and C. Wright Mills, *From Max Weber: Essays in Sociology.* (New York: Oxford University Press, 1958.), p. 180.

place a constraint on the control strategies used within nations and among nations. The "energy crisis" in the United States in the winter of 1973–1974 led to the mandatory allocation of fuels by the federal government, the reduction of speed limits, widespread pleas for curtailment of energy use, and a variety of other behaviors.

Many constraints result from control strategies that were used by groups or individuals in the past. The creation of our complex postindustrial economy can be traced historically to certain groups and individuals. In its present form our economic system places a variety of constraints on the control strategies contemporary individuals and groups can use. For example, resources that could be made abundant are at times kept scarce by those with considerable power who thus use certain control strategies to maintain their positions of power.

The use of certain control strategies by individuals or groups may also change the nature of certain constraints. Thus, a revolution can change the means of production, the use of birth control methods can change population constraints, and the use of advanced technology can change geographic and climatic constraints. The two-way relationship between constraints and control strategies must be considered to understand the complexities of the process of social ordering.

Two points need to be emphasized. First, people are not always or even typically conscious that they are attempting to control the behavior of others. The use of many control strategies becomes so habitual that individuals are not aware of their use. Only when certain control strategies fail to produce the desired results do individuals become conscious that they need to "try" another type of strategy. Some control strategies are rationally constructed and consciously used. Many others are not.

Secondly, the word *control* should not be interpreted as necessarily carrying a negative connotation. Whether or not a specific control strategy is good or bad depends on the evaluation of the strategy. Evaluations must be based on the application of values—which we define as conceptions of what is seen as desirable.

An additional question needs to be answered: Why do people find it necessary to use control strategies to attempt to control others? It will be shown in Chapter 3 that as the newly born infant is transformed into a self-conscious human being certain needs develop. These needs must be gratified. Therefore, individuals use control strategies to attempt to control social conditions so that need gratification is possible. People are motivated to participate in social life to meet their basic human needs.

In this text the process of social ordering as the result of reciprocal control strategies used by individuals and groups under a variety of constraints is explained. This is a synthesis of existing sociological theories, many of which have tended to emphasize only one factor involved in social ordering.

P A R T   I

Social Ordering and Individual Meaning: The Basic Concepts

In Chapter 1 the problems of social order and individual meaning are discussed and the use of control strategies in the process of social ordering is explicated. In Chapter 2 the major types of control strategies people use in attempting to control their social worlds are classified and explained. In Chapter 3 the process of socialization is discussed; how the new infant develops a self in interaction with others and how he learns that control is the basic dynamic of social life also are shown. In this chapter the dynamics by which the individual's needs develop also are discussed. The individual seeking to gratify his needs is motivated to participate in interaction with others. In Chapter 4 various types of groups are classified by the control strategies used to structure them. In this chapter insight is provided into the process of social ordering based on the control strategies used within and among groups.

C H A P T E R 1

Social Ordering
and Individual Meaning

THE TASK OF SCIENCE

All science is predicated on the existence of order. Science assumes that events are not haphazard but occur with enough of a *pattern* so that reasonably reliable prediction is possible. If scientists can observe a specified phenomenon over a sufficient period of time, they can make predictions about the continued existence of this pattern of events as well as about the conditions under which it might be expected to change.

Science wants to *explain* as well as predict. The scientist wants to know which factors or events are related to each other and how these relationships are maintained and how they change under specified conditions. The goal is to explain both the pattern or order in and the change or process of events.[1] Science is a quest, an exploration into the unknown, a process of discovery that makes prediction and explanation possible.[2]

THE CONCERN AND TASK OF SOCIOLOGY

Sociology, as a science, studies the patterned *process* of social ordering. One of the fundamental goals of sociology is to discover those factors and their interrelationships that produce social ordering—the patterns of human behavior that make social life predictable. The word *process* is emphasized because social life is never static. It undergoes continuous change.

3

In simpler societies with small populations and economies organized around hunting and gathering or primitive agriculture, changes are slower and less immediately apparent than in complex societies with large populations and advanced industrial economies. All societies, however, whatever their complexity, continually change, as do all social groups and social relationships within them. The variety of patterns and the continual changes of social ordering complicate the sociological task and by the same token make it more challenging.

The goal of sociologists is to isolate and explain the constraining and controlling forces and their interrelationships that produce social ordering. The beginning student in sociology should not be confused by terminology. The social ordering we are talking about is the same type of ordering experienced in everyday life. This ordering makes your activities and those of the persons with whom you interact predictable. You are able to predict with reasonable reliability how another person or persons will act in response to your behavior. Thus you know what behavior you can get by with because you can predict how others may react to your actions.

Perceptive Explanation and the Sociological Imagination

Even though you make these predictions about your own behavior and the behavior of others with a fair degree of certainty, you may not be able to *explain* the behaviors. The sociological task is to bring you to the point of perceptive explanation. C. Wright Mills (1916–1962) has aptly stated this goal as the development of "a sociological imagination." Mills says:

> The sociological imagination enables its possessor to understand the larger historical scene in terms of its meaning for the inner life and the external career of a variety of individuals. It enables him to take into account how individuals, in the welter of their daily experiences, often be-

The Patterned Process of Social Ordering

Every science studies pattern, order, and change (process). Sociology is no exception, thus, when we say that sociology explores the patterned process of social ordering, we are saying that the sociologist wishes to isolate and explain those *patterns* that produce a constantly changing social order.

come falsely conscious of their social positions. Within this welter, the framework of modern society is sought, and with that framework the psychologies of a variety of men and women are formulated. By such means the personal uneasiness of individuals is focused upon explicit troubles and the indifference of publics is transformed into involvement with public issues.[3]

An individual who is unemployed has a personal problem that affects him and his family. If ten million persons are unemployed, these personal problems become a social issue for the entire society. The sociological imagination enables us to comprehend the relationships between personal and collective experiences. Explicating the intricate network of linkages among individuals and groups in society requires the fullest exercise of the sociological imagination.

Mills not only highlights the possibilities for insight for the person who gains the sociological imagination, but he also points to a second crucial sociological area: *the problem of individual meaning.*

The Problem of Individual Meaning

Even though individuals live within the framework of society and thereby participate in its structuring, they sometimes find their lives frustrating and meaningless. The problem of meaning is addressed to how individuals "within the welter of their daily experience" make sense of their experiences.

If the experiences of individuals within the society in which they live make little or no sense to them, they can be expected to attempt solutions to change this painful situation. These attempted solutions will take many different forms, depending on existing social and psychological conditions and the alternatives available. Some individuals attempt to radically change the existing society by staging a revolution, hoping that this change will provide a new framework for personal meaning for them. Others join different groups or attempt to organize new ones within which meaning may be found. Still others may withdraw by becoming "mentally ill" and creating an "unreal" world of their own.

If such attempts at solutions fail or are unavailable, individuals may live out their lives ritualistically, not really caring for that with which they are seemingly involved.[4] The worker goes to his job but cares nothing about production goals or quality of the product. The student enrolls in the university and attends classes but cares nothing about learning. The individual without a sense of meaning has lost control over the conditions that impinge upon his life and thus feels alienated from himself and others. He goes through the motions, but his daily round of activities makes no sense to him.

In the best of all possible worlds the process of social ordering would involve each individual at a high level of individual meaning. Individuals would find meaning and, therefore, satisfaction in their participation in the processes of social ordering. They would feel involved and have a high sense of self-worth because each would be in control of his social world to the maximum extent feasible. No known social world, including our own, has achieved this optimal state. Therefore, an exploration of how societies, social groups, and social

Working on the Assembly Line and Individual Meaning

The conditions of work in modern societies seem to prevent many individuals from finding meaning and satisfying other basic needs through their employment. Harvey Swados's description of life on the assembly line in his article, "The Myth of the Happy Worker," is supported by many surveys and empirical studies:

> The plain truth is that factory work is degrading. It is degrading to any man who ever dreams of doing something worthwhile with his life; and it is about time we faced the fact....
>
> Almost without exception, the men with whom I worked on the assembly line last year felt like trapped animals. Depending on their age and personal circumstances, they were either resigned to their fate, furiously angry at *themselves* for what they were doing, or desperately hunting other work that would pay as well and in addition offer some variety, some prospect of change and betterment. They were sick of being pushed around by harried foremen (themselves more pitied than hated), sick of working like blinkered donkeys, sick of being dependent for their livelihood on a maniacal production-merchandising setup, sick of working in a place where there was no spot to relax during the twelve-minute rest period. (Some day—let us hope—we will marvel that production was still so worshipped . . . that new factories could be built with every splendid facility for the storage and movement of essential parts, but with no place for a resting worker to sit down for a moment but on a fire plug, the edge of a packing case, or the sputum- and oil-stained stairway of a toilet.[a]

Persons who are unable to satisfy their need for individual meaning in so significant a segment of their daily lives as how they make their living are experiencing a major frustration that has consequences for their self-esteem, their ability to lead happy and productive lives, and their confidence in their society and its social institutions.

[a]Harvey Swados, "The Myth of the Happy Worker," in *Man Alone*, ed. by Eric and Mary Josephson (New York: Dell, 1962), paperback, p. 111.

interactions are ordered to provide various kinds and levels of individual meaning is a crucial sociological task.

In this chapter four interrelated problems are discussed: (1) scarcity and individual survival, which is related to (2) available alternatives. A discussion of these raises in a new context (3) the problem of individual meaning, which explores the individual's attempt to make sense of the world. This in turn leads to a discussion of (4) the dynamics of the process of social ordering.

SCARCITY AND INDIVIDUAL SURVIVAL

Purely biological survival cannot be taken for granted. For the larger part of human history peoples' major concern has been the search for food either by hunting and gathering or by working the soil using primitive methods of agriculture. Even though large numbers of people in American society have been released from this as an immediate problem, many American still live below the federally established level of poverty. Millions of other people around the world in technologically underdeveloped societies still worry about the source of their next meal.

The problem of economic scarcity, which is basic to any consideration of human survival, remains significant in the modern world. A major focus of the science of economics is the problem of the distribution of scarce goods and services. The sociologist also studies this area. Some social theorists see economic scarcity and the differential distribution of goods and services as the major factor in the structuring of social order.[5]

Where there is a problem of economic scarcity, there is also a problem of control. Decisions must be made and enforced about who is to get the available goods and services, in what amounts, and under what conditions.

The problem of scarcity and individual survival does not disappear when the individual has a full stomach and a roof over his head. It moves to another level. Human beings have a variety of needs that go far beyond the strictly biological. Among these are the need for security and the need for self-esteem. The psychologist, Abraham H. Maslow, has suggested a hierarchy of needs beginning with those that are physiological and culminating in the need for self-actualization.[6] These needs exist and must be in some way gratified if people are to survive biologically, socially, and psychologically.

When individuals do not have sufficient control over the conditions that impinge on their lives, their needs are likely go unmet. If needs go unmet, the resulting deprivation may cause certain types of individual behavior such as withdrawal, aggression, what is called mental illness, and even the ultimate solution of suicide.

The fact of scarcity sets definite limits on the possible forms of social ordering. If individuals are to survive, they must attempt to gain sufficient control over their social and nonsocial environments to meet their basic needs. As indicated in the Introduction, the process of social ordering consists of individuals reciprocally controlling each other and their natural environment within the existing constraints.

It should again be emphasized that whether or not a certain type of control strategy is considered good or bad depends on how it is used, the desired ends, and how these are *evaluated* by the people involved in the specific interaction situation. The control strategy of punishment, for example, may be seen as good, or at least necessary, by some people under certain conditions, (some parents feel it is necessary to punish their children when they disobey). However, under other conditions the same people see the identical strategy as bad. Few people today consider the control strategies used by Moses, Jesus, or Buddha as bad, whereas most people see the control strategies used by Hitler as morally detestable.

AVAILABLE ALTERNATIVES

The problem of available alternatives is closely tied to the problem of scarcity and individual survival. If there were unlimited alternatives the problem of scarcity would obviously not exist. However the fact is that there are not unlimited alternatives. The alternatives that individuals, groups, and societies at any given time and place may choose to follow are restricted. Many of these restrictions are the result of the control and constraint factors that produce social ordering. In this section the more important social factors limiting alternatives are outlined.

Historical Factors

The alternatives available to any individual, group, or society at a given time depend in part on choices, either voluntary or forced, that were made in the past. Once a choice is made subsequent choices are limited.

When a student decides to major in a certain subject during his college career, he restricts, by that choice, the range of alternatives from which he can choose a career upon his graduation. If a group decides on a specific goal, restrictions are placed on other possible group goals. Once the people or leaders of a nation accept a certain ideology, limits are placed on what can be done and how it can be done. The history of black people in American society dramatically illustrates how the past can limit the alternatives presently available for individuals, groups, and the society as a whole. Throughout this text we will show how past choices and experiences shape and influence present alternatives.

Power Differentials

The amount of power an individual, group, or society has influences the available alternatives. An individual, group, or society with little power has only limited alternatives that can be realistically followed. Individuals, groups, and societies with more power can restrict the alternatives open to those with less power.

University faculties typically have more power than students and thus can restrict the alternatives available to students about how they use their time if they want to complete a degree. Similarly, a nation having more power than another can restrict the alternatives of the weaker nation in a variety of ways, such as preventing industrial development by using the weaker nation as a source of raw materials and cheap labor.

We will have much to say about significant uses of power throughout the text. Degree of power is closely related to available resources, which brings us to a discussion of costs and resources and how these restrict available alternatives.

Resources, Cost, and Alternatives

If a person pays a cost, he can usually expect *something* in return. What costs persons can pay depend on the amount and kinds of resources available to them. If they have no talents, wealth, or other types of resources that they can *give* they are restricted in what they can *get*. There is a definite relationship between the resources an individual, group, or society commands and their available alternatives. Poor people have fewer alternatives than rich people and persons with few talents are more restricted than people with many talents. Persons who have more get more and persons who have less get less or may even lose what they have if they lack sufficient resources to protect it.[7] That the shelves of supermarkets and department stores are well stocked means nothing to a person without money, just as a piano does not provide an alternative for an individual who has not developed a musical talent.

George Homans defines cost as "alternatives foregone."[8] In social interaction, if persons have no alternatives to forego they are "poor," because they have no possibility of paying the cost of something they want. Few demands can be made by them and, thus, their alternatives are limited. But, as Homans also points out, everyone typically has something to give in exchange. If persons have no tangibles such as wealth, talent, or service, they can always give *approval* to another person from whom they receive or want to receive a reward. Because those with resources also need self-esteem, they are often willing to make such an exchange. Homans states it pithily, "The greater the total reward in expressed social approval a man receives from other members of his group, the higher is the esteem in which they hold him."[9] In many situations the ability of people with few resources to offer *approval* to those with more resources makes at least some alternatives available to the former. However, the hitch is that the more esteem persons have the greater is the possibility of their controlling the behavior of others.

In *Exchange and Power in Social Life,* Peter M. Blau specifies the alternatives for "the person in need of recurrent services from an associate to whom he has nothing to offer":

> First, he may force the other to give him help. Second, he may obtain the help he needs from another source. Third, he may find ways to get along without such help. If he is unable or unwilling to choose any of these alternatives, however, there is only one other course of action left for him: he must subordinate himself to the other with power over himself as an inducement for furnishing the needed help.[10]

In many small social groups there is a person who is the "gofer." When something is needed, he is the one who "goes for" it, be it a spare part, a cup of coffee, a package, or whatever. Often the person who does this is the low man on the group's totem pole, the youngest child, the newest member, the weakest in the gang, the apprentice in the shop. Because he has few resources to use in exchange for what he needs or wants from the group, he offers his services in a subordinate capacity, clearly illustrating the relationship among resources, cost, and alternatives.

Motivation and Alternatives

The level of individual motivation is important in social life.[11] Lack of motivation can and does severely restrict the availability of alternatives.

The reasons why certain people under specified conditions are not motivated to pursue available alternatives are discussed in later chapters. The relevent point is that lack of motivation in the pursuit of available alternatives makes it possible for others to usurp these alternatives with less effort and cost and thereby enhance their degree of control in a specified situation. Students who are not motivated to join collective efforts on campus against what they see as "evil" make it easier for other students, faculty, or adminstrators to "run the show."

Information and Alternatives

If individuals are not aware of available alternatives, these alternatives are not open to them. Individuals at times use psychological control strategies such as selective perception and repression to ignore or get rid of information that is socially available to them.* These practices have implications for the social behavior of persons and their control potential.

Social restrictions are placed at times on the dissemination of information, thereby restricting the availability of alternatives. There are a variety of ways in which information is restricted. For example, if individuals are denied the possibility of entering college because of a lack of resources, they cannot acquire a variety of information to in turn provide them with various alternatives. If persons cannot afford to travel, they remain ignorant about a variety of situations that might provide them with different alternatives. Thus, resources limit the availability of information, which in turn limits available alternatives.

There are individuals and groups that knowingly restrict the availability of certain information, thereby limiting the alternatives of others. Some persons have control over certain information to which others are not allowed access. The so-called credibility gap between the government and the people, often discussed in the daily news, is an excellent example of restrictions placed on the dissemination of information for purposes of control. Information is often withheld in industrial firms both by management and by workers. Such withholding is an attempt to control the alternatives available to those from whom the information is withheld. This remains true even if the person or group doing the withholding claims as motive the good of the person or persons from whom information is withheld.

The more information persons have available, at least to a certain point, the more alternatives they have. Information thus enhances control possibilities. The familiar saying that "Knowledge is power" is not just a meaningless cliché. Much of the tremendous impact of accumulated scientific knowledge upon modern societies comes from

---

*Psychologists refer to these as defense mechanisms. They protect the individual self. We use the phrase "psychological control strategies" rather than "defense mechanisms" to develop consistency and clarify the relationship between sociology and psychology.

the vast increase in alternatives that this knowledge and the technology that rests upon it have provided.

We have seen how available alternatives are restricted or shaped by historical factors, power differentials, the balance between resources and costs, motivation, and information. It is incorrect, however, to assume that the restriction of alternatives is uniformly or necessarily undesirable. Some restrictions on alternatives always exist and knowledge of their existence is important for understanding social ordering and individual meaning. The significance of understanding the restriction of alternatives for individual meaning and social ordering thus becomes the next topic for discussion.

THE PROBLEM OF INDIVIDUAL MEANING

The work of Emile Durkheim, a French sociologist whose writings bridge the nineteenth and twentieth centuries, is helpful in understanding the relationship between the restriction of alternatives and the problem of individual meaning.[12] Durkheim contended that because individuals have the capacity to move in so many different directions, it is necessary that alternatives be in some way restricted.

In a famous study of suicide, he showed that people who are closely tied to a group, and therefore have their alternatives restricted by the rules of the group, are less likely to commit suicide than are people who are loosely tied to a group.* Durkheim showed that people living under conditions marked by the absence of rules and constraints restricting their behavior were more likely to commit suicide than people living under conditions where their behavior is restricted by rules. For example he found higher rates of suicide in cities than in rural areas and among single rather than with married people. Without restrictions, individuals do not, indeed cannot, know in what direction to turn. The restriction of alternatives, then, is necessary for individual meaning.

The problem of meaning refers to how individuals make sense out of their existence within the world in which they live. All solutions to this problem of meaning are based on values that are constructed and validated within the framework of social interaction. Values, defined as that which is desirable in human life, provide a basis for choice.[13] Meaning is born as choices are made on the basis of values and carried into action.[14] Without a basis for choice, whatever its content, behavior would be random and chaotic, and the world would be meaningless for the individual. Nothing would fit together in a way that made sense. There would be no organizing principles.

---

*This is not true for what Durkheim calls "altruistic suicide," which occurs when the individual is too closely tied to the group. If such an individual breaks the rules of the group, his life loses meaning, and suicide may result.

Both values and the restriction of alternatives are necessary for individual meaning. They are not mutually exclusive. The acceptance of a set of values and making choices based on them restrict other possible choices and thus limit other alternatives. A discussion of how values are "selected" therefore becomes important. Two major schools of thought with opposing views about the basis of individual values have developed: *sociologism* and *existentialism.* We will briefly discuss each and then show that a synthesis of the two provides the best explanation.[15]

Sociologism and Meaning

Durkheim was the leading exponent of sociologism. He maintained that morality was the product, or reflection, of group life. The standards by which individuals judge themselves and others come from their society. The Ten Commandments, the Koran, and the Confucian sayings all reflect the societies within which they developed. Group life was the only source of meaning. For Durkheim, a collective consciousness exists exterior to the individual and constrains him to act from a sense of duty to it. This submission to a collective morality, presupposed by Durkheim's idea of the collective consciousness, provides the basis for individual meaning. The ultimate source of collective morality is the human group, which constantly reinforces and maintains the collective consciousness.

Edward A. Tiryakian summarizes Durkheim's position: "Since mor-

---

The Collective Consciousness

The French sociologist Emile Durkheim (1858–1917) developed the concept of the collective consciousness to explain *social* behavior as distinquished from individual behavior. He held that "The states of the collective consciousness are different in nature from the states of the individual consciousness. . . . The mentality of groups is not the same as that of individuals; it has its own laws."[a]

The collective consciousness, then, exists exterior to individuals who find the collective consciousness completely formed and cannot change it as individuals. From Durkheim's point of view, the collective consciousness *imposes* beliefs and practices on us. This should not be interpreted to mean that the collective conscousness exists independently of people. It is the collective representations of a *group.*

[a]*The Rules of Sociological Method* (New York: Free Press, 1950), p. xlix.

ality is a social phenomenon . . . *we cannot aspire to a morality other than that required by our social condition.* To want another morality than that implied by the virtual or actual nature of society is to deny society and consequently to deny oneself: morality depends upon society and not upon me as an individual agent."[16]

Thus, for Durkheim, individual alternatives were severely restricted by the collective morality produced by the group. Living within the framework of this collective morality and abiding by it from a sense of duty provides the basis for individual meaning. When this collective morality does not exist, or when individuals for some reason find themselves "outside" it, their chances of committing suicide greatly increased.[17] Life outside the collective consciousness of the group is rendered so meaningless that persons may escape by taking their own lives.

Some contemporary sociologists, such as Talcott Parsons, allow the individual a little more freedom from social determination than does Durkheim, but still they lean heavily toward sociologism and anchor the basis of morality in the collective life of the group.[18] They call the collective consciousness culture and see it as providing the organizing principles of group life, including morality. Culture "maintains" the human group or society and provides the basis for meaning. The individual makes decisions and acts in a manner consistent with the dictates of this culture. From this viewpoint, we are all completely creations and creatures of our culture, which determines what we believe, how we behave, what we perceive, and the very meaning of our lives.

Existentialism and Meaning

Existential thinkers range all the way from the Christian, Soren Kierkegaard, to the atheist, Jean-Paul Sartre.[19] These thinkers hold in common the assertion that there is no meaning inherent within the framework of society. They completely reject sociologism.

Life for the existentialist is based on the assumption that human existence is objectively meaningless. To be lost or absorbed into the objectified social world is to lose the possibility of constructing an *authentic* subjective self and thus a meaningful *existence.* For the existentialist, Durkheim's collective consciousness is a world of mediocrity, neither authentic in itself nor allowing the possibility of creating an authentic subjective self within its framework. If the individual is to find meaning he must find it alone. Individuals must come to grips with their own existence and solve the problem of meaning in their own way based on their experiences and the choices and decisions required by these experiences. For the existentialist, a life totally submerged in the social is a life without authentic subjective meaning.

Tiryakian is again helpful in summing up the existentialist position: "The existential perspective views society as the seat of objectivity and therefore antagonistic to the subjective existence of the individual. To find and become himself, the individual must struggle to liberate himself from the yoke of society. Society is seen by existentialism as the captor of the individual, very much in the same way as Greek religious thought viewed the body as the captor of the soul."[20]

"Consequently, all existentialists ultimately share the belief that it is up to the individual to solve his own existential problems, particularly the problem of his own becoming."[21]

Thus, the same collective morality or consciousness that gives individual life meaning for Durkheim renders life meaningless for the existentialist. The existentialist demands that individuals select their own set of alternatives while they keep open the possibility of future choice.

We contend that neither of these positions is completely right or completely wrong. Rather, an explanation of the source of individual meaning lies in a synthesis of these polar positions.

A Synthetic Explanation of Individual Meaning

Under most conditions orderly and predictable social interaction processes occur. The human self is and must be constructed initially within the framework of social interaction through the process called primary socialization. Even the existentialist finds no empirical grounds to deny this.

Objective and Subjective

The difference between objective and subjective is critical in understanding the discussion of sociologism and existentialism. An objectified social world is best understood by referring to the description of the collective consciousness. It is a "world" that exists *independently* of specific *individuals* and that constrains them to act in a particular manner. Individuals as such have no control over this objectified world and thus little or no part in the construction of their individual selves. The social world is *objectively* present.

The subjective self, from the existentialist point of view, is a self constructed by the individual over which he *has* control. It is called subjective because it is constructed *by* the individual. This self-construction permits the individual to create his own essence rather than to be merely a "reflection of" or be "absorbed in" an objective social world.

The argument between existentialism and sociologism begins after the point of the initially constructed self. At what age in the life of the individual this self can be said to exist and the types of dynamics that produce this initial self are grounds for argument between the two schools of thought. However, such intricate arguments do not affect the basic assumptions that an initial individual self develops and that this self has certain needs and desires, including a desire for meaning. In Chapter 3 detailed supporting arguments and evidence for these assumptions are presented.

The individual self is constructed (socialized) within the framework of severely limited aternatives. If restrictions were not present, the self would not develop. Indeed, the biological organism would not survive if some restrictions were not present. As the Romantic poet William Wordsworth, says: "Shades of the prison house begin to close upon the growing boy." It is, of course, this "prison house" that the existentialist wishes to destroy. But to completely destroy the prison house would also completely destroy the possibility of self and, therefore, the subsequent possibility of individual meaning. The restrictions placed on the individual, or accepted by him, along with the available alternatives, permit the possibility of the construction of the self and its continued existence and growth. A self, much less a self-identity, cannot come into existence and develop in a completely chaotic world.

The self cannot continue to develop or be sustained in any meaningful sense unless there is something to test itself against and unless there is a system of values to provide criteria for choice. Others with whom the individual interacts provide this testing ground and attempt to implant values within the developing child. In the early years, this helps the child to make sense of the world into which he is born. This essential point supports sociologism.

However, as the child continues to develop in the home and in the larger social world, he runs up against controls imposed on him by others. These may render his activities and experiences meaningless as judged from the point of view of past conditioning and the values he has accepted or developed. If this occurs the individual is not permitted to be his own person as defined by a self-identity that has been developed and grounded on certain values. This is the condition that existentialists protest against.

On the one hand, there is the necessity for values that must be constructed, or at least validated, in interaction with others. It is these values that provide the basis for meaning. On the other hand, because power is unequally distributed in society, some people can restrict other people from making decisions and acting consistently with their self-identities and values. When this occurs, the lives of the persons who are thus restricted may be rendered meaningless.

We suggest a synthesis of the two positions that state the conditions under which an individual's life will have meaning. Meaning is possible when individuals have self-identities based on values validated in social interaction and when at the same time they have enough *control* over the social situations in which they find themselves to make decisions based on these values and to act on their decisions. This statement about the conditions facilitating individual meaning incorporates both the social-value validation of sociologism and the individual control of existentialism.

This synthesis does not deny the possibility of most or even all people in a society holding common values, as probably occurred in small hunting-and-gathering or agricultural societies. At the same time, it allows the possibility of a pluralistic value system such as is claimed for contemporary American society. In both cases the dynamics of the solution to the problem of meaning are the same.

THE PROCESS OF SOCIAL ORDERING

We have indicated people have a variety of needs and that they try to gratify these needs by attempting to control their social as well as their natural environment. We have referred also to the concept of self-identity and its relationship to values that serve as the basis for decision making and action providing the possibility for individual meaning. Individuals attempt to gratify their needs through the realization of goals in a manner consistent with a self-identity based on a system of values.

Self-identity, however, may change over time. For example, if a woman's self-identity is based on the traditional values of womanhood, she may attempt to gratify her needs by being a "good" wife and mother. She seeks favorable responses from others by doing those things she feels a good wife and mother should do according to traditional values. However, if an alternative presents itself, the same woman may come to reject a self-identity based on the traditional values of womanhood and adopt new values and a new self-identity. She might then behave differently by pursuing a career and rejecting sexist stereotypes. She then would attempt to gratify her needs by seeking favorable responses for different types of behavior. Note that both the social influences emphasized by sociologism and the individual choices of existentialism shape her behavior. As her values change in time (from traditional to liberated) her behavior changes.

The attempt to gratify needs motivates individuals to participate in social interaction because this cannot be accomplished in complete isolation. For example, gratification of the need for self-esteem presupposes that at least some others approve of the behavior in which an individual is engaged. Such approval from others is critical for self-esteem.

The questions thus become how do people go about attempting to have their needs gratified and how is this related to the process of social ordering? Individuals, either alone or in coalition with others (usually in groups), attempt to control the behavior of others to achieve goals and gratify basic needs. These control attempts by individuals or groups are the processes that produce social ordering. At times these processes produce peaceful ordering; at other times they produce a more violent ordering of events.

When we talk about control by individuals or groups we mean the ability to elicit desired responses ranging from receiving money to receiving approval from others. This ability depends in large part on the interrelated factors already discussed, including the history of the individual, group, or society; power differentials; available resources; degree of motivation; and the amount and quality of information available. The problem of scarcity (real or created) is also a significant factor.

Social order occurs, then, as parties in interaction use a variety of control strategies in an attempt to gratify needs and realize their common or separate goals. For example, if the parties involved in interaction want to share a common goal they can be expected to use cooperative strategies. They agree to work together cooperatively so that all can gain from a common effort. On the other hand, if they have a common goal that is not to be shared, they will use competitive strategies or, under some condition, coercive strategies. When competitive strategies are used it is usually the party with the most resources that achieves the goal first and thus captures the prize. Each of us is aware from his own experience that the social ordering that occurs through the use of cooperative strategies is different from the social ordering that occurs from using competitive or coercive strategies.

The Reciprocity of Control Strategies

The control capability of any party involved in an interaction is limited by the control capabilities of all other parties involved and by various types of constraints discussed throughout the text. No person or group is without *some* control capability. Everyone's behavior is controlled to some degree by the presence of others.

Take an extreme case: masters and slaves. On the surface it appears that masters are in complete control of slaves and that the behavior of masters is in no way controlled. However, if masters want to keep slaves in servitude they are forced to engage in certain types of behavior. If they want their slaves to work, masters must use their resources (pay a cost) to provide food and shelter. If they want to keep their slaves from escaping, they must build fences or hire guards. Masters are always aware that slaves may form a coalition—thus increasing their degree of control capability and revolt—and are forced to take steps to prevent this. The behavior of the masters is controlled by the very presence and potential threats of those they are attempting to enslave.

Even in such extreme cases of differential power, therefore, control is always reciprocal. *It is this continuous reciprocity of control attempt that is the process of social ordering.* To attempt to control others is to have one's own behavior controlled.

Some persons obviously have more control capability than others. So do some groups and societies. Even though all parties involved in an interaction have *some* control capability, those with more control capability have a greater possibility of structuring the process of social ordering to their advantage. For example, you have chosen (either on your own or under control pressure from your parents or others) to be a student. As a student you have less control capability in the academic situation than do the faculty and administration. The university offers something you need or want—a degree. You are constrained by that fact to abide by certain rules, regulations, and assignments laid down by the administration and faculty, who have more control capability than you do. If you want more control capability you can enter into an organized coalition with other students. Strong organized student coalitions may be able to change the process of social ordering at the university by changing the reciprocal control relationships among students, faculty, and administrators.

Control Strategies in Interpersonal Relations

The sociologist Erving Goffman, in his aptly titled book *The Presentation of Self in Everyday Life*,[22] throws considerable light on how each of us attempts to gain approval. Goffman talks about *staging* and *performances*. He points out that individuals prepare a theatrical stage upon which they play out a performance before a selected audience. If an upper-middle-class couple plans a party for their friends they prepare the stage by thoroughly cleaning the house, preparing fancy bits of food, placing appropriate magazines such as *Harper's* and *The New Yorker* in a conspicuous place (while hiding *The National Enquirer* and *True Confessions*), and storing the children in bed or with a baby sitter.

Once the stage is set to impress the guests, they are ready for the performance, which begins as the guests arrive. Each guest is greeted appropriately. Things are said and questions asked that are calculated to elicit approval from the guests. Certain guests might be asked their opinion about a recent downward trend in the stock market. Other guests might be questioned about their opinion of the reviews of a current movie or play. Suitable drinks and food are served at an appropriate time. The guests manage their own behavior by how they dress, talk, and act. They too are trying to gain the approval of others through the use of control strategies. The social ordering of the whole party is the result of a well-planned and well-rehearsed variety of control strategies played out at the appropriate time by guests and hosts on the stage prepared by the hosts.

Different types of strategies are used by members of other social classes at their parties or get-togethers, but the goals are typically the same: impression management for the gratification of approval needs either immediately or at a later date.

CONFLICT AND SOCIAL ORDERING

At this point a problem emerges. If everyone is attempting to control the behavior of others either individually or in coalitions, why isn't there more open conflict than in fact occurs? There are a variety of reasons for this relative lack of conflict. Some of the more important are discussed here:

1. People are usually aware of their relative degree of power in a situation and of the limitations on their available alternatives. A person with no money resources who needs to keep a job to put food on the family table is not likely to slap the boss in the face if there are no other jobs available, even if he does not like what the boss is doing or saying. The boss is allowed to be in control without *open* protest on the part of the worker. Labor unions were formed to increase the degree of control by workers, thus changing the process of social ordering in the work place. Workers strike to gain more money or a higher degree of control.

2. Different people have different self-identities and, thus, value different things. What is need gratifying for one person may not be need gratifying for another. Furthermore, the relative intensity of specific needs varies from person to person. If a woman defines her self in the traditional sense rather than in the contemporary women's liberation sense, being "treated like a woman" may be more gratifying for her than making the same wages as a man for doing the same job. Some conflict will occur as the identities of women continue to change and challenge the traditional male domination of society.

3. In many group situations some people are attempting to gratify different needs than are others. Everyone in the group does not want

to be a leader and carry the responsibility of that position, even though the leadership position does typically gratify a need for esteem. Some people are gratified just to be members of a group.

In addition, many people belong to several groups so that they can sacrifice the gratification of a specific need in one group (or even in the larger society) and have that need gratified within the framework of another group. For example, lower-class people tend to be denied many need-gratifying experiences open to classes above them. Because of this, church life may become important for some people in the lower classes. Even though in the larger social world they are garbage collectors or domestics, within the church they become ministers, deacons, and Sunday School superintendents, gratifying their need for self-esteem. Or they may simply make a virtue of meekness anticipating their reward in Heaven.[23] Karl Marx (1818–1883) called this form of religion the "opiate of the people." Perhaps so, but some gratification is better than none at all. If such alternatives as the church or the local bar were not available for the lower class more overt conflict might exist despite the power differentials.

4. In some social situations everyone has something to gain by giving a little to gain more through a common effort. People with like interests tend to join together and work in common for the realization of their goals. All persons involved gain when their goal is reached. In less complex societies such common effort by an entire society is necessary for individual as well as group survival. In comtemporary society, an example is the team effort in athletic contests. Beating the opponent gives esteem to every member of the winning team; thus, cooperative team effort pays off for each individual.

5. In any interaction, psychological dynamics are also involved. When persons cannot risk overt social-control strategies, psychological strategies may become more prominent. In many interactions psychological and social control strategies are typically used together. Some examples of psychological strategies are (1) Projection. If one's weakness or other "negative" traits can be projected onto another person or persons, the individual doing the projecting can gain strength, at least in his own eyes. (2) Rationalization. By making excuses for behavior, persons can avoid seeing themselves in an unfavorable light and thus protect their self-identity and self-esteem. (3) Repression. People can repress from consciousness information or experiences that might do them damage. The strategy is to get rid of unpleasant thoughts about oneself that might damage self-esteem.

There are many other psychological strategies, such as regression and selective perception, that enable persons to endure unfavorable social situations. Under severe stress and deprivation of needs persons may become psychotic and remove themselves from the world of social reality by creating a personal reality in which needs are gratified—or at least where the pain of suffering deprivation is not so severe.

6. People do not interact according to the objective conditions present in a situation but according to how these conditions are subjectively defined.[24] They construct or reconstruct their social worlds by subjective definitions. Thus, individuals in the same society may have their needs gratified by making different subjective definitions of the same phenomenon. Wealthy people may feel as though they deserve their riches and thereby define themselves as virtuous. On the other hand, those without wealth may define the rich as evil and accuse them of having gained their wealth by exploitation. These people see themselves as "just as good as anybody" because, even though poor, they have not exploited others and are, therefore, morally better than the rich who have.[25]

REFERENCES

1. There are several good books about the task of science. Among the best are Braithwaite, Richard Bevan. *Scientific Explanation.* New York: Harper, 1960. Popper, Karl R. *The Logic of Scientific Discovery.* University of Toronto Press, 1959. Nagel, Ernest. *The Structure of Science: Problems in the Logic of Scientific Explanation.* New York: Harcourt, 1961.

Definition of the Situation

The American sociologist William I. Thomas (1863–1947) pointed out that people do not act according to the *objective* conditions present in a situation. Rather, their *actions* depend on how they subjectively define a situation. In a sense, this is a truism because "objective" conditions *mean nothing* unless they are first subjectively defined.

It is important to make this truism explicit because of the tendency to take social life for granted. Unless people realize that it is the subjective definitions that affect social interaction, they are likely to think that social life is an objective entity that exists *independently* of the subjective definitions made.

If sociologists are to understand why people act as they do in certain situations, they must first understand how people define these situations. The run of depositors withdrawing their funds from a perfectly sound bank because of false rumor, thus causing the bank to fail, or the panic-stricken crowd trampling people while fleeing a theater because someone mistakenly yelled "fire" are graphic examples of people's subjective definitions of the situation having drastic consequences for their social behavior.

2. For a classic work on discovery in science, see Hanson, Norwood R. *Patterns of Discovery: An Enquiry into the Conceptual Foundations of Science.* New York: Cambridge U. P., 1958.

3. Mills, C. Wright. *The Sociological Imagination.* New York: Oxford U. P., 1959, p. 5.

4. For a discussion of ritual used in this sense, see Merton, Robert. *Social Theory and Social Structure.* New York: Free Press, 1957, Chap. 4.

5. The most important classical thinker holding this view was Karl Marx. See *Karl Marx and Frederick Engels, Selected Works.* Moscow: Foreign Language Publishing House, 1960. See also, Veblen, Thorstein. *The Theory of the Leisure Class.* New York: Macmillan, 1899. For a more recent work, see Galbraith, John Kenneth. *The New Industrial State.* Boston: Houghton, 1967.

6. See Maslow, Abraham H. *Motivation and Personality.* 2nd ed. New York: Harper, 1970.

7. This is what Robert K. Merton has called the "Matthew Effect," drawing on a familiar saying from the Book of Matthew in the New Testament. See his "The Matthew Effect in Science," *Science,* **159**, No. 3810 (Jan. 1968), pp. 56–63.

8. Homans, George Casper. *Social Behavior: Its Elementary Forms.* New York: Harcourt, 1961.

9. Ibid., p. 149.

10. Blau, Peter M. *Exchange and Power in Social Life.* New York: Wiley, 1964, pp. 21–22.

11. For an introductory psychological treatment of motivation, see Atkinson, J. W. *An Introduction to Motivation.* New York: Van Nostrand, 1964.

12. See Durkheim, Emile. *The Rules of Sociological Method.* Trans. Sarah A. Solovay and John H. Mueller, ed. with an introduction by George E. C. Catline (New York: Free Press, 1938). See also, Emile Durkheim, *Suicide,* trans. by John A. Spaulding and George Simpson. Ed. with an introduction by George Simpson. New York: Free Press, 1951.

13. Kluckhohn, Clyde. "Values and Value Orientations in the Theory of Action: An Exploration in Definition and Classification." In *Toward a General Theory of Action.* Ed. by Talcott Parsons and Edwards A. Shils. Cambridge: Harvard U. P., 1951.

14. Becker, Ernest. *The Birth and Death of Meaning.* New York: Free Press, 1962, p. 51.

15. In the following discussion I have relied heavily on Tiryakian, Edward A. *Sociologism and Existentialism.* Englewood Cliffs, N.J.: Prentice-Hall, 1962. This book is highly recommended.

16. Ibid., p. 30.

17. See op. cit., *Suicide.*

18. Parsons' best known work is *The Social System.* New York: Free Press, 1951. Since this publication his theory has become increasingly abstract, leaving less and less theoretical room for individual freedom. For example, see "Some Problems of General Theory *in Sociology.*" In *Theoretical Sociology.* Ed. by John C. McKinney and Edward A. Tiryakian. New York: Appleton 1970.

19. The best of Kierkegaard's works are *Fear and Trembling* and *Sickness Unto Death.* Trans. by Walter Lowrie. Garden City, N.Y.: Doubleday, 1954. *The Present Age.* Trans. by Alexander Dru and Walter Lowrie. New York: Oxford U. P., 1949.

   The most relevant of Sartre's works is *Being and Nothingness: An Essay on Phenomenological Ontology.* Trans. with an introduction by Hazel E. Barnes. New York: Philosophical Library, 1956.

20. Op. cit., p. 152
21. Op. cit., p. 153
22. Goffman, Erving. *The Presentation of Self in Everyday Life*. Garden City, N.Y.: Doubleday, 1959.
23. For a discussion of one view on this, see Nietzsche, Frederich. *The Geneology of Morals*. Trans. by Francis Golffing. Garden City, N.Y.: Doubleday, 1956.
24. The sociologist William I. Thomas makes the case for the importance of the subjective definition of the situation in terms of social interaction. See Thomas, William I. *Primitive Behavior*. New York: McGraw-Hill, 1937. For a discussion of the self-fulfilling prophecy, which states: "If men define situations as real, they are real in their consequences," see Merton. op. cit., Chap. 11.
25. See Centers, Richard. *The Psychology of Social Class*. Princeton University Press, 1949.

C H A P T E R 2

Classification of Control Strategies

INTRODUCTION

Classification is vital in all scientific endeavors. It enables scientists to recognize and isolate for analysis the units with which they are working. Once these units are isolated, how they affect each other in various interactional combinations and what is produced as these combinations are made can be studied. For example, chemists have classified all known elements by arranging them by their atomic weight and valance in the periodic table. Through much experimentation they know what is produced as various elements are brought together in interaction under specified conditions.

The chemist knows that a molecule of water is composed of two atoms of hydrogen and one atom of oxygen. If the constituent elements of water were not known, the composition of water would remain a mystery. Thus, classification and research permit science to remove the mystery from the world about us. Classification helps make sense of what we observe. This is a big step toward explanation.

In this chapter the units of sociological analysis that explain the process of social ordering are classified and discussed. These units are processes of control. Therefore, we call them control strategies. The interaction of the control strategies, operating within the constraints discussed in later chapters, produces specific types of social order. Put differently, the control strategies are the units of the reciprocal control processes that produce social ordering. As each control strategy is outlined, we will indicate where its significance for social ordering and individual meaning is discussed later in the book.

MAJOR TYPES OF CONTROL STRATEGIES

There are seven major types of control strategies: cultural strategies, exchange strategies, procedural strategies, manipulative strategies, coercive strategies, coalition strategies, and withdrawal strategies. Each will be discussed in turn.

Table 2-1 outlines the seven major control strategies and identifies some of the principal subtypes within each. This table should be referred to often as this chapter is read and referred back to during later chapters.

I. CULTURAL STRATEGIES

The Concept of Culture

The concept of culture is one of the most important—yet the slipperiest and difficult—to define precisely in the social sciences. Two famous anthropologists in a review of the usage of the concept found more than five hundred different definitions in the literature, and many more have been added since their report was published in 1952.[1]

A Note on Terminology

An essential part of the scientific process of classification, explanation, and prediction is the gathering together of related events under clearly defined and useful categories called concepts. They range from the specific, closely related to events in the real world (for example, the American Revolution), to the abstract and generalized (for example, social ordering). Concepts are the threads with which the scientist weaves his hypotheses and explanations.

Sociology is a relative newcomer to the ranks of science. Its concepts are sometimes imprecise, occasionally defined differently by different scholars, and perhaps most confusing, it uses words drawn from everyday language. The physical sciences have been around long enough and are far enough removed from daily life so that few people confuse the physicist's concept of mass with the Roman Catholic religious rite of the same name or believe the astronomer is referring to a new dress style when he talks about a "red shift."

For our purposes, the most useful starting point in defining culture was provided by one of the founding fathers of anthropology, Edward Tylor (1832–1917), who defined culture as "that complex whole which includes knowledge, belief, art, morals, law, custom, and any other capabilities and habits acquired by man as a member of society."[2]

TABLE **2:1**
Major Types of Control Strategies

I *Cultural Strategies*
   A. Norms
   B. Sanctions
   C. Roles and Statuses
   D. Group & Societal Entry
   E. Differentiation & Ranking

II *Exchange Strategies*
   A. Superordinate
   B. Subordinate
   C. Accomodative

III *Procedural Strategies*
   A. Bureaucratization
   B. Professionalization
   C. Science and Technology

IV *Manipulative Strategies*
   A. Verbal
   B. Nonverbal

V *Coercive Strategies*
   A. Nonviolent
   B. Violent

VI *Coalitional Strategies*
   A. Permanent, Temporary, or Partial Unification

VII *Withdrawal Strategies*
   A. Physical, Ritual, or Group Disbandment

Such, however, is not always true for the sociologist. Therefore, when we discuss such concepts as socialization, culture, or institutions, we will assign specific and constant meanings to them different from (although sometimes related to) their usage in the colloquial language. We pointed out in Chapter 1 that when we use such concepts as control strategies or constraints there is no intent to associate these scientific ideas with the moral overtones that the same terms carry in popular speech. Sociological concepts are not intended to convey goodness or badness. We now emphasize that the definitions of these concepts are also different from their popular usages. A social institution is not, for the sociologist, a place where people deposit their unwanted older relatives and their alcoholic friends; culture is not limited to what social snobs believe they possess; nor are control strategies necessarily nasty plots by some people to do in others.

These points may appear obvious, yet even professional social scientists sometimes fall into one or the other of these traps: Either reading moral connotations into concepts or confusing the concepts with similar vernacular terms.

Without changing the meaning or intent of his definition, Tylor could have included such material objects as hand and machine tools, plows, tractors, saws, pencils, and a variety of others far too numerous to mention. He also could have included nonmaterial entities such as language, values, and norms. The items Tylor lists, those we have added, and many others constitute a complex assortment of *tools* used by people and groups to understand, design, and control their physical and social worlds. Some of these tools are material, such as plows and saws. Others are nonmaterial, such as norms and roles.

We define culture as a variety of tools and the agreed on rules for their use that are learned or emerge within the process of social interaction and that carry a shared meaning.

Agreement and shared meaning are critical because they imply that the same meaning will be evoked in all people who are parties to the agreement. For example, language is a basic cultural tool. Unless a word evokes a common meaning in communication it serves no useful purpose in the process of interaction. Language must be learned to be useful. The child first learns the shared sound patterns employed by his social group and then learns to associate combinations of these sound patterns (words) with culturally defined entities and events (meanings).

Agreement and shared meaning are also important for control. If two or more parties agree to the use of a cultural tool, when one party uses this tool, the other party is expected to respond as agreed. The various cultural tools are essential for control and are vitally important in the shaping of social order. The agreed on use of cultural tools limits the alternatives of all parties involved in a relationship as long as they remain parties to the agreement.

Many cultural agreements are taken for granted. Unless attention is drawn to them, they go unrecognized as such. We typically agree to wear clothing in public, call our parents mother and father rather than by their given names, open doors when other persons have their arms full, remain quiet when a speaker is talking to an audience, knock at the door of a stranger, be polite to our friends, and so forth.

People often *act* as if they agree with the use of certain cultural tools when a matter of fact they do not. Thus, under certain conditions, for example, if the cost is too great, they will not respond appropriately to the action of others. One person may act as though he is a friend to another person when friendship is spelled out in a cultural agreement. However, if the other person makes a request for help under this agreement, the friendship may collapse if the cost of meeting the request is too high. If my friend asks for a loan of ten dollars, my response may be positive. If he requests I swear falsely before a grand jury so that he can avoid jail, the cost to me may be too great for me to agree.

In addition, people act as if they agree with the use of certain cultural tools for a variety of other reasons. Some are forced to act as if they agree because they have no viable alternative. A woman may act as if she agrees with staying at home and taking care of the children when in fact she would rather work outside the home.

Others genuinely agree and use cultural tools because they feel they should. A woman may believe her place is in the home and thus happily go along with the agreement. Of course, the "place" occupied by a man or a woman has either been culturally defined or determined by the greater power of one party in the situation. The Womens Liberation Movement seeks change in the old cultural agreement that the *only* place for a woman is in the home. Many women have not been a party to this old cultural agreement for some time, even though they may have gone along with it for practical reasons.

THE CONCEPT OF SUBCULTURE

Before discussing specific types of cultural strategies, the concept of subculture needs to be explained. A subculture is a relatively unique and clearly differentiated pattern of behaviors and cultural arguments shared by members of a subgroup within a society. The cultural agreements are sufficiently different from the agreements contained in the dominant culture that they are seen as distinct. In the United States the Hutterites are one example of a subculture.

There are shadings of difference in the cultural agreements of many different types of people. These differences are becoming more pronounced in our complex pluralistic nation. A pluralistic nation by definition contains a variety of subcultures. In the United States it is increasingly difficult to draw clear lines separating subcultures from a dominant culture. There may no longer be a truly dominant culture (if there ever was), but rather loosely knit congeries of separate groups or peoples with different cultures tied together by political and economic considerations. Indians, blacks, and Jews form subcultures; the descendants of immigrants from southeastern Europe and elsewhere are subcultures; there is an adolescent subculture, a criminal subculture, and many others. The concept of subculture will be useful when we discuss social stratification in Chapter 7 and ethnic and minority groups in Chapter 8.

Types of Cultural Control Strategies

A cultural tool in use will be called a cultural strategy because it is used to control the behavior of the self and others. Included among these cultural strategies are: norms, sanctions, statuses, and roles, group and societal entry strategies, and differentiation and ranking strategies. (See Table 2-1.) Each of these cultural strategies plays a significant role in both the process of social ordering and the development of individual meaning.

Norms

Norms are agreed on expectations about how individuals should or should not act under specified conditions. They set standards and limits for behavior, because they are part of shared cultural agreements. Norms vary in the *extent* to which they are shared, the *intensity* with which they are held, and the individuals and groups they *benefit*.

Some norms are widely shared within a given society. Almost everyone is expected to use them as specified by the cultural agreement. Monogamous marriage, for example, is widely shared as a norm in American society. Most Americans marry only one person at a time. Adaptations such as repeated divorces and remarriages are important and must be analyzed, but they fall within the broad normative agreement about monogamy as the preferred marital pattern. Exceptions to this cultural agreement, such as group marriages or communal living arrangements, occur but are relatively rare.

The *intensity* with which the norm of monogamy is held in our society is illustrated by the vigorous reactions to other forms of marital arrangements. The Mormons, whose religion prescribed the form of polygyny in which one husband has several wives, were persecuted during the nineteenth century for practicing this marital arrange-

---

The Hutterites: A Subculture Within American Society

Joseph Eaton and Robert Weil in their study of mental health among the Hutterites provide us with an excellent capsule description of the Hutterite subculture, setting forth the distinctive cultural tools and patterns for living displayed by this small social group:

> The Hutterities, whose origin as a sect goes back to 1528, are a closely knit group of German stock who had lived together in neighboring villages in Europe for a long time before they migrated to the United States from southern Russia between 1874 and 1877. The immigrants—101 married couples and their children—settled in eastern South Dakota. Their descendants have now spread over a wide area in the Dakotas, Montana, and the prairie provinces of Canada. They live in ninety-eight hamlets, which they call colonies. But they remain a remarkably cohesive group; each grownup is intimately acquainted with hundreds of other members in the settlements. The Hutterites believe it sinful to marry outside the sect, and all of the present descendants (8,542 in 1950) stem from the original 101 couples.
>
> Cardinal principles of the Hutterites are pacifism, adult baptism, the communal ownership of all property and simple living. Jewelry, art and overstuffed

ment. The Mormons finally fled to Utah and, at least overtly, ceased practicing their preferred form of marriage. Although our notions about preferred and acceptable marriage patterns are more flexible today, the strongly preferred pattern remains monogamy.

Norms vary in the extent to which they are shared. Occupational groups, for example, have norms that are relatively unique to each. Carpenters, teachers, airline pilots, and farmers share norms that refer to the specific kinds of things they do. Some of these norms are technical and refer to how jobs should be done. Other occupational norms state standards of behavior for the occupation. Teachers are typically expected to dress in conventional middle-class style; truck drivers are not.

Subcultures by definition possess norms that differ from each other. Religious subcultures, ethnic subcultures, and age subcultures have different patterns of expectation and resulting behavior.

In addition, norms often provide a highly efficient way to achieve individual or group goals in a situation because of the shared agreement. The use of norms under some conditions gratifies basic needs. If using norms does not provide enough control over a situation to gratify basic needs, individuals or groups may use other control strategies. Many people do not use norms if they have more to gain, as they see it, by using other control strategies.

chairs are regarded as sinful luxuries. Radio sets and the movies are taboo. Children are the only possessions to which there is no limit: the average completed family has more than ten. The Hutterites cling to their own customs and are considered "different" by their neighbors. But they are not primitive in the ethnographic sense. They get a grammar-school education and speak English fluently. They read daily newspapers, have a telephone in most colonies and own trucks. Since their own members are not encouraged to seek formal education beyond the primary grades, there are no doctors or lawyers among them, but they utilize such professional services from outside. Each hamlet engages in a highly mechanized form of agriculture. Their business with the "outside world," as Hutterities are apt to refer to their neighbors, usually exceeds $100,000 per year per colony.[a]

Eaton and Weil note that "The survival of this sixteenth-century peasant culture in the most twentieth-century-minded continent is a vivid demonstration of the power of values and beliefs."[b]

[a]Joseph Eaton and Robert Weil, "The Mental Health of the Hutterites" in *Man Alone*, ed. by Eric and Mary Josephson (New York: Dell, 1972), p. 499.
[b]Ibid., p. 504.

NORMS AND POWER: WHO BENEFITS?

Because of the power differentials that exist among individuals and groups, some have a greater vested interest in the use of certain norms than do others. They stand to gain if they and everyone else use the agreed on norms. It is to the advantage of rulers if subjects accept as binding the norms that define the relationship. It is perhaps the most efficient and effective way of insuring compliant behavior by subjects if they accept the norms as morally desirable. Clearly such norms benefit those who hold the power—the rulers. In Chapters 7, 8, and 10 many examples of such normative control strategies that benefit those who hold power will be discussed.

NORMS OF EVASION

There are also norms of evasion that define what can be typically gotten away with. These patterned evasions, used by groups they benefit, are themselves normatively defined—their legitimacy is based on not getting caught. Honesty as measured by not lying or cheating, for example, is a widely shared norm in American society. Yet, many Americans lie on thir income tax returns, some college students cheat on exams, advertising is often deceptive, corporations mislead the public about their financial status when selling stocks or setting prices, workers develop elaborate arrangements to loaf on the job, and political leaders often engage in flights of rhetorical excess that result in credibility gaps.

Most of these behaviors, which violate the norm of honesty, are considered acceptable by some members of society so long as the persons who engage in them do not get caught. Getting caught appears to consist of a forced public recognition of the violation of the norm, which may result in the punishment of those identified as violators. The bulk of those who use the norm of evasion continue business as usual.

The preceding discussion suggests the following conclusions:

1. Individuals will use the agreed on norms of their groups or society so long as they provide sufficient control for the gratification of needs, the achievement of goals, or a sense of individual meaning.
2. Individuals will stop using the norms of their groups or society if the use of these norms does not provide enough control for need gratification and goal achievement, or if there is present a greater possibility for control and subsequent need gratification, goal achievement, or meaning through the use of other types of control strategies.

Folkways, Mores, and Laws

William Graham Sumner (1840–1910) in 1904 differentiated three subtypes of norms: folkways, mores, and laws.[3] *Folkways* are norms that define the preferred patterns of behavior of a society. They cover a wide variety of different cultural agreements that are useful but are not seen as morally imperative. Most folkways relate to everyday life. Cutting one's hair short (or not cutting it), wearing a shirt and tie on appropriate occasions, and eating with a fork or with chopsticks are folkways. These customary patterns of behavior vary widely in complex societies such as ours and may change relatively rapidly.

Folkways are used so long as the shared agreements to use them persist and compliance with them evokes favorable responses from others. They save us considerable time that we would have to spend in decision making if these agreements were not present. Thus, even though folkway agreements tend to be restrictive, they are useful and save much time in controlling the responses of others.

Mores are more binding agreements than folkways because they represent directly the basic cultural values of the society. The mores severely restrict the alternatives of individuals and are also more likely to be important for individual meaning. In our society, marriage, sexual behavior, honesty, murder, and patriotism are among the important areas of behavior regulated by the mores.

Mores are culturally important norms and therefore are widely shared. However, they are not adhered to by everyone in the society, nor are they completely resistant to change. Changes in mores have important implications for social ordering and thus for individual meaning.

Laws are written down and codified. Many embody the folkways and mores of a society and thus reflect cultural agreements. The mores about monogamous marriage in our society, for example, are codified into laws.

However, some parts of a specified legal system contain regulations codified or passed by persons with the power to do so and do not represent cultural agreements. These parts of the legal system, although technically laws, are not part of shared cultural agreements but reflect other control strategies written into law because of the power of those who provide them. For example, the South African segregation laws (apartheid) do not reflect agreement by the black majority but result from power held by the white minority.

Cooperation and Competition

The norms regulating cooperation and competition are important cultural control strategies in many societies and groups. *Cooperation* occurs when two or more persons or groups work together to accomplish a common goal or obtain a reward to be shared by all participants. *Competition* occurs when two or more persons or groups struggle to achieve a goal or receive a reward that will go to the successful competitor.

Societies and groups vary widely in the extent to which competitive or cooperative norms are valued and shared. American society places a high value on competition. Our rewards for successful competition begin in the home, extend through the school and the athletic field, and receive their culmination in the market place, where the presumed philosophy is "To the victor, belong the spoils." By sharp contrast, the balance is strongly in favor of cooperation in many primitive societies, where youngsters are taught to assist each other rather than to stand out and excel.[4]

The German sociologist Georg Simmel[5] and others have pointed out that competition must rest on a normative foundation of cooperative agreement if open conflict is to be avoided. The ground rules setting the boundaries and acceptable forms of the competition must be shared by the participants to the interaction, even though the competitive strategy calls for working separately to achieve the desired goal.

Sanctions

Sanctions are rewards and punishments used in connection with agreed on norms. Individuals who use a norm in the agreed way can reasonably expect an approrpriate reward. If they do not, they can expect some form of punishment. Sanctions are cultural, so individuals *typically* know what rewards and punishments to expect when they use or fail to use an agreed on norm at the appropriate time.

The fear of losing security, prestige, and economic goods is a powerful force maintaining cultural agreements. The willingness to punish those who would change these agreements and to reward those who act to maintain them supports social ordering. Those who have more to gain by maintaining cultural agreements will more willingly use available sanctioning strategies than those who have less or nothing to gain by their maintenance.

Sanctioning strategies also support individual identities and meaning systems. The use of sanctioning strategies indicates the presence, for at least some persons, of something that is worth maintaining and that provides individual meaning.

NEGATIVE SANCTIONS

Negative sanctions are punishments for failure to use an agreed on norm when circumstances demand its use. The severity of the punishment depends on the importance of the norm. A punishment for not using an agreed on *mos* (singular of mores) is more severe than a punishment for not using an agreed on folkway. Negative sanctions may range all the way from death or expulsion from the group for not using a mos, to a mere frown or look of disgust by others for disregarding a folkway. Each law usually has a designated punishment for its violation.

In practice, negative sanctions are not applied equally to all people in a group or society. Persons holding high social positions or having more power are usually not punished as severely as are people holding lower social positions or with less power for comparable normative violations. For example, middle- and upper-class people who break laws, if arrested, are more likely to obtain probation or lighter prison sentences; if imprisoned they are paroled earlier than are lower-class people.[6] The causes and consequences of this for social order and meaning are developed in Chapter 7, "Social Stratification," and Chapter 14, "Deviance."

POSITIVE SANCTIONS

Positive sanctions are rewards that are forthcoming when people use norms as the cultural agreement specifies. Positive sanctions include approval, praise, the granting of esteem, and other rewards of various kinds. People of higher social position or with greater power are likely to receive more and greater positive sanctions than are people of lower social position or lesser power. Gerhard Lenski[7] points out that power begets privilege and privilege begets power. Possession of privilege and power makes it possible to gain more praise, approval, and esteem. Those who have more get more; those who have less get less.

Statuses and Roles

When most of us think about society and our place and that of others in it we tend to visualize a collection of "positions" and activities. "I am a student." "She is a teacher." "They are the parents of five children." These are common statements expressing this intuitive understanding of the structuring of social relationships. Sociologists use formal concepts of status and role to describe these positions and activities.

A *status* is a designated social position defined by a group or society. A *role* consists of the agreed on expectations about how a person occupying the status should act. There are many social statuses, including husband, wife, father, mother, son, daughter, teacher, student, farmer, machine operator, lodge member, and literally thousands of others.

Complex societies tend to have great numbers of specialized statuses and roles. The division of labor that accompanies the increase in size of a society causes a vast proliferation of social statuses and roles. In a primitive society, a man's occupation may be a farmer or chief. In a complex modern society he is more likely to occupy a specialized status such as breeder of Holstein-Friesian cattle or judge of the Third Circuit Court of Appeals.

Because the concepts of role and status are so important in the study of social behavior, we will examine several aspects of them now and subsequently refer to these concepts many times. Throughout our discussion, we emphasize the dynamic and processual aspect of roles and statuses. They change over time and through interaction. Individuals not only occupy statuses and use roles but in the course of interaction with others they also redefine and shape the statuses they occupy and the roles they use.

Reciprocity of Roles: Role Set

Roles are reciprocal. We cannot think of one role without at the same time thinking of another role or roles. The role of mother makes no sense apart from its relationship to the role of child. The role of teacher is reciprocal with the role of student. Other reciprocal roles include doctor-patient, boss-worker, aunt-nephew or niece, wife-husband, buyer-seller and clergyman-parishioner.

There are typically a number of roles that people are expected to use when they occupy a specific status. When a person occupies a designated status he stands in a reciprocal control relationship to others who occupy different statuses that are reciprocally attached to the status he occupies. Thus, a status may have two or more different sets of role expectations, the exact number depending on the number of reciprocally attached statuses. The total number of different role expectations attached to a given status is called the role set for that status.[8]

For example, students are expected to use a variety of roles in their interaction with people on campus who occupy other statuses that are reciprocally attached to the status of student. As he interacts with a faculty member the student uses one role. He uses another with other students, another with the residence hall director or other administrators, and so forth. If the student is actively involved in student government, in school plays, or on the student newspaper staff, the number of roles in his role-set increases. Figure 2-1 shows this relationship.

Roles and Control

The reciprocal nature of roles is important for control and thus for social ordering. The role of parent is, in part, controlled by the obligations toward the child. If parents want children to survive physically and socially, they expect certain behavior from their children and attempt to control their behavior accordingly. If the child wishes to control the responses of the parents, he must act in a way that will produce the desired response.

FIGURE 2-1
Example of a Student Role Set

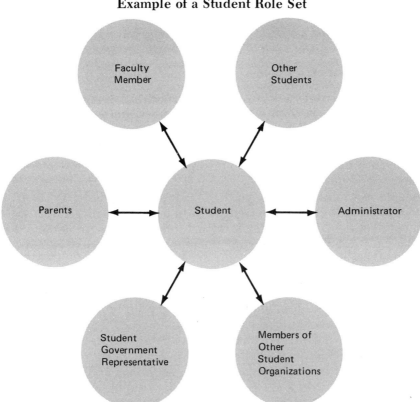

Each arrow indicates a reciprocal relationship

Another control component deriving from the use of roles is the granting of esteem. People who use their roles in the agreed on manner can expect to receive esteem from others. The good doctor is held in high esteem by his patients and the good worker is held in high esteem by his employer. One way of gratifying the need for self-esteem is to use one's role in such a way as to elicit these gratifying responses from others. People use the agreed on norms that make up a role when doing so produces desired responses from others. They can be expected to change their behavior when this is not the case, unless the cost of changing is too great.

Role Taking and Role Making

We have emphasized that people not only use roles, but that they use them in reciprocal interaction with other persons as control strategies to gratify basic needs such as gaining approval and esteem.

The sociologist, Ralph Turner, emphasizes the dynamic aspects of role performance in his concepts of role taking and role making.

> *The idea of role taking shifts emphasis away from the simple process of enacting a prescribed role to devising a performance on the basis of an imputed other-role.* The actor is not the occupant of a position for which there is a neat set of rules—a culture or set of norms—but a person who must act in the perspective supplied in part by his relationship to others whose actions reflect roles that he must identify . . . the tentative character of the individual's own role definition and performance is never wholly suspended.[9]

Turner's suggestion is that role taking in effect becomes role making over a period of time. The person literally *makes* his role in interaction with others. Our theoretical perspective emphasizes how people use roles to gain what they want and to meet basic needs. If traditional roles do not permit them to achieve their goals or meet their needs, people are likely to use other control strategies, thus changing their role behavior and the reciprocal role behaviors of those with whom they interact.

There is often a *negotiated* or bargaining aspect to role use. In many situations the traditional, generally expected behaviors are modified through a process of mutual accommodation to behaviors that more nearly meet the needs of the persons who interact. Workers, for example, often adjust the work situation to meet their needs by seeing what kinds of behaviors are possible in their interaction with other workers and with their bosses. Similarly, the roles in many families between husbands and wives and between parents and children are the result of ongoing negotiations and bargainings about what behaviors are mutually acceptable. Roles are dynamic and change over time as the needs, the goals, and the relative power of the participants in the interaction change.[10]

Role Conflict

Most people use a variety of roles. A woman may be a wife, lawyer, a mother, a club member, and a church member and thus use all of the roles attached to these positions. Because of this, *role conflict* becomes possible. Role conflict occurs when the expectations using one role are incompatible with those using another role. The role conflict may result in impossible time demands or in expectations that are inconsistent. Role conflict also occurs when there is disagreement about how a certain role should be used. In a complex and changing society such as ours, role conflict is common because many people use several different roles to accomplish what they want and role expectations change rapidly. Individuals who experience role conflicts often feel torn between the contradictory expectations that impinge on them. The woman who wants to be a mother and to work often experiences role conflict in our society. The expectations of her husband, her children, and her employer cannot always be satisfactorily met.

Ascribed and Achieved Statuses

The ascription or achievement of social positions is a basic cultural strategy that is used in some fashion or other in almost every society and group to structure the process of social ordering. *Ascribed statuses* are those acquired at birth or later in life without effort by the individual or are assigned because of some criterion such as age, sex, race, ethnicity, social class or some other external criterion over which the individual has little control. *Achieved statuses* are those the individual occupies because of his own efforts or, often, through his choice. A member of the untouchable caste in the Indian caste system occupies a status ascribed by birth. The self-made president of an American corporation who has risen from "rags to riches" occupies an achieved status.

ASCRIBED STATUS

Ascribed statuses are those that are forced on individuals by others; they usually rest on widespread cultural agreements in the society. Age and sex criteria, for example, are used as bases for the ascription of social statuses in all known human societies. The specific norms associated with ascribed social statuses vary widely from society to society, but the use of ascription as a cultural strategy is common.

For example, in most societies men are expected to behave in a specific way, and so are women. Positive sanctions reward conformity and negative sanctions punish deviance. The contemporary Women's Liberation movement is attempting to change certain aspects of behavior expected of women just because they are women. Changing these norms, of course, will change the ascribed statuses for men. Reducing the importance of sex as a basis for ascription frees both sexes from age-old ascriptions.

Historically many occupational statuses were ascribed. (This still exists in some societies.) The child was expected to follow the same occupation as the parent of the same sex. Race and religion have in different times and in different places also served as the basis for ascription.

Much ascription results from the differential distribution of power in a society. In medieval society, the sons and daughters of lords became lords and ladies, whereas the status of serf was ascribed to most others. In our own society the ascription of most black people to the status of slave before the Civil War resulted from the great power differentials between blacks and whites. Whites owned the property and possessed the force to support this power differential and maintain the ascriptive pattern. The black revolution is, in large part, a movement aimed at removing race as a basis for ascription.

ACHIEVED STATUS

Achieved statuses are open to all individuals who meet the qualifications called for by the requirements of these statuses. Even though many positions are still ascribed, the historical trend has been from ascription to achievement. Talcott Parsons notes that the trend is away from assigning statuses on the basis of the *qualities* of individuals to assigning positions on the basis of an individual's *performance*.[11] This historical trend to achievement criteria continues but will never completely replace the ascriptive criteria. Age ascription, for example, will always be present for biological reasons, even though the specific forms may be modified.

So long as power differentials exist in societies and groups, ascription will remain even though specific grounds for ascription can be expected to change over time. At the present, for example, the sons and daughters of the American poor do not have the same opportunities as the offspring of the rich for occupational achievement. Some trade unions and professional associations use a variety of discriminatory strategies to restrict the possibility of achievement. Any type of ascription limits the possible alternatives available to the individual. Even in our society, which places a strong positive cultural value on achievement and performance in occupational positions, the son of a black tenant farmer who aspires to be President of the United States has a far longer and rougher road to travel than the son of an affluent white Anglo-Saxon Protestant attorney. The ascriptive components of being poor, black, or female in our society significantly affect the life-chances of the individual in such highly competitive spheres as politics and employment, even though such positions are supposedly equally available to all.

In Chapter 7 the consequences for individual meaning and the social order of various systems of ranking based on ascription and achievement will be explored. The Indian caste system, for example, represents perhaps the clearest historical example of lifelong ascription of crucial social statuses by birth. Caste status has always been thought to be immutable, but as we will see there have been significant changes in the system in recent decades.

For the disadvantaged—those with less power or more limited access to scarce facilities and rewards—the ascription of social statuses is often the target for programs of social change, as we shall see in Chapter 8, "Ethnic and Minority Groups." Those who benefit most from a system of ascription want to preserve and maintain it.

For all groups and individuals in society, the balance between ascription and achievement in assigning social statuses—and thus distributing social rewards—is a crucial element in the gratification and meaning they derive from their lives.

Group and Societal Entry

Group and societal entry strategies are used both by those who are already members of the group or society and by those who are seeking entry—that is, those who want to become members of the group or society. These cultural strategies are reciprocal processes of control: those who are already members of the society or group set the standards or define the criteria to which aspiring members must conform or be denied access; those who want to secure entry must control their behavior to meet these standards or fit the criteria or else be excluded. The fundamental group entry strategy is *socialization*.

Socialization

Socialization is a process of reciprocal control that, through learning, produces changes in what individuals are—their selves and self-identities—and how they behave in interaction.

The two major types of socialization are primary and secondary. *Primary socialization* occurs as the new infant becomes a member of the society and develops a self and self-identity. *Secondary socialization* occurs later in life after the individual has been through the primary socialization process and wants to join social groups or to change social position, for example, to move from the lower class to the middle class. (Primary socialization is discussed in detail in Chapter 3. Secondary socialization is discussed in Chapter 4.) The following discussion of the two will be general, emphasizing the significance of both forms of socialization as cultural control strategies.

Socialization is one of the most pervasive of the cultural strategies because the use of this strategy by those already in the group is typically backed by a strong public agreement among those previously socialized. Because the public identities and meaning systems of those already socialized are formed by the norms, values, and other information taught newcomers, members have a heavy vested interest in the newcomers' acceptance of what is being taught them. Because newcomers typically want to become members of the group, they are under heavy pressure to permit their behavior to be controlled.

The strength of socialization as a control strategy depends on the degree of interest newcomers have in becoming members of the group. For newly born infants this "interest" is intense because they are completely dependent for survival on the response of parents not only for affection and other necessary emotional rewards but for food and shelter as well. Infants have severely limited alternatives because of their biological and psychic dependence.

If newcomers are willing to go along with the socialization strategies used by the group, they in turn can lay claims on the support and acceptance of those who, through socialization strategies, are attempting to control their behavior. As newcomers go along, group members are expected to make good on the claim that if they go along they will be accepted. Socialization then becomes double-edged: newcomers control, to a degree, the behavior of group members. They become a structuring part of the group through this process of reciprocal control. If a group for some reason badly needs the services of newcomers, these newcomers do not need to allow their behavior to be controlled to the extent they would if their services were not so badly needed. If newcomers are essential for the continuance of the group they can often name the requirements for their acceptance. Some new members are, after all, required for the continuance of the group. If there are many available new members, they will not be as valued and thus will lose some degree of potential control. If available new members are scarce, the degree of potential control on their part will be increased. Both quantity and quality of available new members are important in understanding the control dynamics of socialization strategies.

Assimilation

Assimilation occurs when individuals from one society become members of another society. Two founders of American sociology, Robert E. Park (1864–1944) and Ernest Burgess (1886–1966), defined assimilation as "interpenetration and fusion in which persons and groups acquire the memories, sentiments, and attitudes of other persons or groups, and, by sharing their experience and history, are incorporated with them in a common cultural life."[12]

Individuals who want to be assimilated into a society begin taking on the characteristics required by the society to which they aspire. The implicit promise by members of the host society is that if these characteristics are properly assumed assimilation will result. The members of a society typically hold that their ways of doing things are the best and most valid (this is called ethnocentrism) and thereby implicitly say that all who take on these ways will become acceptable. Individuals who assume these ways feel that a claim for acceptance can be made. If members of the society do not honor this claim, rationalizations must be provided to justify this departure from the norms regulating societal entry.

Assimilation does not always work for the individuals and groups who are attempting to become part of a society. Black people in America, for example, have been denied access to the means for successful assimilation. When, by great effort, they have conformed to many of the entry criteria, extraneous reasons have often been invented to deny them success. If implicit promises are not met, those who have kept the bargain but are not accepted may turn to the use of violent control strategies such as riots against the very society they initially aspired to join.

INITIATION CEREMONIES (RITES OF PASSAGE):
A TYPE OF SECONDARY SOCIALIZATION

Initiation ceremonies or rites are associated with secondary socialization and include a public mutual declaration of faith by the group members and the new initiates. Old members state publicly that the newcomer has met the test and thus has agreed to the group's control strategies, which often are stated in rules and codes. This strategy is also double-edged because once accepted the new members can claim all the rights and privileges of membership for permitting this control. Initiation ceremonies play an important part in controlling the behavior of individuals once public declarations of faith are made.

Ethnocentrism

Ethnocentrism is a feeling on the part of the people in a society or members of a group that their values and total way of life are better than those of other groups or societies. Not all people are ethnocentric, but most of us tend to harbor feelings of ethnocentrism in various degrees. The values and ways of life of the groups and societies to which we belong come to be part of our self-identities, and most of us like to see ourselves as good and to feel that in "the grand scheme of things" that which we "are" has a degree of validity. When other people are different from us this tends to challenge our assumption concerning the "eternal validity" of that which we are or claim to be.

When, from an existentialist point of view, as discussed in Chapter 1, people get a glimpse of the possible ultimate absurdity of things, it is easy to see why they tend to become ethnocentric. The values and way of life of their groups and society are the only things shielding them from this absurdity. When these are challenged by the differences of others, self-identities and basic meaning systems are exposed as potentially meaningless.

Extreme degrees of ethnocentrism are expressed in such statements as "My country, right or wrong" and "America, love it or leave it!"

Example of rites of passage include puberty rites, such as adolescent circumcision in primitive societies; religious ceremonies making the transition from child to adult, such as confirmations and bar mitzvahs; pledging in fraternities and sororities; initiation ceremonies in lodges; and graduation ceremonies in schools.

PHYSICAL SYMBOLS AND RITUALS

Physical symbols and rituals often are used as cultural strategies. These symbols and rituals are used to evoke responses that reinforce group solidarity and the existing society.[13] Symbols and rituals help maintain the usefulness of other cultural strategies over time. The cross for Christians or the Star of David for Jews not only evokes certain emotions in the worshiper but also reinforces loyalty to the congregation and reaffirms its religious orientation.

Some members of a group or society have a greater vested interest in the perpetuation of these symbols and rituals than do others. Potential leaders, for example, often find many uses for national symbols.

In less complex societies the use of ritual tends to be more important than in complex societies. Ritual not only maintains the process of social ordering in these societies but also plays a large part in the formation and perpetuation of individual meaning systems. The use of ritual also reduces levels of anxiety under conditions of uncertainty when the use of other types of control is not possible. A rain dance may not always produce rain, but at least the participants feel they are doing something about the drought. At the same time they are reaffirming group identification and reinforcing group solidarity.

Differentiation and Ranking

All human societies and most human groups differentiate and rank their members by some criteria. The specific criteria vary widely among societies and groups, but often include such socially defined attributes as beauty or ugliness, skin color, physical strength, athletic accomplishments, age, sex, order of birth, place of birth, race, ethnicity, money, talent, skills, education, and family position.

The extent to which differentiation and ranking are cultural control strategies depends on the degree of agreement with them by the parties involved. In turn, how far individuals or groups that are categorized or ranked will agree with the process depends on the category within which they are placed, the meaning attached to it, their relative place in the ranking, what they hope to gain through agreement or fear to lose through disagreement, and the presence or absence of viable alternatives.

It is often puzzling to observers why groups at the bottom of a ranking system—who are objectively deprived and benefit least from the system—appear to participate in it willingly and to support it as a cultural agreement. Sociologists use two concepts to explain this phenomenon: *false consciousness* and *relative deprivation.*

The concept of false consciousness was developed by Karl Marx to explain why some members of a given social class think and act in a manner inconsistent with their own best interests. For example, factory workers were in Marx's view members of the proletariat exploited by the existing system of industrial production. Yet many factory workers were supporters of the capitalist system rather than revolutionaries seeking to overturn it. From Marx's viewpoint, this was false consciousness.

Some measure of false consciousness is often present among members of any group or society. However, it is difficult to decide whether or to what degree an individual or group is falsely conscious. People have different goals and the same goal may have different meanings. What the concept of false consciousness directs us to do is to explore for individuals and groups the meaning for them of their behavior as participants in systems of social differentiation and ranking.

The concept of relative deprivation suggests that an individual's feeling of being disadvantaged by a system of differentiation or ranking depends on the individual or group to which they are comparing themselves. If persons living in a tenement and earning a low income compare themselves with people living in large houses with well-kept lawns and high incomes, they are likely to feel deprived. On the other hand, if these same persons compare themselves with people living in huts with mud floors or on the streets and having no income, they are not likely to feel as deprived. Because people in the lower middle class have others more deprived below them, they typically go along with the cultural ranking agreement—particularly if there is hope for a higher position for themselves or for their children. Individuals do not typically accept categorization and their place in a ranking system blindly.

The differentiation and ranking we find in societies and in groups exists under either implicit or explicit agreements. They are not God-given and thus can be expected to shift and change over time as agreements among subgroups in the society change. Agreement with a given system of differentiation or ranking is made more likely if viable alternatives are absent.

Categorization Strategies As the Basis for Differentiation

The process of categorization is important and necessary in social life. Categorization is necessary if the individual is to attempt to control and find meaning in his world. Gordon W. Allport points out that

The human mind must think with the aid of categories (the term is equivalent here to generalizations). Once formed, categories are the basis for normal prejudgment. We cannot possibly avoid this process. Orderly living depends upon it.[14]

Many, if not most, categories in social life are based on common cultural agreements by certain segments of a population or a total population.

The process of constructing various categories and placing individuals within them is an important control strategy. When stereotypes are attached to what Allport calls rigid categories,[15] individuals or groups can be relegated to these categories, which tend to "fix" the control process over time. All individuals having a defined characteristic are placed in a category and are treated by others in the same manner.

There are a variety of categories into which people are placed: racial, sex, religious, occupational, educational, and others.

Stratification

The cultural strategy of stratification uses the categorization strategy, ranks the resulting categories, and attempts to maintain this ranking over time. If the stratification system is closed, such as in a caste system, persons are born into a ranked category and stay there. If the system is relatively open, people may move either up or down if they or the social control processes change. A system of ranking will not persist over time unless there is substantial agreement with it or force is used to maintain it. If force is used, however, stratification ceases to be a cultural strategy and becomes a coercive strategy.

Students of stratification systems such as Karl Marx, the German sociologist, Ralf Dahrendorf, and Gerhard Lenski agree that at least some latent force is present in and supports all stratified systems.[16] We classify stratification as cultural strategy because it is difficult to assess the degree of latent force present unless the system is directly challenged. Even then, as Marx was well aware, false consciousness may obscure the degree of objective support for or hostility to the system. Put differently, people will suffer a long time before overturning an old cultural agreement and risking the establishment of a new agreement. "Much" can be lost, even though much is, at times, very little indeed.

If the cultural strategy of stratification is to work, there must be an agreement to sustain it. If people are convinced they belong where they are placed or place themselves through their own efforts, the strategy is working. Those with more power can perpetuate a system of stratification that benefits them.[17]

Under the closed classical caste system of stratification of India, with its religiously based belief in reincarnation, the cost of disagreement could be as high as "being reborn as a worm in the intestines of a dog."[18] For an open system, the agreement can be perpetuated by emphasizing that everyone has the possibility of upward social mobility if they will apply themselves sufficiently. Although this may be factually incorrect, if enough people believe it is true, the stratification agreement will remain in effect.

A detailed discussion of various types of stratification systems is presented in Chapter 7.

CULTURAL STRATEGIES: CONCLUDING REMARKS

We have defined culture as a variety of tools and the agreed on rules for their use that are learned or emerge within the process of social interaction and that carry a shared common meaning. We then discussed five broad classes of cultural control strategies: norms, sanctions, status and role, group and societal entry, differentiation and ranking.

Two important points remain to be emphasized. First, although cultural strategies are basic to social ordering, many cultural agreements in existence today were in the historical past forced on groups by conquest, power differentials, or other factors. They became culturally accepted and agreed to during a period of time. Furthermore, many current cultural agreements rest on a foundation of differential power and latent force and remain used and usable partly because there are no alternatives that appear available and viable to some of the parties to the agreement.

Second, cultural strategies have great importance for social ordering and individual meaning. Social order could not be maintained, nor could individual meaning be perceived, without the use of a culturally agreed on and transmitted symbol system such as a language.

This discussion of cultural strategies has presented many of the basic concepts of sociology: culture, subculture, norms, sanctions, roles and statures, ascription and achievement, socialization (primary and secondary), differentiation (categorization), and ranking (stratification).

II. EXCHANGE STRATEGIES

Exchange strategies involve a trade of goods, services, or other rewards between individuals or groups. What is exchanged can be tangible or intangible, concrete or abstract, long-term or immediate. Exchange strategies are commonplaces in social life, as Peter M. Blau, a leading contemporary exponent of social exchange theory, notes:

"neighbors exchange favors; children, toys; colleagues, assistance; acquaintances, courtesies; politicians, concessions; discussants, ideas; housewives, recipes."[19]

The major differences between exchange strategies and cultural strategies are that exchange strategies tend to be limited to a specific relationship and have a "bargained" component that is more explicit. They exist without the presence of moral overtones. Closely related to the latter point is the fact that in an exchange relationship sanctioning strategies are not used. The *only* loss to the individual or group who breaks the relationship is the loss of the reward that was contingent on the original bargain. Therefore, exchange relationships tend to be more flexible and more likely to change rapidly than do relationships based on cultural strategies.

An example will clarify these differences. Although exchange strategies are of many sorts, the most clear-cut are economic exchanges, such as those between a worker and his employer. In return for his services, skills, and energy during a clearly defined period of time, the worker receives in exchange a certain amount of money from his employer. (Money is a *medium* that the worker is able in another series of exchanges *to convert* into the goods, services, and rewards he desires.)

Compare this with the culturally controlled relations in the immediate family. The obligations of parents to children and of children to parents are diffuse, broad, of extended duration, and usually implicit rather than spelled out in a formal contract. The sanctions, both positive and negative, are powerful. To conform is to be loved, accepted, nurtured, and gratified. Nonconformity invites rejection, ostracism, and indeed, for such extreme violations as incest (sexual relations between kinship members), imprisonment or death. Kinship relations are not seen as legitimate objects for "bargaining." Parents do not go on strike for "more love," nor can children petition the National Labor Relations Board for a hearing. Deep emotions and feelings are involved in family relationships.

Broad agreements may surround exchange strategies and define their outer boundaries. George Homans has called one such agreement that regulates exchange relationships *the rule of distributive justice*, which says that "a man's reward in exchange with others should be proportional to his investments."[20] Alvin Gouldner has identified a similar concept he calls *the norm of reciprocity*, which bounds the "mutually gratifying pattern of exchanging goods and services" by requiring that "people should help those who have helped them, and people should not injure those who have helped them."[21]

Both the rule of distributive justice and the norm of reciprocity are assumed agreements within which social exchanges of daily life occur. During a period of time, exchange strategies may become so invested with normative regulations and emotional sentiments that they become cultural strategies, taking on broad components of agreement and no longer regulated by expedient give-and-take bargaining relationships. The reverse may also occur. Such current manifestations of the Women's Liberation movement as the formal marriage contract, where the husband and wife spell out clearly and in detail their mutual obligations and responsibilities after bargaining about them and arriving at a mutually satisfactory statement, represent a shift in the marriage relationship that was previously regulated almost exclusively by cultural strategies.

With these considerations in mind, let us examine the three broad types of exchange strategies: superordinate, subordinate, and accomodation.

Superordinate Exchange Strategies

Superordinate exchange strategies are those used by persons or groups who are in a position to have command over the allocation or distribution of scarce resources either in the form of rewards or in the use of facilities that provide rewards. These scarce and valued rewards range from tangibles such as food to intangibles such as religious salvation. Persons in superordinate positions, by controling the distribution of those valued and scarce rewards can make demands on their subordinates.

If one person can help other persons by providing the means needed to accomplish a goal or by facilitating what other persons want to achieve he can also make demands. Persons in charge of educational facilities, such as a university, can make demands of faculty and students. Faculty need income and the research facilities of the university and students need the facilities of the university to learn and earn a degree. Change in exchange control potential occurs when the *value* of what is being offered as a reward or a facility rises or declines.

Subordinate Exchange Strategies

If a person is in a *subordinate position* and receives rewards or facilities from a person or group in a superordinate position, he must reciprocate if the rewarding relationship is to continue. The subordinate may control the behavior of the superordinate and thereby continue receiving the desired reward only by offering something in exchange that will be rewarding to the superordinate.

One of the most important control strategies used by the subordinate who wants to maintain the exchange relationship is to *obey* the directives of superordinates who supply the rewards. Blau points out the alternatives:

> The person in need of recurrent services from an associate to whom he has nothing to offer has several alternatives. First, he may force the other to give him help. Second, he may obtain the help he needs from another source. Third, he may find ways to get along with such help. If he is unable or unwilling to choose any of these alternatives, however, there is only one other course of action left for him; he must subordinate himself to the other and comply with his wishes; thereby rewarding the other with power over himself as an inducement for furnishing the needed help.[22]

If a person receiving a rewarding activity cannot exchange anything of like value in return, he can give the superordinate in the relationship *approval* and thus may continue to receive the reward. Social approval controls behavior because approval is rewarding.

Accommodation Exchange Strategies

In many interaction situations an impasse is reached and *accommodation* becomes a possible control strategy. When accommodation strategies are used each party gives up something to gain something. This permits individuals or groups to interact without

---

Bride Price: An Exchange Strategy

Bride price is a widespread exchange strategy regulating marital relations in which the groom or his relatives give money, goods, or services to the bride's family or relatives. This is the customary way to obtain a bride in many societies. This exchange strategy regulates one of the most important aspects of the kinship system: the setting up of new familial and reproductive units. It is not surprising, therefore, that the bride-price exchange process occurs within a framework of cultural norms and values.

The anthropologists Carol and Melvin Ember describe the bride-price exchange strategy and then assess its contribution to the process of social ordering:

> Payment can be made in a number of different currencies. Livestock and food are two of the more common. Among the Swazi of southern Africa,
> The number of cattle varies with the girl's rank: twelve head is the current rate for commoners, princesses command fifteen and more. A boy's father should provide the animals for his son's first wife, and subjects contribute for their chief's main wife.

open conflict. Accommodation strategies are typically used when what one party wants is in some way restricted by the interests or goals of another party to the relationships, but conflict is viewed as being too costly by all parties involved. For example, management enters into accommodation agreements with workers to avert strikes. Nations may enter into accommodation agreements to avoid war. Accommodative exchange strategies include compromise, arbitration or mediation, and toleration.

Compromise is the basic type of accommodation. The use of compromise does not mean that the parties involved are completely satisfied with the solution or that other strategies will not be used to accomplish the desired end. Many times the strategy of compromise is used only as a cover for other strategies that continue to be used. A nation threatened with superior force by a more powerful neighbor may compromise by ceding disputed territory while it quietly builds up its military force, seeks powerful allies, and lays plans to regain the lost land.

If parties using the compromise strategy cannot agree, a third party may be called on to help. The use of a third party is the *arbitration* or *mediation* strategy. Arbitration takes the solution out of the hands of the original parties. The arbitrator considers all sides of the issue and makes a binding decision. Mediation does not take the solution out of the hands of the parties involved. The mediator merely serves as

---

The Gusii of Kenya, the Nyakyusa of Tanzania, and the Tiv of West Africa also pay in cattle; the Siane of New Guinea and the Ifugao of the Philippines provide pigs; the Navajo and Somali pay in horses. Food is used by the Hopi and Arapesh; the Kwakiutl pay in blankets.

The Subanun of the Philippines have an expensive bride price. They compute the sum as several times the annual income of the groom *plus* three to five years of bride service. . . . Among the Manus of the Admiralty Islands off New Guinea, a groom requires an economic backer—usually an older brother or an uncle—if he is going to marry, but it will be years before he can pay off his debts. Depending on the amount of the bride price agreed upon, payments are concluded at the time of the marriage or continue for years afterwards.

Despite the connotations bride price may have for us, it does not reduce a woman to a slave. Actually, she acquires prestige for herself and her family, perhaps compensating them for the loss of her services, and those of her future children. Indeed, the fee paid can serve as a security—for should the marriage fail through no fault of her own, and the wife return to her kin, the price might not be returned; on the other hand, the wife's kin may pressure her to remain with her husband, even though she does not want to, because her kin do not want to or are unable to return the bride price.[a]

[a]Carol Ember and Melvin Ember, *Anthropology* (New York: Appleton, 1973), p. 326.

go-between for the two parties and helps to clarify issues. These strategies often are used in working out labor contracts between workers and management and, at times, to settle international disputes.

A final accommodative strategy is *toleration*. This is an informal agreement by the parties involved to leave each other alone so that each party can go its own way—so long as they do not infringe on each other. Again, the parties involved do not agree with what the others are doing but do agree that it is better to leave each other alone than to engage in continuous disputes.

III. Procedural Strategies

Persons or groups using procedural strategies set up (or work within) the "rules of the game" that hopefully will accomplish or maintain their goals. They then attempt to gain acceptance of the rules by others. If others accept these procedures and follow them, control is accomplished. When challenged, an appeal is made to the established procedural rules. Following the procedure, working within the system, or accepting the framework comes to be its own validation, so that the strategy becomes self-sustaining. Those who can establish the rules—set up the organizational framework—or define the system and secure compliance by other parties have great control potential. There are three major types of procedural strategies: bureaucratization, professionalization, and the use of science and technology.

Bureaucratization

Bureaucratization is the process of establishing rules and organizational forms based on them that are calculated to attain goals.[23] Most modern schools and colleges, labor unions, factories, armies, government agencies, and other large organizations are bureaucratized. Bureaucracy is the hall mark of the advanced, complex, industrial society. Bureaucratization seems to be almost a universal concomitant of modernization.

Bureaucratization is a control strategy that allows those in certain statuses to set the procedures. Once the procedures are set, subordinates must go through channels and use procedures that not only control their behavior but protect the machinery of control.

On the other hand, bureaucratization also provides subordinates in the organization with certain control potential. The existence of rules provides them with a point of leverage. If they follow the rules, they have the right to make certain demands based on their performance according to these rules.

The extent to which bureaucracies are in fact efficient or accomplish their goals, and the negative consequences for those who work in them and those who are affected by bureaucratization, will be explored in some detail in Chapter 4, where bureaucratized organizations are discussed as a type of social group. Many of the sharpest problems of individual meaning and social ordering in the modern world flow directly from the proliferation of bureaucratic social forms. The students who took as their battle cry, "Do Not Fold, Staple, Bend, or Mutilate—I am a Human Being," were expressing a widespread negative reaction to being processed through a bureaucratic system.

Professionalization

Professionalization strategies establish procedural steps to certify as professionals a specified group of people who complete these steps. These procedural steps are supposedly rational, which validates the professional's increased control potential. The steps typically consist of a specified number of years of formal training and some type of formal examination. Individuals acquire great control potential once they have been through the professionalizing procedures. However, just because individuals have been "validated" as professionals by going through certain procedural steps does not *necessarily* mean that they are competent to do what the procedural steps would indicate they can do. In spite of this, individuals have greater control potential once they have been through the professionalizing procedures, and it is often difficult to overcome the control they have. If students want credit for a course, they must do as the teacher says. If persons on welfare want to receive help, they must allow their behavior to be controlled by the social worker.

Science and Technology

Modern technology is based on the application of the knowledge produced by science. City planning, rehabilitation programs, and economic planning are all technologies based on science that are increasingly important control strategies. The many branches of engineering, applied chemistry, applied physics, and—to an increasingly extent—applied biology have had profound effects on human life. Questions about the control of the behavior of children labeled as hyperactive by the use of drugs and the much talked about behavioral control through changes made in genetic structure are indications that the use of technological strategies based on science will become increasingly important in all areas of social life.

Technology, with its constant innovation, is a major source of social change in modern societies, as will be elaborated on in Chapter 15, "Social Change and Collective Behavior." The strategies of science and technology are simultaneously sources of great social benefit and great social disruption. In Chapter 5, "Ecological Constraints, Community, and Mass Society," some of these consequences of technology for the environment and for human communities will be explored.

A Final Note on Procedural Strategies

In discussing each of the three major types of procedural strategies, we have noted that they are in large measure modern phenomena, associated with urbanized, industrialized, large-scale, complex societies. Furthermore, they often exist together. Most professionals are trained in and carry on their careers in bureaucracies, and much of their training is in science and technology. In turn, the organizational systems that support science and technology are themselves bureaucratized and staffed by professionals.

These three modern control strategies are among the most potent social forces that man has developed. They operate within the context of a modern society that values rationality, efficiency, and goal attain-

---

Technology: Blessing or Curse?

The merits and demerits of technology are hotly debated in this era of massive environmental pollution, ecological disruption, and energy shortages. The excerpt that follows is an impassioned argument against technological control by the sociologist and social critic Philip Slater. Precisely because Americans automatically tend to accept technology as a blessing (while viewing its negative consequences as "side effects" best overcome by more technology), we present Slater's slashing critique as a partial antidote to the conventional view.

> Our society . . . has traditionally . . . [given] completely free rein to technological change . . . . Since, however, technological change in fact forces social changes upon us, this has had the effect of abdicating all control over our social environment to a kind of whimsical deity. While we think of ourselves as a people of change and progress, masters of our environment and our fate, we are no more entitled to this designation than the most superstitious savage, for our relation to change is entirely passive. We poke our noses out the door each day and wonder breathlessly what new disruptions technology has in store for us. We talk of technology as the servant of man, but it is a servant that now dominates the household, too powerful to fire, upon whom everyone is helplessly dependent. We tiptoe about and speculate upon his mood. What will be the effects of such-and-such an invention? How will it change our daily lives? We never ask, do we *want* this, is it worth it? (We did not ask ourselves, for example, if the trivial

ment. By their operations as control strategies they influence much of the process of social ordering and raise critical questions about individual meaning.

IV. MANIPULATIVE STRATEGIES

Manipulative Strategies are those used by an individual or group attempting to control the behavior of others through the conscious management of communications or behavior. This management takes many forms, all of which attempt to hide from view the *real* reasons for the communication or behavior so that the recipient is led to believe that the manipulator is acting in good faith. Manipulative strategies are either verbal or nonverbal.

Verbal Manipulation

Propaganda is "the deliberate attempt to control the behavior or interrelationships of members of a social group through the use of devices that are effective in changing feelings, attitudes, and

---

conveniences offered by the automobile could really offset the calamitous disruption and depersonalization of our lives that it brought about.) We simply say "You can't stop progress" and shuffle back inside.

We pride ourselves on being a "democracy" but we are in fact slaves. We submit to an absolute ruler whose edicts and whims we never question. We watch him carefully, hang on his every word; for technology is a harsh and capricious king, demanding prompt and absolute obedience. . . . We have passively surrendered to every degradation, every atrocity, every enslavement that our technological ingenuity has brought about. We laugh at the old lady who holds off the highway bulldozers with a shotgun, but we laugh because we are Uncle Toms. We try to outdo each other in singing the praises of the oppressor, although in fact the value of technology in terms of human satisfaction remains at best undemonstrated. For when evaluating its effects we always adopt the basic assumptions and perspective of technology itself, and never examine it in terms of the totality of human experience. We say this or that invention is valuable because it generates other inventions—because it is a means to some other means—not because it achieves an ultimate human end. We play down the "side effects" that so often become the main effects and completely negate any alleged benefits. The advantages of *all* technological "progress" will after all be totally outweighed the moment nuclear war breaks out (an event which, given the inadequacy of precautions and the number of fanatical fingers close to the trigger, is only a matter of time unless radical changes are made).[a]

[a]Philip Slater, *The Pursuit of Loneliness: American Culture at the Breaking Point* (Boston: Beacon, 1970), paperback, pp. 44–45.

values."[24] Propaganda is the most widely used type of verbal manipulative strategy in our society. Most television commercials use propaganda techniques in an attempt to control the buying behavior of consumers. Politicians use propaganda in an attempt to control voting behavior. Many corporations and other types of organizations, including colleges and universities, have public relations departments whose task it is to enhance the image of the organization and influence the behavior or attitudes of clients by controlling the dissemination of information.[25]

Humor is also a common manipulative strategy. Considerable truth is told in jest. Control strategies based on humor range from political cartoons to cutting remarks made humorously. Humor can blunt the sharp edge of truth so that messages can be conveyed that might not otherwise be delivered. Humor also reduces the credibility of another person, thus reducing his control potential. It can cool a potentially explosive social situation, or build one person up while putting another down.[26]

Lying is another commonly used manipulative strategy. Georg Simmel (1858–1918) has pointed out that

> Every lie, no matter how objective its topic, engenders by its very nature an error concerning the lying *subject*. The lie consists in the fact that the liar hides his true idea from the other. Its specific nature is not exhaustively characterized by the fact that the person lied-to has a false conception about the topic or object; this the lie shares with common error. What is specific is that he is kept deceived about the private opinion of the *liar*.[27]

Simmel continues:

> the lie which maintains itself, which is not seen through, is undoubtedly a means of asserting intellectual superiority and of using it to control and suppress the less intelligent.[28]

Lying controls the behavior of others by providing false information and thus protecting and, at times, enhancing the welfare of the liar. Children lie to keep from being punished. Some merchants use false advertising to enhance their profits. Some politicans lie to gain or to remain in political office.

Labeling another person or group is also a useful manipulative strategy that permits control when the labeling is successful. Children apply a variety of labels to each other such as "sissy" or "tomboy." Such labels are temporary and subject to change. Other labels, such as "mentally ill" or "criminal," are longer-lasting and more potentially damaging. Whether or not a label will stick depends partly on the relative power the person doing the labeling has compared with the power of the person being labeled.[29]

The use of jargon is an important verbal manipulative strategy. Jargon is a special language used by individuals within a group or sub-culture to communicate information, attitudes, or emotions. Jargon is often used to impress or exclude those outside the group who cannot understand what is being communicated. Many occupational groups, including the professions, rely heavily on jargon. The meaning of much jargon could be clearly stated in everyday language, but if this were done it would lose its manipulative advantage. For example, statisticians and those who use statistics in their work, call the average of a group of numbers a mean and designate it figuratively as $\overline{X}$ bar. Most people are familiar with the word *average* so used, but few understand the word *mean* or the designation $\overline{X}$ *bar*. Such jargon separates statisticians from others and enhances their importance. Plumbers, pickpockets, drug addicts, intelligence agents, and many others do the same. Such special languages draw boundaries around groups and reinforce in-group solidarity.

Closely related to jargon is the manipulative use of language to impress or evoke certain *responses* from others. Not only *what* is said but *how* it is said can provide control. Discussing rapping in the black ghetto, Thomas Kochman describes this type of manipulative behavior:

> "Rapping," "shucking," "jiving," "running it down," "gripping," "copping a plea," "signifying" and "sounding" are all part of the black ghetto idiom and describe different ways of talking. Each has its own distinguishing features of form, style and function; each is influenced by, and influences, the speaker, setting, and audience; and each sheds light on the black perspective and the black condition—on those orienting values and attitudes that will cause a speaker to speak or perform in his own way within the context of the black community.[30]

Nonverbal Manipulation

Nonverbal manipulative strategies attempt to achieve control through the conscious management of what is *done* rather than through what is said.

Staging and performances are used where the individual or group attempts to manipulate impressions or information by presenting a planned front, or façade, to others. The cocktail party described in Chapter 1, where the hosts carefully set the stage and then engage in reciprocal performances with their guests, expresses this kind of manipulation. Most social interaction involve some staging and performance. It becomes a manipulative strategy when it is calculated to conceal, hide, or mislead.

Withholding information as a nonverbal manipulative strategy is used in many kinds of interaction. The withholding of valuable information from one's superiors can cause them to make incorrect decisions, appear incompetent, and thus jeopardize their jobs. If persons do not have access to pertinent information, they may "make fools of themselves." In most situations we depend on the flow of critical information. Keeping others ignorant of important information is an important control strategy. It is not unusual for individuals to selectively distribute valuable information to increase their degree of control. Much work remains to be done in what has come to be called the sociology of ignorance.[31] The various uses made of *secrecy* are also important control strategies.[32]

Changing rules and procedures is a nonverbal manipulative strategy often used in organizations. If rules and procedures exist and individuals obey the rules or follow the procedures, they can usually make certain claims. If another person who is expected to make good on these claims changes the rules, the procedures, or their interpretation he does not have to honor the claim being made. Changing rules and procedures or their interpretation is used sometimes openly and sometimes subtly, both to maintain existing power arrangements and to change them.

Avoidance is another common nonverbal manipulative strategy. If

Withholding Information and Secrecy As Control Strategies

The political scientist Daniel Ellsberg, a former Defense Department official, achieved considerable prominence by releasing to the press classified government documents concerning the origin and conduct of the war in Vietnam. Describing that part of the vast governmental apparatus for regulating the flow of information that he was familiar with, Ellsberg told an interviewer that "TOP SECRET" was one of the lowest-level clearances, and that he personally had a dozen clearances for access to restricted information above the top-secret level. The existence of these clearances themselves is kept secret, thereby maximizing control—not only is the classified information secret, but the fact that the information exists and is restricted is itself kept secret.

Ellsberg describes the elaborate organizational apparatus that maintains secrecy:

> The clearance list typically will have a code name, and you have a separate code word to go on the pieces of paper so they don't get shuffled in by mistake with files to which unauthorized people have access—a code word on a cover sheet, perhaps with a special colored border, so that anybody handling the paper will be alerted—without looking at the inside contents—that it has to be kept and stored separately. And you need a separate safe or, if there's a lot of material, a

persons can avoid confrontation or involvement they can at times achieve control by protecting themselves from being forced to do something they do not want to do. They avoid situations in which unwelcome demands would be made on them. This control strategy is often used by administrators who do not want to make a decision on an issue for fear of being wrong or appearing incompetent.

Co-optation is used to control persons or groups by either making it appear that the co-opter is acting in their best interests or by enticing them to join his side. This strategy is often used by persons in power to reduce the threat of opposition. An example is the promotion of a strong union leader who is making trouble in an industrial plant to foreman. Many administrators use this control strategy when opposition to their policies develops and they feel their power is threatened.

V. COERCIVE STRATEGIES

Coercive strategies are ordinarily used only after other attempts at control have failed and the individual or group has still not reached its objectives. Most coercive strategies carry a high potential cost and a

---

separate office. You need a special courier to carry this around, perhaps a whole system of couriers. And some secretaries probably will have to be cleared to work on the papers.

If you're not dealing in one single location, you might need separate communications facilities—separate radio channels, circuits under which coded messages are sent, or separate telephone lines. . . . [if] there's a lot of written material, you have special stationery so that you don't have to type these special code words all the time. . . .

You have entire administrative bureaucracies whose job is keeping the "need to know" lists up to date, to oversee the procedures, to check that the couriers are following out their instructions and the communicators are not being careless, that the pieces of paper are not in fact being left out on desks and so forth.

Ellsberg concludes by pointing up the control potential of secrecy and withholding information:

The whole purpose of these procedures is not merely to keep messages or memoranda away from the eyes of certain people, but to keep such people from ever guessing or wondering whether such information exists, or from having any notion of the type of people who may have access to it.

In other words, it's a management of attention and of speculation, not merely of information.[a]

[a]Daniel Ellsberg, *Rolling Stone* (Dec. 6, 1973), p. 35.

correspondingly high risk. Coercive strategies may be nonviolent or violent. Nonviolent types tend to be used before the ever costlier violent coercive strategy.

Nonviolent Coercive Strategies

Nonviolent coercive strategies are more useful than violent coercive strategies for people with little power because these people neither control nor have access to instruments of massive force. Individual or group values may also dictate the choice of nonviolent strategies. Individuals or groups with considerable power also use these strategies, preferring them because violent strategies are usually costlier, riskier, and overly disruptive for the goals sought. The nonviolent coercive strategies discussed include threats, argument, verbal disruption, antilocutions, withholding rewards, withholding services, withholding facilities, and general disruption.

Threats take two major forms: threatening to move toward a more forceful type of strategy if demands are not met, and threatening to withdraw certain rewards if demands are not met. The conditions under which each of these is most likely to be used depend on what the person or group seeking control has to bargain with. If the person or group has limited resources, the threat of more forceful action will probably be used. If they have adequate resources, they will probably threaten to withdraw rewards.

Argument is a useful strategy only under sharply limited conditions. The opponent must be willing to "listen" or be "forced" into a change of behavior if he "loses" the argument. Typically, an argument is backed up with threats when the chips are down. *Verbal disruption strategies,* such as shouting down a speaker, are used to prevent rational argument or to show contempt for a speaker. *Antilocutions* are degrading or cutting remarks directed at another person or group, ranging from mild jokes to derogatory epithets. Allport points out that "the more spontaneous and irrelevant the antilocution, the stronger the hostility that lies behind it."[33] Words cannot kill, but they can inflict severe damage on an opponent in public or private situations. Ridicule and name calling are common antilocutions.

Withholding rewards is used as a nonviolent coercive strategy if an individual (or group) controls rewards based on resources that another individual or group needs or wants. Firing an employee, boycotts, and the withholding of affection or approval are examples of this strategy. The *withholding of services* is a parallel to withholding rewards as a control strategy. If persons need the services of others and these services are withheld, control can often be achieved. Strikes and slowdowns in industrial plants and the refusal by a spouse to work or to be sexually responsive if the other spouse has "gotten out of line" are examples of this strategy. *Withholding the use of facilities* follows the same dynamics as the two previous strategies. Not allowing persons or groups access to needed facilities can cause them to accede to the demands of the person or group controlling the facilities. The lockouts that occurred during the labor strife of the 1930s are an excellent example of the use of this strategy. Refusing to loan or grant the use of a needed facility can serve as a powerful control strategy. The usefulness of these three withholding strategies depends on the degree to which the rewards, services, and facilities are needed and the degree of disruption that the strategy might cause.

Although the three strategies discussed here are usually disruptive, *general disruption* as such is also a strategy used to coerce others into making concessions. Such actions as blocking streets, staging sit-ins, stand-ins, and similar disruptions can be effective strategies.[34]

Violent Coercive Strategies

Violent coercive strategies use open physical force in attempting to accomplish the desired objective. The specific types and the intensity of violence used depend on the resources, the goals, and the willingness to accept the extremely high costs and risks of those using these strategies. We shall discuss riots and mob actions, revolution, and terror strategies.

Riots and mob actions are violent coercive strategies typically used by people who have little power.* Riots tend to be random in goals and targets, whereas mobs tend to be more single-minded in their pursuit of specific objectives. Both these strategies seem to be used when a high level of frustration is present in a situation and other types of control strategies have been ineffective. Their use is spontaneous and unplanned. Whether riots or mob action will be effective depends on the degree of disruption, the threat of further disruption, and the willingness by those with more power to change the conditions causing the use of these strategies.

Revolution as a strategy occurs when a group of individuals join together and either use or are prepared to use force against those who control the formal machinery of government. Political revolutions are commonplace in many parts of the world, where control at the formal political level changes hands frequently. Brazil, Chile, Libya, and

*We will see later that riots and mob actions are sometimes used by those holding more power in order to maintain this power.

Greece are but a few recent examples of the forceful seizure of state power by an organized group.

Terror strategies include various methods that are used by individuals, groups, or governments. They include widespread spying and executions, random arrests, bombing houses or buildings, random murders, and lynchings. At times terror strategies are used by governments—for example, during the Stalinist period in the USSR—and, at other times, by people outside of government who wish to change the processes of social ordering—for example, the bombings and assassinations in Northern Ireland. Much of the control exerted by terror strategies stems from the widespread fear and social dislocations they produce.

Violent coercive strategies seek to change or prevent change in existing control relationships. Riots often express underlying dissatisfactions that have built up during a long period of time. Mob actions, although limited in scope, also attempt to go outside the existing order of control relationships to effect or prevent changes. Terror strategies may seek immediate goals or may be aimed at achieving so much disruption of the over-all process of social ordering that major changes occur or are prevented from occurring in power relationships. Revolution by definition seeks changes in the process of social ordering. In Chapter 15, the causes and consequences of many violent coercive strategies will be examined.

Bride Price Too High? Coercive Strategy Replaces Exchange Strategy

Our familarity with violent coercive control strategies in modern societies should not blind us to their presence in other kinds of societies. The anthropologist Robert Edgerton studied four East African Tribal societies living in Kenya, Uganda, and Tanzania and found numerous examples of personal and group violence. These tribal societies all have the exchange control strategy bride price already described. Edgerton notes that the conflicts that this exchange strategy creates are often resolved by violent coercive strategies, as are other forms of marital discord:

> In these tribal societies, a woman's choice of her spouse is a good deal less than free. Typically, young women form romantic relationships with young men only to find that their romantic inclinations do not often correspond to those of her family who wish a happy and secure marriage but who also wish one in which a sizeable bride price is paid. When young women refuse to marry the man their family finds most suitable, or best able to pay the bride price, they may (and often

VI. COALITIONAL STRATEGIES

Coalitional strategies involve the joining together of individuals, groups, or societies to increase collective resources and to present a common front—thus increasing the relative degree of control potential. There are three major types: permanent unification, temporary unification, and partial unification.

If *permanent unification* is used, individuals, groups, or societies decide to become one in all matters. This typically occurs when individuals or groups have much in common and will gain substantially and lose little or nothing in joining forces. The ecumenical movement among some contemporary religious denominations is an example here.[35]

Temporary unification brings people, groups, or societies together for a specific short-term purpose, often as a result of a common threat. Once the threat is overcome, separation occurs. The use of this strategy does not require the giving up of separate identities. Differences and even frictions remain within the coalition—but in the face of the common threat the individuals or groups appear as one. This strategy is common in wartime when several nations form a coalition to defeat another nation or group of nations. The North Atlantic Treaty Organization (NATO) and the Warsaw Pact Alliance are two such

---

do) attempt to run away, but since this maneuver has been anticipated, it is seldom successful. Instead, the girl is likely to be apprehended and subjected to varying degrees of force until she accepts the designated husband. This force may consist in nothing more than confinement and haranguing, but it may also involve a prolonged beating at the hands of her brothers and father. Similarly, a woman who deserts her husband, either to run away with another man or merely to escape from an unpleasant marital relationship, may be captured and beaten by her family or by interested clansmen until she agrees to return to her husband. Many women flee their husbands several times, only to be apprehended and coerced back into the marriage. However, it is also the case that a husband who regularly or flagrantly abuses or mistreats his wife may be seized by his clansmen and beaten. In both cases, the family and the clan are concerned that the marriage—and their reputation as people from whom good marriages may be expected—be maintained and that neither husband nor wife do anything to destroy the marriage. The use of violence against runaway women is a good deal more common than it is against misbehaving husbands, but collective violence may be directed against either.[a]

[a]Robert Edgerton, "Violence in East African Tribal Societies," in *Collective Violence*, ed. by James Short and Marvin Wolfgang (Chicago: Aldine, 1972), p. 166.

temporary unifications dating from the cold war between the United States and the USSR.

In *partial unification,* individuals, groups, or societies join to accomplish a common goal or to protect certain interests. Separate identities remain. The coalition typically centers around the achieving of only one goal or interest. Workers, for example, form coalitions to improve working conditions and income.

VII. WITHDRAWAL STRATEGIES

There are various degrees of withdrawal, from tangential membership with limited involvement where membership or physical presence is maintained to complete physical withdrawal.

Withdrawal strategies are typically used where continued involvement is not paying off in anticipated or promised rewards or where safety is threatened. There are times when withdrawal will not be allowed by those with more power. If an individual, group, or society has been actively involved in important relationships, withdrawal can be expected to have severe costs and high risks.

Physical withdrawal involves leaving completely the interactional setting. Group members or individuals remove themselves to another place. This strategy has been used by some persecuted religious groups and is the strategy used to dissolve marital ties that we call divorce.

Ritual withdrawal does not entail complete physical withdrawal. The individual or group remains in the situation and *acts* interested in individual or collective goals but in fact is in the group but not of it.[36] Workers who go to work but care nothing about their jobs and students who go to class but care nothing about learning are practicing ritual withdrawal as a control strategy.

Group disbandment may be used as a withdrawal strategy for purposes of safety or because the group is no longer useful. For example, after a revolution, some old groups seen as threatening to the new regime might disband for the sake of the survival of their individual members. After the Communist revolution in the USSR many religious groups disbanded. Groups may also disband because their goals have been achieved or because remaining together no longer gratifies individual needs. However, withdrawal strategies may not always be what they appear to be on the surface. Individuals or groups may at times withdraw to regroup, give themselves time to retrain, or to formulate new strategies.

CONTROL STRATEGIES AND SOCIAL ORDERING

The seven major types of control strategies (cultural, exchange, procedural, manipulative, coercive, coalitional, and withdrawal) provide a classification of the processes of social ordering. Groups and societies are ordered and change as these strategies are used in various combinations and different intensities under differing types of constraints.

Many of the most significant differences among groups and among societies result from differing patterns produced by the use of differing combinations of control strategies. For example, coercive strategies are more widely used in dictatorships and totalitarian societies than in democratic societies, which depend more heavily on manipulative strategies. Smaller and less complex societies are typically ordered primarily by cultural strategies because of their limited division of labor and the lack of alternatives. People in modern complex societies with their elaborate division of labor are more likely to use exchange, procedural, and manipulative strategies. People in societies with heterogeneous populations are more likely to use coalition and exchange strategies. Control strategies are important working concepts that help us use our sociological imaginations to meaningfully comprehend our social environment. They are powerful instruments of analysis not only at the level of entire societies or large groups, but also for the description and analysis of interpersonal relations and patterns of interaction within smaller groups.

REFERENCES

1. Kroeber, Alfred, and Clyde Kluckhohn. *Culture: A Critical Review of Concepts and Definitions.* Cambridge: Peabody Museum Anthropological Papers, 1952, No. 47.
2. Tylor, Sir Edward Burnett. *Primitive Culture.* New York: Brentano's, 1924, p. 1. This work was first published in 1871.
3. Sumner, William Graham. *Folkways.* New York: Dover, 1959. This work was first published in 1906.
4. See, for example, *Cooperation and Competition Among Primitive Peoples.* Ed. by Margaret Mead. New York: McGraw-Hill, 1937.
5. *The Sociology of Georg Simmel.* Ed. and trans. by Kurt Wolff. New York: Free Press, 1950.
6. See Quinney, Richard. *The Social Reality of Crime.* Boston: Little, Brown, 1970.
7. Lenski, Gerhard. *Power and Privilege.* New York: McGraw-Hill, 1966.
8. See Merton, Robert K. "Role Set: Problems in Sociological Theory." *British Journal of Sociology,* Vol. 8 (June 1957), 106–120.
9. Turner, Ralph. "Role-Taking: Process Versus Conformity." In *Human Behavior and Social Processes.* Ed. by Arnold M. Rose. Boston: Houghton, 1962, p. 23.

66   *Social Ordering and Individual Meaning*

10. For a discussion of roles from this perspective, see Lindesmith, Alfred, and Anselm Strauss. *Social Psychology*. New York: Holt, 1968.
11. See Parsons, Talcott. "Evolutionary Universals in Society." *American Sociological Review*, **29** (June 1964), 339–357.
12. Park, Robert E., and Ernest Burgess. *Introduction to the Science of Sociology*. 2nd ed. Chicago: U. of Chicago, 1951, p. 575.
13. Durkheim, Emile. *The Elementary Forms of the Religious Life*. Trans. by Joseph Ward Swain. New York: Collier, 1961.
14. Allport, Gordon W. *The Nature of Prejudice*. Boston: Addison-Wesley, 1954, p. 20.
15. Ibid., p. 171.
16. See Dahrendorf, Ralf. *Class and Class Conflict in Industrial Society*. Stanford, Calif.: Stanford University Press, 1959, for a discussion of Marx and a modification of Marxian theory. Also, see Lenski, Gerhard. *Power and Privilege: A Theory of Social Stratification*. New York: McGraw-Hill, 1966.
17. See Lenski, loc. cit.
18. See Weber, Max. *The Religion of India*. Trans. by H. H. Gerth and Don Martindale. New York: Free Press, 1958.
19. Blau, Peter M. *Exchange and Power in Social Life*. New York: Wiley, 1964, p. 88.
20. Homens, op. cit.
21. Gouldner, Alvin. "The Norm of Reciprocity: A Preliminary Statement." *American Sociological Review*, **25** (April 1960), 120–121.
22. Blau, op. cit., pp. 21–22.
23. Weber, Max. *The Theory of Social and Economic Organization*. Trans. by A. M. Henderson and Talcott Parsons. New York: Free Press, 1947.
24. Bertrand, Alvin. *Basic Sociology*. 2nd ed. New York: Appleton, 1973, pp. 340–341.
25. For a classic treatment of propaganda, see Lee, Alfred McClung, and Elizabeth Briant Lee. *The Fine Art of Propaganda*. New York: Harcourt, 1939.
26. For example, see Stephenson, Richard M. "Conflict and Control Functions of Humor." *American Journal of Sociology*, Vol. 56 (May 1951), 569–574 and Burma, John H. "Humor As a Technique in Race Conflict." *American Sociological Review*, Vol. 11 (Dec. 1946), 710–715.
27. Wolff, op. cit. p. 312.
28. Ibid., p. 314.
29. For examples, see Schur, Edwin M. *Labeling Deviant Behavior*. New York: Harper, 1971.
30. Kochman, Thomas. "Rappin in the Ghetto." In *Soul Chicago*. Ed. by Lee Rainwater. Chicago: Aldine, 1970, p. 51.
31. See Schneider, Louis. "The Role of the Category of Ignorance in Sociological Theory: An Exploratory Statement." *American Sociological Review*, Vol. 27 (Aug. 1962).
32. For an excellent discussion of secrecy see Wolff loc. cit.
33. Allport, op. cit., p. 58.
34. For a discussion of nonviolent coercive strategies see Sharp, Gene. *Exploring Nonviolent Alternatives*. Boston: Porter Sarbent, 1970.
35. For a discussion of this see Berger, Peter. *The Sacred Canopy*. Garden City, N.Y.: Doubleday, 1967.
36. Merton, Robert K. *Social Structure and Social Theory*. New York: Free Press, 1949, Chap. 4.

C H A P T E R 3

Socialization

Socialization is the process of reciprocal control that produces changes in what individuals are (their selves and self-identities) and how they behave in interaction with others through a process of learning. When individuals enter new and strange situations they must learn new ways of acting to more effectively control the responses of others. Socialization, thus, is a lifelong process. Individuals learn to act differently in different situations and during different stages of their lives. Such continuous socialization is necessary in order for individuals to optimize their control and to participate in the processes of social ordering.

In this chapter the dynamics of primary socialization—the way the new human organism becomes a functioning member of society—will be described.

THE INFANT

At the point of birth the infant is little more than a biological organism. He has no self-identity. Indeed, he is not aware of his own separate existence from that of other people and material objects. If a self is to develop, it must do so within the framework of interaction with other people. This, of course, does not mean that the infant is only an inert piece of protoplasm. He has the *capacity to respond* in a variety of ways to external stimuli, the possibility of development, and the potential to "seek" survival. Sucking, for example, is present at birth. However, if left to their own devices, infants would soon perish.

The Major Concern

Our objectives are to analyze the socialization process that occurs between parent and child, to isolate those interaction dynamics that produce a social self, and to identify the *needs* and desires that *motivate* this self to participate in the *processes of social ordering.*

Even though *specific* socialization strategies differ from society to society and among different groups and social classes within the same society, the general dynamics of the primary socialization process are not infinitely variable. Primary socialization must operate within a range restricted by the *nature of the biological organism* and by the *nature of social ordering.* Certain activities need to be performed by socialization agents (usually parents) in all societies if the new biological organism is to survive, develop a self, and learn the control strategies required to exist within a limited range of alternatives.

Control Is Necessary

For new biological organisms to develop into social beings their behavior must be controlled. Indeed, the attempted control of the infant's behavior and the controlling responses this produces in him, are the core of the socialization process. If infants behave correctly by following the expectations of the parents, they are rewarded. If they behave incorrectly, some form of punishment or avoidance is likely to ensue. Expectations, rewards, and punishments take different forms in different societies and at different times in history.[1] Whatever their form, however, all rewards and punishments serve to control the behavior of infants. From birth infants respond to the control strategies used by parents as they attempt to control the behavior of infants.

Attempts at control by parents are both inevitable and necessary for the process of social order. Control is also necessary if the infant is to survive biologically, become a social being by acquiring a self and participate in the process of social ordering with a degree of individual meaning.

Socialization through control is not a one-way process. Control attempts by parents condition infants to behave in specified ways that in turn have the effect of controlling the behavior of parents. Infants learn through conditioning that if they behave in specific ways they will receive rewards and if they behave in other ways they will receive punishment.

Greater power and potential control are clearly possessed by the parents. But despite this, infants do come to control the behavior of parents through the control of their own behavior. As this occurs, a microcosm of the social order structured by reciprocal control, discussed in Chapter 1, begins to emerge.

In the *very* early stages of socialization this process of reciprocal control is not very different from that present in the conditioning of animals in the laboratory of the experimental psychologist. If experimenters want an animal to behave in a certain way they must reward the animal for the desired behavior. The animal controls experimenters in the sense that experimenters are forced to reward the animal if they want the animal to continue the behavior they are attempting to teach it.

This analogy to animal conditioning holds only in the earliest stages of socialization. As the infant develops, the control strategies used become increasingly complex. The child gains higher degrees of sophistication and becomes amenable to the uniquely human form of reciprocal control that is made possible through the manipulation of shared symbols.

The attempts by the infant and child to control the behavior of parents and other significant persons take many different forms depending on the situation and past experiences. One infant may cry, another may pout, still another may "coo" or "show off" in an attempt to control the responses of others. "Spoiled" children, who always "get their way," are children who are in more complete control of parents. Successful control strategies that gain rewards and avoid punishments are "remembered" by children and are reused when the occasion demands. As children become older they find new and better control strategies to "wrap" parents around their fingers and to get their way. Parents often say such things as, "I should spank him but what he did was too cute." A study by M. J. Radke[2] supports the existence of this control orientation by the growing child. A significant number of the parents he studied reported that their children sulked, pouted, bargained, threw temper tantrums, and even ignored orders in an attempt to keep from doing what they were requested to do.

The Consequences of Behavior Control

The control of infants' behavior by parents conditions them to behave in specified ways. They learn that by behaving in these ways they can control the responses of parents on future occasions, thus avoiding punishment and gaining rewards. *Beginning with the earliest conditioning, children learn that interpersonal relations are based on one person attempting to control the behavior of others.*

As children grow older, their ability to make inferences from their experiences develops. Because their behavior is still being controlled and they also have learned to control the behavior of others, they *infer* that control is the basic dynamic of social life. This inference reinforces what the child has learned through conditioning. Of course, this inference is not typically made explicit. The older child probably reasons something like this: "If I want my parents or others to do a certain thing, I must first do something else." Or, in many situations, reasoning as such may not be involved as long as habitually used control strategies are working by gaining desired responses from others. Nevertheless, the results for understanding the structuring processes of social order tend to be the same. Children learn the necessity of controlling their own behavior if they are to control the behavior (responses) of others.

THE SOCIAL SELF

To assist in the explanation of the development of the social self we will briefly consider the relevant ideas of three major thinkers: Charles Horton Cooley (1864–1929), George Herbert Mead (1863–1931), and Sigmund Freud (1856–1939).

How Culture Is Transmitted in Guadalcanal

Each society has its own ways of transmitting its basic norms and values and its own repertoire of rewards and punishments, both physical and symbolic, that it uses in forms consistent with the age of the young who are being socialized. The anthropologist Ian Hogbin in this excerpt describes how the native culture in Guadalcanal, one of the Solomon Islands near New Guinea, transmits and reinforces its mores:

> Two virtues, generosity and respect for property, are inculcated from the eighteenth month onward—that is to say, from the age when the child can walk about and eat bananas and other things regarded as delicacies. At this stage no explanations are given, and the parents merely insist that food must be shared with any playmate who happens to be present and that goods belonging to other villagers must be left undisturbed. A toddler presented with a piece of fruit is told to give half to "So-and-so," and should the order be resisted, the adult ignores all protests and breaks a piece off to hand to the child's companion. Similarly, although sometimes callers are cautioned to put their baskets on a shelf out of reach, any meddling brings forth the rebuke, "That belongs to your uncle. Put it down." Disobedience is followed by snatching away the item in question from the child and returning it to the owner.
>
> In time, when the child has passed into its fourth or fifth year, it is acknowledged to have at last attained the understanding to be able to take in what the

---

Cooley's "Looking-Glass Self"

Cooley's concept of the "looking-glass self"[3] is accepted by most sociologists. Cooley saw the self developing in reciprocal interaction. The looking glass is another person or persons to whom we look for responses based on our own behavior. If the reflection (responses) we "see" are interpreted as negative (punishing), we are likely to modify our behavior to change the nature of the reflection (response) from negative (punishing) to positive (rewarding). We can *only* see ourselves in the real or imagined responses of others. A conception of self can develop only by observing others' responses and interpreting or reacting to them.

These reflections are seldom if ever completely perfect because the person must interpret them. There are many reasons why similar responses are interpreted differently by different persons. Past experiences and different situational contexts are important sources of differing interpretations of the same response.

The interpretations the individual makes based on observed or "felt" responses influence his self-conception. Although this process lasts for a lifetime it is most significant during primary socialization.

---

adults say. Therefore, adults now accompany demands with reasoned instruction. One day when I was paying a call on a neighbor, Mwane-Anuta, I heard him warn his second son Mbule, who probably had not yet reached the age of five, to stop being so greedy. "I saw your mother give you those nuts," Mwane-Anuta reiterated. "Don't pretend she didn't. Running behind the house so that Penggoa wouldn't know! That is bad, very bad. Now then, show me, how many? Five left. Very well, offer three to Penggoa immediately." He then went on to tell me how important it was for children to learn to think of others so that in later life they would win the respect of their fellows.

On another occasion during a meal I found Mwane-Anuta and his wife teaching their three sons how to eat properly. "Now Mbule," said his mother, "you face the rest of us so that we can all see you aren't taking too much. And you, Konana, run outside and ask Misika from next door to join you. His mother's not home yet, and I expect he's hungry. Your belly's not the only one, my boy." "Yes," Mwane-Anuta added, "Give a thought to those you run about with, and they'll give a thought to you." At that point the mother called over the eldest lad, Kure, and placed the basket of yams for me in his hands. "There, you carry that over to our guest and say that it is good to have him with us this evening," she whispered to him. The gesture was characteristic. I noted that always when meals were served to visitors the children acted as waiters. Why was this, I wanted to know. "Teaching, teaching," Mwane-Anuta replied. "This is how we train our young to behave."[a]

[a]Ian Hogbin, *A Guadalcanal Society: The Koaks Speakers* (New York: Holt, 1964), p. 33.

Infants have a limited frame of reference and few past responses to which they can refer. Thus, their range of possible interpretations is severely restricted. Parents and a limited number of significant others tend to be the only frame of reference or, in Cooley's terms, the only looking glass. For this reason, parents and significant others assume critical importance.

From Cooley's point of view, we tend to see ourselves only as we see others seeing us. In the final analysis, there is no meaningful point of reference other than the interpretations we make of the responses of other people to our behavior. Our conception of our self depends on these responses and our interpretations of them.

George Herbert Mead and Symbolic Interactionism

Mead[4] and his students developed a school of thought called Symbolic Interactionism.[5] Mead shared Cooley's view that the self develops out of the interaction process. Symbolic interactionism suggests that interaction is based on commonly shared meanings given to symbols. It is the meanings of these symbols as they come to be understood by the individual in interaction with others that play a large part in the development of a self.

Nearly everything conceivable may take on symbolic meaning. Two pieces of wood nailed together to form a cross have symbolic meaning for the Christian as does the six-pointed star for the Jew and the Stars and Stripes for Americans. Gestures are another important class of culturally defined symbols, including such commonplaces as facial expressions and waving one's hand as a greeting. The most important symbol system is language.

For Mead, a self develops as children learn the meanings of symbols and apply these to themselves based on the evaluations of significant others with whom they are interacting. Over time a symbol comes to evoke in individuals the same response they want to evoke from others. This can occur only because individuals have first learned the symbolic meaning of the response through interaction.

For Mead, as for Cooley, a self can come into existence only as the child learns the point of view of the other and from the perspective of that other looks back on the self. Mead called this dynamic process taking the role of the other. Taking the role of the other involves imagining the *anticipated* response of another person based on one's *intended* behavior. After anticipating this response, the individual acts and then evaluates the response of the other person to his behavior. A response that is *interpreted* as positive reinforces the person to act in the same manner again under the same circumstance. If there were no other person it would make *no* meaningful sense to act in the first place. If the person did not first take the role of the other, he would not know *how* to act. Furthermore, the individual would have no way of viewing his self if there were no real or imagined response from the other person. It is only from the perspective of others that individuals can see themselves as independent selves. On the basis of this they engage in *meaningful* social interaction.

Reciprocal Control in the Theories of Cooley and Mead

The element of reciprocal control in both Cooley and Mead relates directly to the development of the social self. For Cooley, individuals develop a self as they begin to respond to the controlling responses of others. Interpreting others' responses, they control their own behavior to either maintain favorable responses or to improve unfavorable responses. If the child's behavior changes, this forces a change in the response of others. *The child sees his behavior changing the behavior*

The Symbolic Nature of Human Emotions

Most of us are aware that linguistic symbols (oral and written) are culturally defined and have no intrinsic meaning except that given to them in their cultural context. Such bits of folk wisdom as "I am firm, you are obstinate, he is pig-headed" enshrine this insight. It is important to recognize also that the meanings that we assign to actions and the emotions that they elicit in us are also culturally controlled and are learned during socialization. A chart prepared by two of the leading proponents of the Symbolic Interaction school graphically demonstrates this by showing the various emotions aroused by differing definitions of situations that involve the same physical action, a slap in the face:[a]

Act	Situation	Definition	Resulting Emotion in Victim
Slap in the face	Two quarreling people	Insult	Fury and resentment
Slap in the face	In a play	Play acting	None or simulated
Slap in the face	Father slaps child for lying	Punishment	Shame
Slap in the face	Twenty-month-old child slaps father	Good spirits	Amusement

[a]Alfred Lindesmith and Anselm Strauss, *Social Psychology*, 2nd ed. (New York: Holt, 1968), p. 179.

of others. This is an important dynamic in the distinguishing of self from others and, thus, in the self's development as an entity separate and distinct from others.

For Mead, the child comes to see himself from the perspective of others as he sees that different behavior produces different responses from others. This permits the child to see that he is separate from others and that his activity as a separate self has a controlling effect on their behavior. Thus, the relationship between social selves is based on each attempting to control the responses of the other.

Sigmund Freud: Id, Ego, and Superego

Freud conceptualized three parts to the self: the id, the ego, and the superego.[6] The id is the seat of inborn impulses or drives toward pleasurable releases or experiences. The superego develops during socialization and incorporates what others ("society") would like us to be. The superego includes the group's norms of what is good or bad. These norms are learned from others, especially from parents. The ego is that part of the self that directly interacts with others and with external reality. In this interaction, the id impulses must be controlled so that the self will be "acceptable" to others. The blueprint for this control is contained in the superego. The ego balances the drives for gratification from the id, the restrictions of the superego, and the demands of the external reality.

The Control Element in Freud

Control is the basic dynamic of Freud's self. The main function of the ego is as a control mechanism. Without it the superego would be in direct conflict with the pleasure-seeking impulses of the id.

In Chapter 1 we noted that if the individual is unable to derive gratification within the framework of interaction with others, psychological control strategies such as regression, projection, and rationalization become important. The ego is the mechanism that triggers these psychological strategies to protect the self from unbearable pain.

We will discuss the content of self and self-identity later in this chapter. Before doing so, we need to discuss the development of needs that, once developed, motivate the self to participate in the processes of social ordering.

THE DEVELOPMENT OF NEEDS

In discussing the source of the control orientation in the child, we have examined the dynamics of reward and punishment. Now we want to explore other dynamics. The question is, in addition to behavior control, what other dynamics are necessary to the socialization process and what needs develop because of these dynamics?

The Necessity for Response

First, there must be *response* to the infant from others, usually the parents. When the infant acts, a response must be forthcoming from others if he is to survive and develop. All the infant has when he comes into the world is potential and a limited number of signs that must be interpreted and responded to by parents. The infant cries and by crying offers a sign to his parents who must respond by taking steps to eliminate the cause of the sign, whether it is hunger or something else. It is the *nature* of the response that conditions the behavior of the infant in specific directions.

The responses from parents and others must be *relatively consistent.* Consistency of response is necessary if the child is to construct a sensible (meaningful) world to which he can relate and therefore operate within as a human being. Psychologists have long been aware of the damaging consequences of inconsistent responses toward an infant. If, for example, the infant is rewarded for a certain behavior at one time and punished for the same behavior another time, he becomes confused and is not able to sort out how his physical and social world is constructed. Consistency of response is necessary if the child is to develop normally. Even animals can be made neurotic under conditions of inconsistent response from the conditioning agent.

Where there is a high degree of inconsistency in the response of others, the child finds it impossible to initiate a control orientation because he cannot get hold of the world in a *patterned fashion* in order to control it with a consistent set of behaviors. Extreme inconsistency of response can cause serious mental disorders in the child.[7] If the outside world is too inconsistent to control with one self-orientation, more than one becomes necessary.

The Necessity of Stimulation

The second necessary dynamic in the socialization process is *stimulation* from the socialization agent. Because infants have only a limited number of signs that they can offer for external response (and thus for potential conditioning) it is necessary that they be stimulated from the outside to display behaviors that can then be rewarded and learned. This is prerequisite for the learning of language and forms of behavior.

In cases of extreme isolation, where little stimulation is received from the outside and the infant is not forced to expand his behavior, little development occurs. Evidence indicates that under these conditions the infant does not really become human.[8]

The Necessity for Providing Security

The third necessary dynamic of socialization is to provide basic *security* for the child. The child must be stimulated from the outside to behave. It is also sometimes necessary to punish certain behaviors to keep the child from moving down the wrong behavioral path. However, punishment is always threatening and other forms of external stimulation may also be perceived as a threat. These mechanisms thus pose the danger of causing the child to withdraw into his own world, making adequate socialization impossible. It is therefore necessary to provide basic security for the child within which he can accept the necessary stimulation and use it for continued development. If this basic security is not present, even small punishments may be felt as total threats and cause the child to withdraw.

Talcott Parsons calls the relationship that provides basic security "diffuse attachment":

> It seems highly probable that early diffuse attachments, particularly to the mother, constitute the focus of what is sometimes called the security system of the child. Security in this sense may be taken to mean that there is a certain stabilization of his system of orientation, by viture of which the child is able to develop a certain tolerance of frustration.[9]

Double-bind Responses

A double-bind response carries at least two contradictory "messages." For example, a mother or father may tell a child, "I love you," while *throwing* him into bed, thereby expressing anger or even hatred of the child. Because even very young children are sensitive to the feeling states of parents, the child cannot separate out and make sense of the expression of hatred and the words of love coming forth from the parent at the same time. This is obviously confusing to the child who has no way of knowing which message is more valid. If the child is exposed to a continuous series of double-bind responses severe psychological problems may develop.

The anthropologist Gregory Bateson was among the first to identify the nature and significance of the double-bind response and has used it to attempt to explain a number of psychopathological conditions ranging from schizophrenia to alcoholism. Bateson describes a common double situation in our society:

> [If the] mother begins to feel hostile toward her child and also feels compelled to withdraw from him, she might say, "Go to bed, you're very tired and I want you to

The child with a secure relationship can tolerate the necessary frustrations of socialization. The psychologist Erik H. Erikson summarizes this well:

> Parents must not only have certain ways of guiding by prohibition and permission; they must also be able to represent to the child a deep, an almost somatic conviction that there is a *meaning* to what they are doing. Ultimately, children become neurotic not from frustration, but from the lack of loss of societal meaning in these frustrations.[10]

Socialization under conditions of insecurity and excessive threat causes the child to distrust the world and to attempt to place a barrier between self and the world. A common form this barrier takes in later life is the authoritarian personality with its rigid and sadistic orientation toward others who try to break the barrier, and masochistic orientation toward the self.[11] In severe cases, the individual may come to have a need for punishment.

The Necessity for Recognition

The fourth necessary dynamic is recognition. This is more far reaching than response. To respond to a person is to make him know that you are aware of his existence. Recognition goes beyond this and leads to growth. Whereas responses may be either negative (punishment) or positive (reward), recognition is always positive. Some re-

---

get your sleep." This overtly loving statement is intended to deny a feeling which could be verbalized as "Get out of my sight because I'm sick of you." If the child correctly discriminates her . . . signals, he would have to face the fact that she both doesn't want him and is deceiving him by her loving behavior. He would be "punished" for learning to discriminate orders of messages accurately. He therefore would tend to accept the idea that he is tired rather than recognize his mother's deception. This means that he must deceive himself about his own internal state in order to support mother in her deception. To survive with her he must falsely discriminate his own internal messages as well as falsely discriminate the messages of others. . . .

The problem is compounded for the child because the mother is "benevolently" defining for him how he feels; she is expressing overt maternal concern over the fact that he is tired. To put it another way, the mother is controlling the child's definitions of his own messages, as well as the definition of his responses to her (for example, by saying, "You don't really mean to say that," if he should criticize her) by insisting that she is not concerned about herself but only about him. . . . *The child is punished for discriminating accurately what she is expressing, and he is punished for discriminating inaccurately—he is caught in a double bind.*[a]

[a]Gregory Bateson, *Steps to an Ecology of Mind* (San Francisco: Chandler, 1972), pp. 214–215.

sponses provide recognition, whereas others do not. Recognition comes when the socialization agent lets the infant know that he has made a step in the "right" direction. It is, therefore, a prime motivator in social life. If recognition, such as praise, does not occur at the proper times, the infant is left without direction because no *qualitative* judgment is made about his behavior and it is difficult for him to know which way to turn. Recognition in the forms of a smile, a gentle pat, and verbal recognitions after language is learned are vital in socialization. Recognition helps in the development of a self-identity and a sense of self-worth.

There are other dynamics in socialization, but these four— consistent response, stimulation, security based on love, and recognition including approval—are the most important. These dynamics operate together during successful socialization and can be separated only for the purpose of analysis. Recognition is a form of response reward. The punishment response as well as stimulation must take place within a basic sense of security. The child is not a passive agent but a participant who by his behavior actively influences the interactive nature and quality of these dynamics.

Consequences As Basic Needs: Motivation to Participate in Social Ordering

The necessity and presence of these dynamics in socialization conditions corresponding needs to develop in the child. Individuals develop a need for response, a need for stimulation or new experience, a need for security including belongingness and love, and a need for recognition and approval, including self-esteem.

These needs are conditioned into the child and are present to various degrees in each individual. The individual attempts to control his environment, including his own behavior, to gratify these needs. They motivate the individual seeking their gratification to participate in the processes of social ordering.

The needs we have isolated are consistent with lists of needs that other sociologists and psychologists have suggested as being present in the individual. For example, W. I. Thomas lists the basic needs (he calls them wishes) as new experience, recognition, response, and stimulation.[12] The basic need for approval, response, acceptance, and esteem is implicit in the work of Talcott Parsons.[13] George Homans assumes the needs of approval, esteem, and response in his theoretical work.[14] In developing his theory of motivation, Maslow lists the basic needs in a hierarchy: physiological, safety, belongingness and love, esteem and self-actualization.[15] There is substantial agreement among behavioral scientists about the basic needs that motivate individuals to participate in the processes of social ordering.[16]

ADDITIONAL DEVELOPMENTS IN THE SOCIALIZATION PROCESS

Two additional important components develop from the dynamics of the socialization process: a desire for distributive justice (discussed in Chapter 2) and a desire for individual meaning (discussed in Chapter 1).

The Desire for Distributive Justice

In his book, *Social Behavior: Its Elementary Forms*, Homans argues that animals as well as humans exhibit a "sense" of distributive justice. He points out that if a pigeon has been conditioned to obtain food (a reward) for a certain behavior (a cost), and if the food is not supplied when the behavior is emitted, the pigeon engages in behavior that can be described as anger. Homans adds that: "In the same way, men express anger, mild or savage, when they do not get what their past history has taught them to expect."[17] "The rule of distributive justice says that a man's reward in exchange with others should be proportional to his investments."[18]

This desire develops during socialization. As the growing child is rewarded for a certain behavior he is conditioned to build up an expectation for a reward when he repeats the behavior. If a young child is praised by parents for putting away his toys, he comes to expect praise or other rewards when this behavior is repeated.

This conditioning creates in individuals a desire for distributive justice that becomes a generalized expectation in interaction with others. The desire for distributive justice is a direct result of the relative consistency of response necessary for successful socialization. If a relative consistency of response is not present, the desire for and sense of distributive justice is lacking or confused in the individual.

The desire for distributive justice in social life is important. For example, it provides the basis for exchange relationships between individuals. Without a widespread desire for distributive justice there would be more conflict in social interaction than presently exists. Individuals would not be so willing to "give" (pay a cost) if they did not think they would "get" (receive a reward) in return. The desire for distributive justice is one foundation for reciprocal control.

The Desire for Individual Meaning

The desire for meaning (making sense of one's experiences) also originates during socialization and is reinforced throughout life. This desire develops because responses made toward the child in the primary socialization process are not *always* consistent. The problem of meaning has its source at the points of discrepancy in means-ends relationships. If all behavior (means) led immediately to the "promised" response (previously experienced ends), no problem of meaning would occur. This cannot be the case because there are many discrepancies in means-ends relationships, not only in early socialization but throughout life.

Among those possibilities that will produce discrepancies during socialization are (1) differences between how the mother responds to the child and the way the father or others respond to the child; (2) the necessity of applying different standards for behavior as the child develops; (3) misunderstandings by parents of what the child is trying to communicate to them, which may produce inconsistent responses; (4) the absence of parents at the appropriate time when a certain response should be forthcoming; and (5) outright neglect by some parents.

These discrepancies and others make it impossible for children to make complete sense of the world. They are left with feelings of insecurity and incompleteness. From this, the desire for meaning is born. If all needs were immediately and consistently gratified, the desire for meaning would not develop at this early age. Because it is impossible for any set of interactive relationships that form the framework within which socialization occurs to immediately, completely, and consistently gratify the needs of the growing child, he encounters inconsistencies and experiences frustrations. The desire for meaning emerges as he attempts to make sense out of these inconsistencies and frustrations. As his self-identity grows through interaction with others, the child develops his values, which in turn enable him to make choices among the alternatives available to him.

SOCIALIZATION AND CULTURE

As needs develop in the socialization process, their gratification becomes necessary. Because children have little possibility of gratifying these needs by themselves, they are highly dependent on parents. Thus, children are potentially willing to turn in almost any direction for need gratification, just as they would be willing to eat almost anything provided to satisfy their hunger. However, just as kinds of food are typically restricted within a society, so are the usable strategies for the meeting of other needs. Along with other strategies, parents use the available cultural strategies as they interact with the child. The cultural strategies used or presented are those typically accepted by others in the society or the subgroup to which the parents belong. Children try these strategies and if they find them workable to meet needs, they accept them as the ones to be used again. Because children are taught cultural norms and values at the same time their needs are developing, they have a heavy emotional investment in the use of cultural norms and values to gratify these needs. Being rewarded for the use of a certain norm causes this norm to take on importance because its use gratifies needs. The emotional investment is a major source of cultural continuity. This investment is seldom so great, however, that children will forever continue to use cultural norms and values if needs are not met through their use.

The socialization process is an interaction situation. It contains at least two people, usually the child and a parent. Culture presupposes agreement, so it cannot be said that parents and child share a common culture until the child becomes an active participant in the interactive process. Even though the parents have a culture in common with others and use certain strategies from this culture in their relations with the child, the child does not share a common culture with his parents until this culture emerges within their interaction process. Culture emerges in the child-parent relationship as the child accepts and agrees to the use of the cultural strategies the parents use. The learning of cultural strategies in the primary socialization process is little different than it is in other interaction situations. The control component necessary for learning is useability. However, in the early socialization process, the growing child has few alternative strategies to use and is therefore more likely to "accept" the culture as presented by others with little modification—at least as long as extreme dependency is present. Because the child's needs are developing at the same time culture is being taught there is greater emotional investment in cultural values and norms than is produced in other situations. Despite this, however, children will rapidly and readily deviate from the use of a cultural norm taught by a parent when they join a peer group where other behaviors are demanded as the price of entry or membership.

The French psychologist Jean Piaget presents a similar interpretation of the development and use of norms in the child. He sees the child moving progressively from nonrecognition to the perception of a pattern that is taught by the socialization agent and then mutually agreed to. Beyond this point Piaget finds the child perceiving the pattern as something that can be *manipulated* by parents, others, and himself.[19]

Culture and Self-Identity

In socialization parents use a variety of norms and values that are important for the development of a self-identity in the child. Among these are the cultural values that, if accepted by the child, become a basis for his meaning system. In the early years children come to see themselves as "good" if they agree with these cultural value components because parents reward them if they do so.

Cultural norms and values related to sex are present in all societies. A female child is encouraged to agree with the cultural norms defining how a female should act. The same is true for the male and the male identity. Such normative patterns change in some societies but will probably always be present to some degree even if in radically modified forms.

The learning of language and other symbols and their meanings is also of utmost importance to the development of self-identity. If the meanings contained in language and other symbols are not learned, the child cannot develop a self-identity because it would be impossible to impute meanings to the activities of others.

A variety of other cultural norms are learned from parents during the socialization process, such as the "correct" way of eating and of dressing and many other usages and beliefs. These permit children to develop self-identities as they apply the norms to themselves based on the responses of others. The learning of values, norms, and other cultural agreements not only helps children to construct self-identities, but also gives them a "kit" of cultural control strategies that they find useful in gratifying their needs in a variety of situations. *As*

"Permissiveness" during Socialization and Self-identity

Much of the perennial debate about the specific norms and values that regulate socialization practices among middle-class Americans centers around the notion of permissiveness. All the ills that are attributed to the younger generation are seen as the products of overpermissiveness by parents during the socialization process. Without accepting the moral premises of those who condemn permissiveness, it does appear that they make a valid point that can be formulated using our concepts. The desire for distributive justice and for individual meaning and the development of values and of self-identity emerge out of a process of reciprocal control and of ongoing frustrations and inconsistencies. If there are no constraints—no structure against which to struggle and with which to interact—the result may be an individual with low self-esteem and little grasp on reality.

William Braden, in *The Family Game: Identities for Young and Old*, quotes a number of psychiatrists who reformulate in their vocabularies our emphasis on the significance of structure for the development of identity and values:

"Everybody talks about this new youth—so free, so happy. Well, these permissively raised kids have had to develop their own internal constraints on their

part of the same process, children learn other control strategies as they see them used by parents and others.

Once having constructed a self-identity, the individual attempts to control the responses of others by acting in a manner consistent with this self-identity and in the process attempts to gratify his basic needs. If a male identifies himself as such, he will behave consistent with this identity. For example, he will be "tough" under certain conditions to evoke a positive response from others and thus gratify his need for response and recognition.

Self-identities may change over time depending on the kinds of people or groups one becomes involved with. Furthermore, children learn very early that they must act differently in different situations to gain gratifying responses even though they still see themselves as the "same" persons. Thus, the strategies used in reinforcing a particular self-identity may call for being tough while playing with a gang of other boys and being nice and neat while attending religious services.

If need gratification is not possible by holding a self-identity in the "real" world, a person may adopt a new self-identity in the "unreal" world of the psychotic to gratify needs. In this unreal world he may claim to be Jesus or another famous person and refuse to listen to any evidence to the contrary.

---

behavior—and these are a great deal more rigid and punishing than the average good parent would have given them, if he had taken the trouble to set limits. The good parent sets limits. He helps the child define reality. This means that the child is provided with a problem-solving range, between those limits, that is appropriate to his skills. If this happens, he moves from success to success with a growing sense of well-being and personal competence, and he is never placed in a disastrous situation where the problems are beyond his capacity of solution." . . .

Rebellion against authority in fact may sometimes represent a fear of too much freedom, or indeed a desperate and pathetic plea for authority to impose some kind of limits on the individual's behavior: "For God's sake, how far do I have to go before you stop me?" The analyst Bruno Bettelheim, for example, has observed this phenomenon in some of the troubled young people he has treated at the Sonia Shankman Orthogenic School.

"That's right," he said. "They ask for the limits. I'm running a treatment institution. I've been running it for a quarter of a century. And I know that what all young people need is certainly understanding, certainly gentle handling, but within firm limits. Because, as one of my delinquents said after we had cured him, he said: 'You can't grow up if there are no walls to push against.' And then, after a thought, he said: 'But you can't grow up either if the walls give way when you push against them.' "[a]

[a](New York: Quadrangle, 1972) p. 45.

A variety of control strategies are used as people attempt to gratify needs consistent with a self-identity. If this is not possible they may change self-identities, move from group to group, or "enter another world" in a desperate attempt at need gratification.

Personality

Personality expresses itself in the social world through the control strategies used by the individual in interaction with others. If the individual wants to view his own personality, he can do so only from the outside. As Mead claimed, the individual must see himself as an object, and to see one's self as an object is to take the perspective of others. There is no such thing as a purely subjective point of view unless we want to call subjectivity that which occurs when the individual looks out from "within." Even for this to make any sense, the individual must see self as standing in a relationship with others, and this is an object-to-object relationship. When this object-to-object relationship is not present, as for example in sensory deprivation experiments, the self can hardly be said to exist in any meaningful sense. When all outside sensations are removed, the person begins to hallucinate.[20]

If persons are conscious of something happening to them, they must see it happening to the objects that they are. Conversely, if they are to see themselves as having an effect on others, they must see one object acting on another.

Sensory Deprivation Experiments

In sensory deprivation experiments an attempt is made to eliminate or reduce to a minimum all external stimuli that might in any way stimulate the subject in the experiment. The volunteer subject in a typical experiment is blindfolded and submerged in water with a temperature equal to the temperature of the body. In addition, his ears are plugged so that he cannot hear; nor can he smell or "feel." The subject is "outside" sensory reality. Under this condition, the subject tends to "lose touch with self" because there is nothing present to activate a response. Subjects in these experiments tend to hallucinate, indicating how dependent we are on external stimuli for a sense of self-existence.

These experiments prove the importance not only of sensory stimuli but support our view about the importance of responses from others for the construction and maintenance of self over time.

We do not suggest that individuals are always *in* control of the social situation or even of themselves. Individuals who have a phobia or are suffering from anxiety are obviously not in complete psychological control. Most people suffer at one time or another from some form of psychological noncontrollability, ranging all the way from minor neuroses to severe psychoses.

This approach to personality allows a better understanding of what is referred to as "sick" and "well" or "abnormal" and "normal." The well person, both socially and psychologically, is a person who is viewed by self and others as being in control in relation to a situation.

L. S. Kubie and others[21] have pointed out that normal and abnormal can be understood only in relationship to a single act within a specific situation. An individual may be able to control the self in relation to one social situation but not in relation to a different situation. In some situations the individual may need to use predominantly psychological control strategies, in another social control strategies may be more useful. Societies and social situations within them differ in how wide a range of these strategies is allowed before a definition of either social deviance or psychological abnormality is made. The explanation is the same whatever the outcome. The individual is attempting to control his environment and self, to gratify his needs or achieve his goals based on his self-identity.

Persons are known and know themselves by the control strategies they use and by their reactions to the control strategies used by others toward them. Of course, the definitions made by others are not necessarily the same as the definitions made by the individual. Others do not always see individuals as individuals see themselves. These discrepancies may cause problems, depending on the individual, the situation, and the relative distribution of power. The poor man who takes off his clothes and runs screaming down the streets is likely to be branded as mentally disturbed in our society and shipped to a mental hospital for examination and treatment. The college student who strips and streaks is likely to be dismissed as another student prankster. The rich man is merely eccentric, and his subsequent problems, if any, are handled by his attorney and private psychiatrist.

THE SIGNIFICANCE OF SELF

Our discussion is not mechanistic in its view of the individual. Once individuals develop a consciousness of their own existence and their needs and desires, they are not machines that can be completely programmed by others. Instead, they become social *actors* who attempt to control their external social environments as well as their internal feeling states. This control is based on their *own* perceptions and definitions of situations. Selves are developed in interaction with others, but once a person is aware of his own existence, the self becomes the most valued entity he "possesses." It is the existence of the self, with its various needs and desires, along with important physiological needs that make reciprocal control both necessary and possible.

Furthermore, because a person values the self does not mean that he will not engage in "unselfish" behavior as this term is popularly defined. The substance of the self is the self-identity. This identity may change, but at a specific time this identity is the very essence of the person. If persons define themselves as unselfish and take on this identity, we will expect them to engage in unselfish acts. Not to do so would destroy their self-identities and render their lives meaningless. Socrates and Jesus were willing to die rather than deny their self-identities. The same has been true of countless others. These people died because they were willing to engage in what is popularly defined as unselfish behavior. If they had not died, but "given in" instead, their self-identities would have been destroyed. It is ironic but true that at times an individual will willingly die to "save" the very self for which he has lived.

REFERENCES

1. See for example, Mead, Margaret. *Sex and Temperament in Three Primitive Societies*. New York: Morrow, 1935. *Childhood in Contemporary Cultures*. Ed. by Mar Neal. Chicago: U. of Chicago, 1955.
2. Radke, M. J. "The Relation of Parental Authority to Children's Behavior and Attitudes." University of Minnesota Institute, *Child Welfare Monograph*, No. 22 (1946).
3. Cooley, Charles Horton. *Human Nature and the Social Order*. New York: Free Press, 1956. This work was first published in 1902.
4. His major work is *Mind, Self and Society*. Chicago: U. of Chicago, 1934.
5. For a recent treatment of this school written by one of Mead's students, see Blumer, Herbert. *Symbolic Interactionism: Perspectiveness and Methods*. Englewood Cliffs, N. J.: Prentice-Hall, 1969.
6. Freud, Sigmund. *The Ego and the Id*. Trans. and ed. by James Strachey. New York: Norton, 1961.
7. See Bateson, Gregory, *et al.* "Toward a Theory of Schizophrenia." In *Interpersonal Relations*. Ed. by Warren G. Bennis *et al.* Homewood, Ill.: Dorsey, 1964.
8. See Davis, Kingsley. "Extreme Isolation of a Child." *American Journal of Sociology*, **XXXXV** (1940), 554–56.
9. Parsons, Talcott. *The Social System*. New York: Free Press, 1951, p. 218.
10. Erikson, Erik H. *Childhood and Society*. New York: Norton, 1950, pp. 149–50.
11. See Adorno, T. W., *et al. The Authoritarian Personality*. New York: Harper, 1950; also Fromm, Erich. *Escape from Freedom*. New York: Farrar and Rinehart, 1941.

12. Thomas, William I., and Florian Znaniecki. *The Polish Peasant in Europe and America*. Chicago: U. of Chicago, 1918; and Thomas, W. I. *The Unadjusted Girl: With Cases and Standpoint for Behavior Analysis*. Boston: Little, Brown, 1923.
13. Parsons infers these needs in several places: see op. cit., Chap. 3 and Parsons, Talcott, and Edward A. Shils. *Toward a General Theory of Action*. Cambridge: Harvard U. P., 1951, Chap. 2.
14. Homans, George Casper. *Social Behavior: Its Elementary Forms*. New York: Harcourt, 1961.
15. Maslow, Abraham H. *Motivation and Personality*. New York: Harper, 1954.
16. See, for example, Fromm, Erich. *The Sane Society*. New York: Rinehart and Company, 1955.
17. Homans, op. cit., p. 71.
18. Ibid., p. 235.
19. Piaget, Jean. *The Moral Judgment of the Child*. London: Routledge, 1932.
20. See Solomon, Philip, *et al. Sensory Deprivation*. Cambridge: Harvard U. P., 1961.
21. Kubie, L. S. "The Fundamental Nature of the Distinction Between Normality and Neurosis." *Psychoanalytical Quarterly*, **XXIII** (1954), 167–204. Also, See Redlich, F. C. "The Concept of Health in Psychiatry." In *Explorations in Social Psychiatry*. Ed. by Alexander H. Leighton, John A. Clausen, and Robert N. Wilson. New York: Basic Books, 1957.

C H A P T E R   4

Social Groups

INTRODUCTION

The concept of social group is fundamental to sociology. Many sociologists define the discipline itself as the study of social groups. One, for example, says that sociology is "the science that deals with social groups: their internal form or modes of organization, the processes that tend to maintain or change these forms of organization and the relations between groups."[1] There are literally thousands of groups with various shadings of differences in their size, criteria for membership, internal structure, goals, duration over time, and a host of other variables.

Our lives from birth to death are interwoven and intersect with many groups. We are born into a family group, an intimate small group within which we are socialized. Our physical birth usually takes place within the confines of a hospital—a large formal group. Throughout the course of our lives, the interactions that help to shape our self-identities and within which we seek and find individual meaning occur within groups: the peer group as we emerge from the family; the school; friendship cliques; the work place; military service; the kinship group within which we marry and reproduce. Homans, in his classic study, *The Human Group*, notes that "[the] first and most immediate social experience of mankind is small group experience.... The group is the commonest, as it is the most familiar, of social units."[2] Merton has listed twenty-six different significant properties that can be considered in the classification of groups, and his is an admittedly partial listing.[3]

As a working definition of group, we will adopt Merton's conclusion that, "the *sociological* concept of a *group* refers to a number of people who interact with one another in accord with established patterns."[4] Our primary interest is in the kinds of control strategies used by group members to produce these established patterns of interaction. The use of different control strategies by group members produces different types of groups. Our discussion will be limited to general types of groups and the control strategies that typically structure them.

There are two major types of social groups, *formal* and *informal*, with a variety of subtypes for each. We will first discuss the differences between formal and informal groups, and then consider their major subtypes. The subtypes of informal groups include primary groups, such as the family, and congeniality groups, such as cliques and friendship groups. Formal groups include voluntary associations such as parent-teacher groups and—most important—bureaucracies.

After discussing informal and formal groups in some detail, we will discuss social categories and then survey some broad patterns of intergroup relations. The concept of reference groups, which helps explain how individuals are recruited into social groups, will be elaborated on. We will conclude the chapter by drawing the implications of this discussion of social groups for the development of individual meaning.

DIFFERENCES BETWEEN FORMAL AND INFORMAL GROUPS

Control Strategies

The major difference between informal and formal groups is that procedural strategies are *never* used in the structuring of informal groups, whereas they are *always* used in the structuring of formal groups. Formal groups always have written procedural rules that govern at least part of the behavior structuring the group. The procedural rules in formal groups usually define a series of offices such as president or chairperson, secretary, treasurer, and so on and the rules that other persons in the group are expected to follow. In addition, the steps to become a member of the formal group and the conditions under which one can be expelled from the group are often codified.

The probability of the use of other types of control strategies also varies between informal and formal groups. For example, exchange strategies are used less frequently in informal groups than in many formal groups. Manipulative and coalitional strategies are used to structure both formal and informal groups. The intensity of their use varies according to the subtype. Cultural strategies are used in both types but tend to be used more often in informal than in formal groups. The control strategies that structure each of the subtypes will be discussed subsequently.

Longevity

Another important difference between formal and informal groups is that formal groups usually have a longer lifespan than do informal groups. A bureaucracy (a type of formal group), for example, may last for centuries with "new" members being added as "old" members either die or move out of the group. The Roman Catholic Church is an excellent example of a very old bureaucracy. Because informal groups do not have codified procedural rules and formally specified positions, they are much more likely to go out of existence with the death or moving out of members. A friendship group at the university, for example, usually dissolves as each of its members goes in a separate direction upon graduation.

However, some informal groups last for a considerable length of time, whereas some formal groups last a very short time. Formal groups with a limited goal that is achieved may be of brief duration. Informal groups seldom have names, whereas most formal groups are named. During a period of time, as all or most persons die or leave an informal group and new members take their place, it is difficult to say whether or not it is the same group, even if it occupies the same physical place. An informal drinking group that meets year after year in the same bar may completely change personnel. Is it the same group or a different one?

Formal groups, especially large ones, usually have within them a series of interlocking informal groups that significantly affect their ability to achieve their goals and the style and substance of their operations. Homans states this important relationship between formal and informal groups clearly:

> When, as grownups, we get jobs, we still find ourselves working with a few persons (an informal group) and not with the whole firm, association, or government department (formal groups). We are members of these larger social organizations, but the people we deal with regularly are always few. The informal groups mediate between us and the leviathans.[5]

The problems and possibilities of these relationships between informal and formal groups pose questions about individual meaning and social ordering that will occupy us later in this chapter and throughout the rest of the text.

Informal groups—a number of people who interact according to established patterns that are never structured by procedural strategies—include two major subtypes: primary groups and congeniality groups. Each of these will be defined and examined in turn.

Informal Groups

Primary Groups

Cooley, the sociologist who developed the concept of the looking-glass self, also developed the concept of primary group. Defining primary groups, Cooley says:

> By primary groups I mean those characterized by intimate face-to-face association and cooperation. They are primary in several senses, but chiefly in that they are fundamental in forming the social nature and ideals of the individual. The result of intimate association, psychologically, is a certain fusion of individualities in a common whole, so that one's very self, for many purposes at least, is the common life and purpose of the group. Perhaps the simplest way of describing this wholeness is by saying that it is a "we"; it involves the sort of sympathy and mutual identification for which "we" is the natural expression. One lives in the feeling of the whole and finds the chief aims of his will in that feeling. . . . The most important spheres of this intimate association and cooperation—though by no means the only ones—are the family, the playgroup of children, and the neighborhood or community group of elders.[6]

Primary groups are structured principally by the use of cultural strategies, with manipulative and other types of strategies frequently used. For example, a family is a significant primary group at times structured primarily by cultural strategies. However, the social ordering of families is structured at times by coercive strategies such as threats and punishments, exchange strategies, and manipulative strategies.

For the most part, however, primary groups are structured by deep-seated agreements among the persons involved. In primary groups communication among members is deep and extensive, and there is much mutual trust. There is usually reciprocal concern for the welfare of each member and, ideally, each person is viewed as an *end* rather than as someone who can be used as a *means* to an end.

Primary groups are important because they gratify many of the basic needs of their members. Individuals in a primary group feel secure and feel recognized as whole persons. They can typically depend on positive responses from others, or at least can depend on their deep abiding concern. It is within the framework of primary groups that individuals can express pent-up emotions without fear of arousing too much antagonism on the part of others. It is here that individuals are most likely to be themselves—in the sense that they do not have to abide by the strict rules and severely regulated behavior of more formal groups. The importance of the primary group for personal well-being cannot be overstated.

Men and women literally will die and have died to preserve their primary groups or to defend or assist other primary group members. We are all familiar with the parent who although a nonswimmer dives into a lake to try to save his or her drowning child or dashes back into a burning building to rescue a family member. Numerous studies of combat motivation—that is, what it is that induces soldiers to risk their lives under wartime conditions—show that it is the primary ties established in a small informal group of buddies who support and defend each other that motivate combat performance. The primary group ties far outweigh abstract conceptions of patriotism, the national honor, the flag, or the other sentiments and symbols often appealed to as motivators by political leaders in time of war.[7]

Congeniality Groups

A congeniality group is similar to a primary group, and at times it is difficult to distinguish between them. The major difference is the intensity of emotional involvement among group members and the level of mutual trust. Congeniality group members are less emotionally involved and have a lower level of mutual trust than the members of primary groups. Congeniality groups often develop into primary groups over time as the emotional commitment and mutual trust increase among those involved. Congeniality groups are composed of friends who interact regularly to pursue common interests. Examples include friends who golf or play pool or poker and people who get together to talk about a common interest or to gossip.

Congeniality groups may form within other types of groups such as work groups, residents of a university dormitory, church members, or labor unions. They also form outside these formal groups among neighbors or people having similar interests.

In both primary groups and congeniality groups, the individual gains psychological support and gratification for some of his basic needs. Persons who have no primary group or congeniality group affiliations are often lonely and despondent. They have the feeling that no one cares about them and they are probably correct.

Social isolates, such as the residents of Skid Rows in large cities, many of whom suffer from alcoholism or some form of mental illness, are examples of persons in our society who have been unable or unwilling to enter into or to sustain primary group relationships. Dating bureaus (with all their computer paraphernalia), singles bars, vacation resorts, and other specialized arrangements are among the ways people in our society seek to establish primary ties with each other.*

Formal Groups

As we have indicated, formal groups are made up of numbers of people who interact according to established patterns that are always structured in part by procedural strategies. Other control strategies are also used, but procedural strategies are always present. The two major types of formal groups that will be discussed here are voluntary associations and bureaucracies.

Voluntary Associations

Voluntary associations are groups of persons who share mutual interests or goals. They are "ideally" open to those willing to abide by the rules of the group. Members are free to withdraw if they wish to do so. However, not all *voluntary associations are open to everyone in a particular society.* Some voluntary associations are open only to people who have characteristics acceptable to the existing membership. Thus, voluntary associations can be broken down into two subtypes: *exclusive* voluntary associations and *inclusive* voluntary associations.

The major structuring strategies of all voluntary associations include cultural and manipulative as well as procedural. When cliques form within voluntary associations—a common occurrence—coalitional strategies also become important, as power struggles among the cliques influence the structure of the group. Coercive strategies are rarely used because if these go beyond the rules the members against whom the coercive strategies are being used are likely to drop out of the group.

Withdrawal strategies are used also at times. A number of persons may split off and form a group of their own. Many splits have occurred within Protestantism; sect groups have split off from existing denominations or local congregations. Careful analysis usually shows the existence of a struggle for power behind these splits. On the surface the

---

Secondary group is a concept used by some sociologists as a blanket contrast to the concept of primary group. For example, Charles Allyn defines secondary group as "simply . . . the complement of primary groups. They include those organizations where interaction is more superficial, mechanical, and rationally subordinated to the pursuance of goals. They have little concern for the private emotions of their members." *Sociology: An Introduction* (Englewood Cliffs, N.J.: Prentice-Hall, 1972) p. 315.

Rather than contrast primary and secondary groups, we find it more useful to differentiate formal and informal groups and then establish subtypes within these broader categories, using as our main criterion the kind of control strategies that predominate in each type and subtype.

split is supposedly based on differences in beliefs, but beneath the surface there is an unsatisfied desire for more control by those members who withdraw and form a "new church." Seldom, if ever, do the most powerful persons or cliques in a denomination or local congregation withdraw to form a separate group. People with more control typically stand in a better position to have their basic needs gratified and thus have no need to form a new group.

Exclusive Voluntary Associations

Exclusive voluntary associations will accept as members only persons who have specified characteristics and who are willing to accept the cultural norms and procedural rules of the group. Examples include Italian-American or Polish-American ethnic-group clubs, lodges that exclude by race or religion, university sororities and fraternities, some country clubs, upper-class men's social clubs, and other clubs where voting must occur before an applicant can become a member.

Some exclusive voluntary associations came into existence because some individuals lacked the characteristics specified for membership in existing associations. For example, some Jewish and Catholic voluntary associations were formed because these people were excluded from Protestant groups.[8] Similarly, the black churches came into existence because black people were either excluded from white churches or relegated to positions of inferiority within them.[9]

The strategies of categorization and labeling are evident in many of these exclusionary practices. People who control access to socially desirable positions, services, or facilities may use exclusionary practices to help maintain positions of power and privilege. Exclusionary practices may be used by persons trying to guarantee that their children will marry the "right kind" of people by not permitting them to come in meaningful social contract with the "wrong kind" of people. John Finley Scott, in his article, "Sororities and the Husband Game," notes that many mothers want their daughters to be accepted in sororities so they will increase their chances of marrying the right person, usually a fraternity man.[10]

Inclusive Voluntary Associations

In theory, inclusive voluntary associations are open to anyone willing to use the cultural norms and procedural rules and go along with the initiation strategy. Examples include churches, professional associations, and interest groups such as garden clubs, camping clubs, sports clubs, and hundreds of others.

Even though these associations are ideally open to everyone, in practice they usually are not. Some white churches still exclude blacks—if not officially, at least in practice. Many people cannot afford the cost of joining a variety of voluntary associations. If a country club is open to all, but some cannot afford the yearly dues, the club is effectively exclusionary. Those who cannot afford to go to college are

The Scope of Voluntary Associations

Voluntary associations, both exclusive and inclusive, are a common feature of American life. A partial listing in *The Associated Press Almanac* of 1973 contains hundreds of entries under the heading "Societies and Associations." Their memberships range from the tens to the tens of millions, and their preoccupations and goals are so varied and wide as to boggle the imagination. A brief sampling of organizations and their membership sizes follows:

Name of Voluntary Association	Number of Members
Adult Education Association of the United States	7,000
Air Force Association	100,000
Alcoholics Anonymous	400,000
American Antiquarian Society	245
American Association of Retired Persons	2,700,000
American Feline Society, Inc.	2,700
American National Red Cross	36,000,000
American Ornithologists Union	3,600
Association of Chairmen of Departments of Mechanics	94
Benevolent and Protective Order of Elks	1,500,000
Daughters of the American Revolution	190,000
Epilepsy Foundation of America	50,000
Imperial Council of the Ancient Arabic Order of Nobles of the Mystic Shrine	878,013
National Congress of Parents & Teachers	10,000,000
National Hay Fever Relief Association	2,000
National Council of Churches of Christ in the United States of America	42,000,000
Save-the-Redwoods League	50,000
Supreme Council, Ancient Accepted Scottish Rite of Freemasonry, Northern Jurisdiction	510,587
Writers Guild of America, East	1,500[a]

[a]New York: Quadrangle, 1972, pp. 493–498.

Membership and *active participation* in both exclusive and inclusive voluntary associations varies among Americans by their race, social class, and ethnicity. A compilation of national surveys of voluntary association

by that fact excluded from the American Sociological Association or any other associations requiring a college degree.

In addition to cost requirements, many voluntary associations, publicly open to all, have a variety of subtle ways to make certain types of

---

memberships by Charles Wright and Herbert Hyman showed that "a sizeable group of Americans are not members of any voluntary associations and that only a minority belong to more than one such organization. . . . Nearly half of the families (47 per cent) and almost two-thirds of the respondents (64 per cent) belong to no voluntary association. About a third of the families (31 per cent) and a fifth of the respondents belong to only one such organization. Only about a fifth of the families (21 per cent) and a sixth of the respondents (16 per cent) belong to two or more organizations." Wright and Hyman conclude that "these findings hardly warrant the impression that Americans are a nation of joiners."[b]

The conclusion that is warranted is that *some* Americans are very much joiners. Through further analysis of their data, Wright and Hyman conclude that membership in voluntary associations is more characteristic of whites than blacks; of Jews than Protestants; of Protestants than Catholics; of higher socioeconomic status as measured by level of income, occupation, home ownership, level of living, and education; and of urban and rural nonfarm residents.[c]

Subsequent research by others has tended to confirm these findings and provided additional information about patterns of joining and participation. Persons over sixty, for example, tend to be joiners, and the women over sixty tend to be more active participants than the men. Among those who are joiners, those with college educations tend to be more interested in civic and political issues.[d]

Voluntary associations, like other kinds of social groups, fulfill multiple functions. For some joiners, the informal ties they establish within voluntary associations provide primarylike emotional supports and contacts. For others, joining up is part of upward mobility in the class system. Still others attempt to use such associations as vehicles for furthering social changes and reforms. Part of what constitutes our pluralistic society is the conglomeration of crisscrossing voluntary associations whose goals are often contradictory and occasionally are conflicting.

---

[b]Charles Wright and Herbert Hyman, "Voluntary Association Membership of American Adults: Evidence from National Sample Surveys," *American Sociological Review.* **23**, No. 3 (June 1958), p. 286.

[c]Ibid, p. 294.

[d]See, for example, Murry Hausknecht, *The Joiners: A Study of Voluntary Associations in the United States.* (New York: Bedminster, 1962)

people feel uncomfortable. If these people become members they soon drop their membership or become inactive. These factors partially explain why more middle- and upper-class people belong to voluntary associations than do people in the lower strata of our society.[11]

Bureaucracies As Formal Groups

For many Americans the term *bureaucracy* conjures up painful images of endless delays; buck passing; long lines; red tape and runarounds; complex hierarchies of paper shufflers who feed at the public trough; indifference by corporate, labor, and government executives to the public interest; and the grinding of the poor and the powerless as they wait for their handouts in what have been called the anterooms of the welfare state. For these persons, *bureaucrat* is a fighting word. By the time most of us have passed our second decade of life in our complex society, we have had experiences that make these stereotyped reactions real. Participation or membership in large schools, hospitals, trade unions, factory employment, and military service is a widely shared experience. Coping with the motor vehicle bureau to obtain a driver's license or secure registration plates for an automobile; filing an insurance claim; appearing in a legal proceeding; trying to obtain social security or welfare benefits; or registering with a state employment service exposes us to bureaucracies where we are the clients, "units" to be "processed."

Sociologists, however, are not satisfied with simply reacting negatively to life in a bureaucratized society. Their goal is to understand how this social ordering came about and how it is structured. The reactions described here are important and significant. They give us important insights into the kinds of problems individuals have in finding meaning in groups and societies structured by bureaucratic procedures. However, they are symptoms rather than causes.

Max Weber was one of the first students of society to perceive the enormous significance of the increasing bureaucratization of life in the modern world for individual meaning and social ordering: the increased division of labor accompanying industrialization; the rise of corporate business enterprises; the tremendous worldwide expansion of population after the seventeenth century, especially in the industrializing societies; and the complex systems of transportation and government that tied together all these activities and developments and that therefore required elaborate systems of coordination and control. The result was the spread of the most effective system of administration yet devised: the bureaucracy.

Bureaucracies get things done. Weber states it succinctly:

The decisive reason for the advance of bureacratic organization has always been its purely technical superiority over any other form of organization. The fully developed bureacratic mechanism compares with other organizations exactly as does the machine with the nonmechanical modes of production.[12]

Characteristics of Bureaucratic Formal Groups

We have already discussed bureaucratization as a control strategy in Chapter 2, defining it as the process of establishing rules and organizational forms based on them that are calculated to attain goals in the most efficient manner. This procedural strategy allows those in positions of authority or power to determine the rules and thus force subordinates to go through channels that control their behavior and thus protect the machinery of control and subordination.

Merton, following Weber's lead, has defined bureaucracy as "a formal, rationally organized social structure [with] clearly defined patterns of activity in which, ideally, every series of actions is functionally related to the purposes of the organization."[13]

Weber's ideal-type bureaucracy had the following characteristics:

1. *Specialization.* There is a staff organized into subunits among whom the workload is parceled out according to special skills and tasks. The division of labor is often elaborate.
2. *Hierarchy.* Authority flows from the top to the bottom. At the top there is a small, decision-making elite or executive group. In the

---

Ideal Type

An ideal type is a methodological tool that is used in many sciences. An ideal type does not reflect empirical reality in an exact factual sense but is constructed by the scientist to reflect a conceptually pure form of a condition, event, or type of interaction. The word *ideal* carries no connotation of evaluation in the sense of being best. Examples of ideal types in the field of physics are such concepts as a frictionless surface, a perfect vacuum, and absolute zero. In the science of economics, the rational economic man is an ideal type. None of these entities actually exists, but they serve as useful tools for comparison and for analysis.

The German sociologist Max Weber used the ideal type in much of his work and constructed an ideal-type bureaucracy referred to in the text.

For an excellent discussion of various forms of constructed typologies, see John C. McKinney, *Constructive Typology and Social Theory* (New York: Appleton, 1968).

middle, there are functionaries who interpret and administer the policies set by those at the top. At the bottom are the largest number of persons who carry out the operations of the bureaucracy.

3. *Achieved positions.* The positions in a bureaucracy are obtained on formal, technical criteria and are open to achievement. Competence is the criterion of employment. Positions are secured by appointment.

4. *Rules and procedures.* There are clear-cut criteria for performing the bureaucratic tasks that are independent of individual preferences. Who is to be accepted as a client or what is to be produced and how it is to be done are clearly spelled out.

5. *Career lines.* Bureaucratic positions are ordinarily tenured and secure. The requirements and steps for advancement within the bureaucratic group are spelled out in the rules and procedures.[14]

All these are procedural strategies calculated to maintain efficiency. They attempt to control the behavior of persons in the bureaucracy and those with whom it deals by their specification of who is to do what, when, how, and to whom.

The hallmark of the bureaucracy is its table of organization, which shows in appropriate detail the various social positions within the organization and the hierarchical arrangements among them. Almost every bureaucracy, from army to hospital, boasts a table of organization. Changes in that table are often bitterly fought over if they represent genuine changes in the balance of power and control among bureaucratic units.

Bureaucracies are extreme developments of formal groups. Weber's ideal type, like a table of organization, is too neatly packaged. Bureaucracies are *never* structured as the rule books say they are. Other control strategies are used that not only violate the official rules but also structure the bureaucracy independently.

BUREAUCRACY, POWER, AND PRIVILEGE

Rules are not handed down by some Supreme Being but are made by people with the *power* to do so. The unequal distribution of power directly affects the making and, under certain conditions, the breaking of the procedural rules in bureaucratic organizations. For example, persons at the top of a bureaucracy have more power. Using their power they see to it that they have a greater share of desired rewards and facilities than any of their subordinates. Whether at a large state university, at a hospital, in an army, or at a large corporation, the top executive echelons have more space, fancier offices, personal secretaries, more privacy, larger salaries, and longer vacations than most of their subordinates.

Accompanying the greater power and control ability of top-echelon executives is greater access to and control of the flow of information about the bureaucracy's affairs and operations. If knowledge is in fact power, then control over the flow of information is an important mark of and source of executive power. Military and intelligence bureaucracies with their "need-to-know" doctrine carry this relationship between knowledge and power to an often absurd length, but in even the most benign bureaucracy there are restrictions on the flow of information. The "Catch-22" philosophy of never letting the right hand know what the left hand is doing is pervasive in bureaucratic groups.

If power produces the possibility of privilege, then Weber's ideal-type can be considered as rational *only* if certain value premises are taken as givens. Once positions of power and privilege are attained, people who have them want to retain them and can do so by making new procedural rules or changing old rules.

DOMINATION AND SUBJECTION

Dahrendorf points out that "In an imperatively coordinated association, two and only two, aggregates or positions may be distinguished, that is, positions of domination and positions of subjection."[15] Domination means "the right to issue authoritative commands" and subjection is "the duty to obey authoritative commands."[16] These rights and duties are part of the procedural strategies already discussed that typify the bureaucratic group.

Dahrendorf takes the position that persons in positions of domina-

---

Imperatively Coordinated Associations

Dahrendorf borrows the idea of an imperatively coordinated association from Max Weber, who defines it as "A corporate group, the members of which are by virtue of their membership subjected to the legitimate exercise of imperative control; that is 'authority' will be called an 'imperatively coordinated' group."[a] Imperative control is the probability that a command with a given specific content will be obeyed by a given group of persons." "Discipline is the probability that by virtue of habitation a command will receive prompt and automatic obedience in stereotyped forms, on the part of a given group of persons."[b]

Weber sees imperative control as legitimate. Persons are willing to go along with the command without coercion. Dahrendorf's position and ours emphasize that there are definite limits to the use of imperative control, which, in a bureaucracy, is part of what we call procedural strategies.

[a] Max Weber, *The Theory of Social and Economic Organization*, trans. A. M. Henderson and Talcott Parsons (New York: Free Press, 1947), p. 153.
[b] Ibid., p. 152.

tion and persons in positions of subjection have inherently separate and often opposing interests. At times, these separate interests are latent; individuals are not collectively conscious of their common interests. At other times, however, these interests become manifest, people become conscious of their common interests as a group, and they act to improve or reinforce their interests.[17] As latent interests become manifest, other types of control strategies are used and actions are taken to change the nature of the organization. For example, if a worker in an industrial plant is mistreated by management, other workers may realize that the same thing can happen to them. The workers may then form a strong coalition and demand that the structure of the organization be changed to guarantee better treatment.

We differ slightly from Dahrendorf's position. Certain interests, both *individual* and *collective,* are always manifest in various degrees. The line between positions of domination and subjection is relative and shifting. A junior executive, for example, is in a dominating position over a foreman, while he is in a subordinate position to a senior executive. Under these circumstances—which are typical—manipulative, coalitional, and exchange strategies (all of which are outside the procedural rules) are constantly being used in various combinations and degrees. Dahrendorf focuses directly on the use of coercive strategies in confrontations between dominant and subordinate groups and individuals must choose sides, as in a strike by industrial workers or a sit-in by students. Such coercive strategies are attempts to produce rapid and at times violent organizational change.

The Hawthorne Studies: Human Relations and Bureaucratic Group Norms

When sociologists began to explore bureaucratic groups in the field rather than in theory, they discovered that far more was going on than was revealed by the tables of organization or the manuals of rules. Bureaucracies are formal groups whose social ordering is always partly structured by procedural strategies. However, hundreds of studies over the last decades have demonstrated the significance of the use of other control strategies for goal attainment, individual meaning, and social ordering within bureaucracies.

One of the earliest of these studies was undertaken by Elton Mayo and his associates at the Harvard Department of Industrial Research during the 1930s.[18] They studied the Hawthorne plant of the Western Electric Company to establish what factors affected the output of the workers. Their original interest was to manipulate the physical conditions of the job situation (number of hours, lighting conditions, rest periods) and financial remuneration to see how these factors affected productivity. An isolated work group of six women was established in which these conditions could be changed at will by the experimenters.

The surprising discovery was made after several years of observation that productivity was relatively independent of pay, rest periods, lighting, and physical environment. The women's output rose during the course of the experiment and then stayed at the same relatively high level no matter what the experimenters did. Much cogitation and further research produced the interpretation that has come to be known as The Hawthorne Effect: the interest shown in the workers by the experimenters caused the initial rise in production. The workers felt significant and important, had good rapport with the experimenters, and therefore stabilized output at a relatively high level no matter what minor changes in lighting or work hours were made. The amount of work done in an industrial plant is not determined solely by the official procedural strategies of the organization, but by a variety of other factors, including good human relations. Workers like to be recognized as human beings. When they are, production goes up, as one could predict from the existence of the need for recognition.

The Hawthorne studies and others resulted in the "human relations" approach in industry. Efforts were made to view the workers as human beings performing tasks that require individual meaning and significance, rather than to see them as replaceable cogs in a machine to be exploited and used to the greatest extent possible and then discarded. All these studies accepted the values of management and occurred within the context of the bureaucratic factory or corporation. For this reason, some critics have called this human relations school of industrial sociology "cow" sociology. In effect, it takes as given and unchangeable the goal of the farmer (corporation) to produce more milk (higher output) and then seeks to placate and soothe the cows (workers) to increase the flow, not seriously considering the possibility that the farmer's and cow's interests may not be identical.

INFORMAL GROUP NORMS AND OUTPUT

Another central finding of these studies is the enormous significance of informal groups and their *norms* for the ordering of bureaucracies. Workers control the production process through the use of coalitional strategies in the formation of informal groups. These informal groups develop norms that allow workers to increase their degree of control over the environment and lessen their dependence on management. Blau and W. Richard Scott summarize some of these group norms and the sanctions that support them:

What group norms were there to enforce? In the course of interaction a set of common rules of conduct emerged, which included the following prohibitions: Don't be a rate-buster by working too fast. Don't be a chiseler by working too slow. If you are a straw boss, act like a regular guy; don't try to get bossy. Don't be a squealer. Conformity to norms was rewarded by approval that bestowed a relatively high position in the informal status structure. Norm violations were punished by group members in a variety of ways. Minor violations might be met with "binging"—striking the offender on the upper arm—or with ridicule. Continued violation of important norms resulted in a loss of popularity, a reduction in social interaction, and ultimately in complete ostracism. One worker was isolated because he violated the most serious group norm: he "squealed" on his fellows to the foreman.[19]

Whether in the military service, in a hospital, a religious organization, a prison, a school, or a factory, sociologists have documented the enormous significance of informal groups for the social ordering of formal groups. Because bureaucracies dominate modern societies, much of the research has been directed to studies of the interpenetration of informal groups and bureaucratic organizations, but voluntary associations also are permeated with and affected by informal groups. Individual needs for recognition and security are met by informal groups. Some of these informal groups are almost primarylike in the intensity of the emotional relationships and gratifications (the buddy groups in military service), whereas others more nearly resemble the congeniality groups discussed above (most work groups in industry).[20]

Bureaupathology

Most of the elements that cause the negative stereotypes that make bureaucracy and bureaucrat fighting words for many in modern societies result from what have been called bureaupathologies—that is, extreme developments or exaggerations of bureaucratic tendencies. We will briefly examine two related bureaupathologies here: the means-end inversion and the bureaucratic personality.

THE MEANS-END INVERSION

Bureaucracies are goal-oriented. They are set up to achieve one or more goals. The ideal-type essence of the bureaucratic orientation is the rational adaptation and use of means to achieve these goals. However, the stability and security that are part of the bureaucratic system often become ends in themselves, so that the original goal recedes in the distance and the immediate efforts of those in the bureaucratic group are directed to preserving and often extending the bureaucracy itself; thus protecting their positions and interests.

THE BUREAUCRATIC PERSONALITY

The bureaucratic personality is the occupant of a social position in a bureaucracy who has fallen prey to the means-end inversion. For him, the rules and routines set up to accomplish goals have become ends in themselves.[21] The procedural control strategies are no longer used to achieve an end but are valued intrinsically. Merton has suggested that persons with a psychological predisposition to this ritualistic orientation are attracted to bureaucratic positions and, in turn, the bureaucratic system of routines, regulations, hierarchies, and careers reinforces and rewards the ritualistic tendencies in members.

Examples of these bureaupathologies abound. The librarian who comes to view the books as ends in themselves, to be carefully preserved from the users for whom the library ostensibly exists, is a common phenomenon. So is the middle-echelon functionary whose social role consists of receiving, filling out, and passing along endless forms. It is not uncommon for him to lose sight of the goals of the bureaucracy and to judge "production" and "effectiveness" solely by the quantity of paper processed rather than the quality of goals achieved. The endless committee meetings, written reports, memoranda, and ever-revised books of rules that typify large corporate and governmental bureaucracies are examples of the means-end inversion.

Sometimes the means-end inversions are directly subversive of the organization's goals. Mental hospital attendants who treat patients inhumanly to make their jobs easier are defeating the therapeutic goals of the hospital. Teachers for whom the achievement of tenure is an end in itself may cease to communicate with students.[22]

Tendencies within Bureaucracies

To summarize the many observations by sociologists about what happens in bureaucratizing and bureaucratized groups, Anthony Downs has set forth some general statements that he calls "laws." These laws are empirical generalizations (abstractions from observations) that represent tendencies common in many bureaucracies. They do not always occur and are not inevitable, but they happen often enough to be useful in trying to understand bureaucratic social forms and the control strategies used in their structuring.

1. *Law of increasing conservatism.* In every bureau, there is an inherent pressure upon the vast majority of officials to become conservers in the long run.
2. *Law of imperfect control.* No one can fully control the behavior of a large organization.
3. *Law of diminishing control.* The larger any organization becomes, the weaker the control over its actions exercised by those at the top.
4. *Law of countercontrol.* The greater the effort made by a sovereign or top official to control the behavior of subordinate officials, the greater the efforts of those subordinates to evade or counteract such control.[23]

The law of increasing conservation implies that the majority of officials in a bureaucracy can be expected to use control strategies that will maintain the system and their place within it. The law of imperfect control suggests that because no one can fully control all behavior in a large organization, many people have some control potential. As organizations become larger, the law of diminishing control shows that those in lower positions can increase their control potential because control by those at the top becomes weaker. The law of countercontrol illustrates the reciprocity of control that, in the final analysis, structures all social order.

Downs offers four additional generalizations that clarify bureaucratic control attempts and explain deviations from the use of procedural strategies.

1. Each official tends to distort the information he passes upward in the hierarchy, exaggerating those data favorable to himself and minimizing those unfavorable to himself.
2. Each official is biased in favor of those policies or actions that advance his own interests or the programs he advocates, and against those that injure or simply fail to advance those interests or programs.
3. Each official will vary the degree to which he complies with directives from his superiors, depending upon whether those directives favor or oppose his own interests.

Organization Charts and Informal Groups

As is mentioned in the text, one of the hallmarks of formal groups, and especially of bureaucracies, is the organization chart or table of organization that displays the various social positions arranged according to the hierarchical system of authority. There are many kinds of organization charts. Some identify each position in the hierarchy and indicate the name of the individual or individuals who currently occupy the slot. Others describe the organizational positions in functional terms only. The chart here shows how a manufacturing company might set up operating divisions for its several products.

The sociological perspective about formal groups that has developed during the last several decades of research has emphasized the significance for organizational effectiveness (and for social ordering and individual meaning) of what is not shown on such charts. We can confidently predict that within any formal group that can be represented by such a chart there will exist networks of interlocking informal groups that greatly influence the behavior of members of the formal group. Work output, morale, efficiency, goal realization, communication flow within the organization, and many other aspects of formal structure will be determined not by prescribed lines of formal authority and procedural rules and regulations but by informal group norms and informal interaction and communication patterns.[a]

4. The degree to which each official will seek out additional responsibilities and accept risks in performing his duties will vary directly with the extent to which such initiative is likely to help him achieve his own personal goals.[24]

These four statements suggest the widespread use of manipulative and coalitional strategies in bureaucratic organizations. Individual interests in the gratification of needs or in the reaching of personal goals often take precedence over loyalty to the goals of the organization if the two are incompatible.

Downs' "laws" emphasize the differences sociologists have discovered between how bureaucracies operate in the real world and the ideal-typical Weberian model. The tendencies to expand and to get out of control, the tendencies for the various bureaucratic echelons to lose sight of what the others are doing, for means to replace ends, for security and routine to swamp innovation and adaptation, for communication channels to become clogged, and for individuals to pursue self-serving interests from the top to the bottom are common. Large size and complexity of operations increase these tendencies, but small size is no guarantee of their absence. The smallest social work agency may display all the bureaupathologies and tendencies toward organi-

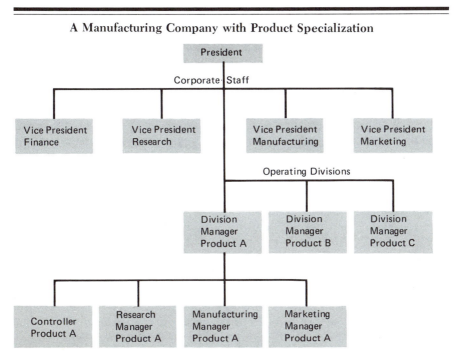

A Manufacturing Company with Product Specialization

[a]*Handbook of Business Administration*, ed. by H. B. Maynard (New York: McGraw-Hill, 1970), pp. 8–12.

zational hardening of the arteries that the enormous Department of Health, Education and Welfare displays.

Individuals seek to gratify their basic needs and to find individual meaning within the framework of bureaucratic groups. Informal groups emerge to meet these needs and, in Homans' word, "mediate" between the bureaucratic colossi and the otherwise likely-to-be-overwhelmed individual human being. Finding individual meaning and need satisfaction among the huge bureaucracies that surround us is a problem for most members of our society. Whether we embrace achievement orientation and seek recognition through rising up the power-and-reward ladder of a large corporation, seek security in the sheltered routine of the clerk's life, or reject both alternatives and try to set up an alternative life-style in a commune, we may be reacting to and conditioned by the pervasive bureaucracies that dominate modern social life.

Max Weber, whose sweeping theories about and influential ideal-type models of bureaucracies formed the basis for most subsequent studies of these formal groups, stepped outside of his preferred role of observer to make this impassioned statement about the implications of ever-increasing bureaucratization:

> It is horrible to think that the world could one day be filled with nothing but those little cogs, little men clinging to little jobs and striving toward bigger ones—a state of affairs which is to be seen once more, as in the Egyptian records, playing an ever-increasing part in the spirit of our present administrative system, and especially of its offspring, the students. This passion for bureaucracy . . . is enough to drive one to despair. It is as if in politics . . . we were deliberately to become men who need "order" and nothing but order, who become nervous and cowardly if for one moment this order wavers, and helpless if they are torn away from their total incorporation in it. That the world should know no men but these: it is such an evolution that we are already caught up in, and the great question is therefore not how we can promote and hasten it, but what can we oppose to this machinery in order to keep a portion of mankind free from this parceling-out of the soul, from this supreme mastery of the bureaucratic way of life.[25]

Weber starkly poses the problem of individual meaning in a world whose social ordering is bureaucratically structured. We have already discussed communes as one alternative group form and in later chapters we will examine other alternative value systems and social groups to the procedural strategies and focus on rational, efficient goal attainment that typifies bureaucracies.

This concludes the discussion of the control strategies that structure types of groups. There is considerable variation *within* the groups discussed in type and intensity of each of the strategies used. For an *exact* analysis, the specific group should be studied in depth, with all strategies considered in the analysis.

SOCIAL CATEGORIES

A social category is a number of people defined as having a specific characteristic. Examples of characteristics often used to define social categories are race and education. A social category cannot properly be defined as a group because people in a social category do not interact. The people in a social category may or may not have the characteristics ascribed to them, but whether they do or do not, the definition affects how they will be viewed and treated by others and, thus, how they may view themselves. Occupying a defined social category has implications not only for life-style but also for life chances and self-identity.

Our classification of cultural strategies included categorization as a control strategy. Using the categorization strategy to place persons with specific characteristics into social categories is typically done for purposes of control based on the defining characteristics of the category. Thus, persons with a certain ethnic background may be placed in a social category to which a variety of derogatory labels are attached. In our society, for example, white Anglo-Saxon Protestants have categorized and pejoratively labeled a variety of ethnic and racial groups. Some of these have in turn categorized and labeled others.

Categorization and labeling so used are attempts to create or maintain power differentials and thus to limit alternatives. Understanding social categories is therefore important to explain social ordering.

Even though the use of the categorization strategy is cultural when there is widespread agreement among those doing the categorizing, this does not necessarily mean that those who are categorized and derogatorily labeled agree with the results of the use of this strategy. For example, many white people in our society have placed all black people into a social category and have attached certain derogatory labels to the category. This does not mean, however, that black people accept the labels.

Under certain conditions, individuals who are placed in social categories develop a "consciousness of kind"[26] and use coalitional strategies, withdrawal strategies, and coercive strategies against those who have categorized and labeled them. If coercive strategies are too costly, certain types of exchange strategies, such as accommodation, may be used. People who have been placed in social categories may also create subcultures and, under certain conditions, contracultures. A contraculture consists of shared agreements held by a number of people who have been rejected by others. These shared agreements can be understood only through their negative relationship to the dominant society or a subgroup existing in that society. Members of a delinquent gang create a contraculture against those who have rejected them.[27] Aspects of the hippies' way of life have contraculture characteristics.

INTERGROUP RELATIONS: THE STRUCTURING OF INTERGROUP ORDERING

Groups exist for a variety of purposes ranging all the way from basic need gratification in some primary groups to making an economic profit in an industrial bureaucracy. Whatever the purpose of the group, its members usually want the group to survive and attain its goal or purpose and to gratify their personal needs.

If members of a group want the group to survive they must not only control each other's behavior to maintain the internal structure of the group, but also attempt to control external conditions. These external conditions include the physical environment and, perhaps more important, the behavior of the members of at least some other groups. Thus, *intergroup relations are structured by the use of control strategies, as are interpersonal relations.*

The types of control strategies one group will use in its relationships with other groups depend on a variety of factors: (1) the values of the group and the purpose for which it exists; (2) the relative numerical strength of the group; (3) the need for the services of other groups; (4) the relative power of other groups; (5) the degree to which members' identities are tied to the group; (6) the degree to which individuals share common memberships among the groups that interact; (7) the degree to which an outside force threatens the continued existence of two or more interacting groups; and (8) the proximity of the groups. Interaction among these and other factors determines the control strategies used by groups in interaction and, thus, the structure of intergroup relations.

Ten propositions relating to intergroup relations are presented here, with brief commentary and examples:

Proposition 1. A group will tend to use control strategies consistent with its values and purposes so long as its existence is not threatened by doing so.

Because a group's values and purposes provide *a* reason for its existence, a group will maintain consistency between its values and purposes and the types of control strategies it uses in relationships with other groups.

For example, we would not expect a Christian church to use violent coercive strategies because these are inconsistent with basic Christian teachings about "loving one's enemies" and "returning good for evil."

Nor would we expect an industrial corporation whose philosophy is based on free enterprise and free competition to use coalitional strategies in relations with government or other industrial corporations. *But we must also simultaneously consider Proposition 2.*

Proposition 2. If a group's existence is threatened and if control strategies consistent with its values and purposes are not sufficient to maintain the group's existence, control strategies inconsistent with its values and purposes are likely to be used in an attempt to insure survival.

Many people within groups have vested interests in positions of power or privilege, money as income, practices gratifying basic needs, and other interests not necessarily related to the values and purposes of the group as a whole. Therefore, if a group's existence is threatened, if it stands to gain something by so doing, or if those who dominate the group believe their vital interests are endangered, control strategies inconsistent with the values and purposes of the group may be used.

Christian churches have often used violent coercive strategies and supported societies that use them. The Inquisition, the Crusades, and the Salem witchcraft trials are examples. During the history of Western civilization probably more people have been killed in "Holy" wars than have been killed in "unholy" wars. Most nations at war find God on their side, at least according to their religious leaders and groups.

If industrial corporations believe their existence is threatened or see possibilities for massive gains by dividing up the market rather than by competing, corporation executives will forget *laissez faire* and free enterprise and enter into profitable coalitions with government and other corporations to develop gigantic monopolies.

Proposition 3. If a group uses control strategies inconsistent with its values and purposes over a long period of time, the values and purposes of the group will change or be rationalized to bring about consistency.

It is difficult for group members to maintain inconsistencies between values, purposes, and practices. Therefore, it becomes necessary to change one or the other, or to at least present reasons why the inconsistency is only apparent.

The church finds it necessary to "destroy the infidels or heretics" because it is "God's will." Industrial corporations argue that their coalitions with government or other corporations are necessary for economic growth or for the public good.

The next four propositions are closely related:

Proposition 4. If the numerical strength or resources of a group are less than those of the groups with which it interacts, the control strategies used will be such as to minimize the possibility of provoking threatening acts by those other groups.

Proposition 5. If a group depends on other groups for certain resources or services, the control strategies used by the group in its relationships with others will be to minimize the probability of alienation.

Proposition 6. If a group has more power than the groups with which it interacts, the control strategies used by the group will be such as to maintain and, if possible, increase its power advantage.

Proposition 7. If a group has less power than the groups with which it interacts, the control strategies used by the group will be attempts to gain more power while maintaining its chances for continued existence.

These four propositions relate the relative amount of power and resources held by interacting groups and their use of control strategies. The degree of power a group has depends on the amount of resources it controls. These resources can be tangible or intangible. A group with few resources and little power interacting with groups controlling needed resources and having greater power will use control strategies that will not alienate the groups on which it depends. At the same time groups with little power will attempt to increase their power without hampering their chances for continued existence. Groups with more power will attempt to maintain, and, if possible, increase their power.

The structure of many relationships among the interacting groups in a society is clarified by these four propositions. Groups with more power and resources have a greater range of alternatives than do groups with less power and fewer resources and therefore can take greater risks. Groups with greater power are more likely to ignore cultural agreements and corresponding cultural strategies and, if severely threatened, to use coercive strategies to maintain their power. They can also set the conditions for the use of certain types of exchange strategies and establish advantageous procedural strategies.

On the other hand, groups with little power can be "forced" to maintain the use of cultural and procedural and certain exchange strategies even though these work against their best interests. Weaker groups may be restricted to the use of such exchange strategies as obedience, approval, or certain forms of accommodation. They may be able to use certain types of manipulative strategies, depending on what the group (or groups) with more power will tolerate. Groups with little power and similar interests may use coalitional strategies, but this is risky if more powerful groups feel threatened by such coalitions. Members of minority groups are often forced to abide by dominant cultural agreements that are against their own interests. We will discuss dominant-minority relationships at length in Chapter 8.

Many groups with little power are never "bothered" by groups with more power because they do not present a threat to the existing structure of reciprocal control. The voluntary associations that form around specific interests, such as garden clubs or sports clubs, are examples.

Proposition 8. The more members of a group depend on the group for their individual identities and meaning systems, the more extreme will be the control strategies used under conditions of threat from other groups.

If the individual identities and meaning systems of a group's members are heavily tied to the values and purposes of the group, and if these individuals have few or no other sources of identity support, they are likely to use extreme control strategies to keep their group intact.

Black groups, searching for more satisfactory public and personal identities, moved away from the use of such exchange strategies as accommodation to the use of a variety of coercive nonviolent and coercive violent strategies. Certain religious groups have been willing to use extreme control strategies because the identities of their members were firmly tied to the belief systems of their religious groups. If a group provides a basis for identity, to deny the group and its beliefs is to deny one's identity, making life meaningless. Thus, if one's group is of extreme importance it must be saved at all cost, "even unto death."

Proposition 9. If several individuals share common memberships among groups that interact, the control strategies used by these groups in interaction will be such as to reduce the probability of conflict among them.

Overlapping memberships within a variety of groups in a society tend to keep polarization from occurring and thus reduce the possibility of open conflict among interacting groups. If union members belong to the same church or social club as do executives in the company for which they work, the unionists and executives are not so likely to be antagonistic on the job. If members of the Chamber of Commerce in a community are on the board of trustees of a welfare program and thus come to know poor people, they are not so likely to take a hard line against proposed social changes to help the poor.

In his book, *Political Man*, Seymour Martin Lipset notes that the overlapping of group memberships that cut across class, religious, and political lines is essential in maintaining a democratic society.[28] If this overlapping of memberships were not present, the polarization of opposing powerful groups might lead to the use of such violent coercive strategies as revolution.

Proposition 10. If an outside force threatens the continued existence of two or more interacting groups, these groups will use coalitional and cooperative strategies in an attempt to overcome the outside threat.

This proposition is related to Simmel's suggestion that out-group threat increases in-group solidarity.[29] It extends his proposition and says that a common threat will increase solidarity among interacting groups.

When a nation is attacked in war, the various groups within that nation often forget their differences and increase their solidarity in the effort to defeat the common enemy. During World War II in the United States groups of all kinds combined their efforts to defeat Germany and Japan. Such coalitions often fall apart when the common threat is removed, as did the coalition between the United States and the Soviet Union after World War II.

Intergroup relations can be usefully analyzed by examining how control strategies are used. We have seen how the use of these control strategies depends, among other things, on the power balance between the interacting groups. The ten propositions that specify some of these relationships apply to both informal and formal groups and to the relationships among subgroups within large formal groups, such as a bureaucracy.

Behavior and attitudes are not, however, solely determined by group membership. To achieve a more complete understanding of why people and groups behave as they do, we must examine another concept: reference groups.

In Group and Out Group

In group and out group is a dichotomy which has long been used in sociology. An in group is the group to which an individual belongs and that helps provide a sense of identity and meaning. The in group produces a feeling of "we-ness" among its members.

An out group, as the name implies, is a group that exists apart from the in group and, under certain conditions, may be a threat to its continued existence. (The out group is an in group for its members.)

A person can be a member of several in groups and the boundaries of in groups and out groups may shift over time. Under conditions of a common threat, a former out group may become a part of one's in group.

REFERENCE GROUPS

Individuals usually behave similarly to other members of groups to which they belong. Thus, their behaviors can be understood within the context of their membership groups. Sometimes, however, the sociologist observes noticeable differences between the behavior of some individuals and that of most other members of a group. Many such differences can be accounted for by knowing the reference group or groups of the individuals whose behavior cannot be understood within the context of their membership group.[30]

A reference group is a group that furnishes standards and attitudes that influence negatively or positively the behavior of individuals. If the behavior of individuals is influenced negatively they attempt to make their behavior *unlike* that of the members of a negative reference group. If the behavior of individuals is influenced positively they attempt to make their behavior *similar* to the behavior of members of a positive reference group. Thus, there are two types of reference groups—negative and positive.

Negative Reference Groups

A negative reference group furnishes standards that influence the behavior of individuals so that they attempt to make their behavior *unlike* the behavior of members of the negative reference group. These individuals do not want to be considered by others as in any way belonging to the negative reference groups.

Under certain conditions an out group may become a negative reference group. Members of the in group then attempt to show their *loyalty* to the in group by being as much unlike members of the out group as possible.

Negative reference groups may also develop when individuals change groups, especially if they are moving upward in a social hierarchy. For example, if a person has been a member of a group of blue-collar working people and is promoted to a white-collar position, his old blue-collar group may become a negative reference group as he attempts to convince his new associates that he is not really like those with whom he used to associate.

Positive Reference Groups

A positive reference group furnishes standards for the behavior of individuals who desire membership in the positive reference group. Positive reference groups, other than membership groups, are used as a point of reference when individuals want to change their group or social position. Individuals are aware that if they are to be acceptable to the group they want to join, they must present a favorable image. They begin to take on characteristics favored by the groups they want to join. This is called anticipatory socialization.

Merton points out that such *anticipatory socialization* is the taking on of the values and behavior of a nonmembership group to which individuals aspire and may be detrimental to the persons using it.[31] When individuals take on the values and behavior of a nonmembership group, they are likely to be rejected by their membership group. If this occurs, and if for some reason they are rejected by the group to which they aspire, they become persons twice rejected—by the group to which they aspire and by their membership group. They become persons left suspended between two groups, neither of which wants them as members. They become marginal people.

In our achievement-oriented society there are many positive reference groups and much anticipatory socialization. On college or university campuses, independents who want to become members of fraternities or sororities must use these groups as positive reference groups and begin acting in a manner acceptable to members of the group they want to join.

In all types of organizations and among a variety of groups we find individuals who have positive reference groups other than their membership groups. People who want to be promoted in the military service or in industrial organizations, who want to be accepted into exclusive voluntary associations, immigrants who want to become citizens and be seen as "good" Americans, and those aspiring to upward social mobility in the society seek out positive reference groups as part of the process of anticipatory socialization. Educational institutions facilitate this process, which we will explore in Chapter 11. Typically, such individuals have either achieved or are attempting to achieve social advancement or at least need-gratifying acceptance.

RELATIVE DEPRIVATION

The concept of relative deprivation introduced in Chapter 2 as part of the discussion of stratification suggests that the criteria that shape a person's or a group's feelings of deprivation almost always tend to be relative. If persons look long enough, they can usually find others worse off in any number of ways. Most of us, however, tend to look upward rather than downward; that is, we compare ourselves to groups or individuals better off than we. As a result, we are likely to feel deprived. These feelings of deprivation are not based on an absolute standard but vary with the frame of reference we use in comparing. If we compare ourselves with members of groups "below" us we are likely to feel elated. Such reference groups are important because they help to determine how individuals and groups feel about themselves and how likely they are to accept the distribution of rewards, facilities, and gratifications of a particular stratification system.

Group Memberships and Individual Meaning

The importance of group involvement for self-identity and individual meaning cannot be overestimated. Self-identities are created and maintained or changed within the framework of social groups and by exclusion from them. The groups to which individuals belong and the intensity of their involvement within them tell us much about the members and their self-identities. Persons intensely involved in religious groups are likely to see themselves and to be seen by others as different from people who have no religious affiliation. The *type* of religious group to which one belongs is similarly important. Persons who belong to exclusive voluntary associations may see themselves as better than others in their community who do not so belong. Some types of groups, including churches, are ranked higher or lower according to the prestige of their members. Upwardly mobile people seek membership in such groups to enhance their degree of prestige and control potential. If they attain membership, this is likely to change their self-identity and their identity as viewed by others.

To explain who we are to a stranger, group affiliations and our place within these groups are likely to be the first things mentioned. Persons who are identifying themselves to others and, thus, to themselves name such things as their religious group affiliation, their work group or school, any voluntary associations they may belong to, and the offices they happen to hold within these.

Individual meaning is created, maintained, or, destroyed within the framework of social groups. The family as a primary group is critical in the development of individual meaning. As the child develops other groups become important for individual meaning, including peer, school, and work groups.

Many social groups are explicitly formed to create, change, or protect values on which individual meaning is based. Examples include religious groups and many other types of voluntary associations such as the John Birch Society and the American Civil Liberties Union.

Individuals tend to be drawn to groups that support the values they already hold. If their values are vague and they have no basis for individual meaning, they may join a group or groups in an attempt to find a basis for meaning. This writer, in an unpublished study of a group of Jehovah's Witnesses in an Indiana county, found that most members of this group had had no prior group affiliation. They were, thus, intensely loyal to this group, which was providing them with a basis for individual meaning.[32]

Even though we find an occasional isolated person who belongs to no group, people for the most part are group creatures. It is within the framework of group interaction that values can be validated, meaning systems worked out, and needs gratified.

REFERENCES

1. Johnson, Harry. *Sociology: A Systematic Introduction.* New York: Harcourt, 1960, p. 3.
2. Homans, George. *The Human Group.* New York: Harcourt, 1950, pp. 1–2.
3. Merton, Robert K. *Social Theory and Social Structure.* New York: Free Press, 1957, Chap. IX.
4. Ibid., p. 285.
5. Homans, op. cit., p. 2.
6. Cooley, Charles Horton. *Social Organization.* New York: Scribners, 1909, pp. 23–24.

The Search for Identity through Group Membership

One sociologist wrote a book called *The Quest for Community.* Another sociologist titled his study *The Eclipse of Community.*[a] In our urbanized, industrialized, bureaucratized society, with its impersonality and its competitiveness, many persons seem profoundly disoriented and disturbed by their inability to establish meaningful group ties. Anthony Lewis has commented that:

> I have no doubt myself that one of the great unspoken forces in the life of Americans today is a longing for community, for human contact and human concern. People feel themselves in the grip of institutions whose values are inhuman, a juggernaut that sweeps them along with no one to hear their cry. Why does that feeling exist? What makes America so uncommunal, so lonely a country?[b]

Lewis may be overstating the case. Many Americans find secure stable identities in their familial and congeniality groups and in the informal groups to which they belong as part of their roles in bureaucratic economic and political institutions. Yet there are also many who actively seek to experience the individual meaning that comes from belonging to a primary group and experiencing the emotional support and warmth that can flow from such participation.

A girl who joined a commune shortly after graduating from high school describes her quest for meaning in group experience:

7. Shils, Edward, and Morris Janowitz. "Cohesion and Disintegration in the Wehrmacht in World War II." *Public Opinion Quarterly*, No. 2 (Summer 1948). Little, Roger. "Buddy Relations and Combat Performance." In *The New Military*. Ed. by Morris Janowitz. New York: Russell Sage, 1965.
8. Herberg, Will. *Protestant, Catholic, Jew*. Garden City, N.Y.: Doubleday, 1960.
9. Frazier, E. Franklin. *The Negro Church in America*. New York: Schocken, 1964.
10. Scott, John Finley. "Sororities and the Husband Game." In *Sociological Realities*. Ed. by Irving Louis Horowitz and Mary Symons Strong. New York: Harper, 1971.
11. For a study of voluntary association membership, see Babchuck, Nicholas, and Alan Booth. "Voluntary Association Membership: A Longitudinal Analysis." *American Sociological Review*, Vol. 34 (1969), 31–45.
12. Weber, Max. *From Max Weber: Essays in Sociology*. Ed. and trans. by Hans Gerth and C. Wright Mills. New York: Oxford U. P., 1958, p. 214.
13. Merton, op. cit., p. 195.
14. Weber, Max. *The Theory of Social and Economic Organization*. Trans. by A. M. Henderson and Talcott Parsons. New York: Free Press, 1947, pp. 333–334.
15. Dahrendorf, Ralf. *Class and Class Conflict in Industrial Society*. Stanford, Calif.: Stanford University Press, 1959, p. 238.

When we first started the commune two years ago, it was really tough. We would spend hours each week talking about what food we were going to buy for the next week, and who was going to pay what, and who would have to wash the dishes and clean up the livingroom. And we all got angry at each other, and a couple of people left, but the rest of us stuck it out, because we knew that we were on the right track, that what we had going was more important than all the little hassles that were hanging us up. And we were right, because now it's almost two years later, and we really have a good thing going. It's not perfect—we all get mad at each other once in a while, but it's a beautiful thing to come home to after being away for a week, and see nine other people who all really know you and love you. You know, I don't think I would ever care to return to the other way and live in a little house with my husband and a couple of kids. It would just be unnatural, somehow. Maybe time will prove me wrong, but I doubt it.[c]

These are powerful emotions, producing strong reactions in those who experience them. If we can not in all accuracy say that "community" in the sense of primarylike group experiences has been eclipsed in our society, we can say that many of us are in quest of such community.

[a]Robert Nisbet, *The Quest for Community* (New York: Oxford U.P., 1953) and Maurice Stein, *The Eclipse of Community* (Princeton, N.J.: Princeton University Press, 1962).

[b]Quoted on the title page of Donald C. Connery, *One American Town* (New York: Simon & Schuster, 1972).

[c]Harrison Pope, Jr., *Voices from the Drug Culture* (Boston: Beacon, 1972, pp. 53–54).

16. Ibid., p. 237.
17. Ibid., p. 239.
18. See Roethlisberger, F. J., and William J. Dickson. *Management and the Worker.* Cambridge: Harvard U. P., 1939. Also, see Mayo, Elton. *The Social Problems of an Industrial Civilization.* Boston: Graduate School of Business Administration, Harvard University, 1945.
19. Blau, Peter M., and W. Richard Scott. *Formal Organizations.* San Francisco: Chandler, 1962, p. 92.
20. See, for examples, *American Bureaucracy.* Ed. by Warren Bennis. Chicago: Aldine, 1970; Blau, Peter. *The Dynamics of Bureaucracy.* Chicago: U. of Chicago, 1955; Goffman, Erving. *Asylums.* Garden City, N.Y.: Doubleday Anchor, 1961; *The Sociology of Organizations.* Ed. by Oscar Grusky and George Miller. New York: Free Press, 1970; and Roy, Donald. "Efficiency and 'The Fix': Informal Intergroup Relations in a Piecework Machine Shop." *American Journal of Sociology,* Vol. 60, No. 3 (Nov. 1954), 255–266.
21. Merton, op. cit. Mannheim, Karl. *Essays on the Sociology of Knowledge.* New York: Oxford U. P., 1952.
22. Blau and Scott, loc. cit; Scheff, Thomas. "Control Over Policy by Attendants in a Mental Hospital." *Journal of Health & Human Behavior,* 2 (1961), 93–105.
23. Downs, Anthony. *Inside Bureaucracy.* Boston: Little, Brown. 1967.
24. Ibid., p. 206, discussed in Chap. VII. For an elaborate listing of propositions dealing with bureaucracies, see Thompson, James D. *Organizations in Action.* New York: McGraw-Hill, 1967. For a discussion of different types of bureaucracy produced by the relative importance of different control strategies, see Gouldner, Alvin W. *Patterns of Industrial Bureaucracy.* New York: Free Press, 1954.
25. *American Bureaucracy.* Ed. by Warren Bennis. Chicago: Aldine, 1970, pp. 6–7.
26. This concept was developed by Franklin Henry Giddings in an attempt to explain why persons with similar characteristics associate with each other.
27. See Cohen, A. K. *Delinquent Boys: The Culture of the Gang.* New York: Free Press, 1955; and Yinger, J. Milton. "Contraculture and Subculture." *American Sociological Review,* **25** (Oct. 1960), 625–635.
28. Lipset, Seymour Martin. *Political Man.* Garden City, N.Y.: Doubleday, 1963.
29. Simmel, Georg. *Conflict and the Web of Group Affiliations.* Trans. by Kurt H. Wolff. New York: Free Press, 1964.
30. This discussion of reference groups relies heavily on Merton, op. cit., Chaps. VII and IX.
31. See Merton, op. cit., Chap. VIII.
32. For a study of this group, see Pike, Royston. *Jehovah's Witnesses.* New York: Philosophical Library, 1954.

Constraints
and Social Ordering

In Part II four major factors critical to the understanding of social order and individual meaning are discussed. These are *ecological constraints* (Chapter 5), which include the formation of communities, community power systems, and the tendency toward a mass society; *demographic constraints* (Chapter 6), which include the growth of population and influences on population movement; *social stratification* (Chapter 7), which includes the differential power that creates and sustains various types of social stratification systems; and *ethnic and minority groups* (Chapter 8), in which the differential distribution of power is significant.

CHAPTER 5

Ecological Constraints, Human Communities, and Mass Society

INTRODUCTION

In this chapter we shall explore how environmental constraints shape the location, characteristics, and development of human communities. Then we will discuss the internal ordering of these communities as it is shaped by their power systems. Finally, we will consider the extent and significance of trends toward the emergence of mass societies in technologically advanced countries that are heavily urbanized and bureaucratized.

THE SCIENCE OF ECOLOGY

Ecology and *environment* have become emotionally charged household words in recent years. Widespread public alarm, especially in industrialized societies, about the threat of increasing pollution, the scarcity of fossil fuels ("the energy crisis") and other resources, and the phenomenal growth of world population has led to the emergence of an ecological social movement. For the scientist the study of ecology is the study of how organisms adapt to and interact with their environments. Human organisms, like all living things, cannot escape the laws of nature. We too exist within a relatively closed ecological system and must live within the constraints this system imposes on us.

An ecological system or *ecosystem* "combines the biotic (living organisms) with the *a*biotic or nonliving environment in a particular place as a unit of interrelated life."[1] Ecosystems are so finely tuned that a change in one component of the system usually produces changes in other parts of the system, sometimes with catastrophic results. Osborn Segerberg, Jr., gives an example of the interdependencies present in the food web, showing how a single intervention produces an almost endless sequence of events:

> These linkages of the food web can be quite intricate and reveal unsuspected ecological relationships when men interfere with nature in blunderbuss fashion. In Borneo, the World Health Organization began a mosquito control program, spraying large amounts of DDT to combat malaria. The campaign proved to be quite effective, but the killing of mosquitos wasn't the only thing that happened.
>
> The DDT was sprayed inside natives' homes, particularly on walls. Public health officers knew that after feasting on the human host, the female Anopheles mosquito, heavy with blood, had a habit of resting on a nearby wall before journeying back home. That contact with DDT was all it took to eliminate the malaria carrier. The DDT also poisoned houseflies. The housefly happens to be a favorite food of a tiny lizard known as the gecko. Geckos ate the flies and died from the DDT. House cats ate the geckos and in turn were poisoned. So many cats were lost that the homes were invaded by rats—and the community was confronted by the threat of another disease, bubonic plague, which is carried by rat fleas.
>
> On top of that, the roofs of the natives' houses began to fall in. In addition to mosquitos, houseflies, geckos, and cats, the DDT killed great numbers of wasps that preyed on caterpillars. With their predators gone, the caterpillars multiplied, and the lot of them proceeded to dine on their *pièce de résistance*—thatched roofs.[2]

Many ecological principles involve activities of reciprocal control to create a balance in nature and in human societies. Human ecosystems also are finely tuned. A change in the power or effectiveness of one person or group produces changes in social ordering throughout the social system.

Such early human ecologists as Robert E. Park, E. W. Burgess, and R. E. McKenzie drew heavily from the work of plant ecologists as they attempted to better understand human communities.[3]

When applied to humans, ecological concepts suggest that every individual needs to gain sustenance to survive. Sustenance includes both physical necessities such as breathable air, drinkable water, shelter, and food and social necessities such as the gratification of basic needs and desires. Because sustenance and gratification are limited and sometimes scarce, individuals are forced to compete with each other. Using our terminology, they attempt to control the conditions necessary for sustenance and the gratification of needs and desires. Unlimited competition, however, leads to conflict that may reduce rather than enhance the possibility of survival and need gratification for everyone involved. Therefore, people cooperate in many activities to mutually gratify common needs. This competitive cooperation is called symbiosis.

Human *symbiosis* refers to the reciprocal control arrangements that have been worked out to gain sustenance and the gratification of needs. People may not want to cooperate but they are forced to if they want to survive. In a symbiotic relationship each person *gains* something by *giving* something. Some, of course, may give or gain more than others.

The interlocking series of symbiotic or reciprocal control relationships results in what ecologists call the web of life: it brings together a *community*, an aggregate of people who are located in spatial proximity. Such a community may achieve an *equilibrium* where the needs of individuals are gratified at the optimum level, given the distribution of power and available resources.

When this equilibrium is upset by the entrance of new factors, a state of *disequilibrium*, or unbalance, occurs. Examples of new factors in the human community include a new factory or the arrival of many immigrants.[4] When disequilibrium occurs, new symbiotic relationships resulting in a different web of life must be developed. In our terms, reciprocal control relationships are changed causing a different social ordering in the community.

Environmental Constraints and Human Communities

One of the fundamental problems of any organism is to survive by adapting to or changing its surrounding environment. The human environment, both natural and as changed by technology, produces certain *constraints* that must be considered to understand the growth of

---

A Note on the Use of Analogies and the Development of Scientific Theory

The use by human ecologists of the terminology of plant ecologists in their attempt to understand human communities is not as strange as it might first appear to be. Scientific theory often progresses in one area by using analogies based on scientific concepts and theory in another area of science or even analogies based on organisms or processes in the world about us. Some late nineteenth-century sociologists, for example, saw society as being "like" an organism. This led to certain theoretical insights that, even though incorrect in particulars, contributed to the development of sociological theory. Scientific theory and models must be based on something that is known.

---

human communities. The most important are (1) geographic and climatic constraints, (2) spatial constraints, (3) time constraints, (4) population constraints, and (5) technological constraints, including the pollution caused by the growth of population and technology.*

We will briefly discuss how each of these constraints affects community development.

Geographic and Climatic Constraints

All places on our small planet are not equally desirable for human habitation and the development of human communities. Geographic and climatic conditions place constraints on people to live in certain places. Some places are too cold, some are too hot. Others are too dry or inaccessible to permit the creation and maintenance of large communities. Geographers point out that

> The greater part of the earth's land surface, somewhere between 50 and 75 per cent, is not well situated for human habitation—being too cold, snowy, and icy; too high and rugged; too dry; too hot and moist. This does not mean, of course, that there are no human beings occupying such lands but rather that their numbers in most instances average less than one person to the square mile. Scientists do not as yet know how to make these restrictive environments permanently productive. Everywhere the cost of reclamation is economically excessive.[5]

Some people do form communities in very hot, cold, dry, or inaccessible places. They do so, however, at a relatively high cost and are forced to live under conditions of severe hardship. People forming and living in these communities may define their place of residence as desirable, but they are under severe constraints in adapting to existing conditions. Their alternatives in life-styles are more restricted than are those of people living under more favorable conditions.

Figure 5-1 gives some idea of where these places are. In time, advances in technology may alter many of the conditions in these places.

Geography and climate also influence *how* a community develops and grows. The presence of such barriers as an ocean, lake, river, or mountain restricts the direction of possible physical growth. These restrictions often determine settlement and traffic patterns. In Cleveland, Ohio, for example, the Cuyahoga River and Lake Erie determined how that city developed. When the city was first settled there was no bridge across the river. The east side was therefore settled

---

*Another important environmental constraint is the scarcity of goods and services. This is treated in depth in Chapter 10.

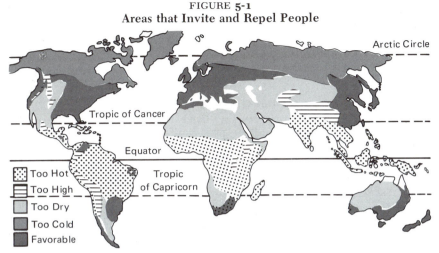

FIGURE 5-1
Areas that Invite and Repel People

SOURCE: Langdon White, George T. Renner, and Henry J. Warman, *Geography: Factors and Concepts* (New York: Appleton, 1968), p. 252. Used by permission.

first, and so the heart of the central business district is on the east side of the river. In short, geography places constraints on land-use patterns as a community develops.

Spatial Constraints

Spatial constraints are related to geographic and climatic constraints. The available *space* for human habitation and community development is reduced by geography and climate.

Amos H. Hawley points out the uneven distribution of human settlements. He states that

> The most striking feature [is] the clusters of population with sparsely settled interstitial areas. The size of these clusters, ranging from tiny groupings to huge agglomerations [varies] in different parts of the world. In some sections small groupings predominate while in others, large concentrations [are] proportionately more numerous.[6]

The spatial distribution and geographical location of large and small communities depends on a variety of factors in addition to geographic and climatic constraints. Among the more important are the availability of food supplies, routes of commerce and transportation, location of natural resources (including tillable land), available consumers' markets, and the level of technology. Cooley points out that communities tend to spring up where there are breaks in routes of transportation, which make it necessary to store goods in warehouses or to unload them from one carrier to another.[7] Laborers are needed to unload and load, carpenters to build buildings, and craftsmen to repair and service the carriers. These workers must be fed and housed, so stores and houses must be built. Administrative offices come into existence along with administrative personnel. The population grows cumulatively until a town or city is born.

In discussing how spatial constraints operate in the development and change of communities we will use the ideal type proposed by Ernest W. Burgess and shown in Figure 5-2. In describing his model, Burgess says:

> This chart represents an ideal construction of the tendencies of any town or city to expand radially from its central business district—on the chart "The Loop (I).* Encircling the downtown area there is normally an area in transition, which is being invaded by business and light manufacturing (II). A third area (III) is inhabited by industrial workers who have escaped from the area of deterioration (II) but who desire to live within easy access of their work. Beyond this zone is the residential area (IV) of high-class apartment buildings or of exclusive "restricted" districts of single family dwellings. Still farther out beyond the city limits is the commuters' zone (V)—suburban areas, or satellite cities, within a thirty-to sixty-minute ride of the central business district.[8]

This describes a city in a relatively advanced stage of development. As Burgess points out, zones I through IV in the city's early history were included in the circumference of the inner zone, the present business district.[9] Some examples will illustrate how cities developed as a result of spatial constraints. Some of these examples show the development of the various zones described by Burgess.

1. Before modern means of transportation came into existence large factories needed to be located close to navigable waters so that boats could be used for transportation. The building of railroads allowed more spatial alternatives in terms of factory location. As trucks came into use, these decreased considerably the spatial constraints in terms of the location of factories.

2. The location of factories determines, in part, where people who work within them live. Again, before modern means of transportation came into existence, factory workers had to live within walking distance of their work place. With the coming of systems of mass transportation and the automobile, this spatial constraint was no longer as important. It is still important to some degree, of course, unless a worker wants to spend many hours every day commuting back and forth to work.

3. The location of the main business district also decided, in part, the location of residential settlement patterns because of transportation considerations.

*This is in Chicago. In other cities it would be referred to as the central business district.

FIGURE 5-2

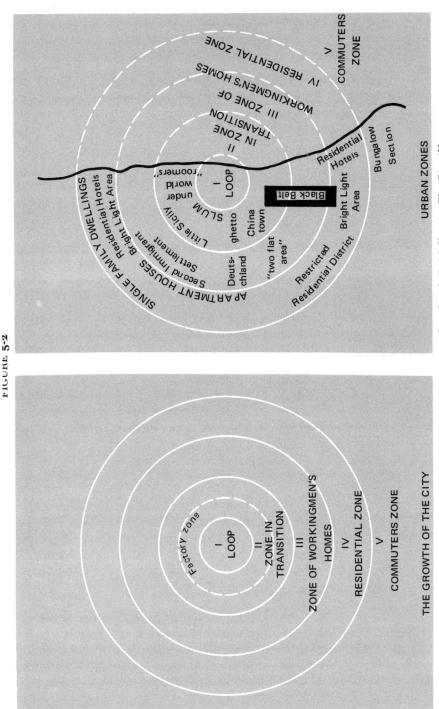

THE GROWTH OF THE CITY

SOURCE: Robert E. Park, Ernest W. Burgess, and Roderick D. McKenzie, *The City* (U. of Chicago, 1968), pp. 51 and 53. First Published in 1925. Used by permission.

4. The location of the main business district, along with the location of factories, also determined, in part, the location of warehouses. Light warehouse areas, for example, needed to be close to business outlets.

5. As the community grew, the business district needed to expand and required more space. Knowing this, land speculators bought up residential properties close to the central business district hoping to sell the land to businesses at a much higher price. Some of these residential properties were formerly owned by wealthy people who were glad to move further out because of the dirt and noise. This left the houses vacant. In order to reap an income from these houses before selling them to encroaching business, the land speculators many times partitioned them off into small apartments or single rooms and rented them to people who could not afford to live elsewhere. Since the speculator hoped to sell the land to a new or expanding business, he was not concerned with the maintenance of the house which stood on the land. Thus the house, crowded with low income people, fell into disrepair and slums were created. Many of these still exist in our larger cities.

6. As modern means of transportation came into existence it was possible for businesses, factories, and people to disperse in a variety of directions. Thus we find sprawling shopping centers located in sprawling suburban areas with freeways crowded as people rush back and forth to work or to do business.

Several ecological processes are involved in the development of the city. Figure 5-2 shows that *segregation* tends to occur, separating various types of activities and people. Lower-income people live in the zone of transition segregated from high-income people who live in the residential or commuter zones. Business tends to be segregated from residential areas, factories tend to be segregated from both of these, and so forth.

Invasion occurs when one segregated area begins to expand and encroach upon another segregated area, a common occurrence as the city expands. If invasion is complete and a type of population, business area, or other activity completely takes over an adjoining area, *succession* has occurred. The ecological processes of invasion and succession occur in nature also—for example, when a forest invades and takes over a meadow.

In the historical development of American cities the zone in transition has been the scene of repeated invasions and subsequent successions. Business expansion helped create slums. Working people left the slums as waves of European immigrants moved in seeking the cheap housing. These areas in many American cities have now been taken over by black people, people of Spanish origin, and Appalachian migrants who because of low incomes or discrimination are forced to live in these deteriorating areas presently referred to as the inner-city.[10]

New and improved modes of transportation, such as railroads, trucks, cars, and commuter trains, made it possible for population, businesses, factories, and other services to disperse. *Centralization* gave way to *decentralization* and created the present urban sprawl.

Time Constraints

Time constraints are closely related to spatial constraints. Modern transportation made it possible to shrink space. A person with a car or using mass transportation can cover a larger distance in a shorter time than is possible by walking. Despite our rapid means of transportation, however, time constraints are still important, especially in our society where people are paid on a time scale and time is money. It is important to move people and supplies from place to place as rapidly as possible. If it takes too much time for a business to deliver goods, money is lost.

How individuals allocate their time is personally important. If too much time is used in commuting back and forth to work, alternative uses of limited time are reduced. In our society, most activities are scheduled at specified times. If individuals are to participate, they must arrange their time to meet these schedules. Because time is important, where people work affects residential patterns and the building of freeways and mass transportation systems. These, in turn, affect where businesses locate. If you work a day shift and cannot get home in *time,* you miss the evening news, or can't make the early movie or attend a night baseball game.

POPULATION AND TECHNOLOGY CONSTRAINTS: THE GREAT TRANSFORMATION

The concomitant growth of population and technology, more than anything else, produced the "Great Transformation" from agriculturally based societies consisting of small folk communities scattered over the countryside with only a few cities of any size to industrial technological societies with many large urban centers. A discussion of population and technological constraints requires a transition in our frame of reference from ecological factors to social factors.

From Geneinscheft to Gesellschaft.

Ferdinand Toennies (1855–1936) was among the first to systematically describe the Great Transformation. He constructed two ideal types of social relations in the historical movement from *gemeinschaft* (community) to *gesellschaft* (society).[11] *Gemeinschaft* is based on primary group relations, including close-knit kinship and congeniality groups whose members interact face-to-face over long periods of time and know each other intimately. Cultural strategies structure, in large part, the social ordering of *gemeinschaft* relations and groups. *Gesellschaft* relationships are based on procedural strategies, exchange strategies, and manipulative strategies. *Gesellschaft* relation-

The Origins and Growth of Cities

As far back as we have knowledge of human origins, men have associated in groups. However, settled communities that can be termed *cities* are a relatively recent innovation in human history. Scott Greer notes that "Historically, man's social life seems to have originated in small roving groups or local bands which hunted and grazed over delimited areas.[a] Village communities were probably the earliest form of territorially fixed human community, going well back into Neolithic times some 8,000 to 10,000 years ago. Greer adds that "Village communities have formed the economic and demographic base for the majority of the world's population since the Neolithic era."[b]

The next major developments were towns that gradually developed into cities in favorable places between 6,000 and 5,000 B.C. The enriched technology of late Neolithic times in the form of ox-drawn plows, wheeled carts, the sailboat, metallurgy, irrigation, and the domestication of new plants permitted an agricultural surplus that allowed urban development; that is, "the concentration in one place of people who do not grow their own food."[c]

Subsequent advances in urbanization appeared in the Nile Delta and in Mesopotamia in about 3,000 B.C. and then in Greco-Roman times, from 600 B.C. to A.D. 400. Yet, as the urban sociologist Kingsley Davis points out, "even the biggest (cities such as Athens and Rome) could scarcely have exceeded 200,000 inhabitants, and the proportion of the total population living in them must have been not more than 1 or 2 per cent. From fifty to ninety farmers must have been required to support one man in a city."[d]

It was not until the Industrial Revolution in the nineteenth century that cities took firm hold and urbanization increased rapidly, first in western Europe and then throughout the world. Davis includes as key elements in

ships tend to be impersonal, transitory, and limited, and do not involve deep emotional commitments.

From Folk Community to Urban Society

Many early sociologists elaborated on the theme developed by Toennies, using different concepts to describe the same fundamental changes in the structuring of social order caused by a burgeoning technology and expanding populations. We will summarize their observations by contrasting two ideal types: folk community and urban society (Table 5-1). The concomitant changes in population and tech-

the Industrial Revolution "improvements in agriculture and transport, the opening of new lands and new trade routes, and above all, the rise in productive activity, first in highly organized handicraft and eventually in a revolutionary . . . new form of production—the factory run by machine and fossil fuel."[e] The results are dramatically displayed in the following table:[f]

Percentage of World's Population Living in Cities

	Cities of 20,000 or More	Cities of 100,000 or More
1800	2.4	1.7
1850	4.3	2.3
1900	9.2	5.5
1950	20.9	13.1

Today the rate of urbanization is slowing down, but the process continues. Today's supercities, with five million or more inhabitants, are a new social phenomenon, the full consequences of which—for social ordering and individual meaning—remain to be explored. Although he is reluctant to make firm predictions, Davis does conclude that "Urbanization is so widespread, so much a part of industrial civilization, and gaining so rapidly, that any return to rurality, even with major catastrophes, appears unlikely."[g]

[a] Scott Greer, "Major Types of Human Groups," in *The Concept of Community,* ed. by David Minar and Scott Greer (Chicago: Aldine, 1968), p. 62.

[b] Ibid.

[c] Kingsley Davis, "The Origin and Growth of Urbanization in the World," *American Journal of Sociology,* **LX** (March 1955), p. 430.

[d] Ibid; p. 432.

[e] Ibid; p. 433.

[f] Ibid.

[g] Ibid; p. 437.

TABLE 5-1
The Great Transformation

From Folk Community	To Urban Society
1. Small populations living mostly in small communities.	1. Large populations living mostly in large and sprawling urban areas.
2. Low level of technology. Handmade articles. Sources of power limited to people and animals.	2. High level of technology. Machine-made articles. Many sources of power, beginning with steam and culminating in atomic power.
3. Homogeneous population. Most people have about the same life-styles, values, and interests.	3. Heterogeneous population. Peoples' life-styles, values, and interests differ.[12] Pluralistic society.
4. Relations based on *status* primarily in the kinship group. Cultural strategies predominate.	4. Relations based on formalized *contract* independent of kinship. Procedural and exchange strategies predominate.[13]
5. Simple division of labor tends to be based on age and sex and to center around hunting and gathering or primitive methods of agriculture.	5. Complex division of labor. The high level of technology demands that many people do many different things.[14]
6. Social positions are ascribed, often by sex and age.	6. Social positions are achieved. Roles are based on performance, which requires expertise.
7. The basis for community solidarity is *mechanical*. That is, loyalty to each other is prescribed by traditional norms. Cultural strategies predominate even though others may be used at times.	7. *Organic* solidarity predominates. Solidarity is produced, in part, by the interdependence of the many roles in the division of labor. Many different control strategies are used in the process of social ordering.[15]
8. *Sacred* orientation. There is an orientation toward the maintenance of the status quo. Change is not sought after and is often abhorred.	8. *Secular* orientation. There is an orientation toward change. People like new models and new ways of doing things. People seek change.[16]
9. Behavior is spontaneous and traditionally based.	9. Behavior tends to be calculated, judged by efficiency, and directed to getting what one wants out of a relationship.[17]
10. Mostly primary and informal group relationships.	10. Mostly secondary and formal group relationships.
11. Barter economy. People trade goods and services for other goods and services.	11. Money economy. People sell labor and goods and services for money to buy other goods and services.
12. Little movement of populations from place to place and over long distances. People tend to die in the community in which they are born.	12. Much movement from place to place and over great distances. Many people move away from the place in which they were born and many move several times during a lifetime.

nology altered the constraints and caused the transition in processes of social ordering from folk to urban. These are *ideal types*, not descriptions of specific communities or societies.

This outline of the Great Transformation is worth careful study. It incorporates much sociological description and analysis in its two contrasting types. The folk community is seen to have a small, homogeneous population, a low level of technology, simple division of labor, ascribed social positions, mechanical solidarity, a barter economy, sacred orientation, informal primary relationships, cultural strategies, and limited physical and social mobility. The urban society has a large heterogeneous population, high technology, an elaborate division of labor, achieved social positions, organic solidarity, a money economy, secular orientation, formal bureaucratic relationships, procedural and exchange strategies, and extensive physical and social mobility.

Not all societies have moved with equal speed toward the Urban Society. The so-called developing nations have not. Development has come to be equated with urbanization and industrialization—which, of course, is a heavily loaded value judgment. Even within our highly urbanized nation some relatively isolated communities remain closer to the folk community type than to the urban society type. However, our society considered as a whole is much closer to the urban society than to the folk community. In 1790 only 5.1 per cent of the population of the United States lived in urban areas. By 1900, this had increased to 39.7 per cent; the projection is that by 1980, 73 per cent of the population will live in urban areas. We are a nation of urban people.

Mass Society or Local Community?

American society, like other postindustrial societies, represents an advanced stage of the Great Transformation. What implications does this have for life-styles, value systems, individual meaning, self-identities, and the structuring of social order in our society? Some sociologists have suggested that societies such as ours are becoming *mass societies* in which local communities are no longer influential.

Mass Society As an Ideal Type

As yet, sociologists do not agree on a uniform definition for a mass society. Some emphasize the *gesellschaft* quality of relationships in such a society. David Dressler, for example, suggests that a mass society "is . . . characterized by relative anonymity and psychological isolation of the individual, and comparative impersonality of existing relationships."[18] Philip Olson draws on a whole body of theory for his definition:

> a mass society is characterized by a core of central institutions that integrate the over-all activities of the total population and provide direction and structure for its daily activities. In key positions within these cultural institutions are persons who have an influence upon institutional activity; those persons C. Wright Mills has called "the power elite."
>
> The integrating factor in this type of society is a technological and industrial order that facilitates communication throughout all "regions" in the society and makes possible a widely specialized and diversified occupational structure.

Urbanism as a Way of Life: The Chicago School

Many observers of the Great Transformation saw urbanization as the key change in this historical shift in the structure of social ordering. Simmel wrote a famous essay on "The Metropolis and Mental Life" in which he explored the content of the blasé urban consciousness caused by "the intensification of nervous stimulation which results from the shift and uninterrupted change of outer and inner stimuli"[a] that typified city life.

A whole generation of American sociologists studied the rapidly expanding American cities of the early twentieth century. Because many of these men studied at or were trained at the University of Chicago, they have come to be known as the Chicago School. Applying Simmel's psychological insights and the concepts of ecology, such men as Robert E. Park, Ernest W. Burgess, and Roderick D. McKenzie developed powerful tools for the analysis of urban social ordering. Urbanization was defined as an increase in the size, the density, and the heterogeneity of population in a limited spatial area. Louis Wirth (1897–1952), a leading member of the Chicago school, asserted, in an influential article, that "On the basis of [these] three variables . . . it appears possible to explain the characteristics of urban life and to account for the differences between cities of various sizes and types."[b]

Philip Hauser summarizes the Chicago School's explanation as follows:

> In the small community, not only are potential and actual contacts fewer, but because they are fewer, they tend also to be quite different in character. . . . According to this hypothesis the small community is characterized by "primary-group" contacts. They tend to be face-to-face, intimate contacts of persons who meet and interact with one another in virtually all spheres of activity. In such a setting personal relations tend to be based on relatively full knowledge of the other person—on sentiment and emotion. In contrast, . . . in the large, high-density population situation, contacts tend to be "secondary" rather than primary, segmental rather than integral, utilitarian rather than sentimental. Moreover, in the large-size, high-density situation, populations are apt to be more

At the same time, its existence provides a basis for a societywide culture (. . . "mass culture" or "popular culture") through the development of a network of culture-disseminating instruments . . . called mass communications.

Urbanization and bureaucracy are characteristic of such a technical and industrial order because they serve as loci from which these institutional forces emanate, and provide an organizational system that structures activity.[19]

There are numerous trends in our society that suggest it increasingly resembles a mass society as defined by Dressler and by Olson. We are all familiar with the enormous influence of the mass media,

---

heterogeneous—to include peoples of greater range and diversity in background, attitudes, and behavior. The person is subjected, therefore, to a greater variety of ways of thought and action.

The combination of heterogeneous and secondary contacts, it is held, tends greatly to modify human behavior. Thus, thought and action tend to become increasingly rational as opposed to traditional, and interpersonal relations become based on utility rather than sentiment. With increased size, density, and heterogeneity of population, the constraints of tradition—the influence of the folkways and mores—diminish. In ever larger spheres of thought and action, behavior is determined by a willful decision taken by the person, rather than automatically determined by the norms of the group. The sphere of personal decision making is greatly extended, including areas of activity previously determined by tradition, such as kind and degree of education, occupation or profession, residential location, choice of mate, size of family, political affiliation, religiosity or even religion.

It follows, then, that increased size and density of population, especially if accompanied by heterogeneity, diminish the power of informal social controls. Informal social control, effected largely through the play of folkways and the mores, gives way to increased formal control, the control of law, police, courts, jails, regulations, and orders. The breakdown in informal social controls is largely responsible for increased personal disorganization as manifest in juvenile delinquency, crime, prostitution, alcoholism, drug addiction, suicide, mental disease, social unrest, and political instability. Formal controls have by no means proved as efficacious as the informal in regulating human behavior.[c]

Contemporary sociologists have discovered far more order and far less chaos in urban areas than suggested by the Chicago School. Informal networks and controls exist in cities, although they are different in form from those in rural areas. Nonetheless, the contributions of the Chicago School remain among the high marks of twentieth century sociology.

[a]Georg Simmel, "The Metropolitan Life," in *Man Alive*, ed. by Eric and Mary Josphson (New York: Dell, 1971), p. 153.
[b]Louis Wirth, "Urbanism as a Way of Life," *American Journal of Sociology*, **49** (1938), pp. 46–63.
[c]Philip Hauser, "Urbanization: An Overview" in *Metropolis in Crisis*, ed. by Jeffrey Kadden *et al.* (Itasca, Ill.: Peacock, 1967), pp. 60, 69.

especially television, which blanket our enormous country and impose uniform messages and symbols transmitted simultaneously to millions of people. The ability of élite groups to control such centralized means of communication is an important element in the development of a mass society. The power of large and growing national corporations that use manipulative strategies in an attempt to control their employees appears to be increasing. The policies of large and growing state governments and of the federal government are increasingly constructed and administered by a variety of experts using procedural and manipulative strategies. Consolidated schools and large state and private universities teach students from many "local" places the latest findings in physical, biological, and social science; what critics have to say about modern art, music, literature, and architecture; and the newest control strategies of corporation management, none of which may be consistent with their previous values. Numerous *national* organizations such as labor unions, professional associations, chain stores, and banks dominate their local units or branches and impose uniform nationwide standards.

Rather than wring our hands (or applaud) these trends as heralding the presumed advent of mass society and the decline of local communities, we prefer to treat these observations as an empirical question. Are local communities, in fact, declining in significance in our society? If so, in what dimensions of community life is decline occurring? How are such declines, if they exist, manifested in community processes of social ordering, and how do they affect life-styles and individual meaning?

To answer these specific questions requires us to elaborate on the significant dimensions of community life, to discuss community control and explore how community power structures are measured, and to examine such social phenomena as suburbanization. As we shall discover, the development of a mass society in the United States is neither simple, direct, nor uniform. The significance of local communities has changed, and in some respects diminished, but they remain important elements in the structuring of our social order.

Dimensions of Local Communities

Roland L. Warren has developed a set of dimensions on which local communities may differ.[20] Table 5-2 shows Warren's dimensions and the continuum on which they can be plotted to describe a specific community.

The dimension of *local autonomy* is the degree to which a community can carry out all the activities necessary for its maintenance and the maintenance of its citizens independently over time. If it can carry out these activities it is independent; if it cannot, it is dependent. *Coinci-*

dence of service areas is "the extent to which the service areas of local units (stores, churches, schools, and so on) coincide or fail to coincide."[21] If individuals shop in one place, send their children to school in another place, go to church in still another place, and use the services of a doctor in a place different from these other three, there is no coincidence of service areas. If all these services are used in the same area there is coincidence of service areas.

Psychological identification with locality is a measure of the degree to which persons identify with the place in which they live. If the community is a positive reference group, psychological identification is strong. If the "inhabitants have little sense of relationship to one another, little sense of the community as a significant social group, and little sense of belonging to the community"[22] psychological identification is weak. *Horizontal pattern* refers to relationships among various local units such as churches, businesses, professional groups, and so forth. If these units support the same values and work together toward their achievement, the horizontal pattern is strong. It is a measure of positive interconnectedness.

If most local communities in a society fall at or near zero on these four dimensions, the local community is still important from an individual and social point of view and must be so considered by the sociologist. On the other hand, if most communities fall at or near a score of four on all the dimensions, a mass society has emerged and the local community has less importance for life-styles, values, meaning systems, and self-identities. In and of itself, the community in such a society is not a center of power. Therefore, it is not an important concept for the sociologist. People from Columbus, Ohio, would be expected to act about the same as people from San Francisco or Charlotte, North Carolina, if ours is a mass society. The local place in which a person was born, socialized, and lives would not significantly affect his behavior in a manner different from a person in another local place.

Warren's dimensions of local autonomy and horizontal pattern are

TABLE 5:2
Four Dimensions on Which American Communities Differ

		0 1 2 3 4	
1. Local autonomy:	Independent	⌞_⌟_⌟_⌟_⌟	Dependent
2. Coincidence of service areas:	Coincide	⌞_⌟_⌟_⌟_⌟	Differ
3. Psychological identification	Strong	⌞_⌟_⌟_⌟_⌟	Weak
4. Horizontal pattern:	Strong	⌞_⌟_⌟_⌟_⌟	Weak

From Roland L. Warren, *The Community in America*, (Chicago: Rand McNally Co., 1963), page 14. Used by permission.

important for assessing the movement toward a mass society. If a community has little local autonomy and is completely dependent on outside sources for all types of goods and services, entertainment, and lifestyles and values, the local community has little internal support. Under these conditions, the people must look outside for those things that provide direction for their daily living.

Of even greater importance is the strength of a community's horizontal pattern in relation to the strength of what Warren calls the vertical pattern. The horizontal pattern has its basis *within* the community, but the basis of the vertical pattern is *outside* the community. "An important characteristic of the vertical pattern is the rational, planned, bureaucratically structured nature of the extracommunity ties."[23] Examples of these ties are those between (1) chain stores and regional headquarters, (2) branch plants and national offices, (3) local schools and state education departments, (4) local unions and national unions, (5) voluntary associations and state or national headquarters, and (6) local church and denominational boards.

The balance of power between the horizontal pattern and the vertical pattern is of critical importance. Where are the important decisions made that affect local values and living patterns? If all or most decisions are made within the local community and are based on local traditional sentiments and common values, the horizontal pattern is strong and so is the local community.

Increasingly, however, vertical patterns are becoming more important than horizontal patterns in our society. Figure 5-3 contrasts a community with a strong horizontal pattern with a community with a strong vertical pattern. A community with a strong horizontal pattern differs significantly from a community with a strong vertical pattern in the locus of control and integration. A community with a strong vertical pattern has lost its local autonomy and become part of a mass society.

Because the question of where and how the basic decisions are made is significant in deciding whether local communities remain important, we must develop concepts that will enable us to identify and measure community power. What we are doing is typical in the process of scientific investigation. Beginning with a broad and general question about mass society, we gradually narrow it down to a specific series of limited questions that are empirically answerable.

COMMUNITY CONTROL AND COMMUNITY POWER STRUCTURES

Many decisions affecting the social ordering of the local community are made outside the community in vertical patterns. However, these

FIGURE 5-3
Horizontal and Vertical Patterns of Community Integration

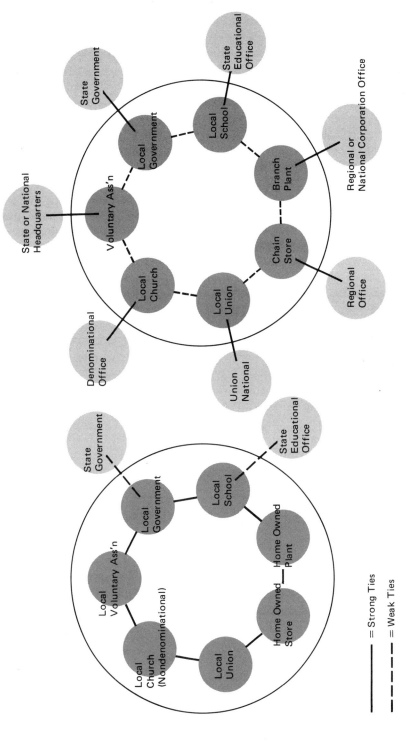

STRONG VERTICAL PATTERN

STRONG HORIZONTAL PATTERN

decisions do not account for the total social ordering of the local community. There are many control strategies used by people and groups within the local community.

Formal Structure

It is widely believed in our society that the social ordering of local communities is based on values, cultural strategies, and the legal procedural strategies used by elected local officials and their appointees.

Local governmental structure is the *formal* community power structure. Along with the various administrative offices, it constitutes a bureaucracy that in large cities is extremely complex. In both large and small American communities the formal power structure typically insures the collection of the garbage; insures the operation of the police force, the schools, and hospitals; paves roads; supplies water; distributes welfare payments; and performs other municipal services.

The elected officials in the community, and the bureaucratic structure, significantly affect the social ordering of that community through the use of procedural strategies. The use of cultural strategies is also important to community social ordering. However, to fully understand the processes of social ordering at the local community level we must examine not only what occurs within the formal power structure but also what occurs "outside" of it.

The important question is, does the formal power structure have complete autonomy in making and carrying out decisions for the *common good*? Or, are members of the formal power structure influenced by powerful individuals or interest groups in the community, so that the decisions favor the interests or whims of these powerful individuals or groups rather than the common good?

Informal Community Power Structure

Evidence from many empirical studies of community power structures shows that powerful individuals and groups exist and use a variety of control strategies to influence the decision-making processes of officials about community problems and activities. The informal power structure includes those individuals and groups who are not explicitly part of the formal power structure but who use various control strategies to effectively structure the social order of the community. Among the community activities that sociological studies have shown to be commonly influenced by the informal power structure in many American communities are the raising and allocating of money for hospitals, private social agencies, and other charitable activities through the United or Community Fund; the broad policies and practices of the public school system; the operation of a public welfare system; who runs for public office, and often who is elected (through control over nominating committees and by providing campaign funds and workers); and whether or not and where public roads and recreational facilities are built.[24]

Early studies of informal power structures found them to be pyramidal, with a few powerful people at the top who, through the use of exchange, coercive, and manipulative strategies, made certain that what they wanted to happen did actually happen.[25]

Figure 5-4 shows the pattern of policy-committee formation in a community with a pyramidal power structure. A policy-making structure exists outside the official governmental sector, which draws its most powerful members from the top power personnel in business, government, and professional and civic associations. Less powerful people in these institutions and associations are used to carry out policies. For specific projects, people from the institutions of religion and education and from cultural associations, such as various clubs, may be co-opted to help carry out the decisions made by those with greater power.

Additional research has qualified these earlier findings. In some communities, coalitional strategies are used so that two or more groups form a strong coalition to fight for or against an issue facing the community. In such communities the informal power structure is more diffuse and the sharp pyramidal form is absent. To reconcile these seemingly contradictory findings, John Walton isolated four different types of power structures, ranging from highly concentrated to almost completely diffused power.[26] Table 5-3 shows these four types and their definitions.

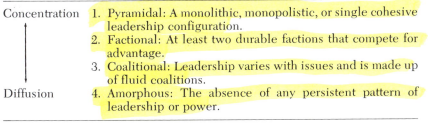

TABLE 5-3
Types of Community Power

Concentration ↑ ↓ Diffusion	1. Pyramidal: A monolithic, monopolistic, or single cohesive leadership configuration.
	2. Factional: At least two durable factions that compete for advantage.
	3. Coalitional: Leadership varies with issues and is made up of fluid coalitions.
	4. Amorphous: The absence of any persistent pattern of leadership or power.

Developed by John Walton, "Substance and Artifact: The Current Status of Research on Community Power Structure," *American Journal of Sociology*, **71** (Jan. 1966). Published in this form by Michael Aiken, "The Distribution of Community Power: Structural Bases and Social Consequences," in *The Structure of Community Power*, ed. by Michael Aiken and Paul E. Mott (New York: Random, 1970), p. 489.

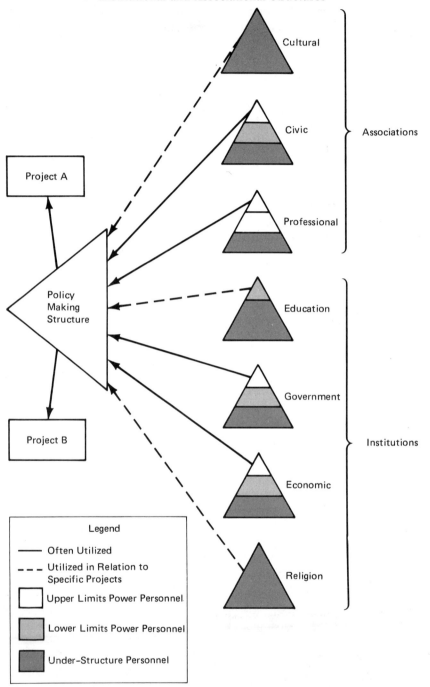

FIGURE 5-4
**Generalized Pattern of Policy-Committee Formation Utilizing
Institutional and Associational Structures**

SOURCE: Floyd Hunter, *Community Power Structure* (Garden City, N.Y.: Doubleday, 1953), p. 90. Used by permission.

Using these four types: pyramidal, factional, coalitional, and amorphous, Walton surveyed the massive literature about community power. He found that (1) studies using the reputational method tend to find pyramidal power structures more frequently than do studies using the decisional method; (2) studies focusing on issues of concern to the general public, such as the creation of a new park, tend to find factional and coalitional structures, whereas studies focusing on private issues, such as the building of a new factory, tend to find pyramidal structures; (3) the smaller the number of community leaders, the higher the likelihood of a concentrated power structure; (4) businessmen are more than twice as likely to be represented in leadership groups than are public officials; (5) the higher the degree of absentee ownership in a community, the less concentrated the power structure; (6) if party politics is competitive, the power structure is less concentrated; and (7) in general, community power structures are changing toward a greater dispersion of power.[27]

Walton's generalizations 5 and 7 suggest that an increase in the vertical pattern is related to a greater dispersion of local community power. Another comparative study of community power by Michael Aiken makes precisely this point:

> Contemporary American communities are not "tight" social systems such as large scale organizations, but are fairly "open" social systems in which some sub-systems may be largely independent of others. The "loss of community autonomy" or "vertical pattern," as described by Warren, is one factor contributing to the modern American community being a relatively "open" social system.[28]

Americans who share the cultural value that an open community is desirable might at first rejoice in this research finding. However, before the rejoicing turns into a premature "celebration of freedom" we must recognize that the probable reason for the increased openness is that *many* of the decisions made at the community level are no longer important to persons and groups at higher levels of power nationally and internationally, where decisions affecting the lives of all of us are made. How and where the $80 billion federal defense budget is spent affects many local communities. The federal decision to sell millions of bushels of grain to the USSR in 1973 was partly responsible for the subsequent sharp nationwide increase in food prices. Local community leaders have little or nothing to say about such major decisions.

Even the nation's largest and wealthiest city, New York, finds itself dependent on federal funds and, therefore, subject to federal control in such traditionally local preserves as schools, roads, housing, and highways. A *New York Times* article (December 1, 1973, p. 1) headlined, "New York's Destiny Tied to Federal Aid Policies," reported these comments by New York's deputy mayor:

The . . . fallacy in the public mind is the thought that an effective local government is enough. For any major improvements, changes, innovations, adaptations or increases, localities have to look to the federal government. The structure of federal appropriations and incentives is the single most important determinant of the policies of the cities and states.

The broad issues—war and peace; budget expenditures for guns or butter; where corporations that employ hundreds of thousands will locate; and how energy resources are distributed that may affect the employment, comfort, and health of most members of the society—are decided by national power groups in the business, governmental, and military institutions.

Reputational and Decisional Methods of Studying Community Power

There are two major types of research methods used to study the structure of community power: the reputational approach and the decision-making approach. Because John Walton and others have found that the method tends to produce different findings, it is important to understand the two approaches.

The Reputational Approach: This method asks people who live in the community to serve as "informants" to list the leaders or most influential people in the community. Those named are then asked to name others who do not already appear on the list. The people who are finally selected as forming the power structure of the community are those who have been named most often by the original informants and by those who have been listed.

The Decision-Making Approach: This method selects specific issues facing a community. An attempt is made to trace the people in the community who become involved in making decisions about these issues and who are listened to in the making of decisions. This tends to be more time consuming because the researcher must trace the process of decision making through committee meetings, secret meetings, and informal contacts.

Clearly, any precise statements about a specific community's power structure require the gathering and analyzing of much empirical data.

An in-depth comparison of these approaches is provided by Charles M. Bonjean and David M. Olson, "Community Leadership: Directions of Research," *Administrative Science Quarterly,* 9 (Dec. 1964), pp. 278–300.

An early example of the reputational approach is Floyd Hunter, *Community Power Structure: A Study of Decision Makers* (Chapel Hill, N.C.: University of North Carolina Press, 1953). An example of the decision-making approach is given in Robert A. Dahl, *Who Governs? Democracy and Power in an American City* (New Haven: Yale University Press, 1961).

The tendencies toward a mass society are pronounced. Critical decisions have been removed from the realm of local community decision makers, although there has apparently been some broadening of the formerly pyramidal local power structures. In effect, community control, a cherished slogan among urban reformers in the 1960s, has amounted to more local people participating in more decisions of less importance. In an article prophetically entitled "The City As Sandbox," the urban analyst George Sternlieb suggests that the tendency is for the central city to become a playground that those who make the basic decisions in our society (and reap the largest rewards) are increasingly content to turn over to the disadvantaged and formerly disfranchised.[29]

Another profoundly important influence shaping the structure and significance of local communities in American society has been the tendency toward suburbanization. The flight of large numbers of persons, especially the middle classes, from the central cities has contributed substantially to the willingness of the powerful to turn the central city into a decaying "sandbox" for the less fortunate.

SUBURBANIZATION, REGIONALISM, AND LOCAL COMMUNITIES

An important factor in any consideration of local community power is the process of suburbanization, which has resulted in the spatial overlapping of many local communities so that it is often impossible to recognize boundaries between communities unless a sign is present to mark the increasingly arbitrary political subdivisions. The older ecological definition of a community as an aggregate of individuals spatially located loses much of its usefulness because no socially meaningful spatial limits can be drawn between local communities.

This overlapping of local communities through suburbanization results in an *urban region.* Figure 5-5 shows a simplified ecological diagram of an urban region. The major roads leading from one place to another in the urban region are typically lined with businesses or factories rather than being open land. It is impossible to tell when you pass from one place to another.

In the northeast from Boston to Virginia and along the California coast, suburban sprawl and overlapping urban regions extend for hundreds of miles. Other parts of the nation appear to be moving toward similar urban regionalization. Such extensive overlapping of communities moves away from local autonomy, coincidence of service areas, and psychological identification with a specific locality toward a vertical pattern of integration. The local community becomes less important and the mass society more salient. Important points of iden-

FIGURE 5-5
A Simplified Ecological Diagram of the Urban Region

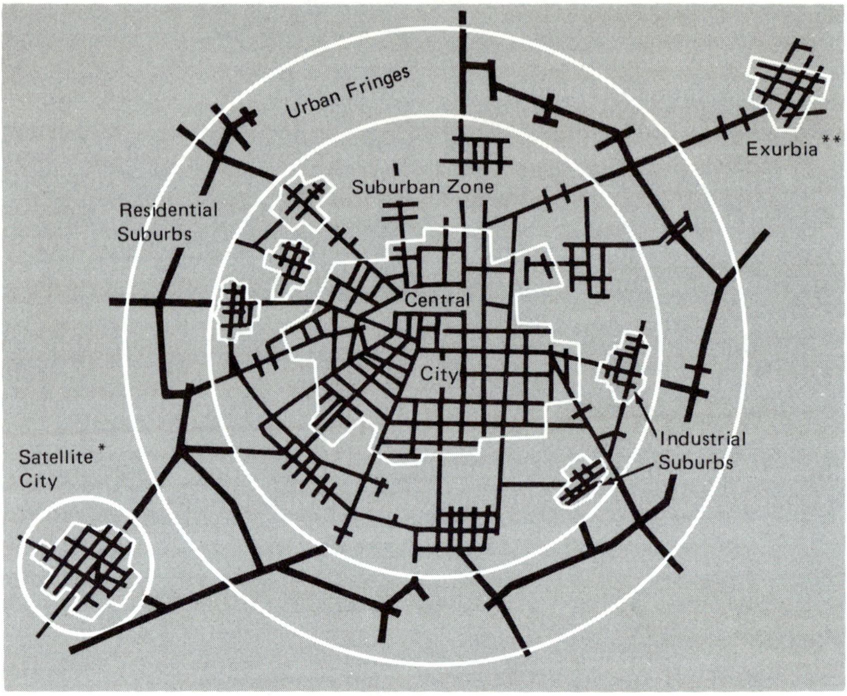

*Satellite cities tend to have their origin prior to and therefore independent of the rise of central cities.

**Exurbia is usually more distant from the central city than is a suburb and the exurbanite can usually do his/her work, or much of it, at home. These people are usually in the "creative" branches of the communications industry, such as advertising, commercial art, television, films, and so forth, and typically command high salaries.

SOURCE: Alvin Boskoff, *The Sociology of Urban Regions* (New York: Appleton, 1962), p. 132. Used by permission.

tity continue to exist in small towns scattered across the nation and in some ethnic enclaves within urban areas, but the overwhelming trend is away from them.

Standard Metropolitan Statistical Areas (SMSA)

To grasp the extent of this redistribution of population the notion of SMSA is useful. As defined by the Bureau of the Census

An SMSA is a county or group of contiguous counties (except in New England) which contains at least one central city of 50,000 inhabitants or more or "twin cities" with a combined population of at least 50,000. Other contiguous counties are included in an SMSA if, according to certain criteria, they are essentially metropolitan in character and are socially and economically integrated with the central city.[30]

In 1970 there were 243 SMSA in the United States containing close to 140,000,000 of the total population of 203,212,000; 75,622,000, or 54 per cent, of the inhabitants of SMSA lived *outside* the central cities.[31] Comparison of the 1970 census data with earlier census data shows that in the last two decades the percentage of the population living in SMSA has risen and, furthermore, that within the SMSA the percentage living outside of the central cities has risen most sharply.[32] Along with the movement of people from the central cities there has been a parallel movement of jobs, so that the old image of the commuter rushing back and forth from the suburb to a central city job is no longer so valid. In 1960, for example, the central cities in the fifteen largest SMSA had 63.0 per cent of the total jobs. By 1970, the central cities had only 52.4 per cent of the jobs, and the downward trend appears to be continuing.[33] The movement of jobs into suburban areas *may* have a tendency to move us back toward a more horizontal pattern of community integration. The irony is that many people moved to suburbia seeking fresh air, open spaces, a "nice" place to raise their children, and an escape from people they defined as "undesirable." Many may have been seeking a romanticized version of the folk community. However, as factories and services move to the suburbs and as freeways are built and become jammed with cars and trucks, these people increasingly find themselves surrounded by an urbanlike physical environment similar to that they sought to escape. The suburban areas, and the regions of which they are a part, appear to be increasingly assuming the characteristics of the mass society. Regional differences remain but are becoming less salient.

The Suburban Poor

The movement to suburbia has been selective. Not *everyone* has moved out of the central city. Many rich and middle-income people live in suburbia, but so do some poor people. The 1970 census shows that for every three poor people who live in the central city, there are two who live in suburban areas, although not in the same suburbs as do the rich and middle-income people. Nor are the lives of the poor improved because they live in the suburbs. The suburban poor live in pockets of poverty separated from the more affluent suburban dwellers by physical barriers such as highways, railroads, or open stretches of land. There are many manipulative strategies that determine where people settle. Restrictive covenants based on race and religion have been outlawed, but control is still exercised by specifying minimum lot sizes and the prices of houses that may be built in certain areas. Such strategies restrict where the poor may live in suburban areas.

Back in the Central Cities

An increasing proportion of people living in the central city are blacks who have migrated there over the years either from rural areas or from one city to another. As black people have moved in, white people have moved out. Figure 5-6 shows the population changes in metropolitan areas by race during 1950 to 1960 and 1960 to 1970. There was a net decrease in the number of whites living in central cities from 1960 to 1970. Figure 5-6 also shows that some black people live in the suburbs and that their number increased between 1960 and 1970, but their number and proportion is *much* smaller than for whites. In 1970, 67.8 per cent of all whites lived in metropolitan areas, but of these only 27.5 per cent lived in central cities. Of all blacks, 74 per cent lived in metropolitan areas but, of these, 57.8 per cent lived in central cities. The proportion of black people living in central cities is more than double that of whites.

Suburbia: Dream or Nightmare?

This is the title of a chapter in the book *The Eclipse of Community* by the urban critic and sociologist Maurice Stein. After surveying many studies he answers his question by suggesting that "suburban life . . . is actually the setting for the dominant 'disorders' of our time."[a] Stein concludes that the mobility-oriented, transient, child-centered, upper-middle-class suburb that is the ultimate aspiration for many persons fleeing the inner-city is itself the cause of serious psychological and social disturbances. Stein cites studies to show that

> The social structure of the prosperous suburb is strangely paradoxical. On the one hand it arranges matters so that the daily life of the individual, no matter what his age or sex, is divided into many compelling tasks that leave little or no time for freely chosen activity. Like modern industrial employment, which it fundamentally resembles, the suburb is frantically devoted to the rhythm of keeping busy. Even the playtime of the children is routinized and many families find that the separate schedules of the various members leave no time for intimate moments with one another. On the other hand, while people are so desperately busy, they do not know or have forgotten how to perform some of the most elemental human tasks. The most glaring evidence for this is the genuine crisis in the American suburb over child rearing. Anxious mothers, uncertain how to raise their children, turn to scientific experts to find out if their children are normal or, even more important, what the standard of normality might be.

FIGURE 5-6
**Population Changes in Metropolitan Areas, by Race: 1950–1960
and 1960–1970**

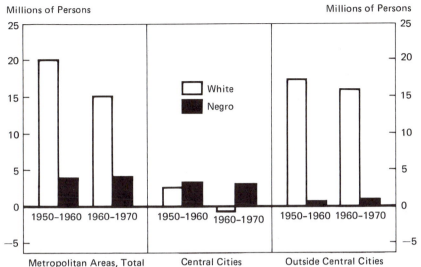

SOURCE: Department of Commerce, Bureau of the Census.

We face a curious and probably unprecedented situation here: a society of material comfort and apparent security in which the most fundamental of human relationships—that between mother and child—has become at the very least problematical. No one is surprised to discover that businessmen treat each other in impersonal and manipulative terms; but surely it should be cause for some dismay to find it habitual, . . . that mothers regard suburban children as "cases" the moment they lag behind the highly formalized routine accomplishments of their peers or, still worse, show signs of distinctive individuality.[b]

Other scholars take a less gloomy perspective and find more room for individual meaning and the development of values in suburban life. The sociologist William Dobriner, a long-time student of types of suburbs and patterns of suburban living, has suggested that the entire problem may become academic because the suburbs are disappearing as distinctive social entities. "The 'middle-class' suburb . . . is fast disappearing. In our efforts to capture the sociological soul of the suburbs, perhaps we turned away from the basic and most fascinating question—the dynamics of the suburbanization-urbanization process, the way in which cities create suburbs only eventually to turn them into cities in their own image."[c]

[a]Maurice Stein, *The Eclipse of Community* (Princeton, N.J.: Princeton University Press, 1960), p. 199.
[b]Ibid., pp. 282–283.
[c]William Dobriner, *Class in Suburbia* (Englewood Cliffs, N.J.: Prentice-Hall, 1963), p. 27.

Many black people migrated to the central city and remained there not by choice but because of constraints produced by technological and social changes and because of control strategies used by whites. These constraints forced blacks out of rural areas and into cities, while the control strategies placed them in an economic position that left them few alternatives but to move into the deteriorated housing in the inner-city. The core areas of many American cities are inhabited by poor black people. Nearly 25 per cent of the black people in metropolitan areas live on incomes below the federally established poverty level, compared with slightly over 7 per cent of the white people in these areas.[34]

Many of the problems faced by central cities result from the movement to the suburbs that accelerated after World War II. Many rich and middle-income people left the central city as did many factories, businesses, and service industries. The tax base, which produced income for the maintenance of all types of services eroded. Thus, the cities, faced with high crime rates, an impoverished citizenry, reduced services, and polluted water and air must increasingly turn for money to state and federal government if they want to survive. *As help comes, so does control.* The city loses some of its local autonomy as it must meet state or federal "standards," which tend to be standardized, leaving little room for local differences.

Back on the Farm

The local rural community in America used to be a service area for the farm families who surrounded it and who came to town on Saturday to trade and greet their friends. Today, however, nearly 70 per cent of all Americans live in metropolitan areas. The local communities serving farming districts have vastly decreased in numbers and importance. This decline in the traditional American heartland has been rapid in recent years. The farm population decreased from slightly more than thirty million in 1940 to slightly less than ten million in 1970. The *number* of farms declined from more than six million in 1940 to fewer than three million in 1970, and the average size of each farm increased from 167 acres to nearly 400 acres.[35] This trend seems to be continuing. Today, about 7 per cent of the population feeds the rest of us.

Big farms require the use of complicated and expensive machinery and a rational approach to agriculture if a profit is to be made. Fewer farmers mean fewer farm communities. A drive through the Midwest shows many once-prosperous small communities in a state of decay. Thus, the last bastion of the folk community is giving way to the constraints produced by technology and the growth of population. If the population is to be fed by a few farmers, agriculture must be highly productive. This calls for an industrialized agriculture that in its turn tends to produce industrialized tastes. The meaning system of the farmer becomes much like that of his city cousin. Our society has entered the era of the corporate farm and what is called agribusiness. The days of the few remaining small family farms appear numbered.

REFERENCES

1. Segerberg, Osborn, Jr. *Where Have All the Flowers, Fishes, Birds, Trees, Water, and Air Gone?* (New York: McKay, 1971), p. 34.
2. Ibid., pp. 40–41.
3. See *The City.* Ed. by Robert E. Park, Ernest W. Burgess and Roderick D. McKenzie. Chicago: U. of Chicago, 1925; *The Urban Community.* Ed. by E. W. Burgess. Chicago: U. of Chicago, 1926; Park, Robert E. *Human Communities: the City and Human Ecology.* New York: Free Press, 1952; McKenzie, Roderick D. *The Metropolitan Community.* New York: McGraw-Hill, 1933.
4. Llewellyn, Emma C., and Audrey Hawthorn. "Human Ecology." In *Twentieth Century Sociology.* Ed. by Georges Gurvitch and Wilbert E. Moore. New York: Philosophical Library, 1945, pp. 471–472.
5. White, Langdon, George T. Renner, and Henry J. Warman. *Geography: Factors and Concepts.* New York: Appleton, 1968, p. 252.
6. Hawley, Amos H. *Human Ecology.* New York: Ronald, 1950, p. 234.
7. Cooley, Charles Horton, "Theory of Transportation." In *Sociological Theory and Social Research.* Ed. by R. C. Angell. New York: Appleton, 1930.
8. Park, Burgess, and McKenzie, op. cit. p. 50.
9. Ibid., p. 50.
10. The Chicago School treated many ecological considerations. See references listed in (3). For a more recent treatment, see Schnore, Leo F. *The Human Scene: Human Ecology and Demography.* New York: Free Press, 1965; and *Studies in Human Ecology.* Ed. by George A. Theodorson. New York: Harper, 1961.
11. Toennies, Ferdinand. *Community and Society.* Trans. by Charles P. Loomis. Lansing: Michigan University Press, 1957).
12. Wirth, Louis. "Urbanism As a Way of Life." *American Journal of Sociology,* **XLIV** (July 1938), 1–24.
13. Maine, Sir Henry Sumner. *Ancient Law.* New York: Holt, 1885.
14. Durkheim, Emile. *The Division of Labor in Society.* Trans. by George Simpson. New York: Free Press, 1933.
15. Ibid.
16. See Becker, Howard. "Current Sacred-Secular Theory and Its Development." In *Modern Sociological Theory.* Ed. by Howard Becker and Alvin Boskoff. New York: Holt, 1957.
17. Tonnies, loc. cit.
18. Dressler, David. *Sociology: The Study of Human Interaction.* New York: Knopf, 1961, p. 312.
19. *American As a Mass Society.* Ed. by Philip Olson. New York: Free Press, 1963, pp. 3–4. See also, Kornhauser, William. *The Politics of Mass Society.* New York: Free Press, 1959.

20. Warren, Roland L. *Community in America*. Chicago: Rand McNally, 1963.
21. Ibid., p. 13.
22. Ibid., p. 14.
23. Ibid., pp. 242–243.
24. For a listing of these studies see *Community Power: A Bibliographic Review*. Ed. by Willis Hawley and James Swarz. Santa Barbara: ABC-CLIO, 1972.
25. See Lynd, R. S., and H. M. Lynd. *Middletown*. New York: Harcourt, 1929; and their *Middletown in Transition*. New York: Harcourt, 1937. For a more recent study see Hunter, Floyd. *Community Power Structure: A Study of Decision Makers*. Chapel Hill, N.C.: University of North Carolina Press, 1953.
26. Walton, John. "Substance and Artifact: the Current Status of Research on Community Power Research." *American Journal of Sociology*, 71 (Jan. 1966), 430–438.
27. ———— "A Systematic Survey of Community Power Research." In *The Structure of Community Power*. Ed. by Michael Aiken and Paul Mott. New York: Random, 1970, p. 452.
28. Aiken, Michael. "The Distribution of Community Power: Structural Bases and Social Consequences." In Ibid., p. 514.
29. Sternlieb, George. "The City As Sandbox." *The Public Interest*, No. 25 (Fall 1971), 14–21.
30. *Statistical Abstracts of the United States*. 1972, p. 2.
31. Ibid.
32. *The New York Times Analysis of Census Tract Reports*. (Oct. 15, 1972).
33. Ibid.
34. *Statistical Abstracts*, loc. cit.
35. U.S. Department of Commerce. Bureau of the Census, *Pocket Data Book, USA, 1971*, pp. 217–218.

C H A P T E R   6

Demographic Constraints

INTRODUCTION

At the same time that ecology became a household word, phrases such as "the population explosion" became common parlance. Groups such as Zero Population Growth emerged to parallel the ecological environmental protection crusade. Ecology as a science studying organism-environment interactions preceded ecology as a social movement. Similarly, demography as a science preceded the recent popular concern for unrestricted population growth.[1]

Demography is the science that studies human populations to isolate the factors responsible for population growth, decline, and stability. In this chapter we will briefly survey the elements of demography and define some of its major concepts, including birth rates, death rates, and migration. Demographic variables define a major body of constraints on the processes of social ordering and significantly determine the control strategies used by individuals, groups, and societies. Population growth, or decline density and movement, affects the use and control of relatively scarce natural resources, the relative economic strength and development of nations, and the balance of political power.

Demographic constraints partially explain the types of control strategy used among nations. If a small nation with high population growth does not have capital for economic development to feed its people but is rich in resources, a richer nation may invest capital in return for a share of the resources that will bring economic profits. A nation with abundant natural resources and capital and a relatively small population can be more independent. The shortage of wheat in the USSR to feed its growing population helped to change the reciprocal control strategies used by that nation and ours from nonviolent coercive and accommodative strategies to exchange strategies. The

155

"energy crisis" in the industrialized nations during the early 1970s changed the political and economic balance of power between them and the Middle Eastern nations that have abundant supplies of oil. Population size and growth, the level of economic development, technological advancement, and natural resources are inextricably combined. Through their interaction they form a set of constraints that shape and limit both the internal and external control strategies and social ordering of societies and groups.

We will examine population growth, discuss the *demographic transition* that refers to the tremendous spurt in population growth that accompanied industrialization in Western Europe, and then examine the population problems of the developing nations. The concept of population pyramids will be introduced as a useful device to summarize important data about populations. Internal and international migration will be examined. Finally, we will discuss the interaction of demographic and ecological constraints with social factors.

POPULATION GROWTH

The history of human beings on this planet has been, until recently, one of gradual population growth. Since 1750, however, the rate and extent of human growth have been so rapid as to justify the term *population explosion* and lend some substance to such queries as that in the title of a recent compendium, *Are Our Descendants Doomed?*[2] Table 6-1 shows in broad outline the population history of the human species.

Even though human beings had been around for more than two million years, the estimated population was only fifty thousand by 400,000 B. C. The average rate of increase per *century* between that date and 8,000 B. C. was only 0.1 per cent, resulting in a population of five million in the latter year. The average rate of increase per *century* between A. D. 1 and 1750 had increased to only 5.7 per cent. From 1750 to 1970, however, the average rate of increase per century rose dramatically to 99.8 per cent. This enormous expansion in actual numbers of people and in the rate of population growth is the central demographic fact of our time.

Technology and Population Growth

Harrison Brown and many others have pointed out that the maximum number of persons who live close together is strictly determined by the level of technology.[3] Before 10,000 B. C. most people

TABLE **6-1**
Population History of the Human Species

	Estimated Population (thousands)	Average Increase per Century in Prior Period (per cent)
400,000 B. C.	50	
8000 B. C.	5,000	0.1
A. D. 1	300,000	5.3
A. D. 1750	791,000	5.7
A. D. 1970	3,620,000	99.8

Kingsley Davis, "The Changing Balance of Births and Deaths,, in *Are Our Descendants Doomed?* ed. by Harrison Brown and Edward Hutchings, Jr. (New York: Viking, 1972), p. 14. Used by permission.
[1]John D. Durand, "The Modern Expansion of World Population" *Proceedings of the American Philosophical Society*, Vol. III (June, 1967) p. 137.
SOURCE: The first figure is speculative. The next three estimates are from Durand (1). The last estimate is made by Davis on the basis of trends up to 1967 and later; it is subject to revision as returns from censuses taken in or near 1970 come in. The rate is (1 − c').

lived by hunting and gathering food. The growth of population was limited by constraints placed on it by the availability of food within a limited radius of the home camp. Brown estimates that, "If humans had continued indefinitely to live as food gatherers, they would have spread over the earth, and their number would have leveled off at about ten million, no matter how effective their tools."[4]

However the human species learned to domesticate plants and animals, permitting more people to settle in one place and population to grow because of the increased food supply. The significant increase in population from fifty thousand persons in 400,000 B. C. to five million in 8,000 B. C. resulted from advancements in agricultural technology.

The population continued to grow from A. D. 1 to A. D. 1750, but the average increase per century was not enormous. The evidence suggests that population during this interval would have grown more rapidly had it not been for the widespread wars, epidemics such as the Black Plague (which swept over Europe in the thirteenth and fourteenth centuries), and sporadic declines in food production caused by droughts that led to famine. Most of these calamities were probably unavoidable, given the existing level of technology. A definite upper limit was set to population growth unless a breakthrough could occur in technological development.

This technological breakthrough took place in the eighteenth century. Table 6-2 shows the results for population growth.

The dynamics of this breakthrough and the enormous subsequent population are called the demographic transition.

THE DEMOGRAPHIC TRANSITION*

The demographic transition is typically interpreted as having three stages. We will discuss each, showing how it arose and its consequences.

Stage 1: High Birth and Death Rates

Stage 1 is the historic stage before the beginning of the Industrial Revolution in the eighteenth century. This stage was characterized by an agriculturally based economy in which children were desired because they were economic assets for planting and harvesting on the farm or for handicraft production. Large families were also desired because of traditional religious or other values. Furthermore, birth

*Not all demographers agree with this theoretical perspective. It is useful, however, in interpreting population dynamics in industrialized nations. Our discussion in this section is about these industrialized nations, so our writing is in the past tense. In the next section we will discuss the developing nations and their population dynamics from the perspective of demographic transition.[5]

Malthus on Population

Alarm about population growth is not recent. Thomas Malthus (1766–1834), an English scholar, identified the significance of population growth in relationship to food supply during the latter part of the eighteenth century. He argued that population would increase in a geometric ratio, as in the numbers 1, 2, 4, 8, 16, 32, 64, 128, 256, with the population doubling every twenty-five years. The food supply, on the other hand, would grow in arithmetic ratio, as in the numbers 1, 2, 3, 4, 5, 6, 7, 8, 9. Under these conditions, the population would soon outstrip the food supply. Malthus predicted that "In two centuries the population would be to the means of subsistence as 256 is to 9; in three centuries 4096 to 13; and in two thousand years the difference would be almost incalculable."[a]

Malthus discussed two major types of population checks, *positive* and *preventive.* Positive checks are those that reduce existing populations, such as disease, famine, and war. Preventive checks are those that reduce the birth rate, such as late marriage and celibacy. Even though his predictions

TABLE **6-2**
Growth of World Population, 1750–1970

	Population (millions)	Increase per Decade in Prior Period (per cent)
1750	791	
1800	978	4.3
1850	1262	5.2
1900	1650	5.5
1950	2517	8.8
1970	3614	19.8

Kingsley Davis, "The Changing Balance of Births and Deaths," in *Are Our Descendants Doomed?* ed. by Harrison Brown and Edward Hutchings, Jr. (New York: Viking, 1972), p. 15. Used by Permission.
SOURCE: Estimates from 1750–1900 are from Durand (1). The 1950 estimate is from United Nations (2, p. 97), and the one for 1970 is by [Davis].
(1) John D. Durand, "The Modern Expansion of World Population," *Proceedings of the American Philosophical Society*, Vol. III (June, 1967), p. 137.
(2) United Nations, *Demographic Yearbook*, 1967. New York, 1968.

control methods were usually unknown. Where birth control methods were available, they were crude, dangerous, and negatively sanctioned by influential religious authorities.

Because of these factors, stage 1 displayed a very high crude birth rate. Indeed, the *fertility rate*—the actual number of babies born during the child-bearing years in a population, usually computed as

about the food supply have not come true, Malthus had important insights: the potential problems of population growth.

Judy Morris points out in an excellent article on Malthus that, despite the failure of his specific predictions, his "fundamental mental concept remains unchallenged: unchecked population growth accelerates faster than the greatest increases of food that man is able to wrest from the earth on a sustained basis."[b] Technology has enabled us to forestall Malthusian disaster through substantial advances in food production and in birth control, but the Malthusian specters of starvation, disease, and war are never far removed even in the modern world. Famine is an ever-present threat and not an infrequent reality for hundreds of millions of people in Asia and elsewhere. As we shall see, the prognosis is not very hopeful.

[a] Thomas Malthus, *An Essay on the Principle of Population* (Homewood, Ill.: Irwin, 1963). This work was first published in 1798.

[b] Judy Morris, "Professor Malthus and His Essay," *Population Bulletin*, **22**, No. 1 (Feb. 1966), pp. 7–27.

from age fifteen to age forty-four—often approached the *fecundity rate*—the theoretically possible number of babies that can be born during the child-bearing years in a population.

Despite the high *crude birth rate* during stage 1, the population did not grow rapidly because of the high *crude death rate*. This high crude death rate was produced by a *high infant mortality* rate, the low level of sanitation, widespread disease, a low level of medical technology, and famine and starvation.

Stage II: High Birth Rate, Declining Death Rate, and Rapid Population Growth

Stage II of the demographic transition was characterized by a declining death rate, whereas the birth rate remained high. The decline in the death rate resulted from (1) advances in medical technology that helped combat death-producing disease; (2) public health measures such as improved sanitation that controlled the spread of disease; and (3) a rising standard of living providing better diets. There was a gradual undramatic decrease in the crude death rate until the nineteenth century. The infant mortality rate declined even more slowly.

Few people want to die or see members of their families die. There is, therefore, little argument about the value of decreasing the death rate. However, the birth rate was far more resistant to attempts to decrease it. Religious beliefs about birth included the Biblical injunction "to be fruitful and multiply." Children were still assets during the nineteenth century. They could be put to work in the mills, mines, and factories and thus increase the family income. Family farms existed on which children remained agricultural assets. Contraceptive devices were extremely crude and most people were completely ignorant about their possible use.

Because the death rate was declining and the birth rate remained

---

Crude Birth Rate (CBR)

Measure: $CBR = \dfrac{\text{number of babies born in a given year}}{\text{mid-year population}} \times 1,000$

Example: USA (1973) $\dfrac{3,480,769}{210,300,000} \times 1,000 = 16.6$

relatively high for a considerable number of years, the population grew rapidly during stage II. *The rate of natural increase* was high.

Stage III: Birth Rate Declines Faster than Death Rate to Slow Population Growth

Stage III of the demographic transition displayed a continuing decrease in the death rate and a lowering of the birth rate. The death rate continued to decline because of improvements in medical technology, sanitation, and other health measures.

The decline in the birth rate was brought about as societies became increasingly industrialized and moved from the religious-oriented folk community, with its traditional values, toward the more secular urban society, with its more rational attitude about family planning. The number of farm families declined as farming became mechanical and children were less valuable economically. Child labor laws also made children living in urban areas economic liabilities rather than assets. The practice of birth control helped to reduce the birth rate among the upper class as well as among people in the growing middle class. As *some* people in the lower class saw the possibility of upward social mobility, they too began to have fewer children. The birth rate in the lower class, however, was more resistent to change. A variety of *constraints* built into the structure of urbanizing societies caused the birth rate to decline.

Stage III, which completed the demographic transition, had a *low* birth rate and a *low* death rate, contrasting with the *high* birth rate and the *high* death rate of stage I. The demographic transition, however, increased population at a very rapid rate during stage II, in which the death rate declined rapidly and the birth rate remained high.

By the 1930s, the populations in many western European nations and in the United States were approaching zero rates of growth. The populations of France and Sweden were actually declining. This was,

---

Crude Death Rate (CDR)

Measure: $CDR = \dfrac{\text{number of deaths in a given year}}{\text{midyear population}} \times 1{,}000$

Example: USA (1973) $\dfrac{2{,}237{,}234}{210{,}300{,}000} \times 1{,}000 = 10.6$

TABLE 6-3

Demographic Profiles of Premodern, Early and Later Transitional, and Modern Populations

Population Characteristics	(Stage I) Premodern	(Stage II) Early Transitional	(Stage II) Later Transitional	(Stage III) Modern
Birth rate	45.6	43.7	45.7	20.4
Death rate	40.6	33.7	15.7	10.4
Annual growth rate, %	0.5	1.0	3.0	1.0
Age structure, %:				
under 15	36.7	37.8	45.4	27.2
15–59	57.6	56.5	50.3	58.2
60 and over	5.7	5.7	4.3	14.6
Average age	25.5	25.1	21.8	32.8
Per cent surviving to age 15	48.8	55.9	78.8	95.6
Expectation of life at birth	25.0	30.0	50.0	70.0
Average number children born to women by age 50	5.7	5.5	6.1	2.9

SOURCE: Ansley J. Coale and Paul Demeny, *Regional Model Life Tables and Stable Populations* (Princeton, N.J.: Princeton University Press, 1966). Used by permission. (Heads in parentheses inserted.)

in part, caused by the worldwide economic depression. The post-World War II "baby boom" caused the population to grow once again. There is typically a baby boom after a war as the soldiers come home. However, this "boom" lasted longer than it should have, according to the demographic transition theory. The evidence indicates that in industrial nations the birth rate is once again declining toward zero growth, even though this point has not actually been reached in many industrial nations.

Table 6-3 summarizes for an ideal-typical series of populations, the changes in population size and composition that accompany the demographic transition.

Perhaps most dramatic among the changes revealed by inspection

Infant Mortality Rate

The infant mortality rate is computed by dividing the number of babies who die in the first year of life in a given year in a population by the number of live births in that year and multiplying by 1,000. The infant mortality rate for the United States in 1973 was 18.5.

of this table are the decreases in the birth and death rates. Of equal significance are the changes in life expectancy at birth from twenty-five years in stage I to seventy years in stage III, with the corresponding change in the average age of the population. These demographic changes in population composition and size accompanied (and partly caused) the transition from the folk community to urban society, with all that implies for changes in values, life-styles, economic forms, and social relationships.

POPULATION GROWTH IN DEVELOPING NATIONS

One of the ironies of the present pattern of world population growth is that the nations that can least afford population growth economically are the very nations whose rates are highest. Table 6-4 compares the extremes and shows that those nations with the lowest per capita gross national product (GNP) tend to have the highest annual rate of population growth. (The GNP is based on United States dollar comparisons.) Those nations with the highest per capita GNP tend to have the lowest annual rate of growth. For example, the United States, in 1973, had a per capita GNP of $4,760, with an annual population growth rate of 0.8 per cent. At this rate of growth it would take 87 years to double the population in the United States. On the other hand, Kenya, with a per capita GNP of only $150, in 1973, had an annual population growth of 3.0 per cent, which would double that nation's population in only twenty-three years.

These glaring differences partly reflect the demographic transition already discussed. The richest nations are the industrialized nations, which have "completed" the demographic transition and thus have relatively low birth and death rates. The poorer nations, on the other hand, are in stage II, with relatively low death and high birth rates. Much of their existing death rate reflects a very high infant mortality.

Rate of Natural Increase

The rate of natural increase in a population is arrived at by subtracting the crude death rate from the crude birth rate. There is, of course, the possibility of having a population decline, but during stage II, this did not occur. Holding immigration and emigration constant, the rate of natural increase shows how many people are added per thousand in a population during a given year based on birth and death rates. The rate of natural increase for the United States in 1973 was 6.0.

TABLE 6-4

Comparison of Selected Nations with High GNP and Low Population Growth and Nations with Low GNP and High Population Growth (GNP based on U.S. Dollars) 1973

Nations with High GNP and Low Population Growth

Nation	Population Estimates Mid-1973 (millions)	Birth Rate	Death Rate	Annual Rate of Population Growth (per cent)	Number of Years to Double Population	Population Projections to 1985 (millions)	Infant Mortality Rate	Population under 15 Years (%)	Population over 64 Years (%)	Life Expectancy at Birth M	F	Per Capita GNP (U.S.$)
United States	210.3	15.6	9.4	0.8	87	235.7	18.5	27	10	67	75	4,760
Sweden	8.2	13.8	10.4	0.3	231	8.8	11.1	21	13	72	77	4,040
Austria	7.5	13.8	12.6	0.1	700	8.0	25.1	24	14	67	74	2,010
Belgium	9.8	13.8	12.0	0.2	347	10.4	19.8	24	13	68	74	2,720
France	52.3	16.9	10.6	0.6	117	57.6	13.3	25	13	69	76	3,100
Germany (Federal Republic of)	59.4	11.5	11.7	0.0	139	62.3	23.2	25	12	68	74	2,930
Denmark	5.1	15.8	10.2	0.5	231	5.5	14.2	24	12	71	76	3,190
Finland	4.8	12.7	9.6	0.3	231	5.0	11.3	26	8	65	73	2,390
Iceland	0.2	19.7	7.3	1.2	58	0.3	13.2	33	9	71	76	2,170
Japan	107.3	19	7	1.2	58	121.3	13	24	7	69	74	1,920

Nations with Low GNP and High Population Growth

Nation	Population Estimates Mid-1973 (millions)	Birth Rate	Death Rate	Annual Rate of Population Growth (per cent)	Number of Years to Double Population	Population Projections to 1985 (millions)	Infant Mortality Rate	Population under 15 Years (%)	Population over 64 Years (%)	Life Expectancy at Birth M	Life Expectancy at Birth F	Per Capita GNP (U.S.$)
Bolivia	5.0	44	19	2.4	29	6.8		42	L*	44	46	180
Brazil	101.3	38	10	2.8	25	142.6		43	L	58	63	420
Columbia	23.7	45	11	3.4	21	35.6		47	L	57	60	340
India	600.4	42	17	2.5	28	807.6	76	42	L			110
Tanzania	14.3	47	22	2.6	27	20.3	139	44	L	41	41	100
Uganda	9.3	43	18	2.6	27	13.1	162	46	L	48		130
Zambia	4.7	50	21	2.9	24	7.0	160	46	L	44	44	400
Togo	2.0	51	26	2.5	28	2.8	159	48	7			140
Guinea	4.2	47	25	2.3	30	5.7	163	44	5			120
Sierra Leone	2.8	45	22	2.3	30	3.9	216	37	L	41	41	190
Sri Lanka (Ceylon)	13.5	30	8	2.2	32	17.7	136	41	L	62	62	110
Kenya	12.0	48	18	3.0	23	17.9	48	46	L	48	48	150

*L = estimated to be less than 5%.
SOURCE: Population Reference Bureau, Inc. 1973 *World Population Data Sheet.* (Modified by author.)

These developing nations, therefore, have *high population growth potential*—a potential for disaster, given their low income level and lack of capital for development.

However, the developing nations are in stage II only in a special sense. Their crude death rate has usually been reduced by external help rather than by internal development. Outside agencies such as the United Nations and some industrialized nations have helped to reduce the death rate in these nations through programs of mass innoculation against smallpox and other killing diseases. In addition, nations facing famines have sometimes been provided with food from outside sources. Some developing nations have a medical technology of their own but are limited by their resources.

The limited resources of some of these nations are the result of massive exploitation during a colonial period. Such exploitation helped to make the industrial nations rich, but it continues to hamper adequate industrial development in poor nations. Colonialism did bring about development in nations such as the Union of South Africa, but this occurred at the expense of the indigenous peoples. Corporations do not invest in developing nations unless they expect to gain more than they invest.

The failure of industrial development has severe consequences. According to the demographic transition theory, it is industrial development and urbanization that create the constraints that reduce the birth rate in stage III. If this does not occur quickly in developing nations, or if their birth rate is not brought under control by the widespread use of contraceptive devices, a country's future appears very dismal. Because of the already low level of the per capita GNP there is little chance of amassing development capital. Any increase in resources is immediately consumed by the rapid increase in population.

Gross National Product (GNP)

The GNP "is *the total market value of all final goods and services produced in an economy in one year.*"[a] This includes those goods that are not sold but placed in inventory.

GNP is not the same thing as *personal income*, which is less. Some goods that are produced are exported or bought by the government. In addition, the portion of the GNP consumed by individuals is not equally distributed among all persons in a particular nation. The very poor usually receive a portion far below the average.

[a]Campbell R. McConnell, *Economics: Principles, Problems, and Policies* (New York: McGraw-Hill, 1969), p. 155.

In some developing societies the birth rate is resistant to change because of cultural values. If these are violated, individual meaning is threatened. In India, where the population problem is intense, some Hindu peasants are reluctant to limit family size because the male Hindu peasant believes that he must have a son who lives long enough to bury him when he dies. If a Hindu is not buried by his eldest living son, it is believed that his soul will be condemned to wander about the earth forever. Therefore, he wants to make sure he has enough sons so that at least one will outlive him. The traditional position of the Roman Catholic church opposes the use of artificial means of contraception. Even though many Catholics do not abide by this teaching, some do. Catholics in developing nations are more likely to follow the church than those in developed nations.

Furthermore, some developing nations may not want to industrialize and consequently to reduce the birth rate. From the point of view of these nations, development is not desirable if it will destroy certain historic values which have provided a basis for meaning. Just because presently industrialized nations equate industrialization with progress does not mean that it is progress from the view point of people in nations that are not industrialized.

The problem of overpopulation, however, persists whatever the attitudes toward industrialization. Table 6-4 shows that the percentage of the population under fifteen years of age in the developing nations is far higher than in the industrialized nations, whereas the percentage of people over sixty-four is higher in the industrialized nations. This younger population in the developing nations has serious consequences for future birth rates because a larger percentage of the population will be entering the child-bearing years and this percentage will increase as the infant mortality rate declines.

The economist and social philosopher Robert L. Heilbroner summarizes the problems and prospects of population growth, which he aptly calls "the race between food and mouths," in these terms:

> World population is today roughly 3.6 billions. About 1.1 billion live in areas where demographic growth rates are now tapering off, so that, barring unanticipated reversals in the trends of fertility and mortality, we can expect these areas—mainly North America, Western and Eastern Europe, Japan, Oceania, and the Soviet Union—to attain reasonably stable populations within about two generations. These populations will be approximately 30 to 60 per cent larger than they are now, and this increase in numbers will add its difficulties to the environmental problems facing mankind. . . .
>
> The [population overload] problem concerns the ability of those areas of the globe where population stability is not now in sight to sustain their impending populations even at the barest levels of subsistence. The dangers involved vary in intensity from nation to nation: there are a few areas of the underdeveloped world that are still underpopulated in their human carrying capacity. But in general the demographic situation of virtually all

of Southeast Asia, large portions of Latin America, and parts of Africa portends a grim Malthusian outcome. Southeast Asia, for example, is growing at a rate that will double its numbers in less than thirty years; the African continent as a whole every twenty-seven years; Latin America every twenty-four years. Thus, whereas we can expect that the industrialized areas of the world will have to support roughly 1.4 to 1.7 billion people a century hence, the underdeveloped world, which today totals around 2.5 billions, will have to support something like 40 billions by that date if it continues to double its numbers approximately every quarter century.

. . .

For the next several generations, therefore, even if effective population policies are introduced or a spontaneous decline in fertility owing to urbanization takes effect, the main restraint on population growth in the underdeveloped areas is apt to be the Malthusian check of famine, disease, and the like.

Heilbroner goes on to identify the dire social consequences of such unchecked population growth:

The race between food and mouths is perhaps the most dramatic (and highly publicized) aspect of the population problem, but it is not necessarily the most immediately threatening. For the torrent of human growth imposes intolerable social strains on the economically backward regions, as well as hideous costs on their citizens. Among these social strains the most immediately threatening is that of urban disorganization. Rapidly increasing populations in the rural areas of technologically static societies create unemployable surpluses of manpower that stream into the cities in search of work. In the underdeveloped world generally, cities are therefore growing at rates that cause them to double their populations in ten years—in some cases in as little as six years.[6]

Even this partial picture of potential social chaos and personal tragedy conveys the seriousness of the current demographic situation and underlines why some scholars refer to it as the population bomb.

POPULATION PYRAMIDS

A population pyramid is a graphic profile showing the age and sex distribution of a population. It summarizes a variety of important demographic data.

If the birth rate of a population were absolutely stable over the years, and if *everyone* lived to the age of seventy-five and then died on his seventy-fifth birthday, the population profile would be a rectangle, as shown in Figure 6-1.

Any deviation from the hypothetical (and never occurring) rectangle profile tells us something about the birth and death rates of a population and what can be expected about future population growth or decline.

If the top corners of the rectangle, starting with the base at each

FIGURE **6-1**
Hypothetical Population Rectangle

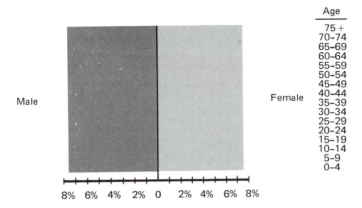

corner, are cut off, as in Figure 6-2, along with a real population pyramid that resembles it, we know that the population has a high birth rate and a high death rate—this is the profile of a population before the demographic transition.

If the top two corners are cut off, as in Figure 6-3, we know that the population has been through the demographic transition. If we then take Figure 6-3 and cut off the bottom two corners, as in Figure 6-4, we display a population in which the birth rate is declining.

Figure 6-5 shows the population pyramid for the United States for 1970 and 1960, showing that our birth rate declined during the 1960s.

FIGURE **6-2**
Hypothetical and Real Population Pyramids Showing a High Birth Rate and a High Death Rate

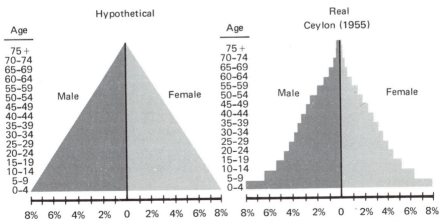

SOURCE: Population pyramid showing Ceylon (1955). From Population Reference Bureau, *Population Bulletin*, Vol. XVI, No. 8 (Dec. 1960), p. 159. Used by permission.

FIGURE **6-3**
Hypothetical and Real Population Pyramid Showing a Population that has Passed Through the Demographic Transition (Low Birth and Death Rates)

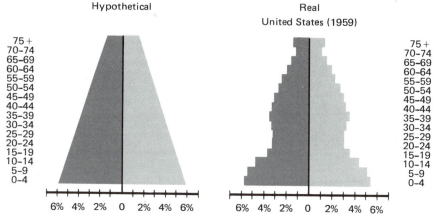

SOURCE: Population pyramid showing the United States (1959). From Population Reference Bureau, *Population Bulletin*, Vol. XVI, No. 8 (Dec. 1960), p. 159. Used by permission.

The age distribution in population pyramids is shown by five-year intervals, from 0 to 4, 5 to 9, and so forth. Such categories are called age cohorts by the demographer. An *age cohort* may be as small or large as the demographer finds useful, but the five-year cohort is the most common. Age cohorts are useful to compare populations among

FIGURE **6-4**
Hypothetical and Real Population Pyramid Showing a Population that has Passed Through the Demographic Transition and is Now in a State of Population Decline

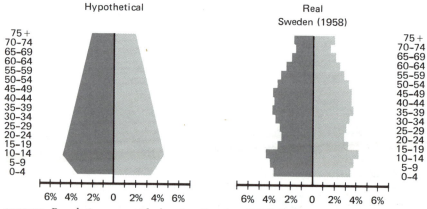

SOURCE: Population pyramid showing Sweden (1958). From Population Reference Bureau, *Population Bulletin*, Vol. XVI, No. 8 (Dec. 1960), p. 159. Used by permission.

FIGURE **6-5**
Population Pyramid for the United States, 1960 and 1970

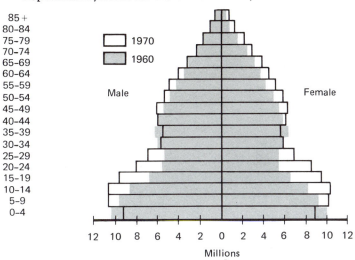

SOURCE: U. S. Bureau of the Census.

nations. Population pyramids also suggest what happened to a population in the past, what is happening now, and what may happen in the
future. The population pyramid for Ceylon in Figure 6-2 has steps that
become smaller as we progress up the population pyramid. This indicates that many children die at an early age as compared with adults in
that nation. In addition, if the death rate in the early years is brought
under control, the population will grow at a very rapid rate.

The population pyramid for the United States (1959) in Figure 6-3
displays the decreased birth rates caused by the Great Depression
(ages twenty to twenty-four, twenty-five to twenty-nine). The results
of the prolonged post-World War II baby boom can be seen in the
cohorts for ages five to nine, ten to fourteen, fifteen to nineteen. The
beginning of our declining birth rate is shown by comparing ages zero
to four with the preceding. Figure 6-5 shows that the United States
birth rate continued to decline during the 1960s, a trend continued
into the 1970s. By March 1973, the replacement level fertility had
fallen to 2.03. Replacement level of fertility is the minimum number
of babies who must be born per woman if the population is to replace
itself over time. The Census Bureau reports that a birth rate of 2.10 per
woman is replacement level fertility. If the 2.03 replacement level
fertility reached in March 1973 continues or declines further, our
population will eventually decline in actual number and the average
age of the population will increase.

Knowledge of the age composition of a population and its birth and
death rates is a prerequisite for social planning. For example, if the

FIGURE 6-6
International Migration Since 1500

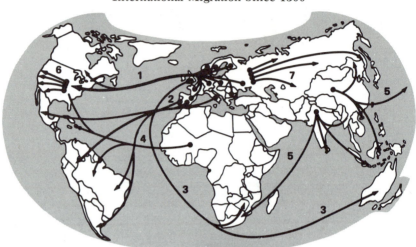

SOURCE: Wladimir S. Woytinsky and Emma S. Woytinsky, *World Population and Production* (New York: Twentieth Century Fund, 1953), p. 68. Used by permission.

birth rate increases rapidly, more schools will be needed and more teachers must be trained. If the population is becoming older, different kinds of services must be provided. The number of jobs needed can be projected, as can expected markets for various goods and services. Thus, the composition of its population places a variety of *constraints* on a nation. A nation such as ours must consider increasingly these constraints in planning for the future. Developing nations, with their limited resources, have an even greater stake in basing planning on population constraints.

MIGRATION

We have considered two of the three principal determinants of population composition and growth: birth and death rates. We now turn to the third principal determinant, *migration*.

Emigration is the movement of persons out of a society. *Immigration* is the movement of persons into a society. Humans have been wanderers since they appeared on this planet. There is no human society that at some point in its history has not been affected by immigration or emigration. First, we shall look at international migration—that is, the movements of people among societies—and then we will examine internal migration—that is, the movements of people within a society.

TABLE 6-5
Immigration by Decade Since 1820

Period	Total In Thousands	Rate*	Period	Total In Thousands	Rate*
1820–1970, total	45,162	3.7	1931–40	528	0.4
			1941–50	1,035	0.7
1820–30	152	1.2	1951–60	2,515	1.5
1831–40	599	3.9	1961–70	3,321	1.7
1841–50	1,713	8.4	1962	284	1.5
1851–60	2,598	9.3	1963	306	1.6
1861–70	2,315	6.4	1964	292	1.5
1871–80	2,812	6.2	1965	297	1.5
1881–90	5,247	9.2	1966	323	1.6
1891–1900	3,688	5.3	1967	362	1.8
1901–10	8,795	10.4	1968	454	2.3
1911–20	5,736	5.7	1969	359	1.8
1921–30	4,107	3.5	1970	373	1.8

*Annual rate per 1,000 population.
SOURCE: U.S. Bureau of the Census, *Pocket Data Book*, 1971.

INTERNATIONAL MIGRATION

Figure 6-6 shows the main currents of intercontinental migration since A. D. 1500.

The main currents have been from (1) all parts of Europe to North America; (2) the Latin countries of Europe, particularly Spain and Portugal, to South America; (3) Great Britain to Africa, Australia, and North America; (4) Africa to the New World, especially the United States (the slave trade was heavy from the seventeenth century through the early part of the nineteenth century); (5) India to Africa, southeast Asia, and the Pacific Islands; and (6) China to North America, southeast Asia, and the Pacific Islands. This gives an overview of where people have come from and where they have gone.[7]

Immigration to the United States

Immigration has been a significant factor in determining the size, population composition, and characteristics of American society. Except for the American Indians, we are a nation of immigrants and the descendants of immigrants. Figure 6-7 shows the origin of immigrants since 1820. Table 6-5 shows the number of immigrants per decade since 1820. Since 1820, 45,162,000 people have entered this country from other nations.

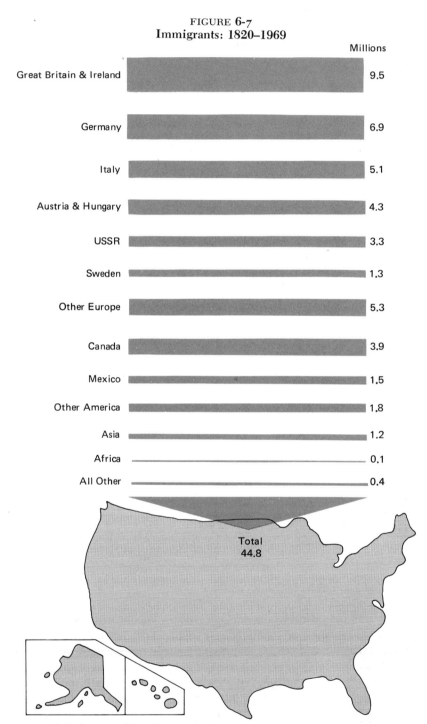

FIGURE 6-7
Immigrants: 1820–1969

Millions

Great Britain & Ireland	9.5
Germany	6.9
Italy	5.1
Austria & Hungary	4.3
USSR	3.3
Sweden	1.3
Other Europe	5.3
Canada	3.9
Mexico	1.5
Other America	1.8
Asia	1.2
Africa	0.1
All Other	0.4

Total
44.8

SOURCE: U. S. Bureau of the Census, *Pocket Data Book*, 1971.

After the decade from 1921 to 1930 immigration dropped sharply. Until the 1920s the United States was open to almost everyone who wanted to come, with the major exception of Chinese people who were restricted by the Oriental Exclusion acts beginning in 1882. The Japanese were excluded by the "gentlemen's agreement" of 1907. A later act, in 1917, barred almost all Asiatic peoples. These laws were clearly discriminatory legislation.[8]

Subsequent discriminatory legislation includes the Immigration Act of 1924 (effective in 1929), which based the quota at 2 per cent of the population from that nation residing in the United States in 1890. This act replaced the first Quota Act of 1921, which based the quota at 3 per cent of the population from that nation living in this country based on the 1920 census. By moving the basis for quotas back to 1890, the total quota for northern and western European countries was cut by only 29 per cent, whereas that for southern and eastern Europe suffered a cut of 87 per cent. The quota for Italy, for example, was reduced from 42,057 to 3,845; for Poland from 30,977 to 5,982; for Turkey from 2,654 to 100.[9] The closer the potential immigrant was to the white Anglo-Saxon-Protestant "ideal," the higher his chance of entering the country. Southern and eastern European countries, whose immigrants had come later, received lower quotas.

The McCarran-Walter Act of 1952 left the quotas established in the 1924 act substantially the same but doubled the extremely low quota for Asian countries. (The initial Asian quotas were so low that this had little effect.) It is ironic that the plaque on the Statue of Liberty is inscribed with this poem by Emma Lazarus that concludes:

Give me your tired, your poor,
Your huddled masses yearning to breathe free,
The wretched refuse of your teeming shore,
Send these, the homeless, tempest-tossed to me;
I lift my lamp beside the golden door.

The Statue of Liberty was declared a national monument in 1924, the year the government moved the quota basis back to the census of 1890.

American Immigrants: "Old" and "New"

Immigrants to the United States are typically divided into the "Old" and "New." The old immigrants came mainly from western European nations before 1870. The new immigrants came mainly from eastern and southeastern European nations after 1870.

The new immigrants were seen as "undesirable" by the old immigrants and their descendants, who were settled and in positions of power. Many of the new immigrants were reduced to minority group

TABLE 6-6
Annual Immigration Quotas by Country, 1929 and 1952

Country	1929 Quota Effective	1952 Immigration and Nationality Act
All countries	153,714	154,657
Europe	150,591	149,667
Austria	1,413	1,405
Belgium	1,304	1,297
Bulgaria	100	100
Czechoslovakia	2,874	2,859
Denmark	1,181	1,175
Finland	569	566
France	3,086	3,069
Germany	25,957	25,814
Great Britain	65,721	65,361
Greece	307	308
Hungary	869	865
Iceland	100	100
Ireland	17,853	17,756
Italy	5,802	5,645
Netherlands	3,153	3,136
Norway	2,377	2,364
Poland	6,524	6,488
Portugal	440	438
Rumania	295	289
Spain	252	250
Sweden	3,314	3,295
Switzerland	1,707	1,698
Turkey	226	225
USSR	2,784	2,697
Yugoslavia	845	933
Other Europe	1,558	1,534
Asia	1,323	2,990
Africa	1,200	1,400
Australia	200	600
All others	400	—

SOURCE: U. S. Bureau of the Census, *Statistical Abstracts of the United States (1958).*

status and used as a source of cheap labor.* The Immigration Act of 1924 was passed to reduce the number of new immigrants who could enter the country. By 1924, their labor was no longer needed and there was a fear that the balance of power might shift away from the dominant white Anglo-Saxon-Protestant group. The act of 1924 can be interpreted as a control strategy used by the dominant group to keep their positions from being threatened. Who arrived here when and in

*As will be developed at length in Chapter 8, the concept of *minority group* refers not to numbers but to subservience in a dominant-subordinate power relationship.

FIGURE 6-8
Center of Population: 1790–1970

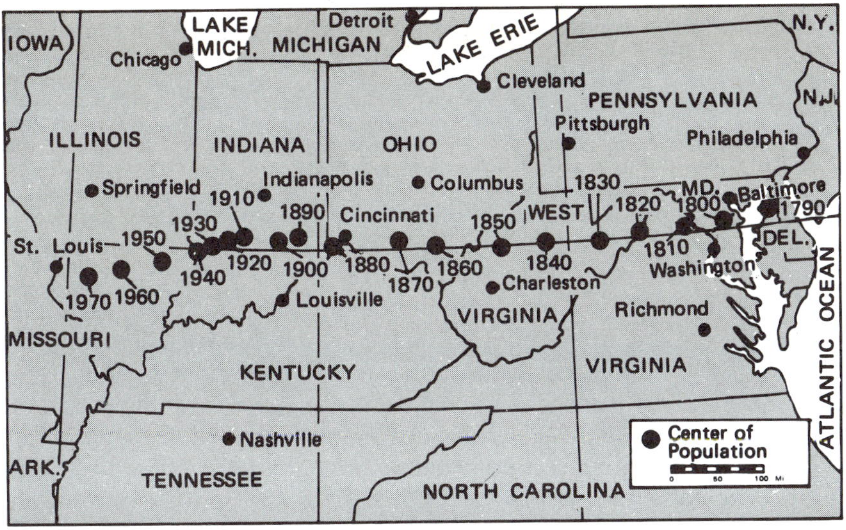

SOURCE: United States Summary, U. S. Census of Population: 1970.

what numbers remains important to understand the distribution of power and prestige in contemporary American society, as will be shown in Chapters 7 and 8.

Internal Migration: The Example of the United States

This nation has been called a nation of nomads for good reason. Since its founding, there has been constant movement of population. The major historical movement was the movement westward, which

Center of Population

"Center of population" is that point which may be considered as center of population gravity of the United States or that point upon which the United States would balance if it were a rigid plane without weight and the population distributed thereon with each individual assumed to have equal weight and to exert an influence on a central point proportional to his distance from that point.[a]

[a] Description by the U. S. Bureau of the Census. United States Summary, U. S. Census of Population, 1970.

continues. Figure 6-8 shows how the center of population has been moving westward since 1790.

The other two major movements of America's population have been from the south to the north and to the west and from rural to urban areas.

The Movement from the South to the North and West

The movement from the south to the north and west began slowly after the Civil War and accelerated rapidly until after World War II. Many of the migrants were black people squeezed off the land and suffering from discrimination who moved north and west looking for jobs and equality. Many poor whites also moved, especially from the economically depressed Appalachia areas. These poor whites, many of whom had lost their jobs in coal mines or could no longer exist on subsistence farming, also sought jobs.

Today, many older retired citizens are moving *to* the south and west, especially to Florida and Arizona. As the south continues to industrialize it will not only continue to increase its holding power but also its drawing power.

From Rural to Urban

In Chapter 5 the extent of the rural to urban migration in this country was outlined. This migration continues along with considerable movement among and within the large metropolitan areas.

In our nation of nomads nearly one fifth of the population moves every year. The largest percentage of movements is within the same county (12.7 per cent in 1969). The next largest is movement into a different county within the same state (6.6 per cent in 1969). Movement between states comprises the lowest percentage of movers (3.3 per cent in 1969), but this still represents more than six million people.

Constraints Causing Movement

There are a variety of constraints causing mass movements of population as well as individual movements. The primary constraints causing *mass* movements include famine, poverty, ethnic or racial discrimination, war, and expulsion. The Irish potato famine of 1849, for example, caused large numbers of Irish people to migrate to other lands, especially to the United States. The promise of a better life caused many Europeans, especially from southern and eastern Europe, to come to the United States. The history of the movement of the Jewish people in Europe and to this country resulted in large part from expulsion and persecution. Modern wars create millions of refugees who either wander about in their own nation or seek safety elsewhere. The war in Vietnam, for example, created an estimated two million homeless people.

Constraints causing individuals to move include job seeking; job promotion; escaping "undesirable" conditions (for example, in the movement from the central city to the suburbs); older people seeking warmer climates in which to retire; and ethnic or racial discrimination. There are also the massive movements of college and university students and nearly 600,000 migrant workers who follow the harvests across the nation.

MIGRATION, SOCIAL ORDERING, AND INDIVIDUAL MEANING

Like other demographic data that can be stated numerically as statistical facts, the data about migration are indicators of profound social changes and personal adjustments. The migrations of the tribes and armies that made up the Mongol "hordes" that swept repeatedly over Europe in the Middle Ages completed the breakup of the Roman Empire and caused profound social dislocations in feudal Europe. The Mongols pursued conquest and new lands and (to use the modern cliché) expanded economic opportunities. It was the Europeans who saw them as invading hordes.

The successive waves of European immigrants to the United States similarly produced profound social changes. The history of many urban neighborhoods in American cities reflects the patterns of European immigrants. The newest immigrants typically settled in the poorest neighborhoods near the central business district. As they be-

---

Push and Pull Factors Affecting Movement

In analyzing population movements many demographers refer to push and pull factors as the causes of movement. *Push* factors are undesirable conditions that cause persons to want to leave a place. Examples include famine, extreme poverty, discrimination, and war. *Pull* factors are conditions in another place that are seen as more desirable than those existing in one's present location. Examples include the promise of a higher standard of living, peace, and the absence of discrimination.

came accepted into and familiar with American society and improved their economic status, they moved out into more desirable locations, only to be succeeded by still newer waves of immigrants. Most recently, black people and southern whites have migrated to the city.

Human Migration and the Marginal Man

The Chicago School of Urban Sociology, founded in a city that was a center for European immigrants, blacks, and southern white migrants, took the social processes of disorganization, conflict, and accommodation that accompanied migrations as its central problems. Robert Park, in his famous essay on "Human Migration and the Marginal Man," noted how the transition from folk community to urban society broke the "cake of custom." The geographic migrant is also a psychological migrant who moves from one society to another and is often not fully accepted into any one of them. This *marginal man* "lives in two worlds." Park summarizes the process and the psychic state of the marginal man:

> The emancipated individual invariably becomes in a certain sense and to a certain degree a cosmopolitan. He learns to look upon the world in which he was born and bred with something of the detachment of a stranger. He acquires, in short, an intellectual bias. Simmel has described the position of the stranger in the community, and his personality, in terms of movement and migration.
>
> . . .
>
> The effect of mobility and migration is to secularize relations which were formerly sacred. One may describe the process, in its dual aspect, perhaps, as the secularization of society and the individuation of the person.
>
> Something of the same sense of moral dichotomy and conflict is probably characteristic of every immigrant during the period of transition, when old habits are being discarded and new ones are not yet formed. It is inevitably a period of inner turmoil and intense self-consciousness.
>
> There are no doubt periods of transition and crisis in the lives of most of us that are comparable with those which the immigrant experiences when he leaves home to seek his fortunes in a strange country. But in the case of the marginal man the period of crisis is relatively permanent. The result is that he tends to become a personality type. The characteristics of the marginal man [are] spiritual instability, intensified self-consciousness, restlessness, and *malaise*.
>
> It is in the mind of the marginal man that the moral turmoil which new cultural contacts occasion manifests itself in the most obvious forms. It is in the mind of the marginal man—where the changes and fusions of culture are going on—that we can best study the processes of civilization and of progress.[10]

In our terms, the marginal man is the person who moves between groups and subcultures, or between societies. The move may be voluntary—for example, the person who aspires to a higher social class—or involuntary—the person who is forced by persecution to flee a familiar place. However, the social dislocations are often similar. As will be apparent in our discussion of ethnic and racial minorities, many of the behaviors and attitudes that members of such groups display are consequences of the marginality that is imposed on them by the power relationships that determine their minority status.

Migration, thus, becomes a major cause of social dislocations and social change. The statistics about migration reflect important aspects of social ordering and individual meaning. For sociologists, the constraints produced by demographic factors become of prime importance in defining the social context within which control strategies shape human behavior.[11]

CONCLUSION: THE PERILS AND PROMISES OF GROWTH

We have provided only an introductory glimpse of demographic complexity. The problems caused by population growth in relation to available resources both now and in the future cannot be overestimated. There are both pessimists and optimists evaluating our chances for survival if the present rate of population growth is not curtailed. The facts are that today two thirds of the world's people have inadequate diets and that *natural* resources are rapidly being exhausted. Unless population is brought under control, or unless there are breakthroughs in the development and use of resources, our descendants will indeed be doomed.

The constraints produced by population growth and density will continue to affect our lives and those of our children. The American birth rate has dropped significantly in the last few years. However, the problem remains critical in developing nations and we cannot divorce their problems from our own. The distribution of natural resources, hunger, considerations of the balance of power among nations, international trade agreements, the growth of multinational corporations, and the increase in world travel are among the many factors that make it so difficult to ignore the growth of world population and the actual and potential problems this presents.

REFERENCES

1. For a general treatment of the population problem, see Ehrlich, Paul. *The Population Bomb.* New York: Ballantine, 1968.
2. *Are Our Descendants Doomed?* Ed. by Harrison Brown and Edward Hutchings, Jr. New York: Viking, 1972.
3. Brown, Harrison. "The Growth and Distribution of Human Populations." In Ibid., p. 4.

4. Ibid.

5. For a lucid discussion of the arguments concerning the demographic transition theory, see Heer, D. M. *Society and Population*. Englewood Cliffs, N.J.: Prentice-Hall, 1968, pp. 6–12.

6. Heilbroner, Robert. "The Human Prospect." *The New York Review of Books* (Jan. 24, 1974), 22–23.

7. For an excellent treatment of international migration, see Taft, Donald R., and Richard Robbins. *International Migrations*. New York: Ronald, 1955.

8. For a concise description of the various immigration acts, see Thomlinson, Ralph. *Population Dynamics*. New York: Random, 1965.

9. Bernard, William S. *American Immigration Policy*. New York: Harper, 1950, p. 27. This book provides an in-depth treatment of immigration policy.

10. Park, Robert E. "Human Migration and the Marginal Man." *American Journal of Sociology*, Vol. XXXIII (May 1928), pp. 888, 893.

11. We do not want to imply that demography is subservient to or a subdiscipline of sociology. Like ecology, demography exists as an independent science. However, also like ecology, the interrelationships between demographic and sociocultural variables are highly significant. For a volume that systematically emphasizes these interrelationships, see *Social Demography*. Ed. by Thomas Ford and Gordon DeJong. Englewood Cliffs, N.J.: Prentice-Hall, 1970.

C H A P T E R 7

Social Stratification

INTRODUCTION

The sociologists C. Wright Mills and Hans Gerth have described the social realities that force an awareness of social inequality on all members of modern societies:

> In New York City some people taxi home at night from Madison Avenue offices to Sutton Place apartments; others leave a factory loft in Brooklyn and subway home to an East Harlem tenement. In Detroit there is Grosse Pointe, with environs, but there is also Hamtramek, without environs; and in a thousand small towns people live on either side of the railroad track. In Moscow, leading party members ride cautiously in black cars along well-policed avenues to well-policed suburbs; other people walk home from factories to huddle in cramped apartments. And in the shadow of swank Washington, D.C., apartment houses there are the dark alley dwellings. In almost any community in every nation there is a high and a low, and in some societies, a big in-between.[1]

Other sociologists have verified the existence of the "high, the low, and the in-between" in every large society. By studying social stratification sociologists try to identify the general principles of such systems of ranking and to explore their consequences for life-styles and life-chances.

In Chapter 2 we identified stratification as one of the principal cultural control strategies and suggested that it is used by individuals and groups with greater power to maintain themselves in their advantageous social positions. A community or society is *stratified* when some people rank higher than others, with the ranking based on some explicitly recognizable criteria. These criteria for ranking differ from community to community and society to society.

Superficially it might appear that societies would be stratified solely by differential power. People with great power would place themselves at the top and those with little power would be *placed* at the bottom of the stratification hierarchy. Such a stratification system would be supported by coercive strategies using force rather than cultural strategies based on shared agreements. However, people and groups with great power have the same basic needs as those with little power, including needs for response, security, self-esteem, and so forth. They also need the services of at least some people with less power. Furthermore, they need to find meaning in the fact and use of their power and want to make it *appear* to themselves and others that distributive justice is being served. They like to feel that they deserve the positions they hold. A society in which raw power alone is used to maintain order and a system of ranking is meaningless in the long run both for those at the top and for those at the bottom.[2]

All social action, including the use of power, is predicated on some type of subjective meaning. As noted in Chapter 1, this meaning is usually derived from the responses of other people. Those with great power need favorable responses from at least some people who surround them or who are subordinate to them. All these needs place substantial constraints on what people and groups who have great power typically do within their communities or societies.

For all these reasons, social stratification is usually a cultural strategy that, if it is to work over the long run, must be sustained by some type of agreement at least on the surface. Those with more power can better initiate and perpetuate these agreements and thereby maintain their privileged positions. People with power, whatever its basis, attempt to create or maintain meaning systems that keep them in power and elicit support from those below them who are taught to view the existing meaning system as "natural" and "right." Not all people learn this lesson. For those who do not, coercive strategies are typically used.

The creation and perpetuation of acceptable and working meaning systems is a major control strategy used by those in power. Gaetano Mosca (1858–1941) in his book, *The Ruling Class*, pointed out that:

> Ruling classes do not justify their power exclusively by de facto possession of it, but try to find a moral and legal basis for it, representing it as the logical and necessary consequence of doctrines and beliefs that are generally recognized and accepted.[3]

We will examine systems of stratification within a framework that assumes that for the most part they will result from the use of cultural control strategies. There is always the latent possibility of the use of coercive strategies if the agreement sustaining the stratification system is not accepted by individuals or groups within it. (Acceptance, in turn, may occur because of the absence of viable alternatives.) We will look first at the three major kinds of criteria that are used as bases for stratification and then examine historical examples of each. We will conclude with a detailed examination of the American system of social stratification and its multiple effects on the life-styles and life-chances of those who live within it, paying special attention to social mobility.

MAJOR DIMENSIONS OF STRATIFICATION

Max Weber suggested that there were three broad orders or dimensions of social stratification within which people might be ranked: *class, status* (prestige), and *power.*

Gerth and Mills, following Weber, define the concepts of class, status, and power succinctly:

> *Class* situation, in its simplest objective sense, has to do with the amount and source (property or work) of income as these affect the chances of people to obtain other available values.
> *Status* involves the successful realization of claims to prestige; it refers to the distribution of deference in a society.
> *Power* refers to the realization of one's will, even if this involves the resistance of others.[4]

We will briefly describe each of these three dimensions of social stratification and then examine their interrelationships.

Economic Order and Class Ranking

For Weber, a person's *class* position "is determined by the amount and kind of ability or lack of such to dispose of goods and services for the sake of income in a given economic order."[5] In the economic order, a person who has a low income, and thus a low access to socially valued goods and services, will occupy a lower class position than a person with access to and disposition of greater income and more goods and services.*

In modern industrial societies, *occupation* is a key determinant of class ranking because it is the principal source of income for most persons; it sets the limits on their ability to dispose of goods and services for the sake of income. In societies where hereditary wealth

---

*Weber's formal definition of class follows:
We may speak of a "class" when (1) a number of people have in common a specific component of their life chances, insofar as (2) this component is represented exclusively by economic interests in the possession of goods and opportunity for income, and (3) is represented under the conditions of the commodity of labor markets. Max Weber, "Class, Status, Party," From *Max Weber: Essays in Sociology,* trans. and ed. by H. H. Gerth and C. Wright Mills (New York: Oxford U.P., 1958), p. 18.

(often in land) is important, class position may be relatively independent of occupation.

Status Order and Prestige Ranking

In discussing status groups within the social order, Weber says:

> In contrast to the purely economically determined "class situation" we wish to designate as "status situation" every typical component of the life fate of men that is determined by a specific, positive or negative, social estimate of honor (prestige).[6]

What is evaluated in giving or withholding prestige is a person's *style of life*. Persons with a style of life defined as "proper"—for example, being a "lady" or "gentleman" or being religious—have high prestige. Persons who are either denied access to such proper styles of life or do not choose them have low prestige in their community or society.

Those persons or groups with the most power often can create and perpetuate the social definition of what is and is not a proper style of life in a particular community or society. People who have the power to prescribe certain styles of life thus may place themselves higher in prestige and others lower. Their power may derive from money, or family heritage, or access to the "gods," or political position. In a pluralistic society with many different subcultures, the agreements for prestige ranking usually differ from subculture to subculture because life-styles are different within each.

Party Order and Power Ranking

Weber points out that "parties live in a house of power." Even though parties may exist in formal groups they are most likely to have their basis within the formal political structure of a community or society. Persons with political power typically have a staff of persons available who are ready to enforce the rules that are laid down.[7] Persons with little political power place low in the party order, whereas those with great political power place high.

The political system in modern societies often dominates other areas of the society. In our discussion of the tendency toward mass society we noted the increase in centralization of control and the emergence of elite groups who can dominate societies containing hundreds of millions of persons through bureaucratic control strategies and use of the mass media. We will return to this in detail when we examine the social basis of political economy in Chapter 10.

Interrelationships Among the Three Major Dimensions

Weber decided that three separate dimensions of stratification systems were required to understand both ancient and modern societies for two major reasons. First, the three dimensions (class, status, and power) may vary independently within a given society, giving rise to problems of consistency and inconsistency in social rank held by persons and groups. Second, the relative importance among the three differs widely in different societies and in the same society over time.

Ranking Consistency and Inconsistency

If the three dimensions of ranking always varied together, persons with high income would also have high prestige and high power. This, however, does not always occur. A successful prostitute may have high income but in modern societies has relatively low prestige (and, thus, low status) and little political power. A Supreme Court justice has high prestige and power but only a middle-level income. A teacher has a relatively low income, but has moderate prestige and, thus, a median rank in the status order along with little political power and, thus, low rank in the party order.

Sociologists call the situation where a person ranks high in one dimension of stratification but relatively low in one or more of the others, *status inconsistency*. This has been a fertile area for much modern social research. Walter Runciman, for example, suggests two possible consequences for individuals experiencing status inconsistency:

> First, the individual will attempt to bring his two (or more) discrepant ranks into equilibrium either by raising his rank on the attribute where his status is low or by denying the validity of the criterion according to which this low rank has been assigned. Second, until he has succeeded in this (and the second alternative depends in any case more on others than on himself), he will remain in a state of psychological stress. It accordingly follows that the many people whose ranks are not all in equilibrium may be expected to evidence social attitudes and behavior significantly different from those whose ranks are "congruent."[8]

Status inconsistency, because of the discrepancy that is present, also has implications for individual meaning. If status inconsistency is present, the individual's world does not fit together in a *meaningful* manner.

In general, there is a relatively high degree of consistency in the ranking of positions across all three orders. Persons ranking high in one order (economic, status, or party) will tend to rank high in the other two.

Societal Variability

The three dimensions of ranking have varying importance under different historical conditions. For example, Weber points out that:

> When the bases of the acquisition and distribution of goods and services are relatively stable, stratification by status is favored. Every technological repercussion and economic transformation threatens stratification by status and pushes the class situation into the foreground.[9]

This fundamental insight will guide us in discussing the three major types of stratification systems and their historical changes. The Great Transformation from folk community to urban society involved this fundamental shift from the dominance of status order and prestige ranking in the folk community to the dominance of economic order and class ranking in the urban society.

MAJOR TYPES OF STRATIFICATION SYSTEMS

We will examine in some detail three major types of stratification systems: the caste system, as exemplified in Indian society; the estate system, as exemplified in feudal societies; and the class system, as exemplified in industrial societies.* In each case we will look at how the use of control strategies affects the three major dimensions of ranking and some of the consequences for the life-styles and life-chances of those who live within such a system.

Before beginning our discussion, we must elaborate further on the concepts of meaning and social consciousness introduced in Chapters 1 and 2.

Meaning and Social Consciousness

Because each type of stratification system is based primarily on cultural agreements, it has significance for individual meaning. *Where in the system of stratification individuals and groups are placed determines not only their life-styles and life-chances but how they view themselves and the world.* In Chapter 2 we discussed Marx's concept of false consciousness, which he used to explain how individuals or groups who are objectively deprived by a stratification system may still support it.

The Polish sociologist Stanislaw Ossowski has expanded and elaborated this idea into a concept of *social consciousness*:

---

*Class used in this sense has a somewhat different meaning than Weber gave it. This will become clearer in the discussion of subsequent class systems.

I shall be using the term as an abbreviation to refer to the ideas that characterize certain milieux, for the concepts, images, beliefs, and evaluations that are more or less common to people of a certain social environment and which are reinforced in the consciousness of particular individuals by mutual suggestion and by the conviction that they are shared by other people in the same group.[10]

This definition includes the necessary components for meaning discussed in Chapter 1: belief, values, and shared convictions. Social stratification is based on the presence of both differential power and social consciousness. Power maintains the stratified order and the social consciousness provides the basis for the required meaning. Under certain conditions the social consciousness may be different for different groups, depending on their place in the hierarchy of ranking. Lord and serf, plantation owner and slave, Brahmin and Untouchable, millionaire and indigent are extreme possibilities within different types of stratification systems. People in each of these social positions have a social consciousness that either supports the stratification system or opposes it, depending on their available alternatives. Their social consciousness, whatever its content, is an attempt by people to make sense of their existence within the framework of a stratified social structure. What Marx calls class consciousness is one type of social consciousness.

The Caste System and the Status Order

A caste system is "a hierarchy of endogamous divisions in which membership is hereditary and permanent."[11] Marriage outside the caste is prohibited. A person is born into a caste and cannot escape from it. The social position of caste member is permanently ascribed. Interaction among members of different castes is restricted and often regulated by strictly prescribed ritual patterns. Widely shared values, often based on a religion, typically stabilize the caste system and provide individual meaning to the members of the various castes.

Because the traditional Indian caste system is the most widely known and pervasive, our discussion is based on it.

Origins of the Caste System

A caste system has its primary basis in the status order. As Weber points out: "The development of status is essentially a question of stratification resting upon usurption. [Usurption is the seizure of power or rights by force or other unlawful means]. Such usurption is the normal origin of almost all status honor."[12] If this usurption becomes complete the status group becomes a closed caste.

There is considerable debate about how the caste system in India began. Some scholars find its origin in the invasions by the more powerful light-skinned Aryans who reduced the darker-skinned indigenous people to positions of subservience. Skin color is seen by some as the important factor in determining status rank. Other scholars believe the conquerors assigned low status occupations to the indigenous population and that, therefore, occupational division of labor is the basis for caste divisions.[13]

There is perhaps some truth in both positions. The Hindu word for caste, *varna,* means color. On the other hand, the names of the four major castes indicate occupations: Brahman-priest, Kshatriya-warriors and governors, Vaisya-merchants and agricultural workers, and Sudra-menial jobs. The outcasts, or Untouchables, were assigned the lowliest work.

The Caste System in India Today

In describing what caste is *not,* Taya Zinkin says:

> It is not class. In every caste there are educated and uneducated, in most there are rich and poor, wellborn and ordinarily born. Most members of the upper classes are in fact from upper castes, most members of the lowest classes are in fact Untouchables; but the correlation is not necessary, and is diminishing.

The Untouchables and the Brahmans: Caste Taboos

The extent and the detail of the ritual regulation of interaction in the caste system are difficult for most of us to imagine. They are conveyed clearly in this description, which should make it easier to understand the slowness with which the Indian caste system has changed and the drastic alterations in life-styles, social consciousness, and meaning systems that these changes entail:

> The whole set of gradations prescribed among castes was based on the idea of purity of the Brahman and the utter impurity of the untouchables. Most fantastic was the belief that the breath, or even the shadow, of an untouchable would pollute another person. In some places untouchables were required to wear clothes over their mouths in order that their breath might not pollute. In Poona they were not permitted within the city walls between 3 P.M. and 9 A.M. because during the early morning and late afternoon sun their bodies cast long shadows. In at least one area there were not only untouchables but unseeables. A caste of washerwomen had to do their work between midnight and daybreak and not show themselves except during the hours of darkness. All castes other than Brahmans were graded in terms of their purity by the extent of provisions to

It is not color, though the old pundits sometimes talk as if it were. A Brahman is no less a Brahman if he is born jet-black; an Untouchable is no less Untouchable if she happens to be fair. Most upper-caste people are fairer than most lower-caste people of their region, and fairness is a quality which is most valued in a bride; but one cannot tell caste from color. People refuse to take water from Untouchables, not from black men. White men, after all, are Untouchables.[14]

Zinkin indicates there is *some* relationship today between caste and occupation.

The four major castes or *varnes* still exist, but within each literally thousands of subcastes or *jati* have developed. The caste system in India has changed over time as persons in different castes and *jati* have used a variety of control strategies to improve their positions in the *status* order.

The Brahmans and the Kshatriyas have formed a power elite and hold many of the important positions of power even in contemporary India. The social consciousness of the caste system is deeply entrenched in and perpetuated by the Hindu religion. Numerous rituals specify the various elements of behavior that structure the caste system over which the Brahmans preside as the high priests. They have a vested interest in maintaining the existing system and its social consciousness because it gives them, and the Kshatriya, maximum status.

Historically, and even today in isolated villages, a person's occupation, whom he may marry, and with whom and how persons of one

safeguard them against pollution by untouchables. The untouchable who could not, for instance, come closer than 124 feet to a Brahman might come within half that distance to an intermediate caste person and as near as seven feet to some lower caste person. In another area the specified gradations of distance were 96 feet down to 36 feet, the specified distance from Brahmans always being the greatest. Wells were polluted if a low caste man drew water from them. The water of a stream was polluted if a Sudra was permitted to walk across a bridge over it. A low caste man could pollute an idol in a temple if he came closer than seven feet and if he did not cover his mouth and nostrils with his hands. Even the glance of a man of low caste falling on a cooking pot would necessitate throwing away the contents of the pot. Public roads which came near temples could not be traveled by untouchables. There were places where untouchables were required to carry sticks or brooms not only so that they might be easily identified but to designate their status.[a]

The physical distance that walled off the untouchables from the other castes reflected the social distance between their position in the caste hierarchy and the positions of the higher ranks.

[a]Carl Taylor, Douglas Ensminger, Helen Johnson, and Jean Joyce, *India's Roots of Democracy* (London: Longmans, 1965), pp. 48–50.

caste may interact with persons of other castes are spelled out in ritually fixed rules. If these rules are disobeyed, a person is ostracized in this life and is believed to have no possibility of being reborn into a higher caste in the next life. These ritual rules, embedded in the social consciousness, keep people in their designated places, perpetuate the high prestige of the Brahmans, and maintain a basis for meaning.

Some *group* mobility has occurred through Sanskritization. In this process a lower *varna* or *jati* takes on the rites and customs of the Brahmans and then makes a claim to higher social position. Furthermore, as India becomes urbanized and industrialized, certain constraints are placed on people to break or change ritual rules. Urbanization produces physical mobility and the possibility of social mobility. Industrialization introduces the constraints of a modernizing economy. An Untouchable, working in the same factory with a Brahman, finds it difficult to maintain the ritually prescribed physical distance. In recent years there have been organized demands by lower-caste people for a chance to compete for high administrative positions that would place them on a *class* level with the Brahmans and Kshatriyas who have tended to usurp these new positions.

The social ordering of India is changing as new control strategies come into use by the lower castes. The new Indian constitution makes the position of Untouchable illegal. Thus, procedural strategies are also being used to form the "new" India. Caste remains important especially in isolated rural areas, but the power of Brahmans, which historically rested on a religiously sanctioned status order and a closed caste system, is breaking down. Just as Weber predicted, industrialization is causing the economic order with its class system to take precedence over the status order and its caste system. This change will cause a crisis in the historic meaning system as it affects the social consciousness of the people. The new social consciousness that will emerge may be based on nationalism, just as it was in industrializing western European countries in the eighteenth and nineteenth centuries.

The Estate System and the Party Order

The estate system of social stratification is typically present within feudal societies, which are based on the control of land and are protected by legal power. Joshua Prawer and Shmuel N. Eisenstadt summarize the "minimal" common characteristics of a fully developed feudal system:

(1) lord-vassal relationships; (2) a personalized government that is more effective at the local level and has relatively little separation of political functions; (3) a system of landholding consisting of the granting of fiefs in

return for services and assurances of future services; (4) the existence of private armies and a code of honor in which obligations in military are stressed; and (5) seignorial and manorial rights of the lord over the peasant.[15]

Feudal systems have existed in many societies, but we will restrict our discussion to the development of the feudal system in Europe, which had its beginnings in the breakup of the Roman Empire and the resulting power vacuum. As the Roman Empire collapsed the great cities and extensive system of commerce that held it together began to disintegrate. People became almost completely dependent on the land for subsistence. Holding political power made it possible to own land. Land became important in the social consciousness of the people, although religion remained of primary importance for meaning, especially among the peasantry.

The lord was placed at the top of the stratification pyramid because he controlled the land of his domain. He granted fiefs (parcels of land) to vassals. The size of the fief depended on the vassal's degree of importance to the lord. In return for the land, vassals agreed to serve in a variety of ways: they became tax collectors, knights, and scribes. Peasants were bound to the land and were at the bottom of the pyramid. They could keep some of what they produced, but owed the major portion to the lord or one of his vassals in return for protection. The importance of land was deeply embedded in the social consciousness because it provided the basis for economic subsistence and for prestige evaluation. The lords, who formed the elite, jealously controlled the land in their domain. Every peasant dreamed of being granted a fief, but this seldom occurred.

The peasantry formed what was legally the Third Estate, the clergy formed the Second Estate, and the nobility the First Estate. Harold M. Hodges points out that:

> Status, economic, and power inequalities occurred within the Third Estate. . . . In general the more rural and isolated a feudal system, the more depressed and homogeneous was the lot of the peasant, and the more servile and serflike his status. But in those areas situated along trade routes, and blessed with prolonged periods of peace and growing agricultural surpluses, a new element—*the bourgeoisie*—emerged. Its evolution was gradual but inexorable.[16]

The emerging *bourgeoisie* gradually moved to the growing trade centers that developed into towns. They formed guilds to protect their interests. Because their skills were needed, their power increased. They slowly acquired a legal recognition separate from that of the peasantry. This group developed the new merchant class and ushered in the commercial revolution. This lengthy process began in the twelfth century and culminated in the French Revolution, which signaled the shift from a system of stratification based on the ownership of land and protected by the power of the nobility to a system of stratification based on economic power with a class system of stratification.

Class System and Economic Order

According to Weber, a person's class is determined by his ability to dispose of goods and services for the sake of income in a given economic order. Low income thus results in low class ranking and high income in high class ranking. Weber identified the dominance of the economic order with its class system as *the* fundamental change that accompanied industrialization and marked the shift from feudal to modern societies. However, Weber also insisted on the independent variability and significance of the other two dimensions of stratification in all societies, including the industrialized.

For Karl Marx, the economic order and social class were the keys to understanding the historical process. Class was the sole significant dimension of social stratification in societies. The history of mankind was the history of the struggle between oppressor and oppressed. Their relationship was determined by the control of the means of production. In industrialized societies, the capitalist class controlled the means of production and the proletariat provided the labor and the surplus value that supported the entire system.

For Marx, social and cultural values, norms, life-styles, life-chances, and all other patterns of social life were determined by the relationships that existed in the economic order. For Weber, cultural values and social institutions could vary independently of the economic order and might themselves determine what occurred there, rather than be "superstructures" determined by arrangements in the economic system.

As an example of a class system based on the economic order we have selected the stratification system of the United States, which will be examined in detail in the balance of this chapter. However, first, we must review and clarify the relationship between social consciousness and meaning systems on the one hand and stratification systems on the other.

SOCIAL CONSCIOUSNESS, INDIVIDUAL MEANING, AND STRATIFICATION SYSTEMS

A major problem for a system of stratification based on political or economic power is the extreme *difficulty* of establishing a stable basis for meaning solely on raw political or economic power. There is, therefore, a tendency for groups having political and/or economic power to establish the criteria for prestige in the status order so that a source of meaning is present not only for themselves but also for the masses who they hope will support them. The social consciousness of all groups would then support the existing ranking systems in the economic and political orders, the ruling groups would receive the prestige they need, and there would tend to be status consistency because those with the greatest income and power would also have the greatest prestige.

The Status Order and Meaning

For Weber, the status order is the primary locus for meaning. A person's style of life is *evaluated*. This style of life must be based on a criterion that tends to produce at least the possibility of meaning and social honor. The Brahmans in the Indian caste system based their power on a religious foundation that provided social consciousness and meaning. During the early feudal period the holders of political power supported the established church, which in turn gave them legitimacy and provided some meaning to the peasants. The Holy Wars and the Crusades served both religious and nonreligious purposes. The crusading knights were given social honor because they were supposedly carrying out the will of God. The status order during the feudal period, at least on the surface, had a religious basis. The peasants were poor, but religion promised them a good life in heaven after death. The nobility enjoyed their wealth and the luxury it brought them as well as the deference they received from those below. They were held, or at least saw themselves as being held, in high honor.

Chivalry and the *noblesse oblige* attitude were prevalent during the feudal period. The lord saw it as his Christian duty to take care of the peasants in his domain and he received some gratification from so doing. Of course, the peasants might not have needed this "care" (except for military protection) if the lords' taxes had been lower.

Power thus works to maintain privilege. The sociologist Toennies sums up this thought:

> Ever since the beginning of culture, this holiness of men has been the most favorable legitimation of authority, based on the reverence and humility of people. And something of this holiness remains as an attribute of the secular ruling estates and their consummations, the princely estates and kingship. Closely related as it is to the original dignity of age, this element of holiness lends dignity to these estates.[17]

The Economic Order and Meaning: Marx and Weber

The basis of power in the economic order presents the same problem of meaning. Karl Marx and Friedrich Engels put the matter squarely in the *Communist Manifesto*:

The bourgeoisie, wherever it has got the upper hand, has put an end to all feudal, patriarchal, idyllic relations. It has pitilessly torn asunder the motley feudal ties that bound man to his "natural superiors" and has left no other bond between man and man than naked self-interest, than callous "cash payment." It has drowned the most heavenly ecstasies of religious fervor, of chivalrous enthusiasm, of philistine sentimentalism, in the icy water of egotistical calculation. It has resolved personal worth into exchange value, and in place of the numberless indefeasible chartered freedoms, has set up that single, unconscionable freedom—Free Trade. In one word, for exploitation, veiled by religious and political illusions, it has substituted naked, shameless, direct, brutal exploitation.[18]

For Marx and Engels, any satisfactory basis for meaning is impossible where differential power is based primarily within the economic order. The bond between people is reduced to "the raw cash nexus." Religion they saw as "an opiate of the people." It promised a blessed life after death, thus promoting false consciousness and preventing the masses from revolting against their oppressors.

The Protestant Ethic

Weber saw the problem of meaning in a system of stratification based on the economic order differently.[19] He maintained that the sufficient conditions for capitalism's emergence had occurred in a religiously based meaning system he called the Protestant ethic. The Protestant ethic derived from the theology espoused by John Calvin, who lived in the sixteenth century.* Calvin taught that from the beginning of time people were either saved or damned by God. Every person's fate in the hereafter was predestined by God and there was nothing one could do to change this decree. Neither faith nor good works could save the damned, nor could those who were saved fall from grace.

People were placed on earth as the servants of God and, as such, should work diligently to subdue nature for His glory. Work became a calling coming from God. Diligent work might bring economic success, but one's earnings were not to be spent frivolously for immediate or personal pleasure or display. Pleasure was the handmaiden of the devil. The money earned was saved, accumulated, and used as investment capital. God's call to each person to work for His glory, no matter how lowly the task, created an organized disciplined work force for the capitalist who had money to invest.

Economic success gradually came to be seen as an outward and visible sign of the inward and spiritual grace of God's election. Those who became successful saw themselves as saved. The economically

*The juxtaposition of the Protestant ethic and the growth of capitalism was a historical accident not intended by the Calvinists.

unsuccessful were seen as damned. Success became equated with virtue: the wealthy were "good" and the poor were damned and "evil." The criterion for evaluation in the status order became economic success. The problem of meaning was solved for the capitalist by the religious processes, which were the seedbed for capitalism. A wealthy person could not wish for a more advantageous solution.[20]

Today the Protestant ethic has become secularized and has lost its religious basis, but the tendency to see rich people as good and poor people as evil remains as part of the social consciousness of many persons and groups. Those who are rich or have the hope of becoming rich hold this point of view more extensively than others. The rich and well off still stereotype the poor as lazy and no good and honor those who work hard even though the work may be meaningless. Thrift, prudence, and saving remain virtues for many people. Although our cultural values about these activities have changed in recent years, the secularized Protestant ethic is still very much with us.

Many of the conflicts and controversies between subcultural groups in contemporary America can be interpreted as collisions between older value systems based on the secularized Protestant ethic and rooted in industrial capitalism and postindustrial value systems supported by affluence and based on values that espouse individual expressiveness. Those who condemn the "long-haired hippies" as being afraid of work, who degrade those receiving public assistance as lazy welfare bums and shirkers, and who continue to believe that a penny saved is a penny earned have difficulty communicating with anyone who is seeking new or different bases for individual meaning.

SOCIAL CLASS IN THE UNITED STATES

Introduction

We will pursue the problems of the economic order and social class by looking at social class in the United States. Other aspects of the American stratification system, including the system of minority group stratification and the relations among ethnic groups will be discussed in Chapter 8.

There are three major problems. (1) The realities of class: do classes in fact exist? If so, how many are there? How are they measured and by what criteria? (2) What are the life-styles and other behaviors associated with the social class system? (3) How does the class system affect the life-chances of those who live within it?

Realities of Social Class

There is considerable debate in contemporary sociology about whether or not there are in fact classes in modern industrial societies. Some sociologists argue that socially distinct classes no longer exist.[21] Instead, they argue that there is a system of gradual ranking where no sharp meaningful class lines can be drawn. From this point of view it is not useful to talk about social classes, even though one may still talk about ranking.

Others take the Marxist view that there are only two major classes: the capitalists who own or control the means of production and the proletariat who have nothing but their labor power to sell. Still other

---

The Protestant Work Ethic, the Renaissance Ethic, and Work in Modern Society

C. Wright Mills, who contributed so much to our understanding of the structure of modern society, contrasted two historical views about work, the Protestant ethic, with its focus on compulsive labor to fulfill God's will, and the Renaissance concept, with its belief in the fulfilling and creative function of work and its exuberant emphasis on skill and craftsmanship:

[For Calvin] It was necessary to act in the world rationally and methodically and continuously and hard, as if one were certain of being among those elected. It is God's will that everyone must work, but it is not God's will that one should lust after the fruits even of one's own labor; they must be reinvested to allow and to spur still more labor. Not contemplation, but strong-willed, austere, untiring work, based on religious conviction, will ease guilt and lead to the good and pious life.

The "this-worldly asceticism" of early Protestantism placed a premium upon and justified the styles of conduct and feeling required in its agents by modern capitalism. The Protestant sects encouraged and justified the social development of a type of man capable of ceaseless, methodical labor. . . .

[The Renaissance] . . . men of that exuberant time saw work as a spur rather than a drag on man's development as man. By his own activity, man could accomplish anything; through work, man became creator. How better could he fill his hours? Leonardo da Vinci rejoiced in creative labor; Bruno glorified work as an arm against adversity and a tool of conquest.[a]

The Renaissance view of work, which sees it as intrinsically meaningful, is centered in the technical craftsmanship—the manual and mental operations—of the work process itself; it sees the reasons for work in the work itself and not in any ulterior realm or consequence. Not income, not way of salvation, not status, not power over other people, but the technical processes themselves are gratifying.[b]

Mills goes on to point out that both the Calvinist view of work as a secular road to redemption and the Renaissance view of craftsmanship and creative

sociologists, although disagreeing on the number, believe there are classes and that even though there is some blurring of class lines, meaningful boundaries can be drawn in a class hierarchy.[22] These boundaries are drawn by using such measures as type of occupation, income level, amount of education, and differential power, which will be discussed subsequently.

Changes in the Ranking System

There is agreement, however, that the present system of ranking (or classes) has a different profile from the preindustrial system. The profile of the stratification structure has changed from one that resembled

---

work as intrinsically valuable have foundered on the shoals of industrialized, bureaucraticized societies with their dreary rounds of routine and often meaningless labor:

> Neither of these views, however—the secularized gospel of work as compulsion, nor the humanist view of work as craftsmanship—now has great influence among modern populations. For most employees, work has a generally unpleasant quality. If there is little Calvinist compulsion to work among propertyless factory workers and file clerks, there is also little Renaissance exuberance in the work of the insurance clerk, freight handler, or department-store saleslady. If the shoe salesman or the textile executive gives little thought to the religious meaning of his labor, certainly few telephone operators or receptionists or schoolteachers experience from their work any Ruskinesque inner calm. Such joy as creative work may carry is more and more limited to a small minority. For the white-collar masses, as for wage earners generally, work seems to serve neither God nor whatever they may experience as divine in themselves. In them there is no taut will-to-work, and few positive gratifications from their daily round.
>
> The gospel of work has been central to the historic tradition of America, to its image of itself, and to the images the rest of the world has of America. The crisis and decline of that gospel are of wide and deep meaning.[c]

Work has become a crucial problem in modern societies. The secularized Protestant ethic no longer sounds a clarion call, especially to younger people. The philosophy has shifted from "A penny saved is a penny earned" to "Fly now, pay later." There is in existence an unending series of studies of job satisfaction, alienation from work, how to improve morale and satisfaction among workers, and the consequences for society of this change in social consciousness and meaning systems.

[a]C. Wright Mills, *White Collar* (New York: Oxford U.P., 1956), paperback, pp. 216–217.
[b]Ibid., p. 218–219.
[c]Ibid., p. 219.

FIGURE 7-1
Changes in the Profile of Social Stratification*

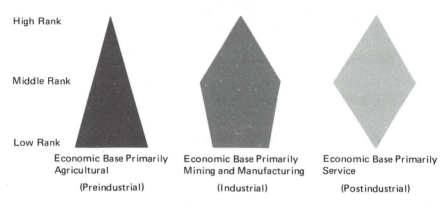

*The shape of each figure is not meant to reflect the exact proportion of people at specific levels. They should be considered as ideal types.

a pyramid to one that is now more in the shape of a diamond.

The change was caused by industrialization. The movement from feudal society whose economic base was agriculture, through an industrial society based primarily on mining and manufacturing, to a postindustrial society increasingly based on providing services changed the profile from a pyramid to a diamond shape as more jobs were created in middle-level positions. Figure 7-1 illustrates the progression.

TABLE 7-1
Money Income—Percent Distribution of Families and Unrelated* Individuals: 1970

Income Level	Families, %	Unrelated Individuals, %
Under $1,000	1.6	11.9
$1,000–1,999	3.0	22.5
$2,000–2,999	4.3	14.2
$3,000–3,999	5.1	10.0
$4,000–4,999	5.3	7.7
$5,000–5,999	5.8	6.4
$6,000–6,999	6.0	5.8
$7,000–7,999	19.9	12.3
$10,000–14,999	26.8	6.3
$15,000 and over	22.3	2.8

*Unrelated individuals are those who live alone. Many of these are older people living on social security.
SOURCE: U. S. Bureau of the Census, *Statistical Abstracts of the United States,* 1972.

Objective Indications of Ranking in American Society

Before examining the evidence for the existence and characteristics of a class system in America, we will briefly review the objective statistical evidence for the unequal distribution of income and related social rewards and facilities.

INCOME

There is clear statistical evidence for the existence of gradations in American society by income. Income, of course, is the principal determinant of class position in the economic order. Our society places a premium on success and success is usually measured by monentary income. Table 7-1 shows the money income distribution of families and unrelated individuals in 1970 and displays a very definite ranking using a purely objective measure with *no* subjective evaluation.

OCCUPATION

Occupations, which are the principal social mechanism through which income is distributed in industrial societies, display income ranking by type of occupation. Table 7-2 shows the median money income for males and females by occupation in 1970.

There is a clear relationship between type of occupation and corresponding income, with persons who are self-employed professional, technical, and kindred workers placing at the top and farm laborers and farm foremen at the bottom on the male side.

The considerable differences between the median incomes of males and females in all occupational categories should be noted in Table 7-2. These differences reflect the results of the historical and present discrimination against women in a male dominated economy along with the traditional pattern of ascription based on sex discussed earlier. More will be said concerning this in the following chapter.

EDUCATION AND INCOME

There are also clear-cut relationships between annual income, expected lifetime income, and level of educational attainment. Table 7-3 shows these relationships for selected years. At the extremes, in 1968 the mean annual income for persons with no education to seven years of education was $3,981 with an expected lifetime income of $196,000; persons with four or more years of college had a mean income of $12,938 and an expected lifetime income of $586,000. Thus, persons with four or more years of college in 1968 could expect to earn nearly three times as much money in their lifetimes as persons with a seventh-grade education or less.

TABLE 7-2
Median Money Income of Persons with Income, by Sex and Occupation—1970

Occupation	Male	Female
	$8,036	$3,844
Professional, technical, and kindred workers	11,577	6,675
Self-employed[1]	17,670	2,463
Salaried	11,249	6,830
Farmers and farm managers	3,859	(B)
Managers, officials, proprietors, except farm	11,292	5,523
Self-employed[1]	7,853	2,910
Salaried	12,304	6,224
Clerical and kindred workers	7,965	4,646
Salesworkers	8,321	2,279
Craftsmen, foremen, and kindred workers	8,833	4,276
Operatives and kindred workers	7,017	3,885
Private household workers	(B)	825
Service workers, except private household	5,568	2,541
Farm laborers and foremen[1]	2,238	1,166
Laborers, except farm and mine	4,839	3,151
Unemployed	3,986	2,040
In Armed Forces or not in labor force	2,159	1,202

B Not shown; base too small.
[1]Includes a small number of unpaid family workers.
SOURCE: United States Bureau of the Census, *Statistical Abstracts of the United States*, 1972.

INCOME AND LIFE-STYLES

These differences in income related, in part, to level of educational attainment and type of occupation are reflected in differential life-styles. Persons with higher incomes can better afford the possession of such amenities as late-model automobiles, color television sets, travel, and the other accouterments of affluent living.[23] As Weber indicated, there is a relationship between differential income in the class order and life-styles which serve as the basis for ranking in the status order.

We have shown that in American society there are unequal distributions of income. Some people get a lot, others get a fair amount, and still others get relatively little money income. Furthermore, some occupations are highly remunerated, whereas others are relatively poorly paid. We have also suggested that amount of education and possession of socially valued goods are correlated with money income and occupation. Ours is clearly not an egalitarian society.

There is, therefore, ranking in the economic order of modern societies distinguishable objectively by income and related indices.

TABLE 7-3
Lifetime and Mean Income of Males 25 Years Old and Over, by Years of School Completed: 1949 to 1968

[Prior to 1961, excludes Alaska and Hawaii. Includes members of the Armed Forces living off post or with their families on post, but excludes a other members of the Armed Forces. Figures for lifetime income based on application of appropriate life tables to arithmetic mean income, by age as obtained for a cross section of population in each year shown.]

Year	Elementary		High School		College	
	0–7 years	8 years	1–3 years	4 years	1–3 years	4 years or more
Lifetime income ($1,000):						
1949	91	123	142	175	202	287
1956[1]	122	166	189	228	268	359
1961[1]	142	192	223	257	325	437
1967:						
Computed from grouped data[1]	183	246	283	338	401	558
Computed from ungrouped data[2]	177	240	275	325	383	529
1968, computed from ungrouped data[2]	196	258	294	350	411	586
Annual mean income:						
1949	$2,062	$2,829	$3,226	$3,784	$4,423	$6,179
1956[1]	2,574	3,631	4,367	5,183	5,997	7,877
1961[1]	2,998	4,206	5,161	5,946	7,348	9,817
1967:						
Computed from grouped data[1]	3,715	5,280	6,529	7,907	9,229	12,532
Computed from ungrouped data[2]	3,606	5,189	6,335	7,629	8,843	11,924
1968, computed from ungrouped data[2]	3,981	5,467	6,769	8,148	9,397	12,938

[1]Based on estimated mean values for specific income class intervals.
[2]Based on actual reported amounts.
SOURCE: United States Bureau of the Census, *Statistical Abstracts of the United States, 1972*

Prestige Ranking

Gradations also exist in the prestige ranking of occupations in the United States. Two nationwide studies, the first in 1947 and the second in 1963, show that this ranking holds quite constantly over time. People in these studies were asked to judge ninety different occupations by social standing in the community on a scale ranging from excellent to poor. The results are shown in Table 7-4.

This table shows that people do accord significantly higher prestige to some occupations than to others, a ranking that remained constant over a sixteen-year period. People in certain occupations are accorded more social honor than people in other occupations and thus have a higher social standing in the community.

All of this appears simple, straightforward, and about what most Americans would expect. However, the existence of rankings that are definable by objective economic indices such as income (which in turn is correlated with occupation and education) and by subjective indices such as the ranking of occupations by prestige, begs an important question. Is it useful in analyzing the American system of stratification to group rankings into social classes?

Measuring Social Class

In the discussion of community power in Chapter 5 we discovered that *how* community power was measured affected what power groups were discovered in the community. The same is true when one attempts to establish the existence and significance of social classses. The literature in American sociology about social class is voluminous, reflecting the central role of stratification as a control strategy in modern society. Two major approaches to measuring (and thus to defining) social class have developed: the *reputational approach* and the *subjective approach*. We will consider them in turn to see what they reveal about the realities of social class in the American stratification system.

The Reputational Approach

The most important studies using the reputational approach have been by W. Lloyd Warner and his associates who attempted to determine the number of social classes and their characteristics in different American communities.[24] The reputational approach uses community informants who rank themselves and others to establish the various class levels in the community.

Warner and his associates used a variety of criteria to assign individuals in a community to a given social class and thus to identify the

TABLE 7-4
Occupational Prestige Ratings, 1947* and 1963†

Occupation	Score 1947	Score 1963	Occupation	Score 1947	Score 1963
U.S. Supreme Court			Musician in a symphony		
Justice	96	94	orchestra	81	78
Physician	93	93	Author of novels	80	78
Nuclear physicist	86	92	Economist	79	78
Scientist	89	92	Official of an		
Government scientist	88	91	international labor		
State governor	93	91	union	75	77
Cabinet member in the			Railroad engineer	76	76
federal gov't.	92	90	Electrician	73	76
College professor	89	90	County agricultural agent	77	76
U.S. Representative in			Owner-operator of a		
Congress	89	90	printing shop	74	75
Chemist	86	89	Trained machinist	73	75
Lawyer	86	89	Farm owner and operator	76	74
Diplomat in U.S. Foreign			Undertaker	72	74
Service	92	89	Welfare worker for a city		
Dentist	86	88	government	73	74
Architect	86	88	Newspaper columnist	74	73
County judge	87	88	Policeman	67	72
Psychologist	85	87	Reporter on a daily		
Minister	87	87	newspaper	71	71
Member of the board of			Radio announcer	75	70
directors of a large			Bookkeeper	68	70
corporation	86	87	Tenant farmer—one who		
Mayor of a large city	90	87	owns livestock and		
Priest	86	86	machinery and		
Head of a dept. in state			manages the farm	68	69
government	87	86	Insurance agent	68	69
Civil engineer	86	86	Carpenter	65	68
Airline pilot	83	86	Manager of a small store		
Banker	88	85	in a city	69	67
Biologist	81	85	A local official of a labor		
Sociologist	82	83	union	62	67
Instructor in public			Mail carrier	66	66
schools	79	82	Railroad conductor	67	66
Captain in the regular			Traveling salesman for a		
army	80	82	wholesale concern	64	66
Accountant for a large			Plumber	63	65
business	81	81	Automobile repairman	63	64
Public school teacher	78	81	Playground director	67	63
Owner of a factory that			Barber	59	63
employs about 100			Machine operator in a		
people	82	80	factory	60	63
Building contractor	79	80	Owner-operator of a		
Artist who paints pictures			lunch stand	62	63
that are exhibited in			Corporal in the regular		
galleries	83	78	army	60	62

TABLE 7-4 *(cont)*
Occupational Prestige Ratings, 1947° and 1963†

Occupation	Score 1947	Score 1963	Occupation	Score 1947	Score 1963
Garage mechanic	62	62	Restaurant waiter	48	49
Truck driver	54	59	Taxi driver	49	49
Fisherman who owns his			Farm hand	50	48
own boat	58	58	Janitor	44	48
Clerk in a store	58	56	Bartender	44	48
Milk route man	54	56	Clothes presser in a		
Streetcar motorman	58	56	laundry	46	45
Lumberjack	53	55	Soda fountain clerk	45	44
Restaurant cook	54	55	Sharecropper—one who		
Singer in a nightclub	52	54	owns no livestock or		
Filling station attendant	52	51	equipment and does		
Dockworker	47	50	not manage farm	40	42
Railroad section hand	48	50	Garbage collector	35	39
Night watchman	47	50	Street sweeper	34	36
Coal miner	49	50	Shoe shiner	33	34
Average	*70*	*71*			

*Cecil C. North and Paul K. Hatt, "Jobs and Occupations: A Popular Evaluation," *Opinion News,* Vol. 9 (Sept. 1947), pp. 3–13.
†Robert W. Hodge, Paul M. Siegel, and Peter H. Rossi, "Occupational Prestige in the United States: 1925–1963," *American Journal of Sociology,* Vol. 70 (Nov. 1964), pp. 286–302. Used by Permission.

social classes. For example, they asked their community informants to identify what they perceived as the number and rank of the social classes and to assign specific persons to each class. They then measured agreement among the informants to establish classes. They also assigned individuals to a given social class if informants said they were equal, superior to, or inferior to persons whose social class had already been established. Gradually they built up a body of data about the various social classes that included the economic status of those in each; their life-styles; their religious and institutional affiliations and behaviors; the sources of their income; the type, size, and location of their homes; and a variety of other data.[25]

In his study of Yankee City, a small city in the eastern part of the nation, conducted in the late 1930s and early 1940s, Warner isolated six classes. Considerable blurring and overlapping is found at the borders of each class. Joseph A. Kahl provides a summary description of each of these six classes and the percentage of people falling into each class:

1. Upper-upper, 1.4 per cent of the total population. This group was the old-family elite, based on sufficient wealth to maintain a large

house in the best neighborhood, but the wealth had to have been in the family for more than one generation. This generational continuity permitted proper training in basic value orientations and established people as belonging to a lineage.
2. Lower-upper, 1.6 per cent. This group was, on the average, slightly richer than the upper-uppers, but their money was newer, their manners thus not quite so polished, their sense of lineage and security less pronounced.
3. Upper-middle, 10.2 per cent. The moderately successful business and professional men and their families, but less affluent than the lower-uppers. Some education and polish were necessary for membership, but lineage was unimportant.
4. Lower-middle, 28.1 per cent. The petty businessmen, the schoolteachers, the foremen in industry. This group tended to have morals that were close to puritan fundamentalism; they were churchgoers, lodge joiners, and flag wavers.
5. Upper-lower, 32.6 per cent. The solid, respectable laboring people who kept their houses clean and stayed out of trouble.
6. Lower-lower, 25.2 per cent. The "lulus" or disrespectable and often slovenly people who dig for clams and waited for public relief.[26]

Another study by the Warner school in a southern city during the late 1930s shows how members of different social classes view each other. The results are shown in Figure 7-2

People see the hierarchy of the social class system differently, depending on where they themselves are located. For example, the upper-upper class and the lower-upper class lump together the upper-lower and lower-lower classes as "po' whites." The upper-middle class sees the two bottom classes as the "no 'count lot," whereas the lower-middle class distinguishes the upper-lower from the lower-lower, viewing only the lower-lower as the "no 'count lot." The upper-lower class sees the lower-lower class as "shiftless people," whereas the lower-lower class sees themselves as "people just as good as anybody."

The specific contents of each category vary from community to community and change over time. The importance of the finding is that people in the various social classes perceive the class system and their place in it differently. This social consciousness and meaning are themselves derived from the class system. The upper classes learn the social consciousness of their class, which defines for them the lower classes as "po' whites" in the example here.

In a study of a Midwestern community, the Warner school found a five-class system, in which the two upper classes found in Yankee City were merged into one upper class. Many sociologists, who believe in social classes rather than in a simple system of ranking, use

FIGURE 7-2
Social Perspectives of the Social Classes

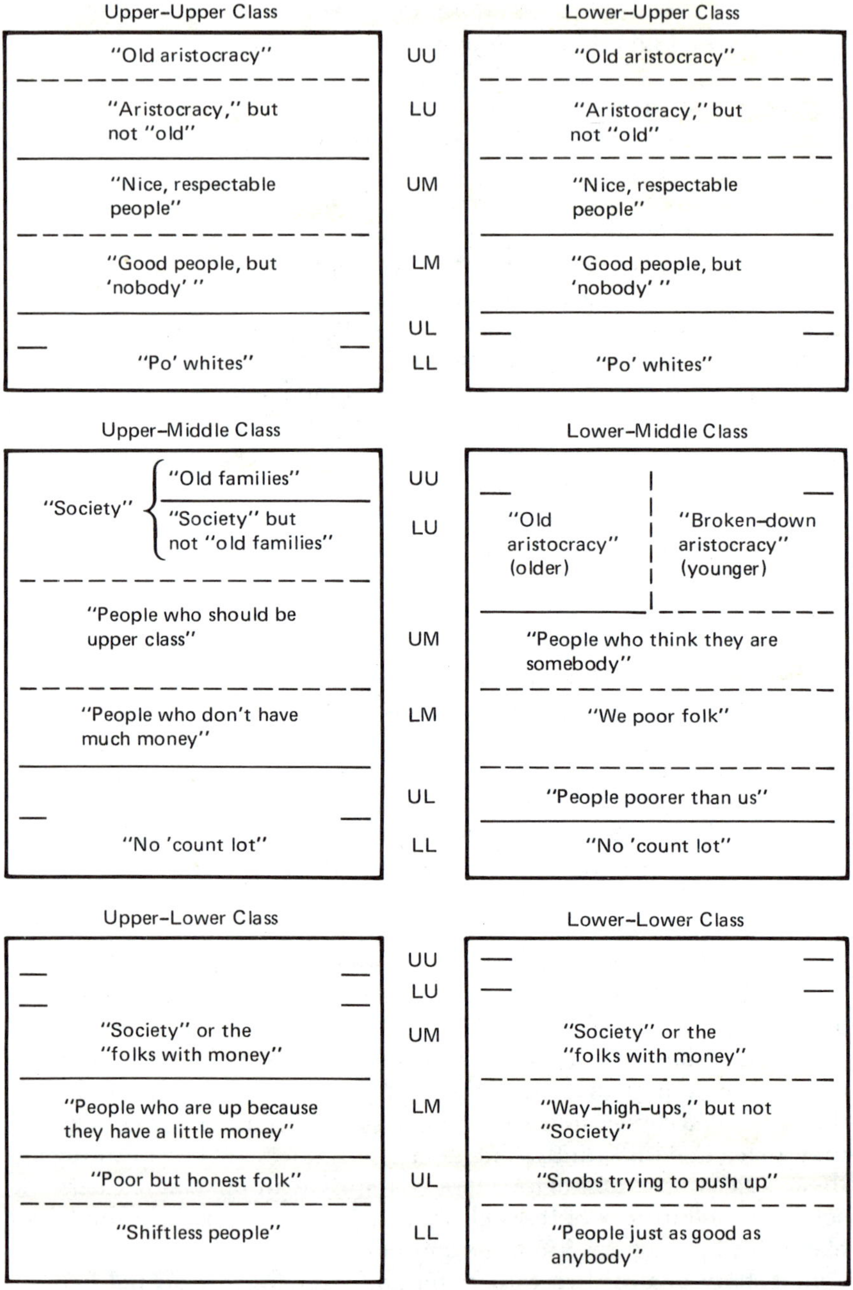

Upper–Upper Class		Lower–Upper Class
"Old aristocracy"	UU	"Old aristocracy"
"Aristocracy," but not "old"	LU	"Aristocracy," but not "old"
"Nice, respectable people"	UM	"Nice, respectable people"
"Good people, but 'nobody' "	LM	"Good people, but 'nobody' "
	UL	
"Po' whites"	LL	"Po' whites"

Upper–Middle Class		Lower–Middle Class
"Society" { "Old families"	UU	
"Society" but not "old families"	LU	"Old aristocracy" (older) / "Broken–down aristocracy" (younger)
"People who should be upper class"	UM	"People who think they are somebody"
"People who don't have much money"	LM	"We poor folk"
	UL	"People poorer than us"
"No 'count lot"	LL	"No 'count lot"

Upper–Lower Class		Lower–Lower Class
	UU	
	LU	
"Society" or the "folks with money"	UM	"Society" or the "folks with money"
"People who are up because they have a little money"	LM	"Way–high–ups," but not "Society"
"Poor but honest folk"	UL	"Snobs trying to push up"
"Shiftless people"	LL	"People just as good as anybody"

SOURCE: Allison Davis, Burleigh B. Gardner, and Mary R. Gardner, *Deep South: A Social-Anthropological Study of Caste and Class* (Chicago: U. of Chicago, 1941), p. 65. Used by permission.

TABLE 7-5
Social Stratification in California Suburbs [1950s]

Level, %	Markings	Personality	Habitat	Diversions
Upper .2	Listing in the Social Register	Conservative; indulges in "inconspicuous consumption"	Doings in "the city"	Partying, gin-rummy, watching baseball; foreign films
Upper-middle 10–15	Professional or executive position, college diploma; $11,000 per year	The "joiner"—gregarious, hyperactive, socially at ease; concerned with "career" and "school"; child-centered and easy-going with children; takes his religion more socially than literally	Service clubs like Kiwanis and Lions	Do-it-yourself projects, *Time*, *Harper's*, Playhouse 90 on TV; bridge, golf
Lower-middle 35	White collar clerk, neighborhood businessman, or foreman; $7,600 per year; a tract home in the suburbs	Togetherness—active church-going; the "typical" American. Says he saves for a rainy day, but more likely than anybody else to own a Cadillac, Lincoln or Buick	Church, lodge, PTA	Bible-reading; gardening (Mr. says he has a greener thumb than Mrs.); the "national favorites" —*Life, Reader's Digest, Saturday Evening Post;* on TV, Perry Mason, Ed Sullivan, 77 Sunset Strip; canasta, watching football
Upper-lower 35–40	A union man; skilled or semi-skilled blue-collar worker; 11 years schooling; $5,500 per year	Closest to the cigarette-ad ideal of the two-fisted, tattooed he-man; ill-at-ease among strangers; wants to improve social position. Likes masculine men and feminine women, but helps with dishes and diapers; has migraine headaches, insomnia	The great out-of-doors Sears, Ward's, Penney's (buying everything on time)	On TV, westerns like Cheyenne and Gunsmoke; poker
Lower-lower 15–20	Usually unskilled laborer; 8 years schooling or less; $3,000 per year	A misanthrope—pessimistic about the future, wary of strangers. Apathetic towards politics. Loyal to family and kinfolk. Wants to be liked; fearful of being an odd-ball or unpopular. "Children should be seen, not heard"	In front of the TV (and waits up for the late, late show)	Bowling; pool; on TV, westerns such as Wagon Train, wrestling and boxing. For wife: romantic magazines

SOURCE: Robert J. Havighurst and Bernice Neugarten, *Society and Education* (Boston: Allyn, 1962), pp. 32–33. Reprinted with permission. (Bracketed material supplied.)

the five-class model, except in communities in which there is a definite "old aristocracy." The power of the old aristocracy, where it exists, is often challenged by the new rich who have considerable wealth and power and control important businesses.

The reputational approach is useful only in those communities small enough for informants to knowledgeably judge many others in the community. In larger cities a variation of this approach is used because people are aware of the prestige ranking of different neighborhoods and of such symbols of prestige as club memberships, occupational differences, and educational and income levels.

Hodges, in his study of 2,000 heads of household in the "peninsula area" from San Francisco to San Jose, California, also isolated five classes.[27] Table 7-5 shows the percentage of his respondents falling into each class and some of the social characteristics of each class.

The percentages of people falling into each class are similar to those falling into Warner's classes. The class characteristics, including lifestyles, that Hodges lists are similar to those found by other

---

Life on the Bottom

The sociologist August Hollingshead conducted a study of a Midwestern community he called Elmtown using the Warner model of the class system to see how the education of adolescents was shaped by the stratification system. As part of his report, Hollingshead provides us with a compelling picture of those at the bottom as seen by the upper classes, whose control strategies serve effectively to keep them "where they belong" and by those who are kept down and show considerable awareness of how and why they are at the bottom of the social heap:

> Class V occupies the lowest-ranking stations in the prestige structure. It is looked upon as the scum of the city by the higher classes. It is believed generally that nothing beyond charity can be done for these people, and only a minimum of that is justified since they show little or no inclination to help themselves. It is the opinion of the upper classes that:
>
> > They have no respect for the law, or themselves.
> > They enjoy their shacks and huts along the river or across the tracks and love their dirty, smoky, low-class dives and taverns.
> > Whole families—children, in-laws, mistresses, and all—live in one shack.
> > This is the crime class that produces the delinquency and sexual promiscuity that fills the paper.
> > Their interests lie in sex and its perversion. The girls are always pregnant; the families are huge; incestual relations occur frequently.
> > They are not inspired by education, and only a few are able to make any attainments along this line.
> > They are loud in their speech, vulgar in their actions, sloppy in their dress,

sociologists in many studies. These characteristics are *approximate profiles* of the general characteristics of the American class structure, although variations occur in some selected communities.

The Subjective Approach

The subjective method of measuring social class placement asks people to place themselves in social classes that are either named by the researcher or left open for a completely spontaneous response by the respondent.

The first major study using this method was carried out in the 1930s by *Fortune Magazine*.[28] Interviewers asked a national cross-section of Americans the question: "What word would you use to name the class in America you belong to?" Among the respondents, 2.9 per cent saw themselves as upper class, 47 per cent saw themselves as middle class, 14.9 per cent defined themselves as working or labor class, and 27.5 per cent indicated they did not know in what class they belonged.

---

and indifferent toward their plight. Their vocabulary develops as profanity is learned.

If they work, they work at very menial jobs.

Their life experiences are purely physical, and even these are on a low plane.

They have no interest in health and medical care.

The men are too lazy to work or do odd jobs around town. . . .

This group lives for a Saturday of drinking or fighting. They are of low character and breed and have a criminal record for a pedigree.

Class V persons, passive and fatalistic, realize that they are "on the bottom" and believe that they can do nothing to improve their position. They desire money, possessions, education, and favorable prestige, but they do not know how these are achieved. When a class V person attempts to improve his position, he is discriminated against by the higher classes, and by many members of his own class who think he is trying to "put on airs." One woman with considerable insight into her class position summarized it thus:

Survival for us depends on staying on good terms with the rich people and the law. Whenever I think about myself and the kids, I am reminded what my father used to say, "We are the ones who are told what to do, when and how" around here. This town takes us for granted. Most people think the people down here [the tannery flats] are too ignorant to do anything and don't care; I guess they're right.

To generalize a little more, class V persons give the impression of being resigned to a life of frustration and defeat in a community that despises them for their disregard of morals, lack of "success" goals, and dire poverty.[a]

[a]Quoted in *Man Alone*, edited by Eric and Mary Josephson. New York: Dell, 1962. Pp. 302–303.

A major nationwide study was conducted in the late 1940s by Richard Centers.[29] His first question was: "If you were asked to use one of these four class names for your social class, which would you say you belonged in: the middle class, lower class, working class, or upper class?" Of his respondents, 3 per cent placed themselves in the upper class, 43 per cent in the middle class, 51 per cent in the working class, 1 per cent in the lower class, 1 per cent responded "don't know," and 1 per cent said they did not believe classes existed.

Centers then compared the respondents' occupational categories with their self-reported class. Table 7-6 shows the split between the respondents in white-collar and higher-prestige occupations who tended to place themselves into the middle and upper class (primarily middle) and the respondents who were skilled workers or in lower-status occupations who tended to place themselves in the working class or lower class (primarily working).

Social Consciousness and Class Perceptions

Centers also asked his respondents: "What would you say places a person in the (upper, middle, working, lower) class?" The self-defined upper-class person chose family origin, wealth, and education as the important criteria for upper-class standing, whereas for others, amount of wealth was the single most important criteria for upper-class placement.

For middle-class placement, money and amount of education were the most important criteria mentioned by middle- and upper-class respondents; working-class people placed a high premium on ownership of a small business, having a profession, or possessing a trade as criteria for placing people in the middle class.

For working-class placement, respondents in all classes mentioned "working for a living," meaning manual, mill, or factory work or labor. Being an employee or wage earner was the most important criterion for working-class placement. Upper- and middle-class people mentioned lack of education as common among working-class people. But "What puts people in the lower class?"

> The most obvious answer is "being poor" and it is by a considerable margin the most frequently received. Poor education or lack of education is next. A surprisingly large proportion of people appear to think of the lower class as a rather despicable group. Poor character and low morals, drink, crime, lack of ability, low intelligence, shiftlessness, laziness, lack of ambition or motivation, menial labor, etc., all indicate the disesteem in which this group is held. The middle and working classes differ little in their responses on the whole. For both of them the term lower class frequently connotes a despised or *declassé* group. The lower class itself is scarcely present in sufficient numbers to defend itself, but those that are present say poverty and lack of education are either the factors that put them there or are the signs by which they distinguish themselves from others.[30]

TABLE 7-6
Occupation and Class Identification

Occupation	N	% Upper Class	% Middle Class	% Working Class	% Lower Class	% Don't Know	% Don't Believe in Classes
Large business	54	13	78	7		2.0	
Professional	73	4	81	10		1.0	4.0
Small business	131	3	70	24		1.5	1.5
White collar	172	2	61	34	0.6	0.6	1.8
Skilled manual	163	2	26	71	1.0		
Semi-skilled	174	1	14	83	1.0	1.0	
Unskilled	77		18	75	7.0		
Farm owners managers	153	3	42	51	1.0	3.0	
Farm tenants and laborers	69	2	16	73	2.0	7.0	

SOURCE: From Richard Centers, *The Psychology of Social Classes* (copyright 1949 by Princeton University Press, Table 20), p. 86.

There is, thus, agreement between these subjective judgments and the Warner school's reputational measurements about life at the bottom of the class system.

CONCLUSION: CLASSES ARE REAL AND SIGNIFICANT

Both the reputational and the subjective approaches point toward the existence of classes as significant and important phenomenon that order areas of social life in America. The two methods disagree about the most effective way to measure these classes and also about the details and number of classes in various places and over time. However, the methods do agree that classes exist and are important. The reputational method is appropriate for use in small communities, whereas the subjective approach can be applied to large national populations.

Hodges suggests a broad definition of social class that incorporates both perspectives:

> [Class is] . . . a distinct reality which embraces the fact that people live, eat, play, mate, dress, work, and think at contrasting and dissimilar levels. These levels—social classes—are the blended product of shared and analogous occupational orientations, educational backgrounds, economic wherewithal, and life experiences.[31]

Hodges's definition incorporates the objective criteria that identify the different strata (income level, years of education, income by occupation, and so forth); the reputational approach (the criteria by which members of the community rank themselves and others); the subjective approach (the perceptions of where one belongs in the class system and of its structure held by members of the community); and the different forms of social consciousness and meaning among the various classes.

There is considerable evidence that a class system does exist in American society, even though the borders between classes are blurred. Furthermore, the chief factors that place people in different classes are family background, type of occupation, and amount and types of income and education. These become translated into specific styles of life that are ranked in the status order to produce differing degrees of prestige in the community and differing types of social consciousness. Granted all of this, however, the problem remains: *why* do we have a social class system?

REASONS FOR SOCIAL CLASS SYSTEMS

We have presented data that suggest that a class system exists and have explored some of its dimensions and characteristics. Now we confront the question of *why* a social class system is typical of modern industrial societies. The theorists who have addressed themselves most directly to this question are Marx and Lenski.

Marx suggested that it is those who own or control the means of production (which in modern societies includes the control of service delivery systems such as hospitals and schools) who have the power to set the procedural rules that define the various occupational levels and their corresponding incomes. This capitalist class exercises control to maximize its gains at the expense of the other classes.

Education is valued because it is one of the procedural strategies used to secure a "higher" place in society. Much of the content of this education is controlled either directly or indirectly by those who own or control the means of production or service delivery systems. Education, especially higher education, is supposed to provide some of the "polish" necessary for a style of life that is "fitting" for a place in the higher social classes. Educational curricula tend to be consistent with the value framework of those who hold positions of power in a community. For example, business schools within universities teach how to best manage existing business enterprises. Students in these schools are not taught how to change the structure of the society to produce a different distribution of income but rather how best to maintain the existing structure while securing for themselves a desirable place within it. Marx was probably accurate when he suggested that the means of production was the infrastructure that determined much of the social superstructure, including educational systems and religion.

Lenski's interpretation is more refined than Marx's.[32] He suggests that an elite either takes over an existing stratification system or creates a new one. It typically begins by using coercive strategies. In the French Revolution, for example, the emergent bourgeois capitalist class or elite came to power by violently overthrowing the monarchy. Once in power the new elite attempted to create a cultural agreement that gave it a legitimate right to power and privilege using the slogan, "Liberty, Equality, Fraternity." Lenski concludes that:

> If the new elite has materialistic goods and is concerned solely with self-aggrandizement, it soon discovers that the rule of might is both inefficient and costly. So long as it relies on force, much of the profit is consumed by the costs of coercion. If the population obeys only out of fear of physical violence, a large portion of the time, energy, and wealth of the elite is invariably consumed in the effort to keep it under control and separate the producers from the products of their labors. *Even worse, honor, which normally ranks high in the scale of human values, is denied those who rule by force alone.*[33] (Italics supplied.)

Nonelite Control Strategies and the Class System

Because societies are structured by reciprocal control, the actions by the elite produce *reactions* from those below.

Lenski identifies four major reciprocal reactions to the control strategies exercised by elite groups. These are (1) the competitive struggle, (2) dropping out, (3) petty thievery, and (4) acquiring technical expertise. Taken together, these reciprocal control strategies exercised by nonelite groups go far to explain the characteristics of the American social class system and the class system of other industrial societies.

COMPETITIVE STRUGGLE

Lenski describes how this strategy supports the social class system:

> Of all the many reactions to the exercise of power and privilege in societies, the most valued by the elites themselves is that of *competition among nonelites for positions in their employ.* In order to attract the best qualified men to these important middle stratum positions, elites make them more desirable than other nonelite positions. In the case of certain key positions, the inducements are substantial. A vigorous competition naturally develops for these positions, and members of the elite are only too happy to encourage it since they are the chief beneficiaries. Whatever expenses they incur can easily be recouped many times over when these positions are filled by capable, zealous, and loyal men.[34]

Those who "win" in the competitive struggle gain high prestige. In our society this includes senior and junior executive positions in large corporations, high positions in government, top positions in service areas, and most professional positions. These people are in the lower-upper or upper-middle classes. Those who do not compete successfully take lower positions but tend to remain loyal to the system because they have gained something and they hope their children will gain even more.

Much competitive struggle occurs in the educational system, culminating in a university degree. The representatives of the various elites come to the university to recruit for their lower-echelon positions. Those who cannot afford to attend the university or are not motivated to do so cannot usually expect to secure high-level occupations and thus are confined to the lower social classes. These people are workers in factories or low-level employees in business, service industries, or government. They comprise the lower-middle and upper-lower classes. The competitive struggle both stratifies the system into social classes and insures its stability and persistence. The relationships between education and occupation and between education and income are outcomes of this struggle.

DROPPING OUT

A second nonelite reciprocal control strategy related to competition occurs among those people who, either because of the inability to compete or the lack of motivation to do so (often caused by a poor environment), drop out of the system and become beggars, criminals, prostitutes, welfare cases, and unemployables.* All these persons are typically held in low esteem by those above them. These are the members of the lower-lower class, placed there by the struggle for survival set in motion by the system of power and privilege. As Lenski points out:

> From the standpoint of the elite, the struggles which developed among the common people have been a matter of little concern, since human fecundity always insured an ample supply of qualified producers. In fact, these struggles probably served the interests of the elite by diverting attention from their own *exploitative role*, thus affording them a considerable measure of security against popular protest and revolution. (Italics supplied.)[35]

PETTY THIEVERY

The third reciprocal strategy is petty thievery by those in subordinate positions. In our society this petty thievery is widespread among factory workers, store clerks, household servants, government and university employees, and a host of others. Such behavior annoys the

---

*There are, of course, criminals in upper-level positions. However, as we will see later, they are not as likely to be caught, labeled, and punished as are those at the bottom.

TABLE 7-7
Comparison of Ruling Classes and Strategic Elites

Comparative Criterion	Ruling Class [the Elite]	Strategic Elites
Number	One	Several
Size	Large	Small, concentrated
Duration	Longer-lived	Short
Modes of entry	Birth and wealth	Expert skill
Modes of exit	Loss of wealth	Incompetence
Scope of authority	Diffuse and wide	Special and limited
Cultural bonds	Schooling, background	No specifiable ones
Accessibility	Relatively closed	Relatively open

SOURCE: Suzanne Keller, *Beyond the Ruling Class: Strategic Elites in Modern Society* (New York: Random House, Inc., 1963), p. 58. Used by Permission. (Bracketed material supplied.)

elites but they seldom do anything about it unless it is flagrant. This reciprocal strategy indicates that subordinates do not always fully agree with the cultural agreements the elite has tried to establish. If they did, they would not steal. The amount of petty thievery in American society currently runs into billions of dollars annually.

Acquiring Technical Expertise and Strategic Elites

The fourth and final reaction of the use of power by the elite is manifested in the *"efforts of the middle classes to gain control over power, privileges, and resources traditionally reserved to the elite."*[36] Because people in the middle classes depend on the good will of the elite, if they lose favor, they lose position. They therefore attempt to gain a measure of control to free themselves from complete dependence. This becomes possible in a complex society because the elite becomes more and more dependent on the technical expertise of those who may be recruited from classes below them. A group of what Suzanne Keller calls strategic elites is likely to develop because of the need for highly trained technical personnel in military, political, business, educational, and other areas.[37] Large corporations, for example, require highly trained management experts. Table 7-7 compares strategic elites with what Keller calls the ruling class and we have called the elite.

Keller points out that "what constitutes need at the top constitutes opportunity below."[38] Not all strategic elites are recruited from below. Some, or even all, may come from the top. However, if those at the top cannot maintain complete control because they lack expertise, they must recruit expertise from below. This permits persons from below some control because they are needed to maintain the system that keeps the elite in power. The ruling elite or class must give up *some* power to strategic elites to maintain itself over time. As Lenski notes, "the distribution of rewards in a society is a function of the distribution of power."[39] Society, including its stratification structure, is based on reciprocal control.

An Alternative Explanation for Stratification Systems: The Davis-Moore Theory

In an influential paper published in 1945, the sociologists Kingsley Davis and Wilbert Moore proposed a general explanation for the apparent universality of stratification systems in all large, complex human societies.[40] They suggested that every society faces the problem of motivating its members to carry out the tasks and fill the positions necessary for its survival. Society has at its disposal a limited set of rewards to distribute among personnel, who are also relatively scarce. Therefore, those positions that are more important to the maintenance of the society or to the fulfillment of its goals receive the largest relative rewards, whether in income, prestige, power or life styles. By this means individuals are placed in positions and motivated to perform the needed roles. Davis and Moore argue that stratification is an "unconsciously evolved device by which societies insure that the most important positions are conscientiously filled by the most qualified persons."[41]

This position (simplified in presentation here) has been criticized and defended in an ongoing series of articles since its publication. Some have suggested that it is merely an elaborate defense of existing inequities in achievement-oriented industrial societies, elevating privilege to a necessity that must be met if society is to persist. Others, including this writer, believe that the authors of this theory ignore the benefits of any stratification system, including the social class system, for those who hold power. One of the results of a stratification system may be to fill social positions, but there is little evidence to suggest that the functional contribution of any given position is clearly related to the rewards accompanying it. Furthermore, there is much evidence, which we developed in the preceding pages, to suggest that the ruling group benefits greatly from a stratification system and therefore employs it as a control strategy to maintain its power and privilege.[42]

SOCIAL MOBILITY AND SYSTEMS OF STRATIFICATION

Social mobility, the relative freedom with which individuals or groups can change their positions within a system of stratification, is one of the principal differentiating characteristics of caste, estate, and class stratification systems. Mobility is lowest in caste systems, with their endogamous strata of ascribed statuses supported by a social consciousness that often is rooted in religion and manifested in fixed rituals and rigidly defined interaction patterns. Mobility is highest in class systems of stratification, with their emphasis on achievement and upward movement within the structure. Estate systems have limited mobility, more than caste systems, but less than class systems.

In our discussion we will concentrate on social mobility in class systems of stratification, especially within the American class system. As we will see, the opportunities for such mobility are themselves prescribed and limited by the class system.

Social Mobility in the American Class System

There are two principal kinds of social mobility in a class system: vertical and horizontal. *Vertical social mobility* is movement upward or downward from one social class to another. *Horizontal social mobility* is movement within the same social class, usually from one occupation to another of roughly comparable income, status, and power.

Each of the two types of mobility can be either intragenerational or intergenerational. *Intragenerational* mobility (sometimes called career mobility) occurs *within* the lifetime of the individual and measures the difference between where a person is at the beginning of a career and where the same person is at its end. *Intergenerational mobility* measures the difference between the class of parents and the class of their offspring at the end of the latters' careers. If the offspring has experienced only intragenerational horizontal mobility, he or she may have a different occupation but remains in the same class as his parents. If the offspring has experienced intergenerational vertical mobility, he or she will be in a different social class from that of the parents—either higher or lower.

Americans place a high value on upward mobility—both intragenerational and intergenerational—and condemn and degrade downward mobility. The Horatio Alger rags-to-riches saga is continually presented as a realistic possibility that all should strive to emulate. No matter how lowly his beginnings, so the myth goes, each American can and should aspire to the top.

The facts, gathered by several generations of sociologists, suggest a different picture. Most persons in our society remain roughly where their parents were in the social class system. A substantial minority move up one step, whereas a smaller minority move down. Only a small group of persons experiences sharp upward or downward mobility, either intra- or intergenerational. We will examine in detail some of the major studies of social mobility from which we have drawn these conclusions.

F. W. Taussig and C. S. Joslyn used the 1928 edition of Pond's *Register of Directors* to select a sample of 19,101 business leaders to whom questionnaires were mailed.[43] They found that more than 70 per cent of the fathers of these business leaders had held positions as minor executives or higher in the business world or were professional men. They concluded "that contrary to an American tradition of long standing, the typical figure among business leaders in the United

The Positive Functions of Poverty

The sociologist Herbert Gans has identified many of the positive benefits of poverty for the advantaged and privileged groups who hold social power in society. "The poor are always with us" not because of some mystic necessity or because of their sins or their genetic deficiencies, but because the stratification system is supported by and to some extent requires the existence of a Class V, of a disadvantaged group on the bottom. Some of Gans's arguments are presented here:

the existence of poverty makes sure that "dirty work" is done. . . . In America, poverty functions to provide a low-wage labor pool that is willing—or, rather, unable to be unwilling—to perform dirty work at low cost. [In] some Southern states, welfare payments have been cut off during the summer months when the poor are needed to work in the fields. . . .

[Poverty] creates jobs for a number of occupations and professions which serve the poor, or shield the rest of the population from them. . . . [The] slum lord and the loan shark are widely known to profit from the existence of poverty. . . . [What] is less often recognized . . . is that poverty also makes possible the existence or expansion of "respectable" professions and occupations, for example, penology, criminology, social work, and public health.

[The] poor buy goods which others do not want and thus prolong their economic usefulness, such as day-old bread, fruit and vegetables which would otherwise have to be thrown out, secondhand clothes, and deteriorating automobiles and buildings. . . .

[The] poor can be identified and punished as alleged or real deviants in order to uphold the legitimacy of dominant norms. The defenders of the desirability of hard work, thrift, honesty, and monogamy need people who can be accused of being lazy, spendthrift, dishonest, and promiscuous to justify these norms. . . .

[Another] group of poor, described as deserving because they are disabled or suffering from bad luck, provide the rest of the population with different emotional satisfactions; they evoke compassion, pity and charity, thus allowing those who help them to feel that they are altruistic, moral, and practicing the Judeo-Christian ethic. . . .

[The] poor, being powerless, can be made to absorb the economic and political costs of change and growth in American society. During the nineteenth century, they did the backbreaking work that built the cities; today, they are pushed out of their neighborhoods to make room for "progress." Urban renewal projects to hold

States is neither the son of a farmer nor the son of a wage earner, but the son of a businessman."[44] Although the way is not completely blocked for a person with superior talents to go from the bottom to the top of the business structure in a single generation, this practice is a rare exception rather than the rule.

A study by Natalie Rogoff in Indianapolis, Indiana, measured the changes in mobility from 1910 to 1940.[45] She found that the likelihood of a son being in an occupational class different from that of his father was about the same in 1940 as it was in 1910.

middle-class taxpayers and stores in the city and expressways to enable suburbanites to commute downtown have typically been located in poor neighborhoods, since no other group will allow itself to be displaced. For much the same reason, urban universities, hospitals, and civic centers also expand into land occupied by the poor. The major costs of the industrialization of agriculture in America have been borne by the poor, who are pushed off the land without recompense, just as in earlier centuries in Europe, they bore the brunt of the transformation of agrarian societies into industrial ones. The poor have also paid a large share of the human cost of the growth of American power overseas, for they have provided many of the foot soldiers for Vietnam and other wars.[a]

Gans identifies a number of other ways in which the existence of a sizeable impoverished class helps maintain the existing system of social ordering and meaning.

He goes on to point out that alternative ways of meeting most of these needs could be devised, but they would be costly. They would require redistributions of income, prestige, or power, so that the poor would get relatively more and the dominant classes relatively less. For example, he notes that

[Society's] dirty work . . . could be done without poverty, some by automating it, the rest by paying the workers who do it decent wages, which would help considerably to cleanse that kind of work. Nor is it necessary for the poor to subsidize the activities they support through their low-wage jobs . . . for, like dirty work, many of these activities are essential enough to persist even if wages were raised. In both instances, however, costs would be driven up, resulting in higher prices to the customers and clients of dirty work and subsidized activity, with obvious . . . consequences for more affluent people.[b]

Gans concludes by stating in different terms the point we have already made about change in control strategies: "phenomena like poverty can be eliminated only when they either become sufficiently costly for the affluent or when the poor can obtain enough power to change the system of social stratification."[c]

[a]Herbert Gans, "The Positive Functions of Poverty," *The American Journal of Sociology*, Vol. 78, No. 2 (Sept. 1972), pp. 278–283.
[b]Ibid., p. 284.
[c]Ibid., p. 288.

TABLE 7-8
Percentages of Men in Urban Occupations with Fathers in
Urban Occupations Who Have Been Mobile Upward and Downward

Category	Centers 1945	NORC 1947	Survey Research Center: 1952
Upward mobile	17	21	19
Downward mobile	8	11	13
Stationary	75	68	67
Number in sample	598	719	463

Note: Upward mobile includes men in nonmanual occupations whose fathers were in manual occupations; downward mobile includes men in manual occupations whose fathers were in nonmanual occupations.
SOURCE: Seymour Martin Lipset and Reinhard Bendix, *Social Mobility in Industrial Society* (Berkeley: University of California Press, 1960), p. 88. Originally published by the University of California Press, reprinted by permission of The Regents of the University of California.

Table 7-8 shows the results of three other major studies of social mobility which included people at all occupational levels.
All three studies showed that at least two thirds of the sons remained at the same class level as their fathers and that there was more upward than downward mobility.
A study completed by Suzanne Keller in 1953 focused on the social origins and career experiences of three generations of men holding leading positions in the top business firms of the United States in 1870, 1900 to 1910, and 1950.[46] For each period she found that business leaders constituted a selected group differing significantly from the population at large. They tended to be of British and colonial stock and to have Protestant religious affiliations. Only a small proportion rose to their positions from humble origins, but the proportion who did was higher for the 1950 generation than for the earlier periods. The author accounts for this interesting finding, in part, by the transition from an economy based on family enterprises to one dominated by corporate enterprises, with the resulting bureaucratization of business careers. This illustrates the recruitment of strategic elites discussed here.

Sociologists differ about whether mobility is increasing or decreasing, but there is little doubt from the preceding studies that, within our stratified society, the chances for occupying positions at the top for each new generation are far from equal.

Vertical Mobility in the United States and in Other Nations[47]

Table 7-9 compares selected nations in which studies have been made in a manner that allows comparisons. The table shows only the movement from manual to nonmanual occupations. Most surpris-

TABLE 7-9
Social Mobility by Nation (Percentages)

Nation	[Upward] Manual into Nonmanual	[Downward] Nonmanual into Manual
Denmark	24.1	36.8
Finland	11.0	24.0
France I	30.1	20.5
France II	29.6	26.9
Great Britain	24.8	42.1
Hungary	14.5	27.5
Italy	8.5	34.4
Japan	23.7	29.7
Netherlands	19.6	43.2
Norway	23.2	28.6
Puerto Rico	14.3	42.7
Sweden	25.5	27.7
USA I*	28.8	29.7
USA II†	28.7	22.6
West Germany	20.0	29.0

*From 1946 data by Richard Centers.
†From 1962 data by Peter Blau and Otis Dudley Duncan.
Reproduced from S. M. Miller, "Comparative Social Mobility," in *Structured Social Inequality*, ed. by Celia S. Heller (New York: Macmillan, 1969), pp. 327, 329. Used by permission of the author. (Bracketed material supplied.)

ing is the large amount of downward mobility that occurs in these nations—almost all of which have reached a relatively high level of industrial development. Downward rather than upward mobility is more common in industrialized societies. All of these societies, however, show far more mobility than do societies that do not have class systems of social stratification.

Factors Affecting Rates of Vertical Mobility

Variations in rates of vertical mobility are caused by five major factors: (1) changes in the economic structure of society produced by technological advancement; (2) differential birth rates among the various classes; (3) the relative number of immigrants; (4) the availability of avenues of mobility; (5) differential power among the various classes. We will briefly discuss each of these.

CHANGES IN ECONOMIC STRUCTURE

Industrial societies with growing economies and expanding divisions of labor will display relatively high rates of upward vertical mobility. As Figure 7-1 illustrates, positions are created at middle and upper levels while those at the bottom are eliminated. If the economy stops growing, or if positions in higher levels reach the saturation point, the rate of upward vertical mobility will decrease.

This may be happening now for the upper-middle class in American society. Public school teachers, for example, typically came from lower-middle-class families and rose into the upper-middle class as they completed college and began working. As teaching positions and others like them, such as engineering occupations, become filled, the rate of vertical upward mobility is likely to decrease. Some people now in college who hope to be upwardly mobile or at least remain in the social class of their parents may be disappointed if they are majoring in subject-matter areas in which the job market is saturated or near saturation. There are already many holders of college degrees, including Ph.D.s, who either are unemployed or are underemployed. The rate of vertical upward mobility *may* decline and vertical downward mobility may increase in American society.[48]

DIFFERENTIAL BIRTH RATES

Historically, people in the upper classes have had a lower birth rate than people in the lower classes. If the birth rate in the upper classes is not high enough to fill positions in these classes with the sons and daughters of upper-class people, then people must be recruited from the lower classes to fill them. This increases the rate of upward vertical mobility. Sons and daughters of upper-class people may, of course, also be downwardly mobile and thereby open places at the top, but this is a relatively infrequent occurrence. Today, the differential class birth rates are beginning to change. If current trends continue, persons at the top will have enough children to replace them in their positions, thereby shutting out some people from the bottom who aspire to these upper positions. There is no reason to believe that upper-class people will not take advantage of their power and privilege to secure advantageous positions for their children.

The rising cost of a college education, along with a decrease in general state support of higher education and of scholarship aids and loans for lower-income people is already beginning to shut out some people in the lower classes who cannot afford to go to college. There is also increased emphasis on the building of technical schools to train people for positions in the lower-middle class. The students who will be "counseled into" such technical schools are not likely to be the sons and daughters of the rich.[49]

THE RELATIVE NUMBER OF IMMIGRANTS

Most of the earlier immigrants who came to the United States were poor and untrained. They took positions at or near the bottom of the social hierarchy. In an expanding economy this tended to give an advantage to native-born whites who were "pushed up," thus increasing the rate of upward vertical mobility. The relatively few immigrants now coming to America tend to be better educated than were those who came in the late nineteenth and early twentieth centuries. They tend to enter the occupational system at the middle levels rather than at the bottom. The drop in the number of immigrants and their higher class affiliation combine to reduce their impact on upward vertical mobility.

Availability of Avenues of Upward Mobility

The existence of avenues of mobility significantly affects the rate of mobility. In this country entertainment and sports have been important avenues for upward mobility. Many actors and professional athletes had their social origins in the lower classes but have risen to national prominence and high incomes. These avenues, however, are very narrow and the competition is great.

Apprenticeships have also provided an important avenue for upward mobility. Currently, some federally supported programs provide limited training for people in the lower classes.

Formal education, however, is the most important avenue for upward mobility. The establishment of the public school system and land grant colleges and universities provided a broad avenue for mobility for masses of people in this nation. It is an avenue that has been and continues to be heavily used. Persons using this avenue may start at or near the bottom of the social hierarchy and climb a considerable distance during the course of their careers. There are presently more than seven million students enrolled in higher education, many of whom have parents in the lower classes. If these students get jobs commensurate with their level of training upon graduation, this will represent a significant amount of upward vertical mobility.

However, as indicated here, many of the jobs for which colleges and universities prepare people may be reaching a point of saturation so that this avenue may narrow in the future unless national priorities are shifted.[50]

DIFFERENTIAL POWER

Differential power affects the rate of mobility as the elite in class societies attempts to maintain itself over time. Once elites are in power they have an advantage because they possess the resources to manipulate, enforce, perpetuate, or change cultural agreements to their advantage.[51] People who control available resources can use manipulative strategies to persuade those below them to accept certain agreements. If manipulation fails, they can move toward the use of coercive strategies. However, these tend to be expensive and to threaten the accepted cultural agreements. It is far less expensive for an elite to perpetuate cultural agreements through the use of manipulative and socialization strategies than through the use of coercive strategies.

The rate of upward vertical mobility tends to be high in a growing economy with an expanding division of labor so long as the positions at higher levels do not reach the point of saturation. Under these conditions, the elite has few problems in perpetuating the existing cultural agreements because most people in the society are convinced that they or their children can be upwardly mobile. Members of the middle class try to convince their children that the existing order of control relationships is valid. Many American citizens live a relatively comfortable physical life and tend to be satisfied with the status quo of control agreements. Those in the lowest class have little power or information that could be used to improve their condition. They are, therefore, not in a position to effectively challenge the existing arrangements of control relationships, although they often are aware that they have been shut out from the culturally defined "good things of life."

Possible Implications of Reduced Upward Mobility

Sociologists have known for a long time that equal opportunity for vertical mobility in an upward direction does not exist in our nation. People in the lowest class have limited opportunities for education, which thus severely restricts mobility. The same is true to a lesser degree for persons in the upper-lower class. Being able to attend a state university is hardly equivalent to attending an Ivy League university for potential upward mobility.

Equality of opportunity has never been a reality, even though considerable upward mobility does occur. If the trends pointed out here continue—a maturing economy, a saturation of positions at the top, and a change in the differential birth rate—we can expect a closing of the traditional avenues of mobility. This may force the stratification system to solidify. The elite will not permit a free flow of people from the lower classes unless they are useful. Of course, some may be needed to staff scientific and technical strategic elite positions in order to keep the society going.

When threatened, groups with power and privilege can be expected to protect themselves. The elite at the top recruit people for high positions who can be trusted. These people are rewarded to the extent that they conform to and support the existing agreements. This value on conformity seeps down to the lower-middle and upper-lower classes. An example is the relatively high degree of right-wing authoritarianism among people in these classes.[52] These people have their foot on the first rung of the class ladder and hope their children will go higher. The source of their income, wages, is insecure. It is easy to drop back to a lower class. Because they exist on the narrowest of margins, we find high conformity among people in these classes and a rigid stance against any kind of social reform that they feel might threaten their present positions and hopes for the future. They do not really want to open up the system for those who are below them.

SOCIAL MOBILITY IN THE USSR

The USSR also has an open class system of stratification, with a social mobility and elite control strategies similar to ours. We are *not* saying that we do not have more freedoms under present conditions than do people in the USSR. We are saying that the elite and social mobility patterns are surprisingly similar.

In the USSR people who are willing to conform to the agreements that were originally established by the Russian revolution and that are maintained by the use of coercive strategies are more likely to experience upward social mobility. Leading members of the Communist party and their families form the dominant elite. This elite recruits people who will conform to the established agreements. Their power is consolidated and we find the same seeping down effects as in the United States. People who are comfortable and have hope for the future cannot be expected to challenge the existing order of control relationships.* The rate of vertical upward mobility has been high in the USSR because of rapid industrial expansion. The emigré study done by the Russian Research Center of Harvard University found the rate of upward mobility in the USSR from working classes into nonmanual positions to be 34.9 per cent, whereas the downward rate from nonmanual to working classes was found to be 12.8.[53]

Intellectuals who criticize the system are still punished, although not nearly as severely as under the dictator Stalin, perhaps because the threat is not seen as so great. The agreements are more toward acceptance based on less coercion *but* the "dictatorship of the proletariat" is not handing over its power to the people, nor would we expect this, despite Marx's optimistic predictions.[54] Rather than withering away, the Soviet state is the dominant social institution. In the USSR the elite uses the writings of Marx just as our elite uses the Bible or the "American Creed" to maintain power.

REFERENCES

1. Gerth, Hans, and C. Wright Mills. *Character and Social Structure*. New York: Harcourt, 1953, p. 306.
2. See Wittfooel, Karl A. *Oriental Despotism: A Comparative Study of Total Power*. New Haven, Conn.: Yale, 1957, especially Chap. 4.
3. Mosca, Gaetano. *The Ruling Class*. Trans. by Hannah Kahn. New York:

*Some intellectuals are an exception to this generalization.

McGraw-Hill, 1939, p. 70. Gerhard Lenski uses this quotation to support his position, which is similar to the position presented here. See his *Power and Privilege*. New York: McGraw-Hill, 1966.
4. Gerth and Mills, op. cit., p. 307.
5. Weber, Max. "Class, Status, Party." In *From Max Weber: Essays in Sociology*. Trans. and ed. by H. H. Gerth and C. Wright Mills. New York: Oxford U.P., 1958, p. 181.
6. Ibid., p. 186.
7. Ibid., p. 194.
8. Runciman, W. G. *Sociology in Its Place and Other Essays*. London: Cambridge University Press, 1970, pp. 176–177.
9. Gerth and Mills, *From Max Weber*, op. cit., pp. 193–194.
10. Ossowski, Stanislaw. *Class Structure in the Social Consciousness*. Trans. by Sheila Patterson. New York: Free Press, 1963, p. 6.
11. Berreman, Gerald. "Caste in India and the United States." *American Journal of Sociology*, Vol. LXVI (Sept. 1960).
12. Gerth and Mills, *From Max Weber*, op. cit., p. 188.
13. For a brief discussion of the conflicting views of the origin of caste, see Bougle, C. "The Essence and Reality of the Caste System." In *Contributions to Indian Sociology*. Ed. by L. Dumont and D. P. Pocock. The Hague: Mouton and Company, 1958.
14. Taya Zinkin. *Caste Today*. London: Oxford University Press, 1958, p. 1.
15. Joshua Prawer and Shmuel N. Eisenstadt. "Feudalism." *International Encyclopedia of the Social Sciences*. New York: Macmillan, Inc., 1968, Vol. 5, p. 394. For a variety of views on various components of the feudal system, see *Feudalism in History*. Ed. by Rustin Coulborn. Princeton, N.J.: Princeton University Press, 1956.
16. Hodges, Harold M. *Social Stratification*. Cambridge, Mass.: Schenkman, 1964, p. 29. The following discussion of the Third Estate draws from Hodges's work.
17. Toennies, Ferdinard. "Estates and Classes." In *Class, Status, and Power*. Ed. by Reinhard Bendix and Seymour Martin Lipset. New York: Free Press, 1966, p. 13.
18. Marx, Karl, and Friedrich Engels. *The Communist Manifesto*. 1848.
19. The following is based on Weber, Max. *The Protestant Ethic and the Spirit of Capitalism*. Trans. by Talcott Parsons. New York: Scribner's, 1958.
20. There has been criticism of Weber's idea that the Protestant ethic provided the subjective meaning permitting the growth of capitalism. The best criticism is probably Samuelson, Kurt. *Religion and Economic Action: A Critique of Max Weber*. New York: Harper, 1957.
21. Robert A. Nisbet. "The Decline and Fall of Social Class." *Pacific Sociological Review*, Vol. 2 (Spring 1959), 11–17.
22. For an excellent summary treatment of the discussion concerning the number of classes, see Ossowski, loc. cit.
23. U.S. Bureau of the Census.
24. These studies include the following: Warner, W. Lloyd, and P. S. Lunt. *The Social Life of a Modern Community*. New Haven, Conn.: Yale University Press, 1942; Warner, W. Lloyd, and Leo Srole. *The Social Systems of American Ethnic Groups*. New Haven, Conn.: Yale University Press, 1945; Warner, W. Lloyd, and J. O. Low. *The Social System of the Modern Factory*. New Haven, Conn.: Yale University Press, 1947; Warner, W. Lloyd. *The Living and the Dead*. New Haven, Conn.: Yale University Press, 1959. These studies are summarized in *Yankee City*. Ed. by W. Lloyd Warner. New Haven, Conn.: Yale University Press, 1963.

Also see, Davis, Allison, B. B. Gardner, and M. R. Gardner. *Deep South.* Chicago: U. of Chicago, 1941; Warner, W. Lloyd, and associates. *Democracy in Jonesville.* New York: Harper, 1949.

25. Warner, W. Lloyd, Marchia Meeker, and Kenneth Eells. *Social Class in America.* New York: Harper, 1960, pp. 37–38.

26. Kahl, Joseph A. *The American Class Structure.* New York: Rinehart and Company, Inc., 1957, p. 26. For a recent study, see Coleman, Richard, and Beatrice L. Neugarten. *Social Status in the City.* New York: Atherton, 1967.

27. Hodges, Harold, Jr. "Peninsula People: Social Stratification in a Metropolitan Complex." In *Education and Society.* Ed. by W. Warren Kallenbach and Harold M. Hodges, Jr. Columbus, Ohio: Merrill, 1963.

28. Fortune Surveys, "The People of the United States—A Self-portrait." *Fortune* (Feb. 1940).

29. Centers, Richard. *The Psychology of Social Classes.* Princeton, N.J.: Princeton University Press, 1949.

30. Ibid., pp. 95–96.

31. Hodges, Harold, Jr. *Social Stratification: Class in America.* Cambridge, Mass.: Schenkman, 1964, p. 13.

32. Lenski, Gerhard E. *Power and Privilege.* New York: McGraw-Hill, 1966.

33. Ibid., pp. 51–52.

34. Ibid., p. 64.

35. Ibid., pp. 65–65.

36. Ibid., p. 65.

37. Keller, Suzanne. *Beyond the Ruling Class: Strategic Elites in Modern Society.* New York: Random, 1963.

38. Ibid., p. 199.

39. Lenski, op. cit., p. 63.

40. Davis, Kingsley, and Wilbert Moore. "Some Principles of Stratification." *American Sociological Review,* Vol. 10 (April 1945), 242–249.

41. Ibid., p. 243.

42. For continuations of the argument pro and con, see Tumin, Melvin. "Some Principles of Stratification: A Critical Analysis." *American Sociological Review,* Vol. 18 (Aug. 1953), 387–394; and Davis, Kingsley. "Reply." Pp. 394–397. See also the article by Wesolowski, Wlodzimierz. "Some Notes on the Functional Theory of Stratification." *Polish Sociological Bulletin,* No. 3–4 (1962), 28–38.

43. Taussig, F. W., and C. S. Joslyn. *American Business Leaders.* New York: Macmillan, Inc., 1932.

44. Ibid., p. 188.

45. Rogoff, Natalie. *Occupational Mobility.* New York: Free Press, 1953.

46. Keller, Suzanne. *The Social Origins and Career Lives of Three Generations of American Business Leaders.* (Ph.D. diss., Columbia University, 1953).

47. One of the most comprehensive statements is Lipset, Seymour Martin, and Reinhard Bendix. *Social Mobility in Industrial Society.* Berkeley: University of California Press, 1960. This book summarizes many studies and compares mobility among different industrial nations.

48. See *The Graduate: A Handbook for Leaving School.* Knoxville, Tenn.: Approach 13-30 Corporation, 1973.

49. Warner, W. L., R. J. Havighurst and M. B. Loeb, *Who Shall be Educated?* New York: Harper, 1944.

50. For a discussion of some of these factors, see Fox, Thomas G. and S. M. Miller. "Economic and Social Determinants of Mobility: An International Cross-Sectional Analysis." *Acta Sociologica,* Vol. 9 (1965).

51. See Lenski, loc. cit.
52. See Lipset, Seymour Martin. *Political Man: The Social Basis of Politics.* New York: Doubleday, 1960.
53. Reported in Miller, S. M. "Comparative Social Mobility." *Current Sociology,* Vol. IX, No. 1 (1960). For a description of social stratification and mobility in the USSR, see Inkeles, Alex. "Social Stratification and Mobility in the Soviet Union." *American Sociological Review,* Vol. 15 (Aug. 1950), 465–479.
54. See Armstrong, John A. *The Soviet Bureaucratic Elite: A Case Study of the Ukranian Apparatus.* London: Stevens and Sons, 1959; and Towster, Julian. *Political Power in the USSR, 1917–1947.* New York: Oxford U.P., 1948. For Communist nations outside the USSR, see Djilas, Milovan. *The New Class: An Analysis of the Communist System.* New York: Praeger, 1959.

CHAPTER 8

Ethnic and Minority Groups

INTRODUCTION

The discussion of ethnic and minority groups will enable us to bring to bear on one of the most pressing and baffling parts of social life many of the analytic tools we have developed. The major classes of control strategies clarify the ordering of intergroup relationships. As pointed out in Chapter 4, relations among groups are structured by the use of control strategies, just as are interpersonal relations and intragroup relations.

The pertinence of our inquiry can hardly be questioned. The mass media are filled with reports and alarms about intergroup tensions and conflicts of all sorts, both within societies and among them. Without exception, every large industrial society has within it groups that are in open conflict with each other, or whose patterned relations of subordination and superordination are being questioned, or are riven by social problems directly related to the ordering of intergroup relations. Catholics and Protestants in Northern Ireland, Jews and Arabs in Israel, blacks and whites in South Africa and the United States, Basques and Spaniards in Spain—the list and the litany of problems are endless.

Our discussion will begin with conceptual clarification to determine how such terms as *ethnic group, minority group,* and *race* can be most usefully defined to facilitate understanding intergroup relations. Then we will examine the principal control strategies used to structure dominant-minority relations. The reasons for intergroup conflict and discrimination will be explored, and the relationship of this to the problem of meaning and identity will be discussed. Finally, as a case study, we will outline the history of the control strategies that order black-white relations in America.

Major Concepts

Ethnic Group

There is a current revival of "ethnicity." All sorts of people are rediscovering or reaffirming previously ignored or disliked ethnic ties, there has been a resurgence of ethnically-based organizations, and sociologists have rediscovered the significance of ethnic identities. Our goal is to define the concept of ethnic groups to maximize its utility for the analysis of how control strategies structure relations among ethnic groups.

We will adopt, in a slightly modified form, R. A. Schermerhorn's definition of ethnic group: An *ethnic group* is a group within a larger society that has real, supposed, or "created" common ancestry, memories of a shared or created historical past, and a cultural focus on one or more symbolic elements defined as representing their peoplehood.[1] Schermerhorn includes among the symbolic elements:

> kinship patterns, physical contiguity (as in localism or sectionalism), religious affiliation, language or dialect forms, tribal affiliations, nationality, pheno-typical features (the way one looks), or any combination of these.[2]

Finally, Schermerhorn points out that, "A necessary accompaniment of [ethnicitity] is some consciousness of kind among members of the group."[3]

By this definition, a wide variety of factors can be the determining criteria for the existence of an ethnic group. Such groups exist within larger societies and are set off from others by the distinguishing criteria in the definition. By definition, then, such groups occur only in pluralistic societies. Where all groups in the society are alike and share the same consciousness of kind, no ethnic groups as we define

---

Consciousness of Kind

Franklin Giddings (1855–1931), one of the pioneers of American sociology, introduced the concept of "consciousness of kind." This exists when people who are alike in some way form what Giddings called "a community made up of like spirits." They are "drawn together by their common response to a belief or dogma"[a] or other cultural agreement. A consciousness of kind, of course, may bind any group together around any type of common interest or common condition. But we are concerned here only with its importance to the creation or maintenance of ethnic groups.

[a]Franklin Henry Giddings, *Civilization and Society* (New York: Holt, 1932).

them exist. Our definition casts a broad net sufficient to include within it religious groups; such nationality groups as Italian-Americans and Polish-Americans; and such groups popularly believed to be "racial" as Chinese-Americans and black Americans.

Equally important, the ethnicity of a group may vary over time and change with circumstances. There are many ethnic groups in our society whose cultural agreements and consciousness of kind differs in various ways and in different degrees of intensity. Irish Catholics, for example, differ in general from Italian Catholics, and in various cities the strength of these differences varies. Indeed, our society has often been referred to as a "nation of nations."

Sometimes an ethnic group living within a larger society may follow its distinctive way of life without conflict with others. Theoretically, at least, such an ethnic group may have relatively complete control over its members and its destiny as a group. Generally, however, members of ethnic groups must interact with others. For example, most ethnic groups are not economically self-sufficient and must compete with others in the job market. They must also find places to live. Furthermore, they are expected to obey the society's laws even if these conflict with their own cultural agreements or coercive strategies may be used against them. Mormons in our society were forced by law to stop practicing polygyny (one husband with two or more wives). The Amish are forced by law to send their children to school until they complete the eighth grade.

When members of an ethnic group interact with others not of their own group, their very presence may be perceived as a threat. This perceived threat by others may be produced, at times, solely by the fact that the ethnic group is *different*. It is, thus, by implication a threat to the cultural values or cultural agreements of others.

When this occurs and when members of a more powerful group (or groups in coalition) begin to use their power in an attempt to suppress, restrict, or change the life-style of an ethnic group, that ethnic group becomes a minority group.

Minority Group

A minority group is a group that has been reduced to subordinate status. The definition of a minority group by Raymond W. Mack and Troy S. Duster is widely accepted:

A minority is a set of people who, capable of being distinguished on the basis of some physical or cultural characteristic, are treated collectively as inferior. Since they look or act differently from other people, it is possible to identify them as a minority and exclude them from full participation in the society of which they are a part.[4]

Others in the society have the *power* to exclude the minority from full participation in the society of which they are a part.

Mack and Duster point out that, "A sociological minority need not be a mathematical one."[5] The best example of this is the Union of South Africa. Bantu-speaking blacks outnumber the European-descended whites in that nation by millions, yet the whites are the dominant group because they control the means of force and can thus maintain themselves in power, subordinating the numerically superior Bantu-speaking blacks into the position of a sociological minority group.

A minority group comes into existence when two or more different ethnic groups meet and the group with more power (either alone or in coalition with other groups) reduces the less powerful group to a position of subservience. This process is often dynamic, as coalitions of groups shift and change over time. For example, E. Digby Baltzell, discussing the relationships among Protestants, Catholics, and Jews in this country, reminds us that before 1850 members of all three groups could belong to the "aristocracy" through inheritance or through social mobility.[6] However, after massive waves of Catholics from Ireland and southeastern Europe and Jews from eastern Europe entered the nation during the latter part of the nineteenth century, white Anglo-Saxon Protestants began discriminating against Catholics and Jews and reduced them to positions of relatively low status and low

The Revival of Ethnicity: The Armenian-Americans

The Wall Street Journal reported on the current revival of ethnic identity and consciousness among many small nationality groups in America by describing in some detail this development among the Armenian-American community. This change is described by some members of that community:

> "When I was a boy, my parents used to despair that we would be dead as a community in twenty years—but that's all changed now," says Jack Antreassian, the middle-aged executive director of the Armenian Church of America in New York. And Dr. Zaven H. Daderian, an Armenian dentist on Long Island, says: "Every group is bragging about its heritage now. Today, it's glamorous to be different.". . .
>
> "When I was a girl, I tried to be as American as possible," says Lucille Kimatian, an Armenian-American in New York. "My cousins and I would even go into another car on the subway just so we wouldn't be embarrassed by our parents speaking Armenian," she recalls.
>
> Today, the fifty-eight-year-old Mrs. Kimatian teaches in an Armenian Sunday school. "These kids are far more interested in their heritage than I ever was as a teen-ager. Everything has changed," she says.

power. Minority groups were created from the earlier ethnic identification.

By 1950 increasing social mobility had placed many Jews and Catholics in positions of high income and power, although the white Anglo-Saxon Protestants (comprising about one third of the total population) still held the major positions of prestige. Baltzell projects a future in which the white Anglo-Saxon Protestant group will lose more power but maintain high prestige. The process will come full circle to the original structure of control relationships and all three groups will have roughly equal access to income, prestige, and power. However, changes in the larger society could drastically affect Baltzell's prediction.

We will return subsequently to a more detailed examination of the structuring of ethnic and minority dominant relationships. First, however, we must clarify one of the most overused, misused, and slippery concepts around: race.

Race

The concept of race is a prime example of the importance of what people *believe* to be true, without regard for scientific truth. Adolph Hitler and the Nazi party in Germany adopted and elaborated the

---

The development of consciousness of kind and memories of a shared historical past is an essential part of such an ethnic revitalization:

The Sunday schools consider it important to stress Armenian culture as well as religion. "When you say 'Armenian,' most people still just think 'shish kebab,' " says Dr. Daderian, the Long Island dentist, who also teaches at the school. Students seem to like the cultural approach. "I get a sense of cultural identity from the school. A lot of people are looking for an identity," says Richard Guevrekian, a sixteen-year-old student. Brenda Nalbandian, a classmate, adds: "One of the main reasons we come here is to help keep Armenian culture going."

In the classes, the youngsters also study the centuries of invasions and persecutions that have devastated the tiny country—but strengthened its will to survive. Once there was an Armenian empire that stretched from the Caspian Sea to Syria. But that was in the 1st Century B. C. Since about 66 B. C., Armenia's political fortunes have been mainly in a slump.[a]

Whether such ethnic revivals are likely to be successful and the circumstances under which they occur will become clearer after we discuss the circumstances under which an ethnic group becomes a minority group, the control strategies that structure dominant-minority relations, and what is meant by the "ethnic solution" in a pluralistic society.

[a]*The Wall Street Journal* (July 11, 1973), pp. 1, 21.

ideas developed during the nineteenth century by Count Gobineau
and Houston Stewart Chamberlain about the higher and lower races
and the necessity for preserving a mythical racial purity.

Racial epithets, racial tensions and racial conflicts are commonplaces of life in many contemporary soceieties. It has been said that,
"Against stupidity, the gods themselves contend in vain." Several
generations of anthropologists and biologists have echoed that sentiment as they sought with minimal success to educate the public to sort
out fiction from fact about race.

In 1950, an expert panel of physical anthropologists and geneticists
was convened by the United Nations Educational, Scientific, and Cultural Organization (UNESCO) to formulate a statement about current
scientific knowledge on race. Their conclusions about "what is at
present scientifically established concerning individual and group
differences" remain substantially correct and equally important
today:

1. In matters of race, the only characteristics which anthropologists have so
   far been able to use effectively as a basis for classification are physical
   (anatomical and physiological).
2. Available scientific knowledge provides no basis for believing that the
   groups of mankind differ in their innate capacity for intellectual and
   emotional development.
3. Some biological differences between human beings within a single race
   may be as great as or greater than the same biological differencces between races.
4. Vast social changes have occurred that have not been connected in any
   way with changes in racial type. Historical and sociological studies thus
   support the view that genetic differences are of little significance in
   determining the social and cultural differences between different
   groups of men.
5. There is no evidence that race mixture produces disadvantageous results
   from a biological point of view. The social results of race mixture,
   whether for good or ill, can generally be traced to social factors.[7]

Anthropologists disagree about the utility of a concept of race to
analyze the distribution and movement of human populations. They
agree that we are a unitary species. Classifications of human beings by
geographic subgroup, blood type, and epidermal pigmentation may
be useful to understand human history. However, they have little
relationship to or bearing on the *social meanings* that ideas and
ideologies about race carry in the modern world. Indeed, some scholars believe that even the effort to scientifically classify races should
be dropped because of the impossibility of making satisfactory clas-
sificatory judgments.

It is ironic that even though biologists and physical anthropologists
have great difficulty placing people into racial categories, people with

little or no expertise in these areas have no difficulty in doing so. People do have different physical characteristics. There are people who have lighter or darker skins, different colored eyes or hair, different facial features, and different hair texture. These differences, however, have *social meaning* only when they are categorized, labeled, and used to assign people or groups to subordinate or pejoratively characterized social positions—that is, to make minorities of them.

In our society, people who categorize themselves as Caucasian (white), categorize others as Negro (black) or Mongolian (yellow). These people in turn may also categorize others. This usually is done for *social* reasons. Historically, whites categorized people with certain physical characteristics and labeled them to exploit them as laborers. The Negro (black) was categorized and subordinated into the social position of slave.

The United States government continues to use racial categories in taking the census and for other purposes. Racial categories have become firmly fixed in the minds of many Americans. Such categories still have important social consequences for people who are categorized and labeled in such a way that they remain a minority.

Many black people and others who are categorized may accept the category but reject the derogatory labeling and subordination into minority status that accompanies it. When we discuss the history of blacks in America we will see how minorities seek to change their relationships with dominant groups by altering the control strategies used to dominate them. Racial categorizations and labeling are control strategies that have been and continue to be widely used. For the sociologist, the concepts of ethnic group and minority group provide the technical apparatus to study intergroup relations. Notions, beliefs, fictions, fantasies, and fears about race are important *social data* that have meaning only because they affect behavior and attitudes.

CONTROL STRATEGIES USED TO STRUCTURE DOMINANT-MINORITY RELATIONS

Minority Group Strategies

The control strategies used by minority groups and dominant groups in ordering their relationships vary with the type of minority groups. Louis Wirth has classified minority groups into four types, each of which uses different control strategies in their relationship with the dominant group: (1) assimilationist, (2) pluralistic, (3) secessionist, and (4) militant.[8] We will briefly discuss each type of group and its control strategies.

Assimilationist Minorities

Assimilationist minorities are those that either do not want to maintain their separate group identity and consciousness of kind or believe it is to their advantage to become a part of and indistinguishable from members of the dominant group. They use the cultural strategy of assimilation and attempt to become like the members of the dominant group. They adopt the cultural agreements of the dominant group hoping that they will become enough like its members to be accepted by them. In our society individuals in groups taking this orientation have often altered their name to an Anglo-Saxon form so that their origins could not be recognized. People have also changed their religion, their congeniality groups, and renounced members of their own group to secure acceptance by the dominant group.

The final test of the success of the assimilation strategy is intermarriage between members of minority groups and members of the dominant group. Once this occurs on a large scale the minority ceases to exist. It is no longer recognizable and has lost its defining characteristics. This process may take from one to several generations, or may never be allowed by members of the dominant group, depending on the acceptability of the minority to members of the dominant group.

W. Lloyd Warner and Leo Srole estimated how long it might take different assimilationist minorities in America to be accepted as members of the dominant group.[9] The most important determinant of time taken for assimilation is the degree of similarity of the characteristics of the ethnic or minority group to those of white Anglo-Saxon Protestants. At the extremes, it takes a light-skinned, English-speaking Protestant only a very short time to become assimilated, whereas the assimilation process for dark-skinned blacks of African descent is very slow.

The degree of subordination of the assimilationist minority and the strength of its subcultural agreements also affect the likelihood and speed of assimilation. Light-skinned, English-speaking Protestant immigrants, for example, experience only slight subordination and are not tightly bound by extremely closely knit subcultural values. On the other hand, blacks in America have experienced extreme subordination and have developed subcultural agreements that make assimilation less likely and less rapid as a viable strategy to order dominant-minority relations. Racial categorization plays an important role in reducing the viability of the assimilationist strategy. The inability of some ethnic and minority groups to achieve assimilation because of discriminatory strategies has led some of these groups to take pluralistic orientations.

Pluralistic Minorities

Pluralistic minorities want to maintain a separate identity and consciousness of kind organized around one or more characteristics that are important to them as members of a group. While maintaining these differences "The aim of the pluralistic minority is achieved when it has succeeded in wresting from the dominant group the fullest measure of equality in all things economic and political and the right to be left alone in things cultural."[10]

Whether or not the pluralistic minority will be able to achieve its goals depends on the successful use of accommodation strategies by its members in their interaction with memmbers of the majority group. Both groups must be willing to tolerate continued differences in the other. Typically, the minority group restricts its *range* of differences and thus gives up certain historic symbols and culural usages to maintain the characteristics that it sees as most important. If other differences are maintained, they tend to be hidden from public view.

The major American religious minorities, Jews and Catholics, have pursued this strategy. Ethnic differences associated with religious difference that remains visible in interaction with members of other groups is religion. Religious differences have become so accepted that American socieity has been referred to as a "tripe melting pot."[11] Members of the three major religions *tend* to use the control strategy of toleration in their intergroup relations. Some latent hostility remains, especially toward Jewish people, but for the most part, the toleration strategy taken by members of these religious groups has worked. Identities and consciousness of kind that have not been given up are "hidden" from public view and therefore pose little threat. An example is the celebration of religious holy days within the home by many Jews.

Secessionist Minorities

Secessionist minorities reject both assimilation and accommodation strategies. "The principal and ultimate objective of such a majority is to achieve political as well as cultural independence from the dominant group."[12] A recent American example of this type of minority is the black nationalist movement which, in its most extreme forms, demands the establishment of a separate state for black people with political and cultural autonomy. The Hutterite people, a closed religious group, briefly described in Chapter 1, also take this orientation.

Secessionist minorities, usually small in size, have a difficult time achieving their goals. Many Hutterites are now moving to Canada because they are not being allowed to expand their communities.

This type of minority might succeed in its strategy if it were to cause so much disruption that the dominant group would let it have its way just to be rid of it. This presumes that the dominant group does not first resort to the use of genocide. Another possibility of success lies in forming a coalition with other groups to tip the balance of power in their direction. In general, however, the secessionist strategy of complete withdrawal is not allowed by the dominant group. For example, during the 1970s, many Jews in Russia wanted to emigrate to Israel, but only a few were allowed to go. Even this limited movement required immense international pressure to achieve.

Militant Minorities

Militant minorities want to escape minority group status by achieving domination and reducing the previously dominant group to minority group status. Even though many minorities may use coercive strategies in an attempt to gain equality, few can muster the necessary power to overcome the power of the dominant group. If this is to happen, they must have help from outside the society. Robin Williams points out that:

> A militant reaction from a minority group is most likely when (1) the group's position is rapidly improving, or (2) when it is rapidly deteriorating, especially if this follows a period of improvement.[13]

Williams' proposition makes sense because under both conditions the minority group will perceive itself as more relatively disadvantaged than previously. If its position is rapidly improving, it will take as its reference group the dominant group. If its position is rapidly deteriorating after a period of improvement, the same comparison will indicate even greater relative deprivation and provoke greater militancy.

In an article titled, "Black Progress and Liberal Rhetoric," Benjamin Wattenberg and Richard Scammon argued that blacks made substantial progress during the 1960s. They cited evidence suggesting increased black median family and single person incomes, entrance into previously closed trade unions and apprenticeship programs, expansion of black enrollments at institutions of higher education, and other data. A storm of controversy ensued, most of it generated by anger that the authors defined "progress" by comparison with past inequities rather than present goals. A typical comment by a critic suggested that:

> What emerges without stretching the facts is that in a society which preaches egalitarianism, incomes are grossly unequally distributed along lines which are fundamentally racial. And this is what the struggle is all about: although significant progress has been made, there is much left to justify discontent.[14]

DOMINANT GROUP STRATEGIES

Having examined typical strategies used by minority groups in ordering dominant-minority relations, we will now examine some typical dominant group strategies that keep minority group members in their place as that place is defined by the dominant group. Resistance by the dominant group takes many forms. Allport, in his discussion of prejudice, suggests a scale of intensity of control strategies used by dominant group members against minority groups. (These same strategies can also be used by minority group members, but usually at a higher cost if they are used publicly.) He lists and defines each, beginning with the lowest intensity:

1. *Antilocution.* Most people who have prejudices talk about them. With like-minded friends, occasionally with strangers, they may express their antagonism freely. But many people never go beyond this mild degree of antipathetic action.
2. *Avoidance.* If the prejudice is more intense, it leads the individual to avoid members of the disliked group, even perhaps at the cost of considerable inconvenience. In this case, the bearer of prejudice does not directly inflict harm upon the group he dislikes. He takes the burden of accommodation and withdrawal entirely upon himself.
3. *Discrimination.* Here the prejudiced person makes detrimental distinctions of an active sort. He undertakes to exclude all members of the group in question from certain types of employment, from residential housing, political rights, educational or recreational opportunities, churches, hospitals, or from some other social privileges.
4. *Physical attack.* Under conditions of heightened emotion prejudice may lead to acts of violence or semiviolence. An unwanted Negro family may be forcibly ejected from a neighborhood, or so severely threatened that it leaves in fear. Gravestones in Jewish cemeteries may be desecrated. The Northside's Italian gang may lie in wait for the Southside's Irish gang.
5. *Extermination.* Lynchings, pogroms, massacres, and the Hitlerian program of genocide mark the ultimate degree of violent expression of prejudice.[15]

Responses of Minority Group Members to Dominant Group Discrimination

Discrimination is the commonest dominant group control strategy in our society. We have selected minority group responses to discrimination to illustrate the types and range of psychological and social control strategies used by minority group members in reaction to discrimination. Allport suggests that the control strategies used depend on whether the individual in the minority group is basically extropunitive or basically intrapunitive. The *extropunitive individual* tends to blame others for his victimization, whereas the *intrapunitive person* tends to blame himself or to take it on himself to adjust to, rather than attempt to change, the situation.

If the individual member of the minority group is extropunitive, he may adopt one or more of the following strategies: (1) develop an obsessive concern and suspicion about any action by dominant group members; (2) engage in sly or cunning activities in an attempt to gain control over the situation; (3) help to strengthen the in-group ties of the minority group; (4) engage in aggressive activity ranging from stealing to active revolt or rebellion, or (5) engage in enhanced status striving by working hard in order to show majority members that he is as good as they are.

Attitudes and Behavior

Prejudice is an attitude, a set of shared, unfavorable beliefs and feelings people have about other groups of people. *Discrimination* is a pattern of behavior that deprives members of a socially defined category of opportunities or rights because of their membership in that category. The two often accompany each other, but in many important and significant circumstances they do not.

Among the earliest studies indicating this discrepancy between attitudes and behavior is one by Richard LaPiere, conducted during the early 1930s. Traveling in the United States with a Chinese couple, LaPiere and his associates stayed or ate without incident or question in 250 hotels, auto camps, tourist homes, and restaurants. Only one motel refused to accommodate them. Six months later a questionnaire was sent to each establishment asking, "Would you accept members of the Chinese race as guests in your establishment?" Only one "yes" response was received.[a]

LaPiere's exploration into the discrepancies between attitudes and behavior in intergroup relations was followed up by other investigators. Melvin Kohn and Robin Williams, Jr., summarized much existing research when they noted that

> an ever-accumulating body of research demonstrates that allegedly prejudiced persons act in a thoroughly egalitarian manner in situations where that is the socially prescribed mode of behavior, and that allegedly unprejudiced persons discriminate in situations where they feel it is socially appropriate to do so. It is also well known that patterns of "appropriateness" in intergroup behavior have been changing with increasing tempo in recent years. The unthinkable of a short time ago has in many areas of life become the commonplace of today.[b]

Individuals and groups who express extreme attitudes of prejudice often behave in an accepting or nondiscriminatory fashion to members of supposedly despised minority groups in certain situations, whereas individuals who claim attitudes of tolerance have practiced control strategies of discrimination. Joseph Lohman and Dietrich Reitzes explain this

If the individual member of the minority group is intropunitive, he may adopt one or more of the following strategies: (1) attempt to deny membership in the minority group into which he has been placed; (2) attempt to withdraw from contact with the dominant group or become passive in his interaction with members of the dominant group; (3) engage in clowning activity in an attempt to gain a positive response from members of the dominant group; (4) engage in self-hatred; (5) become aggressive against members of the minority group in which he is a member; (6) develop sympathy with other people who are victimized by the dominant group; (7) engage in symbolic status striving, such as buying expensive clothing or cars he cannot afford in an

---

phenomenon as the result of the bureaucratized nature of modern society, with its plethora of formal groups and widespread use of procedural strategies:[c]

> While there are some situations in which the behavior of persons toward others can be explained individual *qua* individual, in terms of specific attitudes, in the major and significant areas of social life—namely, jobs, business, and the community—this conception is not adequate. Thus, most situations of racial contact are defined by the collectively defined interests of the individuals concerned and do not merely manifest their private feelings toward other races, for example, Negroes.
>
> Thus, the residential neighborhood is the special locale in which individuals attempt to realize such specific interests as personal and social deference and the protection of property values; in the commercial districts and in neighborhood shopping centers, it is profits, value received, and convenience; and, on the job, it is wages, security, and working conditions. In terms of these several kinds of interests, the activities of individuals are mobilized and collectively shaped in modern mass society. Of necessity, these interests bring individuals together in organizations and cause the members to reflect in themselves, as individuals, the *raison d'être* of the collectivities. These deliberately organized groups structure and define the situations for the individual and offer him ready and available definitions of behavior. Individual behavior is, for all practical purposes, made a fiction. Hence, a distinctly personal attitude toward minority groups may be of little consequence in explaining an individual's behavior.[c]

A worker may express extreme attitudes of prejudice toward minorities when questioned verbally, yet accept and work with them amicably on the job and willingly shop in the same shopping center they do. However, he may react violently if a minority group member tries to move on his block. His behavior is determined by the situational context that defines his interests for him rather than by his prejudiced attitudes.

[a]Richard T. LaPiere, "Attitudes vs. Actions," *Social Forces* (March 1934), pp. 230–237.
[b]Melvin Kohn and Robin Williams, Jr., "Situational Patterning in Intergroup Relations," *American Sociological Review*, Vol. 21 (April 1956), p. 164.
[c]Joseph Lohman and Dietrich Reitzes, "Note on Race Relations in Mass Society," *American Journal of Sociology*, Vol. LVIII (Nov. 1952), pp. 240–246.

attempt to enhance his self-esteem; or (8) become mentally ill as a result of discriminatory treatment and the low self-esteem it can produce in individual members of a minority group.[16]

The control strategies used by various types of minority groups, the control strategies used by dominant groups against the minority groups, and the social and psychological control strategies used by individual members of minority groups who are the victims of discrimination have been presented. These are reciprocal control strategies that structure the relationships between dominant and minority groups and thus contribute to the social ordering of the society.

STRUCTURAL SOURCES OF INTERGROUP CONFLICT

Why do groups that differ from one another find it difficult to live together in peace in a pluralistic society where all people have equal access to the good things of life and equal control over their lives and destines? We will restrict our discussion to the more important answers to these queries.

In general, the most important cause of dominant-minority group antagonisms is perceived threats to the satisfaction of basic needs by members of the dominant group. When individuals or groups feel threatened, they react by using control strategies against the perceived threat in an attempt to contain or eliminate it. We will briefly examine some basic needs of individuals and groups that may be threatened by the presence of a minority group in the society. These basic needs include security (especially economic), self-esteem, and individual meaning.

Threats to Security

Threats to individual security and especially to economic security are the most important sources of hostility toward a minority group. Considerable evidence indicates that if people's jobs are threatened and if there are no available alternatives they will strike out against the *perceived* source of the threat, which, of course, is not always the real source.[17] For example, if persons in the dominant group cannot get jobs, or lose their jobs, or fail to get what they believe are deserved promotions, they are likely to blame others rather than themselves, thus protecting their self-esteem. Minority groups are relatively powerless and so can be blamed and used as a scapegoat. Under most conditions, they cannot effectively fight back. Blaming them rather than the real cause is relatively safe.

Whites in the lower classes discriminate against black people more than do whites in the upper classes. This may change as the number of blacks occupying professional and managerial jobs increases, especially if there is a tightening of the job market at the upper levels. During the latter part of the last century and the early part of this century it was lower-class people who discriminated the most against newly arrived immigrants. People with their feet on the bottom rung of the status ladder tend to be highly insecure and afraid of falling. They perceived the waves of new immigrants coming into the cities as direct threats to their jobs. The availability of jobs is limited always, and increased competition from members of minority groups strikes fear in the hearts of those whose jobs might be endangered. Not only are their present positions seen as threatened, but also the upward mobility they seek for themselves and for their children.

Another threat to security is the threat of crime. Certain minorities are *stereotyped* as criminal and are uniformly seen as a threat to life and property. People in the dominant group often use the strategy of avoidance to remove themselves as far as possible from these people.

Anything that is perceived as a threat to the security of the dominant group can produce the use of discriminatory strategies. Many Germans supported Hitler because of the widespread economic and political insecurity among the German people in the late 1920s and early 1930s.[18] In this country, the number of anti-Semitic organizations increased phenomenally during the Great Depression of the 1930s because Jews were erroneously blamed by many as having caused it. When security is threatened, people are likely to blame someone less powerful than themselves and a minority is a convenient scapegoat. This practice is often encouraged by those with more power so that blame will not be placed on them, where it frequently belongs.

Threats to Self-esteem

There is a basic need for self-esteem. If people perceive their self-esteem as being threatened in any way by the presence of a minority group, they can be expected to use control strategies in an attempt to reduce this threat. These may take the form of avoidance, as with whites who attempt to escape from the inner-city as black people move in, or the form of antilocutions, in which one attempts to build himself up by tearing down the image of minority group members through derogatory terms or ethnic jokes.

Because self-esteem is fragile, especially among people with low prestige or few membership groups that reinforce their self-esteem, keeping members of minority groups down is a useful strategy. As people put others down they see themselves as maintaining or increasing their own self-esteem. If someone is below them, they see their self-esteem as enhanced and assume others see them that way too.

Threats to Individual Meaning

Each of us has a desire for individual meaning. Often the basis of our meaning system is embedded in cultural values that, at times, include religious and nationalistic values.

When many large ethnic groups appeared on the American scene bringing with them different cultural values (including, in some cases, different religious values) they were perceived by many as a direct threat to basic meaning systems. The implication was that if ethnic groups maintained their values they considered them to be as good as or perhaps better than those of the dominant groups that had been in America for a longer period of time. The ethnic presence (different cultural values and meaning systems) thus posed a threat to the *validity* of the white-Anglo-Saxon-Protestant value system. Although black people had been here equally as long as many whites, they had been enslaved and were so recently emancipated they had little opportunity to dent the power structure and meaning system of the dominant group.

This threat to an established meaning system caused these ethnic groups to be reduced to minority group status. They were encouraged and at times forced to give up many of their ethnic ways to become "good Americans." These ethnic groups did not completely reject all of their old cultural values and usages. Elements of pluralism remained. However, even the presence of the remaining differences was perceived as a threat to the existing cultural values and individual meaning systems and identities of the dominant group.

Additional Factors Affecting Discrimination

There are additional reasons why minorities tend to stay in a subordinate position: (1) Economic gains accrue to a dominant group that are based on discrimination and the economic exploitation of minority groups. American slavery, for example, clearly benefited the dominant group. Despite improvements, American blacks on the whole remain economically exploited; they are numbered disproportionately among the poorest paid, the last hired, and the first fired. In the Union of South Africa and Southern Rhodesia blacks are severely exploited for economic gain. (2) When ethnic group members are largely lower class, class dislike can be translated into ethnic group prejudice and subsequent discrimination. This reduces the ethnic group to minority group status. (3) Once stereotypes about a minority group become part of a cultural agreement among the dominant group, they are often uncritically accepted, believed in, and acted on over time. This has tended to occur with the Jewish population in America as well as Polish-Americans, Italian-Americans and a variety of other ethnic groups.

If there is not to be continuous conflict where ethnic and minority groups are present, solutions must be forthcoming. We turn now to a discussion of positive solutions that have been attempted in this country.

A Solution to the Problem of Meaning and Identity: Ethnicity in the Pluralistic Society

In his discussion of immigrant ethnic groups Will Herberg sees the solution as a three-generation process.[19] The first generation of immigrants tends to keep its old cultural ways and is perceived as a threat. The second generation tends to reject the ways of their parents, due, in part, to discrimination and in order to use the strategy of assimilation. The third generation, feeling more secure, tends to return to at least some of the cultural traditions of its ancestors. By this time, they are no longer seen as a threat even though, as indicated earlier, the sharp edge of humor remains in the form of ethnic jokes. Thus, American society maintains a degree of pluralism in certain areas.

Milton M. Gordon's work shows that the identities and meaning systems of many ethnic groups remain embedded in their ethnic past while they function within the framework of the larger society.[20] Figure 8-1 illustrates how self-identity is "embedded" within the framework of national origins, religion, and race, all of which are encapsulated within the framework of the national society.

This is possible without any continuous threat either to the dominant group or to many other ethnic groups because ethnic identities are sustained within the framework of primary group relationships. Differences are not too threatening to others because they are not highly visible in the formal groups where members of ethnic groups and the dominant group are most likely to meet. Figure 8-2 and Table 8-1 show how Gordon believes this process works.

In the formal group areas of political and economic institutions ethnicity is mostly mixed, whereas in education it is partly mixed. Primary group areas, however, such as religion, family, and recreation tend to be ethnically enclosed. The problem of threat is, in part, solved by

FIGURE 8-1

Ethnic Identity of an American

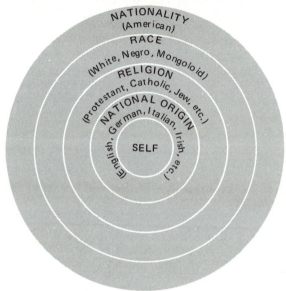

SOURCE: From *Assimilation in American Life*, by Milton M. Gordon. Copyright © 1964 by Oxford University Press, Inc., reprinted by permission.

ethnic groups hiding their ethnic customs within the framework of primary groups, which are not typically open to public view. In these areas ethnic groups can maintain their sense of group identification. The meaning systems of the various ethnic groups are protected from others and the threat to what Gordon calls the white-Anglo-Saxon-Protestant core is reduced.

Gordon suggests that the ethnic group

TABLE 8-1

Ethnicity and Institutional Activity

Institution	Ethnicity
Political	Mostly mixed
Economic	Mostly mixed, with significant exceptions
Education	Partly mixed—parochial schools and some segregation in social activities qualify mixing influence of formal structure of public and private nonparochial school systems
Religion	Ethnically enclosed
Family	Ethnically enclosed
Recreation	Ethnically enclosed in participation, except for impersonal relationships at mass entertainment functions

From *Assimilation in American Life*, by Milton M. Gordon. Copyright © 1964 by Oxford University Press, Inc. Reprinted by permission.

FIGURE 8-2

Ethnic Groups in American Society

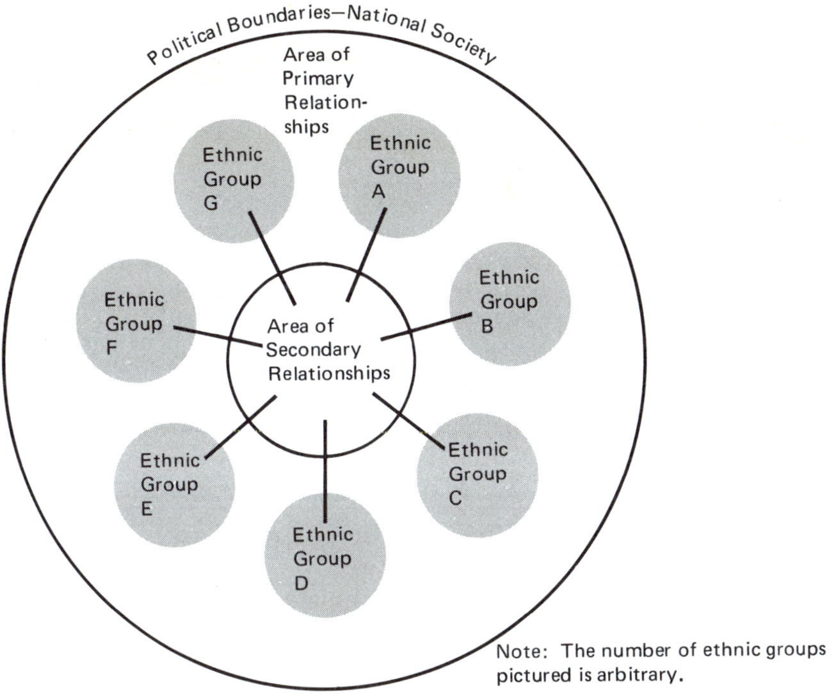

Note: The number of ethnic groups pictured is arbitrary.

SOURCE: From *Assimilation in American Life*, by Milton M. Gordon. Copyright © 1964 by Oxford University Press, Inc., reprinted by permission.

refracts the national cultural patterns of behavior and values through the prism of its own cultural heritage. This unique subnational heritage may consist of cultural norms brought over from the country of recent emigration, it may rest on different religious values, or on the cumulative domestic experiences of enforced segregation as a group within American borders over a number of generations, or on some combination of these sources of cultural diversity. It is this phenomenon which is patently the basis for the term *cultural pluralism*, used to describe the model of American society as a composite of groups which have preserved their cultural identity.[21]

The movement toward a mass society is partly tempered by the presence of ethnic enclaves that have enriched and continue to enrich American life.

This solution to the problem of meaning and identity is clearly pluralistic and appears to be suitable only for those groups whose differences or subordinate status or threat to the dominant majority are not so great that the solution is not permitted. For some groups in our society, "private" ethnicity and "public" conformity to the dominant groups norms has not been an effective solution. We shall now briefly examine one such severely disadvantaged minority: black Americans.

A CASE STUDY OF MAJORITY-MINORITY RELATIONS: THE BLACK EXPERIENCE IN AMERICA

The black experience in America began in the utmost degradation. Pierre van den Berghe points out that "The Negro was defined as a subhuman, disfranchised part of the polity, as a special form of chattel, assessed at three fifths of a man by Constitutional compromise between South and North."[22] He estimates that

> In 1860 on the eve of the Civil War, some 4.44 millions in a total population of 31.44 millions were Negroes, and only some 488,000 were free. Some 47 per cent of the free Negroes lived outside the South. Some of the slaves worked in cities as craftsmen or domestic servants; but the plantation based on the monoculture, first of tobacco in Virginia and later of cotton throughout the Black Belt, was the involuntary home of the mass of Negro Americans.[23]

A Failure of the Ethnic Solution: A Chinese-American

In a fascinating study of San Francisco's Chinatown, Victor and Brett de Bary Nee portray the variety and complexity of the strategies that Chinese-Americans have employed in the history of their tortuous relations with the dominant white majority in America.[a] Perhaps because physiological differences make for high visibility similar to that for black Americans, the Chinese have had to go much farther in abandoning their ethnicity to secure acceptance than ethnic groups who could conform more easily and completely to the white-Anglo-Saxon-Protestant norms.

The authors quote the talented Chinese-American writer Frank Chin, who described his dilemma clearly:

> But the [conflict with whites] taught me something, you know. That I was Chinese-American, whatever that meant. That I was not an individual, not just a human being. Just a human being in this culture, in this society, is a white man, he can disappear. I couldn't disappear, no matter how enlightened I was, no matter how straight my English was. Someone, just because they saw my skin color, would detect an accent. Someone would always correct me. And well, then I began to look at my writing, what I'd been writing about in my letters and everything was just to this point. The Chinese-American, well, schizophrenia. That I'd been playing a kind of ping pong game, you know. Now I'm Chinese, now I'm American. But up against real Chinese in this isolated setting I saw that I had nothing in common with them. That they didn't understand me, and I didn't understand them. We both used chopsticks, okay, that's recognizable. But that's mechanics, not culture. On a personal gut level that doesn't make us brothers.[b]

[a]Victor and Brett de Barry Nee, *Longtime Californ': A Documentary Study of An American Chinatown* (New York: Random, 1973).
[b]Ibid., p. 383.

Black people did not accept the yoke of slavery with docility. John W. Blassingame points out, in his excellent book, *The Slave Community*, that:

> In spite of the slave's general submissiveness, he might at any time resist his master or overseer. In every daily confrontation with his master violence threatened to erupt. Any spark could set off the reaction: carping criticism for work the slave knew had been done well, or a clearly unjustified flogging, or almost anything else. The slave might submit to any and all abuse for years, then, suddenly fed up, fight any man who attempted to punish him. In many instances the slaves fought with or killed their masters and overseers when their temporary anger overcame their customary caution.[24]

The Fourteenth Amendment to the Constitution enacted after the Civil War freed black people *from* legal slavery; however, it did not free them *for* full participation in American life. The dominant white group continued to use many types of discriminatory control strategies in an attempt to keep black people in their "place." This place was defined by whites to keep all black people below all white people and thus out of the race for income, prestige, and power. Black people, as defined by the dominant white group, were second class citizens.

The *Plessy* v. *Ferguson* separate-but-equal Supreme Court decision of 1898 gave the strategy of educational segregation legal approval. Segregation was used in many other areas of American life and black people were increasingly restricted to their own communities.

Booker T. Washington, a black leader at the beginning of this century advocated his "separate as fingers on the hand" philosophy and told black people to be satisfied with menial jobs to prove to white people that they were capable of, and therefore should have, better jobs. Thus they might someday be treated as equals. Washington's advocacy of accommodation strategies was challenged by W. E. B. Dubois, another famous black leader and founder of the National Association of Colored People, who argued for the use of legal procedural strategies and coercive strategies to gain equality for black people. Black leaders during the early part of this century obviously were advocating the use of different strategies for the solution of their problems.

Some attempts were made to use withdrawal strategies. The most famous was the "Back to Africa Movement" led by Marcus Garvey. Garvey's movement had considerable appeal to a segment of the black community, but it failed and Garvey ended up in prison. As was pointed out in Chapter 5, more and more black people moved to northern cities seeking better jobs and living conditions, especially during and following World War II. Riots, threats of boycotts, and other control strategies were used by blacks in their continuing attempt to gain equality and opportunity.

A 1954 United States Supreme Court decision reversed the separate-but-equal decision of 1898. Increased educational and employment opportunities, at least for some blacks, gradually appeared. During the 1950s the probability of reducing discrimination was high. Black people began to mobilize. Leaders such as Martin Luther King emerged and began to effectively use nonviolent coercive strategies. Jacqueline J. Clark made the following discoveries in her study of three Alabama communities:

> The most significant of these measures, both in terms of the organizational policies and programs and the uses made of them in Alabama, are (1) mass

---

Black-White Relations in America: Caste or Class?

One of the most enduring conflicts in the sociological literature revolves around whether the relations between the white majority group and the black minority group in America can be conceptualized best as caste or quasi-caste relations or whether black Americans are assimilated into the social class stratification system. Certainly there are aspects of both systems of stratification. The restrictions on intermarriage, the obsession with social contact and racial purity, and the intricate patterns of black-white etiquette that reinforced the superior legal and economic position of the whites in the South prior to the Civil Rights movement of the 1960s bore more than a faint resemblance to our description of the Indian caste system.

Warner and his colleagues developed a view that combined caste and class to explain majority-minority relations in the American South by suggesting that white-black relations were organized by a caste strategy but that within each class there were social classes. All of the classes in the black caste were subordinate in prestige to all of the classes in the white caste. In an influential paper based on research conducted in the 1930s, Allison Davis suggested that

> Caste in the Deep South integrates into one system all aspects of white-Negro behavior: social, sexual, economic, political, educational, religious, legal, associational, and recreational. The basic subsystem—caste—is a rigid stratification, maintained by physical, social, and psychological punishments and rewards. Everywhere in the South, caste establishes and maintains an endogamous and socially separate system of white-Negro relationship in which by birth the Negroes are all of lower, and the whites all of higher, status. This social caste system is more rigid than that described in the classic literature on Hindu castes.
>
> All white or colored institutions of the southern community, including the church, the school, and the courts, systematically organize and defend the caste system. The only institution which is not completely so organized is the economic.
>
> Not all the members of a color caste . . . possess equal rank and similar ranges of participation. Within the Negro and white castes, all individuals are further

meetings; (2) nonviolent techniques, especially boycotting, or rather what Negroes refer to as "protest" inasmuch as boycotting is illegal in Alabama; and (3) legal-judiciary measures, including voting.[25]

Many nonviolent coercive strategies such as sit-ins, stand-ins, and mass marches were used by blacks in an attempt to improve their conditions. These strategies produced as a response by the dominant majority legal procedural strategies, such as the Civil Rights Act of 1964 and the Voting Rights Act of 1965.

The fires of hope were kindled among many black people but these hopes, at best, were satisfied only partially. Nonviolent coercive

---

stratified by their caste members into a social class hierarchy. Whereas there is a chance that they may move out of their class, there is no possibility, as the system now operates, that they may change their color-caste membership or participation. Through physical birthmarks an individual is assigned his caste position; whether he is white or Negro, he also dies in his birth caste.[a]

Davis goes on to describe intercaste etiquette in terms that are clearly dated, even for the Deep South, and that probably never prevailed widely as control strategies between blacks and whites in any other part of the country:

Whites in this area must not shake hands with Negroes or address them as "Mr.," "Miss," or "Mrs." They address all Negroes either as "girl" or "boy" or by their first names. On the other hand, Negroes must address all whites honorifically. Even an upper-class Negro planter or physician will always address a lower-class white as "Mr.," "Mrs.," or "Miss," whereas whites will not address Negroes in this way, although they may address them as "Professor" or "Doctor." The few exceptions to these rules are limited to Negro domestics who may address their white employers by their first names plus the honorific form, such as "Miss Alice" or "Mr. John," and to some upper middle-class whites who occasionally address a Negro as "Mr." or "Mrs."

Deference to whites by Negroes also includes a conciliating and often whining tone in speaking, removal of the hat, and acquiescence to statements or demands by the white. An absolute taboo prevails against any Negro's contradicting, cursing, or shouting angrily at any white.[b]

Oliver Cox and other sociologists have correctly criticized Davis's approach for overemphasizing the presumed cultural agreements supporting the castelike Southern system and ignoring the considerable evidence for conflict and refusal by blacks to comply.[c] Surely the millions of blacks who voted with their feet against the southern system by going to northern cities seeking better jobs, living conditions, and lessened discrimination bear witness to the reluctance of many to comply.

[a]Allison Davis, "Caste, Economy and Violence," *American Journal of Sociology*, Vol. LI (July 1945), pp. 7–8.
[b]Ibid., p. 10.
[c]Oliver Cox, *Caste, Class, and Race* (Garden City, N.Y.: Doubleday, 1948).

strategies gave way to the use of violent coercive strategies. Riots broke out in many major American cities in the mid-1960s.

Black Power

In their aptly titled book, *Black Power: The Politics of Liberation in America,* Stokely Carmichael and Charles Hamilton say:

> The concept of Black Power rests on a fundamental premise: Before a group can enter the open society, it must first close ranks. By this we mean that group solidarity is necessary before a group can operate effectively from a bargaining position of strength in a pluralistic society.[26]

Carmichael and Hamilton's point can be rephrased in our concepts. Society is structured by reciprocal control relationships. If one group lacks a sufficient amount of power to effectively influence these control relationships, they may at any time be placed or kept in a position of subservience. Black power based on black solidarity is necessary if blacks are to make effective use of control strategies.

Black power is also important for black people's self-identity and individual meaning. Historically, black people have been evaluated by white standards. An *individual* black could never be sure if his treatment by whites was based on his being black or based on what his qualities were as an individual. History forced black people to use whites as a positive reference group, but the responses from this group could never be completely trusted. If it was "white" it was good; if it was "black" it was bad. The "mark of oppression"[27] weighed heavily on many black people who were unable to develop acceptable definitions on their own terms as individuals with self-identities and individual meaning systems. Black power based on black solidarity offers the possibility of separating individual merit and meaning from color in a society dominated by a white majority.

Black Nationalism

There is a definite split among black people in this country about the best way to proceed toward gaining equality. Charles V. Hamilton defines the split as the nationalist versus the integrationist:

> The nationalists see a "black community" that should be strengthened and controlled by blacks; the integrationists see a "black ghetto" that should be broken up and integrated into the mainstream.[28]

The problem with the nationalist position is that the meaningful power in our society is presently held by whites, who control the resources and make the decisions that tend to order black-white relations. The problem with the integrationist position is that whites are not completely convinced that they want integration and they have the power to stop it.

A possible compromise solution is contained in Gordon's ethnic solution. If black people can be guaranteed equal opportunity in the formal political and economic institutions, and the educational institutions can remain mixed, black people may be able to find individual meaning and identity within the framework of the primary group relationships of family, religion, and recreation. Whether even this solution is feasible depends on many factors, especially its acceptability to the dominant white majority.

Some Remaining Black-White Inequities

The 1970 census showed that 35.0 per cent of all black people, as compared with 10.9 per cent of white people, live below the poverty level. Furthermore, even though the median income of black families rose 99.6 per cent between 1960 and 1970 (compared with a 69.0 per cent increase for white families), the median income for black families is still far below that of white families in all sections of the country. The average difference is about $3,000.[29]

The results of three hundred years of discrimination are not easily or immediately overcome. Giant steps must be made if the gap between blacks and whites is to be closed so that blacks will have an equal chance in the competitive struggle and solution of an ethnic type can become possible.

OTHER MINORITY GROUPS

American Indians, Puerto Ricans, Spanish-Americans, and other minorities have had group and individual experiences caused by the differential distribution of power in American society that parallel in significant respects the experiences of black people. Each minority group, of course, has its unique history, subculture, and problems, but they share a common deprivation that is caused by their powerlessness and the control strategies used to subordinate them. For example, Table 8-2 presents some indices that dramatize the plight of the American Indian.

TABLE 8-2
The Plight of the Indian

	American Indian	*U.S.*
Suicides (1970)	32.0 per 100,000	16.0 per 100,000
Life expectancy (1970)	47 years	70.8 years
Unemployment rate (1972)	45% estimated	5.8%
Median family income (1971)	$4,000	$9,867
Infant mortality (1970)	30.9 per 1,000 live births	21.8 per 1,000 live births
Per cent entering college (1971)	18%	50%

SOURCE: *The New York Times* (Nov. 12, 1972). © 1972 by The New York Times Company. Reprinted by permission.

The Black Experience

Being black in America means quite probably the inheritance of inequality in virtually every aspect of life that makes a difference. Much the same also can be said for Mexican, Puerto Rican, and American Indian people living in the United States, but since a discussion of these minority groups raises other aspects of inequality, the discussion will be limited to blacks alone.[a] These are some of the hard facts of race and what it means to be black in the United States today.[b]

1. The chances are 1 in 3 that you will be poor, compared with 1 in 10 for white persons.
2. There is almost twice the likelihood, as compared with whites, that you will be unemployed and an even greater likelihood that you will be underemployed.
3. The chances are 1 in 10 of being a professional or a manager, compared with 3 in 10 among whites.
4. The chances are 1 out of 5 that, if you are a black woman who is working, it will be as a domestic; if you are a man, it will be the same chance that you are working as an unskilled laborer.
5. If you are between the ages of fourteen and nineteen, there is about 1 chance in 6 that you are a high school dropout, compared with about 1 chance in 13 if you were white.
6. If you are a black mother, yours could be one of the 23 out of every 1,000 infants that will die within the first month of life, compared with a rate of 14.7 per 1,000 for whites.
7. For every 1,000 unmarried black women, there are 86.6 illegitimate births, compared with a much lower 13.2 for every 1,000 unmarried white women. The rate for black women, by the way, has fallen in the last decade while it has increased sharply for white women.
8. For every 100,000 black women, 849 of them have been the victims of a violent crime, compared with 164 white women. For men, the respective rates are 523 and 394.

Women As a Minority Group

Women have been categorized by a physical characteristic and often are labeled and treated collectively as inferior. To this extent, they are a minority group. Women have been discouraged and often prevented from entering traditionally male occupations. Furthermore, they make less money than men do working within the same major occupational categories. (Paying a woman less than a man for the same job is now illegal.) Much of this difference is caused by restrictions against females entering the higher paid jobs within these categories. The median income for females in 1970 was less than one half that for males. In 1950, it was a little *more* than one half. As a total group of workers, females have lost rather than gained in relationship to males

These are but some of the vital statistics of black existence; they represent a portrait of unequal probabilities for death, employment, poverty, and education. However, bad as these statistics look, they show improvement in relation to the past, and in some instances there are marked improvements over conditions a decade ago. The situation for blacks in America has improved, but this appraisal engenders optimism only if you look backward to the ground that has been covered. On the other hand there is, perhaps, pessimism if one looks forward to the ground that has yet to be covered to decrease the remaining inequalities.

Whether or not the situation has improved, the inequalities suffered by blacks have been colossal, ranging in a long history from public violence and deadly assault to the more subtle forms of discrimination, disregard, and neglect that have been part of the experience of other minority groups in America as well.

Comparative Proportions of Minority Groups

	Number (in millions)	*Percent of Total Population*
Negro	22.3	11.0
Mexican	5.1	2.5
Puerto Rican	1.5	.7
Indian	.5	.3

Bureau of the Census, "Spanish-American Population: November 1969," *Current Population Reports,* Series P-20, No. 195 (Washington, D.C.: U.S. Government Printing Office, February 20, 1970). Indian population figures from U.S. Census, 1960.

[a]In addition to cultural differences, these minorities also differ as to their numbers, which would complicate a comparative analysis.

[b]From Leonard Reissman, *Inequality in American Society* (Glenview, Ill.: Scott, Foresman, 1973), pp. 71, 72.

since 1950. Taking salesworkers as an example, the median income for males in 1970 was $8,321 and for females $2,279. Males are typically recruited for positions such as sales representatives, whereas females are recruited as salespeople in department stores or supermarkets and paid a much lower wage. For salesworkers, this difference results in more than $6,000 per year less for females than for males.

Women have gained little ground in the occupations usually held by males since 1950. They have gained significantly in such occupations as bank tellers, bakers, and bartenders but these are relatively low-paying occupations and have little prestige. The gain has not been nearly as significant in the higher paying and more prestigious occupations of doctor, lawyer, and judge. They have gained in some middle-level occupations such as editors, reporters, and accountants. The traditional female occupations as nurses, secretaries, typists and telephone operators are still more than 90 per cent female, whereas the skilled worker categories, electricians, auto mechanics, and professional engineers remain more than 98 per cent male.

In the economic sphere, women as a total group of workers, have lost ground in mean money income since 1950 in relationship to men. They have not made significant progress toward filling traditionally male-dominated occupations.

Women and Politics

In the political institution, few women have been actively recruited by male-dominated political parties to run for political offices and few have volunteered to run. They either do not see it as the "proper thing to do" because of the weight of tradition or they are afraid of possible recriminations if they aggressively enter politics. It took an amendment to the United States Constitution to give women the right to vote and the fight for this was led by women, not men. With the defeat of Margaret Chase Smith in the 1972 election, the United States Senate became once again an all-male body. In the 92nd Congress there were only fourteen women in the House of Representatives.

Discrimination has also been present in religious groups. Only recently have women been allowed to become members of the clergy in some major Protestant denominations, and they are still not actively recruited for these positions. Women are also discriminated against in the Catholic and Jewish religions by not being permitted to hold the major positions of religious authority.

In most institutional areas outside the family, women have been relegated to positions of subservience. Even in the family, traditionally women have been expected to be subservient to men.

Women and Sexual Identity

The problem of sexuality is perhaps the most destructive of all the problems faced by women. In many situations a woman never knows whether she is being accepted, honored, or offered a job as a *person* or as a *sexual object,* especially if she is a physically attractive person. As a result, many women have the same problem as black people in establishing a secure self-identity. It is difficult for them to separate "personhood" from sexuality. Indeed, some women have no meaningful identity other than a sexuality that is prominently displayed. This is a double tragedy. Sexuality is a flimsy basis for meaning, and revealing clothing and cosmetics do not wear well as women become older in a society that venerates youth and honors the "Pepsi generation."

Some may respond by saying that this is how most women want it. However, for generations women have not had the opportunity to have it any other way in a male dominated world. When alternatives are restricted, people tend to emphasize their allowable strengths and women are no exception to this. Just as many lower-class males must prove themselves by emphasizing their physical strength because they lack alternative ways to gratify their need for self-esteem; women, who are denied other ways of enhancing their self-esteem, emphasize their sexuality. This is a tragic consequence of a society that does not offer equal opportunity in all spheres of activity.

Many of the activities of the Women's Liberation movement and the other activist groups that have grown up to fight for women's rights represent attempts to provide individual meaning and stable self-identities. Parallels with other minority groups are clear, although the differences must not be overlooked. Women and men interact within the kinship institution and find their principal bonds in primary group ties. For this reason, the ethnic-type pluralistic solution suggested by Gordon is not feasible here.

REFERENCES

1. Schermerhorn, R. A. *Comparative Ethnic Relations: A Framework for Theory and Research.* New York: Random, 1970, p. 12. Schermerhorn's original definition reads: "An ethnic group is defined here as a collectivity within a larger society having real or putative common ancestry, memories of a shared historical past, and a cultural focus on one or more symbolic elements defined as the epitome of their peoplehood."
2. Ibid., p. 12.
3. Ibid.
4. Mack, Raymond W., and Troy S. Duster. *Patterns of Minority Relations.* New York: Anti-Defamation League, 1964, pp. 11–12.
5. Ibid., p. 12.

6. Baltzell, E. Digby. *The Protestant Establishment*. New York: Vantage, 1964. Also, see Glazer, Nathan. *American Judaism*. Chicago: U. of Chicago, 1957; and Handlin, Oscar. *Adventure in Freedom: Three Hundred Years of Jewish Life in America*. New York: McGraw-Hill, 1954.
7. Shapiro, H. L. "Revised Version of UNESCO Statement on Race." *American Journal of Physical Anthropology*, Vol. 10 (1952), 368.
8. Wirth, Louis. "The Problem of Minority Groups." In *The Science of Man in the World Crisis*. Ed. by Ralph Linton. New York: Columbia U.P., 1945.
9. Warner, W. Lloyd, and Leo Srole. *The Social Systems of American Ethnic Groups*. New Haven, Conn.: Yale, 1945.
10. Wirth, op. cit., p. 357.
11. See Kennedy, Ruby Jo Reeves. "Single or Triple Melting-Pot? Intermarriage in New Haven, 1870–1940." *American Journal of Sociology*, Vol. XLIX, No. 4, (Jan. 1944), 331–339.
12. Wirth, op. cit., p. 361.
13. Williams, Jr., Robin M. *The Reduction of Intergroup Tensions*. New York: Social Science Research Council, 1947, Proposition 43, p. 61.
14. Wattenberg, Benjamine, and Richard Scammon. "Black Progress and Liberal Rhetoric." *Commentary* (April 1973). An ensuing exchange with readers appeared in the Aug. 1973 issue. P. 4.
15. Allport, Gordon W. *The Nature of Prejudice*. Cambridge, Mass.: Addison-Wesley, 1954, pp. 14–15.
16. Ibid., p. 160.
17. Allport, op. cit., p. 15.
18. See Fromm, Erich. *Escape from Freedom*. New York: Rinehart, 1941.
19. Herberg, Will. *Protestant-Catholic-Jew*. Garden City, N.Y.: Doubleday, 1955.
20. Gordon, Milton M. *Assimilation in American Life*. New York: Oxford U.P., 1964. Also, see Glazer, Nathan, and Daniel Patrick Moynihan. *Beyond the Melting Pot*. Cambridge, Mass.: M.I.T. Press, 1963.
21. Gordon, op. cit., p. 38.
22. van den Berghe, Pierre. *Race and Racism*. New York: Wiley, 1967, p. 78.
23. Ibid., pp. 79–80.
24. Blassingame, John W. *The Slave Community*. New York: Oxford U.P., 1972, p. 212.
25. Clark, Jacqueline J. "Standard Operational Procedures in Tragic Situations." *Phylon* (4th Quarter, 1961), 323.
26. Carmichael, Stokely, and Charles V. Hamilton. *Black Power: The Politics of Liberation in America*. New York: Vintage, 1967, p. 44.
27. See Kardner, Abram, and Lionel Ovesey. *The Mark of Oppression*. New York: World, 1951.
28. Hamilton, Charles V. "The Nationalist vs. the Integrationist." *The New York Times Magazine* Oct. 1, 1972, p. 52.
29. *General Social and Economic Characteristics: United States Summary*. U.S. Department of Commerce: Bureau of the Census, 1972.

PART III

Social Institutions

Part III is concerned with a discussion of social institutions. There are two major ways in which sociologists study institutions: (1) *descriptively,* by explaining the structure of institutions and how they work, either singly or in comparison with other institutions and (2) *critically,* by using as a basis for analysis the stated or implicit goals of the institution and comparing these with actual institutional practices. Our discussion will use both approaches, emphasizing one or the other as seems appropriate.

In Chapter 9 the concept of institution will be defined and the historical development of institutions will be explored, emphasizing the change from informal to formal controls. How institutions are structured and change over time, creating a blurring across institutional lines and occasionally causing antagonisms, frictions, and struggles for power, will be described. Finally, how some people find meaning by following routinized institutional procedures will be noted.

In Chapter 10 both economic and political institutions are described. The expression *political economy* that appears in the chapter title is one whose usage was prevalent in the nineteenth century. This chapter is primarily concerned with how political and economic power are used (or not used) to allocate goods and services and to maintain order within the framework of American society. A brief history of classical capitalism and classical democracy serves as background for this analysis.

In Chapter 11 the educational institution is described, emphasizing the public school system and how it is structured. The importance of political and bureaucratic constraints on school administrators and teachers will be analyzed along with the control strategies used by students. Social class and race also will be explored as important factors in American education.

In Chapter 12 the types of family structuring found in human societies are described. Analyzing the changes that have occurred in the American family structure suggests that the family has lost many of its important historical reasons for existence. Models of the contemporary American family, constraints that act on the family, the control strategies used in family interaction, and the possible future of the family are discussed.

The institution of religion and how religion contributes to meaning and control are discussed in Chapter 13. Aspects of religion that are shared with science and magic will be briefly considered. An ideal typology of church and sect, the structure of American religious institutions, the specific control aspects of religion, and the possible future of religion will be discussed.

CHAPTER 9

Institutional Analysis

INTRODUCTION

In popular usage the word *institution* often refers to a building housing some form of human activity or to a *specific* organization such as a *particular* college, university, or industrial corporation. The sociologist's use of the term as a concept differs from the popular usage. Sociologists use the concept to refer to broader and more generalized ranges of human behavior. They take the total range of human behaviors and break these down into institutions which are segments of related social processes that have importance for social ordering. The five most important are political institutions, the institution of family, religion, education, and economic institutions. These cover a large portion of human behavior.

These five, however, do not cover the full range of institutions, especially in modern industrial societies. There are also institutions of leisure, science and technology, medical care, welfare, and others. We will, however, restrict our discussion, for the most part, to the five most important institutions listed here.

Sociologists break the total society apart into institutions *only* for the purpose of analysis. In the real world, all institutional areas of human activity influence each other. For example, an income tax law passed by a government has implications for the amount of money that can be spent by families. If many persons lose their jobs because of a depressed economy, the family institution is profoundly affected. A major shift or change in behavior or activity in one modern institution will change, in some way, patterns of behavior in other institutions. Figure 9-1 illustrates the complexity of the institutional web. The political institution focuses on the maintenance of order. The economic institution is concerned with the production and allocation of goods and services and providing gratification for esteem needs.* The educational and family institutions focus on socialization and the provision of gratification for basic individual needs. The religious institution is oriented around providing meaning, purpose, and basic need gratification.

As the discussion of institutions progresses, we will see that the connections between needs, order, and meaning on the one hand and institutions on the other are idealized. In actual practice, institutions do not always meet the needs they are supposed to serve. Nonetheless, these connections provide a place to begin our analysis and will enable us also to criticize institutions insofar as they fail to meet these goals.

THE HISTORICAL DEVELOPMENT OF INSTITUTIONS: FROM INFORMAL TO FORMAL CONTROL

Primitive Fusion: The Extended Family

In primitive societies, there was only one major institution, the extended family, a group that included all those socially defined as kin and their offspring. Extended family members, *within the context of the family,* attempted to provide for all necessary needs and to maintain order. This arrangement is called *primitive fusion.* Family members hunted or grew their own food, built their shelters, socialized their children, met other needs, often had their family or clan religion,[1] and maintained order among family members.

The use of cultural control strategies predominated. The division of labor was within the family group and typically was based on ascribed sex and age roles. Work was done according to informal agreements. There were few alternatives that could gain separate coalitional support because there were few people. Common threats from nature or other groups produced high group solidarity. Such peoples tended to subsist by hunting and gathering or by primitive forms of agriculture. With little economic surplus, there tended to be common sharing of the necessities.

Population grew as agriculture developed and more food was produced. This made possible an elaborate division of labor in which everyone did not have to gather or grow his own food, build his own shelter, and so forth. Some people were freed to engage in other activities. At this point the extended family began losing some of its

*Economists have often overlooked the gratification of esteem needs by the economic institution. One who did not was Thorstein Veblen. See his *The Theory of the Leisure Class* (New York: Macmillan, 1899).

FIGURE 9-1
The Complexity of the Institutional Web

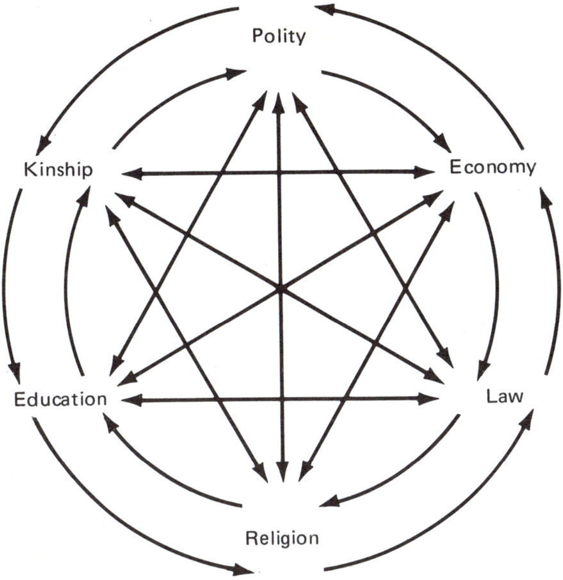

SOURCE: Copyright 1972, McGraw-Hill Book Company. Used with permission of McGraw-Hill Book Company. From *Patterns of Social Organization*, by Jonathan H. Turner.

power over certain areas of human behavior and *primitive fusion* began to break down.

Emergence of Separate Institutions

There is considerable debate about the order in which various institutions evolved out of the extended family over the course of human history.[2] Religion was perhaps the first, often being placed under the jurisdiction of a shaman who was thought to have greater access to supernatural powers. As population increased, some type of control outside the family also became necessary to maintain over-all order among families and individuals. Thus, the rudiments of a political institution came into existence.[3] Economic institutions appeared as *exchanges* of goods and services among people increased and it became necessary to establish the relative value of the different kinds of goods and services that were produced and exchanged. Educational institutions developed as people were taught the rituals and lore required for rites-of-passage ceremonies outside the family.[4]

Some of these institutions reached relatively high levels of separate development in ancient societies in the eastern Mediterranean area and in Asian societies, especially China.[5] The Aztec and Mayan civilizations in Mexico and Meso-America also reached a high level of institutional development.[6] Thus, in some societies, separate institutions have existed for thousands of years.

Change to Formal Control Strategies

As separate institutions developed the control strategies used in their structuring moved toward higher and higher degrees of formalization. Procedural, manipulative, and other types of control strategies began to replace the predominant use of cultural strategies under primitive fusion. States with strong governments came into existence and either mandated or passed laws. Schools staffed by faculties were built as knowledge was accumulated. Churches were established with separate buildings and a trained clergy. Formal creeds based on sacred writings came into existence. In the economy, barter gave way to formal money exchange. Means of production and distribution became rationalized. Home handicraft was moved to the more efficient factory, the division of labor in the industrial system became more complex, and sophisticated techniques to sell goods and services developed.

As institutions became specialized and formalized, the attainment of privilege and power within them became increasingly important. Procedural, manipulative, and coercive strategies came into use to maintain position and power. Modern institutional resources are often used not to maximize the idealized institutional goals but to maintain institutional forms of behavior that guarantee the maintenance of power and privilege for selected individuals and groups. Institutional goals may be partly reached, but the formal structures that come into existence as a *means* of achieving them tend to become ends in themselves.

Critical Perspectives on Modern Institutions

In modern urban-industrial societies specific organizations within many institutions have developed bureaucratic structures and have become highly formalized in their operation. Within these bureaucratic structures positions of power and privilege are created and perpetuated. Their goal becomes to protect the organization rather than to meet the idealized or real needs of the people they ostensibly serve. To clarify this point we will look briefly at some examples within each of the major institutions.

The Economic Institution

The economic institution in the United States increasingly consists of a highly bureaucratized system of huge industrial corporations; it displays a similar well-advanced trend in the selling of goods and services through national drug store chains, national food store chains, national restaurant chains, and so forth. The primary goal of these bureaucratic organizations within the economic system is to make a profit. The meeting of the economic needs of people is secondary. Thus, we find factories operating at less than their potential output even though people need the products they manufacture. Corporations close factories and relocate plants without regard to the severe social dislocations of the workers. Goods are produced, prices are set, and corporate decisions are made by criteria that place the economic needs of most people in a secondary position.

Restrictions are placed on what *could be done* to meet the needs of *all the people*. The perpetuation of a specific type of economic institution, the large corporation and the power and privilege it embodies, takes priority over the basic human needs the economic institution is ideally supposed to meet.

The Religious Institution

In the religious institution means often become more important than stated ends. Large and expensive buildings are built and a hierarchy of clergy is developed who come to count "silver" and the number of members rather than deal with the problem of meaning and the individual's relationship to his or her God. There is little concern with social justice among many of the larger religious bodies, although historically this is part of the Judeo-Christian tradition. There is widespread indifference rather than militant hostility toward established religion in American society, partly because it is doing little that threatens the *status quo*.[7]

The Educational Institution

In an idealized sense the educational institution exists not only for secondary socialization but also to help people create fuller and more meaningful lives. Schools in our society are vehicles for secondary socialization but few of them help individuals build any possible basis for what Maslow has called self-actualization.[8] Like other modern organizations, schools at all levels are bureaucratic and relatively inflexible in the application of procedural rules that are administered without regard to their psychological and social consequences. Our educational institution tends to support and maintain the existing system of stratification and social ordering.

The Political Institution

The political institution in our society is highly bureaucraticized and exists not just to maintain order but to maintain *the existing order*. The political institution tends to support other institutions in their existing states whether or not they serve the idealized reasons for their existence. In return for this support, persons in positions of power in other institutions support the political institution. At a gen-

Public Trust in Leadership

The pollster Louis Harris conducted nationwide surveys of a random sample of the population in 1965, 1972, and 1973 to get some measure of public confidence in those who held leadership positions in various areas of political, social, and business life and to measure changes in those attitudes. The question posed to each respondent was, "As far as the people running [each area of political, business, or social life] are concerned, would you say you have a great deal of confidence, only some confidence, or hardly any confidence at all in them?" Figure 9-2 shows the percentage of respondents who expressed great confidence in the leadership in each area of social life for the three years the survey was conducted.[a]

The findings of the study are highly suggestive, although as with all such surveys, caution must be used in making sweeping interpretations. Clearly, there has been an over-all *decline* in the number of people expressing great confidence in the leaders of most areas between 1965 and 1973. Clearly also, in each of the three years a substantial number of people appeared to have little confidence in those who occupy many formal positions of leadership in our society.

Such polls are highly susceptible to the influence of immediate events. The scandals surrounding the break into the Democratic national headquarters and the subsequent televised hearings and extensive public uproar during 1972, 1973, and 1974 (summed up as "The Watergate Affair"), probably had much to do with the fluctuations in the ratings given the executive branch of the federal government (down dramatically) and television news (up sharply from 1965 after a drop in 1972). Although the pollster titles his findings a measure of "confidence in various institutions," professional sociologists would probably want firmer and more substantial data before interpreting these poll results so broadly.

Harris's over-all findings, nonetheless, are interesting. He suggests that "most Americans generally supported the basic system of government in

eral level, the order of *formal* control relationships that exists within each of the institutional areas gains support from the existing formal order of control relationships that exist in other institutions.

The Institution of Family

Because the institution of the family has lost many of its former purposes to other institutions, the modern family tends to be *constrained* into patterns of behavior fixed by other institutions. Children are forced by law to attend schools and learn what teachers teach them. Jobs, and therefore income and place in the stratification sys-

---

the country and believed that with the right people running it, it could be made to work properly. But the survey's principal findings showed a disillusioned, disenchanted, and cynical public. . . ." Harris supports this conclusion by noting that in 1973, 53 per cent of his respondents agreed that "there is something deeply wrong with America," and that this feeling cut across income lines and was widespread in every segment of the population.[b]

It appears that the individuals in positions of power and privilege in important areas of social life have probably suffered a loss of public confidence, most severely among government leaders but running generally across the board. The implications of this apparent change for control strategies and for the likelihood of social change, however, are hard to analyze. Most persons most of the time go along with the existing arrangements because they derive some benefits, however minimal, from them and are uncertain that changes would improve their lot. If there was a total lack of support for strategic elites and ruling groups, social change would presumably be inevitable and probably occur relatively rapidly, even if the elites relied on coercive strategies solely. For reasons enumerated in our discussion on social stratification, coercion is inherently unstable and unsatisfactory for all parties, including the ruling groups. However, in between the extremes of total support and complete cultural agreement about the validity and desirability of existing social arrangements and rule based on naked force is a vast gray area where it is much more difficult to draw firm conclusions. Harris's findings are suggestive, but as we will see in our detailed examination of institutional arrangements in Chapters 10 through 13, the problems of social ordering and individual meaning are complex and subtle and definitive answers are elusive.

[a]David Rosenbaum, "Public Trust in Institutions Found to Decline," *The New York Times* (Dec. 3, 1973), p. 34.
[b]Ibid.

FIGURE 9-2

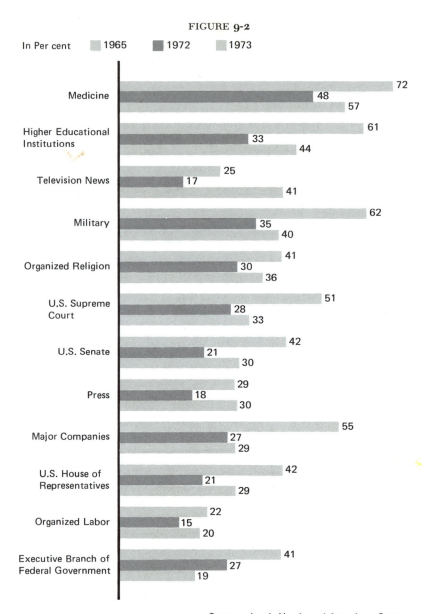

In Per cent ▓ 1965 ▓ 1972 ▓ 1973

Medicine — 72, 48, 57
Higher Educational Institutions — 61, 33, 44
Television News — 25, 17, 41
Military — 62, 35, 40
Organized Religion — 41, 30, 36
U.S. Supreme Court — 51, 28, 33
U.S. Senate — 42, 21, 30
Press — 29, 18, 30
Major Companies — 55, 27, 29
U.S. House of Representatives — 42, 21, 29
Organized Labor — 22, 15, 20
Executive Branch of Federal Government — 41, 27, 19

Source: Louis Harris and Associates Survey

tem, are primarily determined by the economic institution rather than by the family.

The society "works," but not in the idealized sense of optimizing the possibility of need gratification for all people. Some people are clearly more privileged than others.

All this should not be construed to imply that formalized institutions in the United States are much different from institutions in other industrialized nations. At least we can criticize in a relatively open manner institutions that do not meet the needs of people. Such recourse is not available in societies that are openly totalitarian. There is no utopian society in which all human needs are met optimally at all times by all social institutions.

Furthermore, if the formal arrangements of control relationships among institutions were not somewhat supportive of each other, society would be in a state of continuous open conflict. However, this does not alleviate the needs of people that formal institutional structures may fail to gratify. A partial solution to this problem is the development of informal controls.

Informal Adaptations to Formal Institutional Control

When institutions reach a high degree of formal complexity, they are difficult to change. Resistance to change is built into the structure of the formal control relationships that maintain these institutions. Such institutions do serve some of the needs of a considerable number of people, although not in an idealized manner. Thus, even though many people might be dissatisfied with how institutions are structured, they are usually not only relatively powerless to bring about change but they are also reluctant to attempt to do so. Change *might* produce an even worse structure of control relationships. If a person has a job, his family can at least eat. If the political institution is not too repressive, persons can still publicly criticize. Even if a student does not like the way in which a university is run, he can get a degree after four years. In addition, feelings of deprivations are almost always relative. Most people always can find other people who are worse off.

Thus, there tends to be a general acceptance of how institutions work, even though people might not have much confidence in them. To compensate for the lack of need gratification within formal institutions, individuals use a variety of informal control strategies in an attempt to gratify their needs and to attain their goals.

People who have more power within these formal institutions are typically intelligent enough to recognize the limits to which people can be pushed before they rebel. Before this occurs, *ameliorative measures* are taken by those in power in an attempt to maintain their positions.* These ameliorative measures are control strategies that, along with the control strategies used by people with less power, play a part in the structuring of institutions and in slowly changing them over time. Like social order in general, the ordering of the formal organizations that make up the various institutions is structured by reciprocal control.

*These are measures designed to improve conditions without changing the fundamental structure of the institution.

Some of these informal control strategies used by people within the framework of institutions and the ameliorative measures used by those in power in response will be discussed briefly. Many will be discussed in more depth in the chapters on specific institutions.

The Economic Institution

Within the economic institution, there are many informal control strategies that workers use on the job in an attempt to gain some control over the work situation and to gratify their needs. In factories, workers often "run scrap" and slow down the production process to a point below the level specified by formal management. People miss work when they are not sick, take extended coffee breaks, and in general allow their work output to slacken. Workers strike to gain pay increases or to improve their working conditions. Informal friendship groups form that help people to tolerate their jobs and also provide support for the use of informal control strategies.

Ameliorative measures taken by those in power within the economic institution include reduced work weeks, overtime pay, paid vacations, sabbatical leaves after a number of years of service, seniority rules to provide job security, rest breaks, clean-up time in factories, paid lunch periods, health and life insurance coverage, pension plans, job rotation, and a variety of other benefits.

Many of these benefits have been instituted as a result of organized pressure from work groups, labor unions, and governments, but they nevertheless help to keep people performing on the job even though the job itself may not be satisfying.

The Religious Institution

Within modern religious institutions one finds such informal control strategies as low attendance at religious services by members, a variety of social events that have little to do with the historical goals of religion, rejection of formal creeds or their recitation with tongue in cheek, and the firing of unwanted clergy. At the extreme, groups of people withdraw from established religious bodies and form new ones that provide them with a greater source of meaning and need gratification.[9] The Jesus People movement and Humanistic Judaism are contemporary examples.

A variety of reforms have been instituted among modern religious bodies in an attempt to keep members loyal. Among some Protestant groups, these have included lifting prohibitions against smoking, alcoholic beverages, dancing, and gambling, and changes in the time of religious services. The Catholic church has made many far-reaching reforms, including changing the Mass, lifting prohibitions against eating meat on Friday, and increased toleration of local autonomy in matters once rigidly controlled by the church hierarchy. Among Jews, reform groups have dropped many of the older restrictive practices about diet and the keeping of the Sabbath.

Most established religious groups have made accommodations to modern pressures for change. If these ameliorative measures had not been forthcoming from the official bodies, membership and attendance would probably have reduced to even lower levels.

The Educational Institution

In the educational institution informal control strategies include students making demands of their teachers in return for quiet in the classroom; widespread truancy, especially in the upper grades; and a general inattention to what goes on in the classroom. Students have considerable if subtle control over their teachers. The formation of informal friendship groups among students also helps to relieve tensions within the school. Many students look forward to going to school not to learn but to be with their friends.

Ameliorative measures in the school situation include extracurricular activities such as athletics, clubs of various sorts, school plays, open classroom programs, and the like. These provide outlets for students and keep some students from dropping out of school who are of legal age to do so. At the higher levels of the educational system, student representatives may sit in on faculty and administrative committees and be consulted about limited kinds of decisions.

The Political Institution

Informal control strategies used by citizens within the political institution range from breaking laws to employing powerful lobby groups to attempt to secure special favors. Protests against some political action or laws are a commonplace occurrence. The mass protests against the war in Vietnam and the demonstrations against the bussing of school children are recent examples of informal control strategies. Voting allows some possibility of control, but its effectiveness is relatively limited unless there is mass organization to push an issue or candidate that a group feels can help its cause. Only 54 per cent of all adults voted in the 1972 presidential election, which indicates a great deal of political apathy and perhaps a feeling of hopelessness about being able to control the machinery of government to any significant extent.

The old political machines and bosses provided considerable control, even though, at times, many of their practices were extremely shady legally.[10] They got things done that met the needs of some people that the formal structure of government would not. Most have lost their effectiveness. The strongest machine remaining is in Cook County, Illinois, but indications are that it is also declining in power.[11]

The formal political institution has found it necessary to initiate a variety of ameliorative measures that cut across many areas of modern life. These include such social legislation as social security, welfare programs, unemployment compensation, public housing, public transportation, school integration, and others. Without these, the needs of many people would have gone completely unmet and much open conflict might have occurred. The patronage system also serves to reduce potential trouble as does the civil service system instituted at all levels of government to provide security for people working in the middle and lower echelons of the political institution.

There are a variety of factors that place pressures on formal institutional structures to meet the needs of the people. These help to strike a balance between the idealized goals of institutions and what they might be if left completely at the disposal of those with great power within them.

Increasing Overlapping Among Institutions

In modern societies, the extent of each institution's control often becomes problematic. There is an overlapping among institutions so that their boundaries and their purposes become increasingly blurred.

1. Children are being socialized outside the home at earlier ages in day care centers and nursery schools as more and more mothers work outside the home. Thirty per cent of all mothers with children under six years of age are now holding jobs outside the home.[12]

2. Young people are attempting to find meaning in a variety of places other than in formal religious structure, including political ideologies, within their peer groups, in leisure time activities, or through individualized religion.[13]

3. The formal political institution is increasingly providing many jobs as its various bureaucracies grow. In 1970, there were more than twelve million people employed by governments at federal, state, and local levels. In addition, more than twelve million families and nearly seven million unrelated individuals receive either social security monies or some form of public assistance income from the government.[10] The government spends billions of dollars each year to secure a variety of economic goods and services for its use and provides direct or indirect subsidies to a variety of corporations and individuals. Thus the government's involvement in the economic institution is of significance.[14]

4. Large corporations establish educational facilities to train their employees. Some of these are of considerable size and importance, such as the General Motors Institute.
5. Religious institutions have public school counterparts to educate young people. The Catholic church has the most extensive parochial education system, but other religions also have substantial school systems.

As we will see in detail in our examination of social institutions in the following chapters, this blurring of boundaries and overlapping of functions serve to precipitate institutional change and conflict as well as to create problems for individuals seeking meaning and gratification for their needs.

In modern industrial societies, new institutions of leisure, science and technology, medical care, and welfare have developed, causing even more blurring across institutional lines. This overlapping of institutions can create friction, antagonisms, and struggles for power. However, where the new institutions meet basic needs or provide individual meaning, they also add to the cohesiveness of the society.

Antagonisms between religious and political institutions have been common in Western societies and remain present to some degree in the battle over state support of religious schools and over legalized abortions. The present conflicts are mild compared with the struggles for power between church and state that dominated Europe for centuries.

The Welfare Institution

As an example of institutional development and interinstitutional conflict, we will briefly examine the history of the welfare institution and the current battle between welfare and political institutions. This example provides insight into what institutions are, how they develop and change over time, and how they affect each other.

Historically, welfare in western Europe and in America fell under the jurisdiction of the religious institution. The poor were dependent on the church not only for salvation and meaning but also for their daily bread. As the political institution gained power in society, and as the numbers and problems of the poor increased, welfare increasingly came under the auspices of either local or national governments. The religious institution lost this reason for its continued existence and, therefore, some of its potential power.

The political institution vacillated about how to handle the problem of the indigent. They were put in jail, or in poorhouses, or used as a source of cheap labor. No one, except the indigent themselves, had a vested interest in improving their condition. Because they lacked resources, the poor had little power.

The "social gospel movement" and the writings of the muckrakers during the first part of this century placed the problems of the poor in the spotlight. The writings of such people as Charles Dickens and Lincoln Steffens highlighted their deprivation. Jane Adams established Hull House in Chicago and other settlement houses began to spring up in other cities.

Specialized positions were created to deal with the problems of the poor. Social workers and others received special training to assist the indigent population. These people were paid *as professionals* to help solve the problems of the poor. The emerging welfare institution sought more autonomy as its personnel—social workers and others—increasingly claimed that they were the people who could most adequately deal with the problem of welfare.

The federal government created a Department of Health, Education and Welfare. In addition, every state and many counties within states

Public Welfare

In an important study of the origins and operations of the modern public welfare system, the political scientist Frances Fox Piven and the sociologist Richard A. Cloward suggests that

> The key to an understanding of relief giving is in the functions it serves for the larger economic and political order, for relief is a secondary and supportive institution. Historical evidence suggests that relief arrangements are initiated or expanded during the occasional outbreaks of civil disorder produced by mass unemployment, and are then abolished or contracted when political stability is restored. We shall argue that expansive relief policies are designed to mute civil disorder, and restrictive ones to reinforce work norms. In other words, relief policies are cyclical—liberal or restrictive depending on the problems of regulation in the larger society with which government must contend.[a]

After a careful survey of the historical origins of welfare systems in European industrialized societies, the fluctuations in the numbers of persons given "relief" of various kinds, and the sums of money they receive, the authors concluded that the two main goals of the welfare system have been and are to maintain civil order and to enforce the work norms of society by maintaining the existing system of stratification. The authors sum up their detailed findings in these terms:

> When mass unemployment leads to outbreaks of turmoil, relief programs are ordinarily initiated or expanded to absorb and control enough of the unemployed to restore order; then, as turbulence subsides, the relief system contracts, expelling those who are needed to populate the labor market. Relief also performs a

established departments of welfare and hired professional personnel to staff them. Thus, the welfare institution became increasingly formalized, with a large professional staff and bureaucratic rules and regulations. Even though the financial base of the welfare institution, for the most part, has remained in the political institution, its values, general orientation, and the vested interests of its paid personnel have become separate and distinct.

In the 1970s, there are many different points of view about what is called the welfare problem. The number of people receiving welfare has increased as rapidly as has the number of people who administer the various programs in the welfare institution. Now, a relatively strong basis of power exists in the welfare institution because of the millions of people who have a vested interest in its perpetuation.

Friction, antagonisms, and struggles for power are emerging between the personnel of the welfare institution and certain personnel in the political institution at many levels of government. Professional welfare workers feel they know best how to deal with welfare. They

---

labor-regulating function. . . . Some of the aged, the disabled, the insane, and others who are of no use as workers are left on the relief rolls, and their treatment is so degrading and punitive as to instill in the laboring masses a fear of the fate that awaits them should they relax into beggary and pauperism. To demean and punish those who do not work is to exalt by contrast even the meanest labor at the meanest wages.[b]

This argument is the reverse side of the argument made by Herbert Gans when he identified the social "functions" of poverty. He showed how the existence and perpetuation of a poor underclass serves the needs of other groups in the society. Piven and Cloward identify some of these "needs" in concrete historical terms and show how the social regulation of the poor serves to preserve the existing system of social stratification (and therefore of existing social inequality and inequity) by providing a safety valve in times of civil disorder and by motivating people to perform dirty jobs at low wages.

Many people have vested interests in the welfare system, including some of those who rail and rant longest and loudest for its abolition and the importance of getting people off of welfare and into what they deem gainful employment. Once again, we see that "the poor are always with us" and seem to always remain poor not because of some divine administrative decree but because of concrete social arrangements and control strategies that intersect and interact to produce a social underclass.

[a]Frances Fox Piven and Richard A. Cloward, *Regulating the Poor: The Function of Public Welfare* (New York: Random, 1971), p. xiii.
[b]Ibid., pp. 3–4.

have used the strategy of professionalization to get where they are and thus make certain claims to expertise and power. People in the political institution, however, disagree and withhold the funds for some welfare programs and dismantle others.

There is a continuing battle between two institutions. People in both have vested interests to protect and positions of power to maintain. Both sides hope to get the general public on their side to increase their degree of power. This battle will continue as long as different views prevail among people in the two institutional spheres and as long as both sides have conflictive positions to protect.

S. N. Eisenstadt sums up the general problem of institutional growth and differentiation:

> The more differentiated and specialized institutional spheres become more interdependent and potentially complementary in their functioning within the same over-all institutionalized system. But this very complementarity creates more difficult and complex problems of integration. The growing autonomy of each sphere of social activity, and the concomitant growth of interdependence and mutual interpenetration among them pose more difficult problems. Each sphere must crystallize its own tendencies and potentialities and regulate its normative and organizational relations with other spheres. And at each more "advanced" level or stage of differentiation, the increased autonomy of each sphere creates more complex problems of integrating these specialized activities into one systemic framework.[15]

These problems of integration are clearly manifest in the conflict-ridden relations of the emergent welfare institutions with their constituencies of professionals and clients and the political institutions of our society.

Routine Institutional Practices and Meaning[16]

Routine institutional practices often provide meaning in themselves for individuals even though these practices have been completely or almost completely divorced from the reason for their original creation. People feel a sense of accomplishment or fulfillment by going through a certain series of routine activities within the framework of an institution. Participation in a routine practice provides meaning regardless of the content of the activity.

In the economic institution people may feel a sense of need-gratifying accomplishment for having done a good day's work, even though what is done or made on the job has little use and involves no creative effort. Henry Van Dyke's poem entitled *Work* expresses this clearly:

> Let me but do my work from day to day,
> In field or forest, at the desk or loom,
> In roaring market place or tranquil room;
> Let me but find it in my heart to say,
> When vagrant wishes beckon me astray,

"This is my work, my blessing, not my doom:
Of all who live, I am the one by whom
This work can best be done in the right way."
Then shall I see it not too great, nor small,
To suit my spirit and to prove my powers;
Then shall I cheerful greet the laboring hours,
And cheerful turn, when the long shadows fall
At eventide, to play and love and rest,
Because I know for me my work is best.[17]

In the political institution some people gain a sense of self-esteem by "living by the law," even though the law itself may be contrary to their values. This appears clearly in the popular slogan, "My Country: Right or Wrong."

In education students may gain a sense of accomplishment by attending every class and reading all the assigned material, even though they neither learn anything in class nor understand what they read. Receiving a college degree is satisfying for some, even though they remain ignorant of the materials they were supposed to master.

In the religious institution, people may feel "good" after attending a religious service if the proper form of worship was followed, even if they have little understanding of the symbolism or theology that supports the form of worship followed. Thus, for example, many older Catholics were very disturbed when the form and language of the Mass was changed.

In the family, a father and mother may feel a sense of self-esteem if they do what they think "good" parents should do. In the middle classes, this includes keeping the children clean and out of trouble, encouraging children to learn to play a musical instrument, to do their homework, and a variety of other ritualistic practices that "make a good parent." Even though parents do all these things their children may be very unhappy. The result of this ritualistic following of routine practices for their own sake often ends with parents making the statement, "I don't know where I failed" if the child goes "wrong."

Many institutional practices are kept alive *not* because they are producing the results for which they were intended but because sheer participation in institutional practices takes on a value that produces meaning for the individuals who use them. Participation in the use of institutional practices gives validity to the experience.

Different Specific Activities for the Same Purpose

The control strategies that structure institutions take different specific forms in different societies and in the same society over time. There is great variability in specific institutional activities over both space and time. For example, there are many ways in which goods and services can be produced and distributed. Among the different institutional forms created to accomplish this are capitalism, state socialism, communism, and cooperatives. Among political institutions that maintain order are democracies, monarchies, dictatorships, and a variety of others. There are also many types of family structures, numerous ways of educating people, and many different religions in the modern world.

Our discussion of the movement from primitive fusion to the formalization of institutions is an example of how institutions change over time. In the following chapters, although we concentrate on the structure of institutions in the United States, we will occasionally make comparisons with different institutions in other societies both past and present.

REFERENCES

1. See De Coulanges, Fustel. *The Ancient City.* Trans. by Willard Smith. Garden City, N.Y.: Doubleday, this work was first published in 1864.
2. For one view, see Parsons, Talcott. *Societies: Evolutionary and Comparative Perspectives.* Englewood Cliffs, N.J.: Prentice-Hall, 1967.
3. See Carneiro, Robert. "A Theory of the Origin of the State." *Science*, **169** (Sept. 1970), 737–738.
4. See Childe, V. Gordon. *Social Evolution.* London: Watts, 1951.
5. See *Ancient Mesopotamia: A Socio-Economic History.* Ed. by I. M. Diakonoff. Moscow: Nauka, 1969; and Levenson, Joseph R. *China: An Interpretive History from the Beginnings to the Fall of Han.* Berkeley: University of California Press, 1961.
6. See Von Hagen, Victor. *The Ancient Sun Kingdoms of the Americas.* New York: World, 1961.
7. Williams, Jr., Robin M. *American Society.* New York: Knopf, 1960, p. 336.
8. Maslow, Abraham H. *Motivation and Personality.* New York: Harper, 1970. Also, see his *Toward a Psychology of Being.* New York: Van Nostrand, 1968.
9. For a discussion of sect groups, see Troeltsch, Ernst. *The Social Teachings of the Christian Churches.* New York: Macmillan, 1931. Niebuhr, H. Richard. *The Social Sources of Denominationalism.* New York: World, 1957; and Pope, Liston. *Millhands and Preachers.* New Haven: Yale, 1942.
10. For a brief treatment of the role played by political machines, see Merton, Robert K. *Social Theory and Social Structures.* New York: Free Press, 1957, Chap. 1.
11. For a treatment of the Chicago political machine and the man who runs it, see Royko, Mike. *Boss, Richard J. Daley of Chicago.* New York: New American Library, 1971.
12. U.S. Bureau of the Census, *General Social and Economic Characteristics, United States Summary,* 1972.
13. See Luckmann, Thomas. *The Invisible Religion.* (New York: Macmillan, 1967.
14. U.S. Bureau of the Census, loc. cit.
15. *Readings in Social Evolution and Development.* Ed. by S.N. Eisenstadt. Oxford: Pergamon, 1970, p. 16.
16. The following is based on *The Sociology of Georg Simmel.* Trans. and ed. by Kurt H. Wolff. New York: Free Press, 1950.
17. *The Poems of Henry Van Dyke.* New York: Scribners, 1911, p. 256.

The Social Basis
of Political Economy

INTRODUCTION

For some years it has been fashionable in the academic world to analyze separately political and economic institutions. This arbitrary intellectual division has caused political science and economics to be organized as separate departments in most universities. This separation has not always existed, however, and we believe it is a mistake. A better understanding of both institutions can be achieved by treating them together. This is especially true for existing and emerging post-industrial societies in which these institutions interact so heavily that they almost merge.

The major concern of each institution reflects their interdependence. The economic institution involves the production and distribution of goods and services—some of which may be scarce. If there were no scarcity, people could simply pick up what they needed or wanted. Everything would be as "free" as the air we breathe. Scarcity, of course, may be real or created. It is real when the forces of production are being used to their full capacity and there is still not enough to meet basic needs. It is created when the forces of production have the capacity to produce a surplus but, usually to protect certain vested interests, are not used to do so.

Scarcity can also be created in certain areas of the economy by how the forces of production are used. Both in the United States and in the USSR the massive productive capacity used in the arms race diminishes the productive capacity to meet domestic needs. Scarcity can also be created when productive capacity is used to produce new products although "old" and perhaps necessary products remain in short supply for some people. If productive capacity were used to produce only necessary products, the law of supply and demand would reduce prices and those without the necessities could better afford to buy them. The law of supply and demand however is a fiction in many modern economies because both supply and demand are manipulated by those who own or control the means of production, assisted by government policies.

Because some goods and services are scarce, the problem of allocation emerges: which people are to get what goods and services under what conditions. If there are twenty people who want them and only twelve automobiles, a decision must be made as to which persons under what conditions get the twelve available automobiles. Politics in this sense has been defined as the process of deciding who gets what, when, and how.

In turn this raises the major concern of the political institution, maintaining order in a society. Conceivably the twenty people who want the twelve automobiles could fight it out to the bitter end with the winners getting the automobiles. This type of distribution process, however, would hardly create a workable social order. Part of the problem of maintaining order within a society is setting down rules for how goods and services are to be produced and allocated.

The problem of maintaining order in the production and distribution of goods and services involves reciprocal control. What are the elements that enter into the reciprocal control between the political and the economic institutions? To answer this important question, we must take a historical view. This will eventually bring us to an analysis of the political and economic institutions in our society and how they are interrelated.

THE HISTORICAL PERSPECTIVE

Lenski points out that *"men will share the products of their labors to the extent required to insure the survival and continued productivity of those others whose actions are necessary or beneficial to themselves."*[1] Lenski calls this his first law of distribution and goes on to say:

This first law, however, does not cover the entire problem. It says nothing about how any surplus, that is, goods and services over and above the minimum required to keep producers alive and productive, which men may be able to produce will be distributed. This leads to what may be called the second law of distribution. If we assume that in important decisions human action is motivated almost entirely by self-interest or partisan group interests, and if we assume that many of the things men most desire are in short supply, then, as noted before, this surplus will inevitably give rise to conflicts and struggles aimed at its control. If, following Weber, we define power as the probability of persons or groups carrying out their will even when opposed by others, then it follows that *power will determine the distribution of nearly all of the surplus possessed by a society.*[2]

Lenski then argues that there are two principles that govern the distribution of goods and services in a society: *need* and *power.*[3] He suggests that *"in the simplest societies, or those which are technologically most primitive, the goods and services available will be distributed wholly, or largely, on the basis of need."*[4] There is high scarcity in these societies and thus "no surplus to be fought over and distributed on the basis of power."[5]

As surpluses become available with the advance of technology, *decisions* must be made as to which persons will get the surplus that is being produced. At this point goods and services begin to be distributed on the basis of *power.* Because the use of raw force in fighting over this surplus would keep a society in constant conflict, one of two things must happen. Persons with enough physical force at their disposal must keep the rest of the population subdued by the constant use of coercive strategies, or a government must come into existence and maintain order.

Usually the latter occurs and some form of government emerges. The agreements used to maintain order are typically based on some type of *ideology* or belief system that legitimates the system of government. The constant use of open force is expensive, dangerous, and does not lend itself to the gratification of other needs among those with great power. The establishment of a government does not guarantee that it will not be overthrown as new people and groups muster enough force to take over. When this happens, the new people in power attempt to convince the masses that they should be where they are through the use of a new ideology.

Max Weber has pointed out that once a government has established itself as legitimate, it alone has the *right* to use force. *Ultimate* power, therefore, rests in the political institution. The government must decide in one way or another how the surplus is to be distributed. It may lay down laws specifying in concrete terms who is to get what under what conditions, it may *permit* what has been called a free market—a market that supposedly operates on supply and demand—or it may take a middle position between these two extremes. But whatever the system, final power rests with the government to allow or not to allow certain types of activity in the economic sphere. If practical politics is the attempt to control the government, the important question becomes: who does, in fact, control the government and in whose interests is it controlled?

Before we examine the historical development of modern economic and political systems, however, we must introduce some concepts that will enable us to understand the control strategies that underlie both political and economic institutions.

Legitimacy and Power

How do political institutions secure the consent of those they govern? Max Weber distinguished three types of legitimacy—that is, three systems of belief that obedience to those who have power is morally right. The three types of legitimate authority Weber distinguishes are *traditional*, in which authority is based on sacred norms or established customs; *legal*, in which authority is established by a codified set of rules; and *charismatic*, in which the authority is based on the extraordinary personal qualities of some leader.[6]

Most primitive societies have political systems in which legitimacy is conferred on the leaders by traditional authority. The positions of power are based on what the sacred book says or on inheritance or some other system rooted in cultural norms and values. A complex variant of such a system was the divine right philosophy that provided legitimacy for the authority of monarchs in the Middle Ages.

Legal authority is the system of legitimacy most characteristic of modern societies with their formalized social institutions, bureaucratic control strategies, and emphasis on procedures and rules. A constitution or other body of rules defines the system of government and how it can be changed. Procedures are set up for interpreting the constitution (for example, a Supreme Court) and for enforcing its provisions (a police force or army). Typically, the system of rules or constitution becomes part of a widely shared cultural agreement.

Charismatic authority confers legitimacy by virtue of the outstanding qualities of the leader. Mahatma Gandhi, John F. Kennedy, Martin Luther King, Fidel Castro, and Mao tse-Tung are among the persons who, because of their personal qualities and their ability to present themselves as symbols, were able to profoundly influence the political structures and power systems of their historical eras. Charismatic authority always poses a serious threat to political institutions that rest on traditional or legal bases of authority. The charismatic leader is followed not because he holds an office or because he has inherited a position of leadership but because he has specific gifts of body and spirit. The personality and spirit of the charismatic leader are such that others are drawn to him, particularly in times of crises. Historically, it was not unusual to ascribe to these leaders supernatural qualities, as in the case of Old Testament prophets or Jesus. Weber points out that the holder of charisma "seizes the task that is adequate for him and demands obedience and a following by virtue of his mission."[7]

Governments, systems of legitimated political power, thus possess *authority*. To some measure, they rest on the consent of the governed, whether that consent is given because of conformity to traditional norms, to a legal-rational constitution, or to a charismatic leader—at times this consent rests on the lack of viable alternatives. Where does the basis for this consent develop? How is it that people defer to, respect, obey, and thereby ascribe legitimate power—authority—to their leaders? One set of answers to these questions emerge from the study of political socialization.

Political Socialization

Political socialization studies the processes in the training of youngsters that cause them to identify with the power systems of their society or to reject those systems and seek to change them. Many research studies suggest that "most youngsters appear to be overwhelmingly favorably disposed toward political objects that cross their vision. Officers and institutions of government are regarded as benevolent, worthy, competent, serving, and powerful."[8]

Subsequent events in the lives of these children may change their images and attitudes of government (as the study of confidence in public officials cited in the preceding chapter demonstrates), but most stable societies inculcate among the young acceptance of and obedience to the existing stratification system and distribution of power.

The roots of this acceptance may lie in the lengthy period of helpless dependency of the human infant. Robert L. Heilbroner suggests that:

> We find evidence of this in the ascription of majesty to kings and queens who are obvious substitutes for our parents, or in the childlike attitudes of mingled resentment and admiration with which the lower orders of society characteristically regard the higher orders, or in the "cult of personality" to which the peoples of the world show such willingness to succumb. Anyone who has seen the wild excitement of a crowd caught up in the adulation of a political leader cannot fail to recognize the rekindling of childhood feelings of awe and obedience in the behavior of these cheering adults.[9]

Whatever the specifics of how people come to accept authority and to ascribe legitimacy to their rulers, the process illustrates the complexity and the importance of the interplay between the social institution of the family and education on one hand, and the political institution and the stratification systems on the other. For the sociologist and the political scientist, legitimated power in the form of authority must be understood if we are to understand the social ordering of modern societies.

Now we turn to an examination of the historical development of modern economic and political institutions.

CLASSICAL NINETEENTH-CENTURY CAPITALISM

The idea of free markets, or laissez faire, the *historical* basis of our economic institution, is an ideology that was not only supported by governments but initiated by them. Karl Polyani, discussing the nineteenth century, points out the following:

> There was nothing natural about laissez faire; free markets could never have come into being merely by allowing things to take their course. Just as cotton manufacturers—the leading free trade industry—were created by the help of protective tariffs, export bounties, and indirect wage subsidies, laissez faire itself was enforced by the state. The thirties and forties saw not only an outburst of legislation repealing restrictive regulations, but also an enormous increase in the administrative functions of the state, which was now being endowed with a central bureaucracy able to fulfill the tasks set by the adherents of liberalism.[10]

The laissez-faire model of capitalism was believed by many to be not an ideology but *the natural order of things*. Adam Smith (1723–1790), in his *Inquiry into the Nature and Course of the Wealth of Nations*, saw it as a *natural* law that if each person was to pursue his own self interest, this would in the long run produce the best of all possible social worlds. "The invidivual intends only his own gain, and he is in this, as in many other cases, led by an invisible hand to promote an end which was not part of his intention."[11] Because of the working of this "invisible hand" in history, any interference by the government was seen as hampering "natural development" and, in the long run, adversely affecting people.

> To the question, "What can the law do relative to subsistence?" Bentham (another English philosopher) answered, "Nothing directly." Poverty was nature surviving in society; its physical sanction was hunger. "The force of the physical sanction being sufficient, the employment of the political sanction would be superfluous. . . . Bentham believed that poverty was part of plenty. "In the highest stage of social prosperity," he said, "The great mass of the citizens will most probably possess few other resources than their daily labor, and consequently will alwlays be near indigence."[12]

The market was thought to be inherently self-regulating. Thus, "Man under the name of labor, nature under the name of land, were made available for sale, the use of labor power could be universally bought and sold at a price called wages, and the use of land could be negotiated for a price called rent."[13]

Darwin's work on evolution, which introduced the principle of the survival of the fittest in nature, was applied to social life by the English sociologist Herbert Spencer (1820–1903) and the American sociologist William Graham Sumner (1840–1910). They added fuel to the fire that burned the poor by proclaiming that laissez faire *ideology* was "validated" by "science" and therefore was incontestable.

The English government allowed and encouraged the laissez faire ideology, at the same time that many workers made below-subsistence wages and very young children were used as cheap labor in the mines and factories.

In America, during the late nineteenth and early twentieth centuries, the heyday of laissez faire, captains of industry (as they called themselves)—robber barons (as others called them)—paid their workers, including children who worked 14-hour days, wages so low that many were forced to live in shacks and basements with little or no heat in the winter and to suffer malnutrition from inadequate diets. Plenty of "cheap labor" was supplied by the massive waves of immigrants from southeastern Europe. Those who owned the factories, mines, and businesses built luxurious homes and amassed huge fortunes. Andrew Carnegie, a robber baron par excellence, brought sociologist Herbert Spencer to this country for a series of enlightening lectures about the virtues of laissez faire. Power and knowledge met in mutual admiration and Spencer was well received by the captains of industry. He did not lecture to (or for) the poor in their hovels.

The government permitted and supported these conditions and even passed tariffs to protect domestic markets. The federal government had the power to prevent the use of child labor and to establish a minimum wage for workers. We *know* this because child labor and minimum wage laws were finally passed after considerable public outrage.

The basis for legitimacy in the nineteenth-century capitalist economic institution thus rested in laissez faire *ideology,* which proclaimed that the government (the ultimate source of power by virtue of its possession of a monopoly on the legitimate use of force) had to keep hands off the economy except to support its "natural" workings in the interests of the dominant economic elite. Before returning to a discussion of the development of capitalist economic institutions, we must examine the political ideologies of the Western world. These ideologies received their clearest expression in the writings of the great political philosophers Thomas Hobbes, John Locke, and Jean Jacques Rousseau.

THE PHILOSOPHICAL BACKGROUND OF EIGHTEENTH- AND NINETEENTH-CENTURY POLITICAL INSTITUTIONS

During the seventeenth and eighteenth centuries there was considerable debate about why governments are instituted among people. Thomas Hobbes (1588–1679), an English philosopher, argued that in a state of nature there was continuous strife among people based on competition, fear that one person would surpass another in the usurpation of power to gratify needs and the seeking of glory.[14] In a state of nature, life is "solitary, poor, nasty, brutish, and short."[15] In this state of nature there is neither right nor wrong, good nor bad, justice nor injustice, because there is no supreme power (the state) present to define and establish values. To solve this problem of brutishness and continuous war, governments are instituted to impose control and to define justice and goodness. Once established, government, whatever its form—aristocracy, democracy, or monarchy (Hobbes preferred monarchy)—is sovereign. Thus, it is not to be challenged no matter how oppressive, for to destroy the sovereignty of government would once again reduce interaction among people to a state of war and brutishness. For Hobbes, a tyrannical government is better than a state of nature.

The French philosopher Jean Jacques Rousseau (1712–1778) disagreed with Hobbes about the interaction of people in a state of nature. For Rousseau, people in their "natural" state, unfettered by governments, are good and life is tranquil and happy. Rousseau contended that, like air and water, land was *naturally* free. He saw in the creation

---

FIGURE 10-1

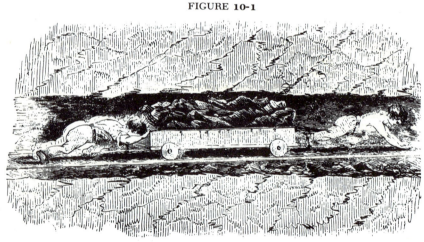

SOURCE: William Peterson, *Population* (New York: Macmillan, 1975), p. 444. Used by permission.

An illustration from one of the many white papers reporting governmental investigations of labor conditions in nineteenth-century England. The accompanying text reads as follows:

of private property the basis of many evils. This is summed up in what is perhaps his most famous statement:

> The first man who, having enclosed a piece of ground, bethought himself of saying "This is mine," and found people simple enough to believe him, was the real founder of civil society. From how many crimes, wars, and murders, from how many horrors and misfortunes might not anyone have saved mankind, by pulling up the stake, or filling up the ditch, and crying to his fellows: "Beware of listening to this imposter; you are undone if you once forget that the fruits of the earth belong to us all, and the earth itself to nobody.[16]

The establishment of private property produced "usurpation by the rich, robbery by the poor, and the unbridled passions of both, suppressed the cries of natural compassion and the still feeble voice of justice, and filled men with avarice, ambition, and greed."[17] Rousseau believed that this state of affairs led both rich and poor to form an explicit contract creating society and the state. But once formed the state "bound new fetters on the poor, and gave new power to the rich; which irretrievably destroyed natural liberty, eternally

---

By far the greater number of Children and persons employed in coal mines are engaged in propelling and drawing tubs laden with coal, from the face to the pit-eye, or the main levels in those pits where they have horses. This is done by placing the hands on the back of the waggon, and propelling it forward with as great velocity as the inclination of the mine, the state of the road, and the strength of the waggoner admit of. The mines in this district [Lancashire and Cheshire] are for the most part laid with rails, and the waggon runs on wheels. . . . There are, however, mines . . . where the old mode of drawing the baskets or wooden sledges (called in Lancashire "sleds") is still retained. The drawer is in this case harnessed by means of a chain attached to the "sled"; the other end of the chain passes between his legs, and fastens in front to a belt round the waist. When thus harnessed, and moving along on his hands and feet, the drawer drags after him and loaded basket; if he is not sufficiently strong he has a helper rather younger than himself. . . . [Figure 10-1] represents three young Children hurrying or drawing a loaded waggon of coals. The Child in front "is harnessed by his belt or chain to the waggon; the two boys behind are assisting in pushing it forward. Their heads, it will be observed, are brought down to a level with the waggon, and the body almost in a horizontal position. This is done partly to avoid striking the roof, and partly to gain the advantage of the muscular action, which is greatest in that position. It will be observed the boy in front goes on his hands and feet: in that manner the whole weight of his body is in fact supported by the chain attached to the waggon and his feet, and consequently his power of drawing is greater than it would be if he crawled on his knees. These boys, by constantly pushing against the waggons, occasionally rub off the hair from the crowns of their heads so much as to make them almost bald" (Great Britain, Children's Employment Commission, *First Report of the Commissioners: Mines*, H. M. Stationery Office, London, 1842, pp. 81–82).

fixed the law of property and inequality, converted clever usurption into unalterable right, and, for the advantage of a few ambitious individuals, subjected all mankind to perpetual labor, slavery, and wretchedness."[18]

Because the forming of the political institution had left people "everywhere in chains," Rousseau called for a new social contract. This new contract was to base the state on the sovereignty of the people, which in turn is based on what Rousseau called the general will:

> The first and most important deduction from the principles we have so far laid down is that the general will alone can direct the State according to the object for which it was instituted, for example, the common good: for if the clashing of particular interests made the establishment of societies necessary, the agreement of these very interests made it possible. The common element in these different interests is what forms the social tie; and, were there no point of agreement between them all, no society could exist. It is solely on the basis of this common interest that every society should be governed.[19]

For Rousseau, the state does not stand *above* the common interests of the *people*. It is the people. Their rights are inalienable.

A third writer, John Locke (1632–1704), believed that in a state of nature people were equal, peaceful, and willing to help each other under most conditions.

> To understand political power right, and derive it from its original, we must consider what state all men are naturally in, and that is a state of perfect freedom to order their actions and dispose of their possessions and persons as they think fit, within the bounds of the law of nature, without asking leave or depending upon the will of any other man. . . . The state of nature has a law of nature to govern it which obliges everyone; and reason which is that law, teaches all mankind who will but consult it that, being equal and independent, no one ought to harm another in his life, health, liberty or possessions.[20]

Yet, in this state of nature, natural rights are violated and there is no way to administer justice. Locke argued that governments came into existence to right the wrong that people might do to each other in a state of nature. Governments exist to *guarantee* that which the law of nature has already given: life, health, liberty, and possessions.

If government becomes tyrannical, it must be overthrown. The only reason for its existence is to guarantee all people what by nature is theirs. A state of nature, for Locke, was far better than a tyrannical government. Unlike Hobbes, Rousseau and Locke saw government as serving, protecting, and perhaps extending what nature had already given. Both called for revolution if a government did not fulfill its purposes.

With this background, we are now ready to examine our classical democratic political heritage and the values it espouses. *Given these values,* we argue that there is injustice if the power of the state is used to permit some people to exploit other people in the economic institution. Without socially established values the world is rendered absurd and there is no possibility of making sense out of one's existence. The establishment of values is of critical importance in the political institution for it is only by these values that the performance of political leaders can be judged.

CLASSICAL AMERICAN DEMOCRACY

The Declaration of Independence, along with the Constitution, laid the foundation for our political system. In part, the Declaration said:

> We hold these truths to be self-evident, that all men are created equal, that they are endowed by their Creator with certain inalienable rights, that among these are life, liberty, and the pursuit of Happiness. That to secure these rights, governments are instituted among men, deriving their just powers from the consent of the governed. . . .
> That whenever any form of government becomes destructive of these ends it is the right of the people to alter or abolish it and to institute new government, laying its foundations on such principles and organizing its powers in such form as to them shall seem most likely to effect their safety and happiness.

Our Declaration of Independence incorporated some of the ideas of Rousseau and Locke. The French political philosopher Montesquieu (1689–1755) advocated the separation of powers into the legislative, executive, and judicial, an idea embedded in the American Constitution. The overriding conception behind the American political system is that government exists to guarantee that people will get what "by nature" is already theirs: life, liberty, and the pursuit of happiness under conditions of equality.

At the birth of our nation the ideals of political democracy and the realities of laissez-faire economics *tended* to fit together well. The outstanding exceptions were black people, who were enslaved. "In 1780, just after the American Revolution about four fifths of the non-slave labor force in the United States were independent property owners or professionals—farmers, merchants, traders, craftsmen and artisans, businessmen, lawyers, doctors, etc."[21] Under these conditions, the Declaration of Independence made sense, for the large majority of people were independent and free to pursue their own fortunes as they wished. Some people had more money than others. However, the majority, self-employed people, could find *meaning* in their economic endeavors under the protection of the political institution.

C. Wright Mills has pointed out that:

Under the pattern of individual success there were political and demographic conditions, notably the land policy, which opened economic routes to the masterless individual. The wide distribution of small property made freedom of a very literal sort seem, for a short time, an eternal principle. The relation of one man to another was a relation not of command and obedience but of man-to-man bargaining. Any one man's decisions, with references to every other man, were decisions of freedom and equality; no one man dominated the calculations affecting a market.... Political authority, the traditional mode of social integration, became a loose framework of protection rather than a centralized engine of domination; it too was largely unseen and for long periods very slight. The legal framework guaranteed and encouraged the order of small property, but the *government was the guardian, not the manager, of this order.*[22]

The economic ideal of laissez faire worked well and was protected by the political institution of democracy.

From Self-employment to Employment by Others

However, this ideal state did not last for long. In 1780, 80 per cent of the nonslave population were self-employed. Today, more than 90 per cent of all people are employed by someone else. Table 10-1 shows this change. Associated with this dramatic process of change in the labor force have been changes in our political and economic institutions and the reciprocal controls between them. We will first look at the development of the economic institution.

Development of the American Economic Institution

Classical economists included three types of resources in their analysis of the production and distribution of goods and services: (1) *land,* which includes agriculture and such natural resources as oil, iron, coal, copper, and so forth; (2) capital, which includes the *means of production,* such as tools, machines, factory buildings, warehouses, and the *money* that can be invested to buy these means of production, and (3) *labor.* Later economists added to these three resources organizational know-how or *entrepreneurship,* which combines all the preceding to make an economic system work efficiently.

In 1780, 80 per cent of the free population were self-employed and thus had some resources over which they had control. Because power is based on available resources, power was roughly equally distributed. Each person was autonomous, responsible only to the government as an individual citizen. Each competed with others to sell goods and services on the free market. Government control was limited. The law of supply and demand operated and thereby structured the market place.

TABLE **10-1**
Change in the United States Labor Force[a]

Year	Percent Wage and Salaried Employees[b]	Percent Self-Employed Entrepreneurs[c]	Percent Salaried Managers and Officials	Total
1780[d]	20.0	80.0		100.0
1880	62.0	36.9	1.1	100.0
1890	65.0	33.8	1.2	100.0
1900	67.9	30.8	1.3	100.0
1910	71.9	26.3	1.8	100.0
1920	73.9	23.5	2.6	100.0
1930	76.8	20.3	2.9	100.0
1939	78.2	18.8	3.0	100.0
1950	77.7	17.9	4.4	100.0
1960	80.6	14.1	5.3	100.0
1969	83.6	9.2	7.2	100.0

Notes: [a]Defined as all income recipients who participate directly in economic activity; unpaid family workers have been excluded. [b]Excluding salaried managers and officials. [c]Business entrepreneurs, professional practicioners, farmers and other property owners. [d]Figures for 1780 are rough estimates. Slaves, who comprised one-fifth of the population, are excluded; white indentured servants are included in the wage and salaried employees category.

SOURCES: Data for 1780 from Jackson T. Main, *The Social Structure of Revolutionary America* (Princeton, N.J.: Princeton University Press, 1965), pp. 270–77. Data for 1880–1939 from Spurgeon Bell, *Productivity, Wages and National Income* (Washington, D.C.: Brookings Institution, 1940), p. 10. Data for 1950-1969 computed from U.S. Dept. of Labor, *Manpower Report of the President*, various years; and U.S. Dept. of Commerce, Bureau of the Census. *Census of Population*, 1950 and 1960, and *Current Population Reports*, Series P-60, various years.

SOURCE: Michael Reich, "The Evolution of the United States Labor Force," in *The Capitalist System*, written and ed. by Richard C. Edwards, Michael Reich, and Thomas Weisskopf (Englewood Cliffs, N.J.: Prentice-Hall, 1972), p. 175. Used by permission.

This arrangement, however, was doomed. Technology and industrialization required the accumulation of capital for the construction of factories, the buying of other instruments of production, and the extraction of large amounts of natural resources to be used in the manufacturing process. Through banks large sums of money determined for savings were made available for investment. Money was also pooled by forming corporations in which each person invested money hoping to make a profit. In the early years some individuals had enough money of their own to found small enterprises.

A second factor necessary for industrial development is a pool of labor that can be *hired*. In 1780, this pool consisted of roughly 20 per cent of the population. It increased rapidly during the nineteenth century when capital and labor were increasingly brought together under organizations created by people having high entrepreneurial skills. For the most part, the early factories and mining operations were relatively small. A system of what is called family capitalism developed. One family, with enough capital, set up a factory, business, or mining operation and hired people to work.

As immigrants continued to arrive, the labor force expanded, operating under a relatively free market. With no minimum wage specified by the government, labor was cheap. More profits can be made with cheaper labor because the difference between what it costs to make a product and what it sells for can be greater. A poor immigrant without a job needed to eat and feed his family and thus could be hired at low pay. He had severely restricted alternatives.

Under these conditions, profits can be made and capital accumulated very rapidly by those who own the means of production. This is precisely what happened in the nineteenth century. By 1900, 67.9 per cent of the population were working, not for themselves, but for someone else. Small, individually owned enterprises and family capitalism gave way to corporate capitalism. Capital became increasingly consolidated and controlled by a smaller and smaller proportion of the population compared with earlier years.

Monopolies developed that restricted the free play of the competitive market. Where monopolies exist and their products are needed, higher prices can be charged, making it possible for those who have wealth to accumulate even more. The government at the beginning of this century passed antitrust legislation to break up the developing monopolies, but the application of these laws was ineffectual. Those who owned and controlled the monopolies possessed considerable power and were able to exert control over government officials to restrict the application of these laws.

Changes in the Labor Force

Marx predicted that the proletariat would revolt against depressed wages, mass unemployment, and the deplorable working conditions under capitalism. Two factors prevented this from happening. The first was the development of the labor union movement, which began to extract higher wages through the use of coalition and coercive strategies.

The number of workers belonging to unions grew rapidly but sporadically during these years, reaching a peak in 1920, declining in the 1930s as the Great Depression set in, and then increasing rapidly. Today more than twenty million people belong to labor unions. The number of strikes or work stoppages used to make wage demands and for union organization reached a peak of 4,450 in 1917, but declined after that. From 1950 to the present, work stoppages have averaged between 3,500 and 5,000 per year.

The use of coalitional and coercive strategies by the unionized labor force was significant during the early part of the century in making gains for workers as well as in structuring the nature of control relationships in the economic sphere. Unions remain an important element in the economic institution.

The second factor that forestalled Marx's predicted revolution was the change in the composition of the labor force, especially after the beginning of the twentieth century. New machines took the place of most backbreaking labor. As the economy matured a major shift in types of jobs occurred, permitting upward social mobility for a significant number of people. Even though these people continued to work for someone else, the nature of their work changed and became more satisfying. With increased chances for upward social mobility, more and more people came to have a vested interest in the perpetuation of the system. They saw themselves or their children gaining even though many remained poor. Their sense of relative deprivation lessened.

Table 10-2 shows the change in the composition of the labor force from 1900 projected to 1975; and Table 10-3 shows the change from 1910 to 1970 by categories of occupations: white collar, blue collar, service workers, and farmers and farm workers.

These tables demonstrate a significant amount of upward social mobility in the labor force. Table 10-2 shows that the percentage of professional, technical, and kindred workers increased from 3.4 per cent of the labor force in 1900 to a projected 14 per cent by 1975. Roughly the same changes occurred among managers, officials, and proprietors. Clerical and sales workers also increased significantly from roughly 1 per cent in 1900 to 4.6 and 3.6 per cent, respectively, projected to 1975. The percentage of white-collar workers increased from 21 per cent in 1910 to 48 per cent in 1970. By 1975 more than 50 per cent of the labor force will be employed in white-collar positions. Correspondingly, the percentage of farmers declined from 31 per cent in 1910 to 4 per cent in 1970. People moved off the farm to the factory as farming became more productive, more specialized, and required large capital investments.

Increased productivity in factories, mines, and farms made possible by new technology (including automation) expanded the economy rapidly, increased the standard of living for many, created many new higher-level occupations, and increased the number of people needed in older higher-level occupations. Social mobility increased and kept the society somewhat stable. If machine technology had not made this possible, revolution might have occurred as Marx predicted.

Labor unions played a significant role in increasing the wage level of those who remain in many blue-collar positions. The coalitional and coercive strategies of unionization increased the standard of living of workers in these positions. Those who owned or controlled the

TABLE 10-2
Employment of Men by Major Occupation Group: 1900–1975°

	Estimated			Reported	Projected
Major Occupation Group	*1900*	*1920*	*1940*	*1960*	*1975*
Per Cent Distribution					
Total	100.0	100.0	100.0	100.0	100.0
Professional, technical, and kindred workers	3.4	3.8	5.8	10.8	14.0
Managers, officials, and proprietors, except farm	6.8	7.8	8.6	11.3	14.0
Clerical and kindred workers	2.8	5.3	5.8	7.4	8.1
Sales workers	4.6	4.5	6.4	7.1	6.4
Craftsmen, foremen, and kindred workers	12.6	16.0	15.5	20.5	19.3
Operatives and kindred workers	10.4	14.4	18.0	20.9	18.2
Service workers	3.1	3.7	6.1	6.4	8.0
Laborers, except farm and mine	14.7	14.0	12.1	7.1	6.4
Farmers and farm managers	23.0	18.4	13.3	5.7	3.2
Farm laborers and foremen	18.7	12.1	8.4	3.0	2.3

SOURCE: Data for 1900, 1920, and 1940 are from David L. Kaplan and M. Claire Casey, *Occupational Trends in the United States, 1900 to 1950,* Bureau of the Census Working Paper No. 5, Washington, D.C., 1958. Data for 1960 are from 1960 Census of Population, Vol. I, Part 1, U.S. Summary. Projections for 1975 are based on unpublished data provided by the U.S. Bureau of Labor Statistics, and are consistent with projections of occupations for both sexes published in the March 1963 issue of the *Monthly Labor Review.*

*Data for 1900 and 1920 refer to civilian gainful workers 10 years old and over; data for 1940 refer to persons 14 years old and over in the experienced civilian labor force; data for 1960 and projections to 1975 refer to employed persons 14 years old and over.

SOURCE: Adapted from John K. Folger and Charles B. Nam, "Trends in Education in Relation to the Occupational Structure," *Sociology of Education,* Vol. 38 (Fall 1964). Used by Permission.

means of production were forced to pay higher wages, passing much of the higher cost of labor on to the consumer. The standard of living among blue-collar workers improved.

Despite these changes, which perhaps forestalled revolution, the extreme concentration of wealth and the unequal distribution of income have not changed, as we will see subsequently. Before this, however, we need to discuss developments in the political institution.

Development of American Political Institutions

Growth of Federal Power

At the birth of the nation the federal government had little power. Each of the new states jealously guarded its own vested interests. The federal government did not need too much power because there were

TABLE **10-3**
Changes in the United States employment structure, 1910–1970

Occupational Category	Per cent of employment			
	1910	*1930*	*1950*	*1970*
White collar	21	29	37	48
professional and tech.	5	7	9	14
managerial and prop.	7	7	9	11
clerical and sales	10	15	19	24
Blue collar	38	40	41	35
craftsmen, foremen, etc.	12	13	14	13
skilled machinists, etc.	15	16	20	18
unskilled labor	12	11	7	5
Service workers	10	10	10	12
Farmers and farm workers	31	21	12	4

SOURCE: *Historical Statistics of the United States: Colonial Times to 1957* (Washington, D.C.: U.S. Bureau of the Census, 1960), p. 74; for 1910–1950; and *Statistical Abstract of the United States 1970* (Washington, D.C.: U.S. Bureau of the Census, 1971), p. 222.

few entities in social life that were thought to require regulation. People became concerned with public issues only if the issues were thought to affect their lives and private interests. The prototype of democracy during this early period was the New England town meeting at which an individual could express his opinion publicly and attempt to affect the opinions of others before a public vote was taken.

As the population increased, the federal government grew. The movement away from local autonomy developed. Total expenditures by the federal government were quite low in the early years. In 1791, for example, the federal government spent only $4,269,000. By 1940, this had increased to $9 billion (with the 1940 dollars worth much less in purchasing power than 1791 dollars).

Since 1940, the federal budget has grown phenomenally. Annual expenditures by the federal government now exceed $300 billion. The military budget alone for fiscal year 1973 was nearly nine times the total budget in 1940. The growth of the federal government is reflected in the number of people it employs. This has increased from only five thousand persons in 1816 to nearly three million today.

The tremendous size and complexity of the federal government makes its influence felt in many areas of life once considered to be private. In discussing this, Emmanuel G. Mesthene says:

> it must certainly be conceded that the power, authority, influence, and scope of government are greater today than at any time in the history of the United States. The principal concerns of governments in the past have been to provide for national defense and to act as agents of social justice. Much more than that is demanded of modern government and much more is

attempted by it. In today's highly industrialized mass societies, government takes on responsibility for education, for public health, for cultural development, for provision of housing, for the functioning of the economy, and for the support of scientific research and technological development. To the extent that government does so it encroaches on domains that were once exclusively private.[23]

The results of these developments are an economic institution increasingly organized into giant conglomerates that produce a GNP of more than a trillion dollars annually, large union organizations, and a powerful federal government, including a large military establishment. Each of these is a center of great power. Even though each citizen theoretically is a small part of one or more of these large centers of power, it is difficult for an individual voice to be heard.

Each power center attempts to exert control over the others and in the process creates an ordering of control relationships that affects the lives of all of us. The federal government is supposed to be the guardian of the people because its historical legitimacy rests on its being "a government *of* the people, *by* the people and *for* the people." Using this criterion, we will examine the present arrangement of control relationships in the economic and political institutions to see how they affect the life-styles, life-chances, and individual meaning of the American people.

THE POLITICAL ECONOMY OF THE CONTEMPORARY U.S.

Many people still espouse the free-enterprise system, and it remains the official ideology of American society. This ideology bears only the faintest resemblance to current economic realities. Even though many people may receive relatively high wages or salaries they are not "their own men." More than 90 per cent of the labor force are employed by someone else and thus take orders either directly or indirectly from those for whom they work. Some people are satisfied with their positions and find meaning by performing their work but many others are not satisfied and do not find meaning in what they do.[24] Most of these seek economic security through the income produced by their employment. In an economy subject to recession and a job market affected by automation they may not even find that. Everett C. Hughes has pointed out:

> One may find himself earning his living at work that neither he nor those who guided him (teachers, parents and knowing peers) had heard of when he was in school. He may find that the cherished object of his and his parents' ambition and hard work is "automated" to splinters; or that the profession which was to make him free nowadays makes him a cog in a great machine.[25]

The typical American is free only to sell his labor on the market. Polanyi defines the market economy that developed under the laissez-faire ideology as "an economic system controlled, regulated, and directed by markets alone; order in the production and distribution of goods is entrusted to this self-regulating mechanism."[26] (This definition must be modified to the degree that markets are manipulated.) Polanyi points out that a market economy can only exist in a *market society* in which *all* of social life is geared to the continuous working of the market.

This brings us to the crux of our attempt to understand the relationship between the economic and political institutions in our society and all other institutions. We live in a market society and the *social ordering of all institutional spheres is constrained in many ways by the influence of the market* and the market mentality that develops in a market society. The economic institution, with its market economy and its free enterprise ideology, *is the dominant social institution in American society*. The government regulates and protects the economic institution as part of the reciprocal ordering of control relationships. Other institutions also reciprocally affect it, but the key to understanding American society is to recognize the dominance of the economic institution. We will support this statement and explore some of its consequences.

Inequality in American Society

In Chapter 7, when we discussed the American social class system, we clearly established the existence of inequalities in the distribution of income among Americans, the differences in income by occupational groups, and the resulting differences in life-styles and life-chances among the classes in the American system of social stratification.

Table 10-4 shows per capita personal income from 1950 to 1971 (preliminary). The average per capita income for all Americans in 1970 was about $4,000. This means that if the total personal income was divided equally among the population, a family of four could have an income of $16,000 per year, a family of two would have an income of $8,000 per year, and so forth. If we compare this distribution of income in 1970 with the actual distribution of income in that same year, we find a wide disparity. In 1970, 58.6 per cent of unrelated individuals had incomes below the average level. If we take the average size of a family as 3.3 persons, the average family would have an income, under equality, of $13,200, based on the $4,000 per capita income average. In 1970, about 65 per cent of all families fell below this figure.

TABLE 10-4

**Per Capita Income and Product for Selected Items in Current Dollars:
1950–1971**

[Prior to 1960, excludes Alaska and Hawaii. Based on Bureau of the Census estimated population as of July 1, including Armed Forces abroad. See also *Historical Statistics, Colonial Times to 1957*, series F 2, and, for data in 1929 dollars, series F 4]

Item	1950	1955	1960	1965	1967	1968	1969	1970	1971 (prel.)
CURRENT DOLLARS									
GNP	1,877	2,408	2,788	3,526	3,997	4,308	4,586	4,756	5,057
Personal income	1,501	1,881	2,219	2,774	3,168	3,434	3,704	3,924	4,140
Disposable personal income	1,364	1,666	1,937	2,436	2,751	2,946	3,130	3,358	3,581

SOURCE: U.S. Bureau of the Census.

Why is the Corporation the Dominant Economic Form?

When we discussed bureaucratic groups as a kind of formal social group in Chapter 4 we asked why bureaucratic social forms were so successful and dominant in the modern world. The answer was that, with all their drawbacks, they were the most efficient means man has yet devised for coordinating large-scale complex social activities. A similar answer must be given to the question of why the large corporation has become the specific kind of bureaucratic entity that has come to dominate economic institutions both in those societies that espouse free-enterprise ideologies and in those that espouse socialist or state-planning ideologies. The Soviet Union has social forms similar to the corporate economic bureaucracies owned by small groups of the population that exist in the United States. The predominance of the economic institution and the dominance within the economic institution of huge, bureaucraticized, centrally controlled productive apparatuses is quite similar in both societies.

The economist and social philosopher Robert J. Heilbroner has suggested the broad reasons for this striking similarity in two societies whose ideologists never tire of proclaiming their fundamental differences:

The corporation, with its vast powers at best half-controlled, is a form of social organization from which there will be no escape for many generations to follow. . . .

The reason for this lies in the technology of our time. In all industrial societies, the provision of steel and power, computers and automobiles, even bread and water, today requires the coordination of enormous numbers of men, welded together by complex processes of extraction and assembly and transportation. From one nation to another the legal forms, the powers and immunities of the

The percentage of aggregate income received by each fifth and the top 5 per cent of families from 1950 to 1970 is shown in Table 10-5. A vast disparity is again displayed. The highest fifth of the population received 41.6 per cent of the aggregate income in 1970—more than 200 per cent in "equal" share; whereas the bottom fifth received only 5.5 per cent; about 25 per cent of their equal share. The top five per cent received three times its share; whereas the bottom 60 per cent received less than their average share. Table 10-5 also shows that the distribution of income has not changed significantly since 1950.

Poverty

In 1969, 13 per cent of all persons in the nation were living *below* the poverty level, and another 4.9 per cent were living at or slightly above it.[27] Thus, nearly 19 per cent of the population, or forty million

---

organizations that supervise this technology vary, but in all industrial societies, socialist as well as capitalist, something like the corporation dominates the economic process. That is, in all advanced societies we find semiautonomous, bureaucratic, profit-oriented (even in socialist nations) enterprises carrying out these vast technological operations—and bringing in their train an accumulation of power and influence that eludes effective control.[a]

Fully aware of the dehumanizing nature of the corporate bureaucracy (whether capitalist or socialist) and the problems it poses for the satisfaction of individual needs and the provision of individual meaning, Heilbroner goes on to starkly pose the dilemma we face when we contemplate the political economies of modern societies:

A more terrible fact is that we do not know any better way to organize mankind in the immense numbers needed to operate our technology, other than by utilizing the motives of acquisitiveness or bureaucratic conformity through which the corporation exerts its dominion over men.

I do not know which institution it is more blasphemous to challenge—the nation-state with its flag and parades, its solemn mystical unity, and its latent ferocity; or the corporation with its insatiable wealth, seeking, its dehumanizing calculus of plus and minus, its careful inculcation of goals and impulses that should at most be tolerated.

As things now stand, the corporation that binds men together by appealing to their acquisitive natures, and the state that binds them together by appealing to their patriotic natures, are the only means we have for insuring our survival, even if by a terrible irony they are also the institutions by which our survival is most seriously endangered.[b]

[a]Robert J. Heilbroner *et al.*, *Profiles in Corporate Irresponsibility.* Garden City, N.Y.: Doubleday, 1972), pp. 261–263.
[b]Ibid.

TABLE 10-5
Percent of Aggregate Income Received by Each Fifth and Top 5 Percent of Families and Unrelated Individuals: 1950–1970

Item and Income Rank	1950	1955	1960	1965	1967	1968	1969	1970
Families	100.0	100.0	100.0	100.0	100.0	100.0	100.0	100.0
Lowest fifth	4.5	4.8	4.9	5.3	5.4	5.7	5.6	5.5
Second fifth	12.0	12.2	12.0	12.1	12.2	12.4	12.3	12.0
Middle fifth	17.4	17.7	17.6	17.7	17.5	17.7	17.6	17.4
Fourth fifth	23.5	23.7	23.6	23.7	23.7	23.7	23.5	23.5
Highest fifth	42.6	41.6	42.0	41.3	41.2	40.6	41.0	41.6
Top 5 per cent	17.0	16.8	16.8	15.8	15.3	14.0	14.7	14.4

SOURCE: U.S. Bureau of the Census, *Statistical Abstracts of the United States*, 1972.

people, were living below or close to the poverty level. Table 10-6 shows the poverty-level guidelines established by the federal government for farm and nonfarm families of various sizes. A nonfarm family of four is considered in poverty if its income falls below $4,300 per year. Compare this with Table 10-7, which shows annual budgets at three "levels" of living for a four-person family to see the wide disparity. The poverty level set by the federal government is nearly $3,000 below the lower level of living defined in Table 10-7 as adequate for this size family. Of course, if income equality existed and a family of four received its proportionate share of the national income, it would have $16,000 per year.

Table 10-7 also shows how families at various income levels spend their money. For example, a family of four at a higher level of living spends $3,198 on food per year, whereas a family of four at a lower level of living spends only $1,964. Thus, we see again that patterns of consumption and life-styles vary widely depending on the size of family income.

TABLE 10-6
OEO Poverty Guidelines for All States Except Alaska and Hawaii

Family Size	Nonfarm Family	Farm Family
1	$2,200	$1,670
2	2,900	2,465
3	3,600	3,000
4	4,300	3,655
5	5,000	4,250
6	5,700	4,815
7	6,400	5,410

For families with more than 7 members, add $700 for each additional member in a nonfarm family and $600 for each additional member in a farm family.
SOURCE: *Federal Register*, Vol. 38, No. 109 (June 7, 1973).

TABLE 10-7
Annual Budgets at Three Levels of Living for a 4-Person Family, Autumn 1971

| Area | Total Budget | Cost of Family Consumption | | | | | | | | Special Security and Disability Payments | Personal Income Taxes |
		Total	Food	Housing	Transportation	Clothing and Personal Care	Medical Care	Other family Consumption	Other Costs		
Higher Level of Living											
Urban United States	$15,905	$11,935	$3,198	$3,980	$1,260	$1,740	$638	$1,129	$937	$419	$2,614
Metropolitan areas	16,408	12,282	3,274	4,137	1,273	1,765	659	1,172	955	421	2,761
Nonmetropolitan areas	13,657	10,385	2,857	3,277	1,147	1,625	543	935	861	409	2,002
Intermediate Level of Living											
Urban United States	10,971	8,626	2,532	2,638	964	1,196	612	684	569	419	1,366
Metropolitan areas	11,232	8,823	2,575	2,723	964	1,214	633	704	567	421	1,121
Nonmetropolitan areas	9,805	7,746	2,338	2,258	941	1,113	521	575	530	409	1,111
Lower Level of Living											
Urban United States	7,214	5,841	1,961	1,516	536	818	609	368	357	387	826
Metropolitan areas	7,330	5,926	1,996	1,543	512	862	630	383	359	395	654
Nonmetropolitan areas	6,694	5,461	1,821	1,396	611	787	517	299	315	352	573

U.S. Department of Labor.

TABLE 10-8
Per Cent Distribution of Family Personal Income before and after Federal Income Tax by Fifths and the Top 5 Per Cent

	Poorest Fifth	Second Fifth	Middle Fifth	Fourth Fifth	Richest Fifth	Richest 5%
Before tax	4.0%	10.9%	16.3%	22.7%	45.5%	19.6%
After tax	4.9%	11.5%	16.8%	23.1%	43.7%	17.7%

SOURCE: Reprinted from *Inequality and Poverty,* edited and with an introduction by Edward C. Budd. By permission of W. W. Norton & Company, Inc. Copyright © 1967 by W. W. Norton & Company, Inc.

In 1973, the federally established minimum wage was $1.60 per hour. Working a forty-hour week this provides $3,328 per year. If only one member of a family of four was working at this wage, the family income would be nearly $1,000 per year *under* the federally established poverty level and nearly $4,000 per year under the lower level of living adequate for a family of four as shown in Table 10-8.* The contradictions between the ideal of equality and the inequitable reality are clear.

The Income Tax

Many believe the federal income tax is designed to produce a more equitable distribution of wealth in the nation. Table 10-8 shows that even though there is a slight decrease in the proportion of income after taxes in the richest fifth and the highest 5 per cent, the balance of the population gains only very slightly.

Who Owns the Wealth of the Nation?

The wealth of the nation is highly concentrated in the hands of a very few people. Table 10-9 shows the distribution of various types of personal wealth in 1962.

(There is no reason to believe that this has changed significantly since.) The wealthiest 1 per cent own 31 per cent of all wealth and the wealthiest 20 per cent own 76 per cent. In ownership of corporate stock, a significant source of power, the top 1 per cent own 61 per cent and the top 20 per cent own 96 per cent. A relatively small group of people clearly have great power. This power is used to maintain the

*In early 1974 the minimum wage was increased to $2.00 per hour after one Presidential veto. This still places a family of four under the poverty level. The minimum wage will increase to $2.20 in 1975 but the inflationary spiral of the 1972–74 period will wipe out any gain for the poor.

TABLE 10-9
Distribution of Varous Types of Personal Wealth, 1962

	Wealthiest 20%	*Top 5%*	*Top 1%*
Total wealth	76%	50%	31%
Corporate stock	96%	83%	61%
Business and professions	89%	62%	39%
Homes	52%	19%	6%

SOURCE: Projector and Weiss, *Survey of Financial Characteristics of Consumers*, pp. 110–114, 151; and Irwin Friend, Jean Crockett, and Marshall Blume, *Mutual Funds and Other Institutional Investors: A New Perspective*, p. 113.
Reproduced from Richard C. Edwards, Michael Reich, and Thomas Weisskopf, *The Capitalist System* (Englewood Cliffs, N.J.: Prentice-Hall, Inc., 1972), p. 211. Used by permission.

existing market society and its government with all the gross inequalities and inequities in income distribution and therefore in lifestyles and life-chances that we have portrayed.

Reciprocal Control Relationships between Economic and Political Institutions

Data to show the control relationships between the economic and the political institutions in our society in *specific* terms are not available. General data are available, however, and we will use these to make inferences about the structure of control relationships between the economic and political institutions.

The government *did* allow inequality in the economic sphere to develop. The government allowed the "captains of industry" to amass huge fortunes that were generated from the exploitation of natural resources, low wages, and the miserable living conditions of the laborers and the poor. These fortunes have been passed down within the families of the rich from generation to generation. Great wealth remains concentrated in the hands of a few in relationship to the total population.[28]

Social Welfare

During the New Deal and since, the government has made attempts to alleviate some of the human suffering that occurs under conditions of economic inequality. Social Security laws, minimum wage laws, unemployment compensation laws, civil rights laws, welfare laws, inheritance tax laws, and graduated income tax laws have been passed.

Many of these laws were passed over the objections of the rich and powerful. In addition, labor unions were allowed to grow, despite severe initial opposition. But the power of unions has been somewhat limited by the passage of right-to-work laws in some states and by the federal Taft-Hartley law that gives the federal government the right to stop some strikes, thus limiting the most effective control strategy available to workers. Some labor leaders have themselves become rich and it is difficult at times to tell which side they are on.

Table 10-10 shows social welfare expenditures by the federal, state, and local governments for selected years beginning with 1935. Even though many welfare laws have been passed, unions have been or-

The Super-Rich and Corporate Power

Another way to answer the question "Who owns the wealth of the nation?" is to examine the super-rich and their relationship to corporate economic power. In his study of the great private American fortunes, *The Rich and the Super-Rich,* Ferdinand Lundberg notes that "Nearly all the current large incomes, those exceeding $1 million, $500,000 or even $100,000 or $50,000 a year are derived in fact from *old* property accumulations, by inheritors—that is, by people who never did whatever one is required to do, approved or disapproved, creative or noncreative, in order to assemble a fortune."[a] The wealthy DuPont, Harriman, Rockefeller, Vanderbilt, Astor, Mellon, and Ford families today are the descendants of the great freebooting entrepreneurs of the heyday of expansive American capitalism in the nineteenth and early twentieth centuries.

The inherited family wealth of the superwealthy is shown by Lundberg to be invested in family holdings that control important banks and industries (the Rockefellers and Chase Manhattan Bank; the DuPonts and General Motors and the DuPont corporation); to have established charitable foundations (such as the Ford, Carnegie, and Rockefeller foundations); to support large universities and the major American political parties; and often to have extensive foreign investments that give the superwealthy and their advisers an ongoing interest in foreign and military policy.[b]

Members of these familial economic dynasties often play important roles in state and federal government, in leading and influential banks and brokerage houses, and on the boards of directors of the major American corporations. Their controlling interests in the dominant corporations are passed from one generation to another, insuring a continuity of power in all other institutional areas.

[a]Ferdinand Lundberg, *The Rich and the Super-Rich* (New York: Bantam, 1969), p. 155.
[b]Ibid., pp. 160–164.

TABLE 10-10

Social Welfare Expenditures under Public Programs for Federal, State, and Local Level in Selected Years: 1935–1971 (In millions of dollars)

Year and Source of Funds	Total Social Welfare	Social Insurance	Public Aid	Health and Medical Programs	Veterans Programs	Education	Housing	Other Social Welfare	All Health and Medical care
Federal									
1935	3,207	119	2,374	50	597	53	13	2	103
1940	3,443	394	2,243	97	620	75	4	11	178
1945	4,339	735	420	1,801	1,118	187	11	66	1,909
1950	10,541	2,103	1,103	604	6,386	157	15	174	1,362
1955	14,623	6,385	1,504	1,150	4,772	485	75	252	1,948
1960	24,957	14,307	2,117	1,737	5,367	868	144	417	2,918
1965	37,712	21,807	3,594	2,781	6,011	2,470	238	812	4,625
1966	45,379	25,663	4,366	3,146	6,337	4,580	251	1,035	5,384
1967	53,267	30,515	5,244	3,681	6,875	5,279	283	1,360	9,833
1968	60,314	35,390	6,455	4,233	7,214	5,000	325	1,697	13,060
1969	68,379	40,847	7,835	4,540	7,583	4,947	411	1,915	15,227
1970	77,321	45,245	9,637	4,773	8,952	5,878	577	2,260	16,598
1971 (prel.)	92,411	53,599	13,119	5,282	10,330	6,460	841	2,771	18,767
Percent	54.1	81.1	60.1	49.7	99.1	11.6	86.6	52.2	65.9
State and Local									
1935	3,341	287	624	378	(X)	1,955	(X)	97	440
1940	5,351	878	1,353	519	9	2,487	(X)	106	604
1945	4,866	675	610	553	7	2,889	(X)	132	670
1950	12,967	2,844	1,393	1,460	470	6,517	(X)	274	1,704
1955	18,017	3,450	1,499	1,953	62	10,672	15	367	2,473
1960	27,337	4,999	1,984	2,727	112	16,758	33	723	3,477
1965	39,464	6,316	2,690	3,466	20	25,638	80	1,254	4,911
1966	42,622	6,271	2,935	3,792	21	28,244	84	1,274	5,449
1967	46,444	6,794	3,567	3,947	23	30,529	95	1,489	5,989
1968	53,525	7,349	4,637	4,226	33	35,589	103	1,589	6,970
1969	59,395	7,917	5,610	4,463	51	39,359	107	1,888	7,707
1970	68,029	9,408	6,839	4,795	67	44,454	120	2,346	8,434
1971 (prel.)	78,341	12,476	8,700	5,338	90	49,073	130	2,534	9,696
Percent	45.9	18.9	39.9	50.3	0.9	88.4	13.4	47.8	34.1

SOURCE: U.S. Social Security Administration, *Social Security Bulletin* (Dec. 1971).

ganized, and the monies spent on social welfare increased significantly, the distribution of income in the nation has not been significantly changed. Much human suffering has been alleviated by these ameliorative control strategies, but the basic inequities remain.

Business Subsidies and Support

The federal government has subsidized farmers, with the richest farmers getting the largest proportions of the total government benefits. Many of these benefits have been given as compensation for

TABLE **10-11**

Share of Assets Held by the Largest Manufacturing Corporations: 1948–1971
[In per cent. Corporations ranked on value of assets in each year. Prior to 1969, excludes newspapers.]

Corporation Rank Group	1948	1950	1955	1960	1965	1968	1969	1970	1971
100 largest	40.2	39.7	44.3	46.4	46.5	49.1	48.2	48.5	48.9
200 largest	48.2	47.7	53.1	56.3	56.7	60.8	60.1	60.4	61.0

SOURCE: U.S. Bureau of the Census, *Statistical Abstracts of the United States*, 1973.

the restriction of farm production despite widespread inadequate diets in the United States and starvation elsewhere in the world. The government either pays direct cash subsidies or gives tax or credit subsidies to companies dealing in international trade, transportation, and commerce and allows oil companies large depletion allowances before taxes are computed. Capital gains, which allow fortunes already made to increase, are not proportionately taxed.[29] Large corporations are allowed to increase in size despite antitrust legislation passed to guarantee competition and a free market.

Table 10-11 shows the growth of the 100 largest and 200 largest manufacturing corporations since 1948. The 200 largest corporations, which are controlled by a relatively few people, now hold 60.4 per cent of the manufacturing assets of the nation.

The federal government also supports the investments of American corporations abroad, although investments are made for the profit of the small minority of people who own stock in these corporations. Overseas investments exploit cheap labor markets abroad, take profit from nations that are attempting to develop, and reduce the number of domestic jobs available, as products made overseas using cheaper labor are shipped back to the United States for sale. Table 10-12 shows the increase of American investments abroad from 1950 to 1969. If a foreign government confiscates corporation property the United States government compensates the corporation for its lost investment. In addition, the military is sometimes used to protect these private investments abroad.

Furthermore, all levels of government allow *public* utility corporations, which are monopolies and whose rates are directly controlled by government, to make large profits. In 1969, electric companies made a profit before taxes of nearly $5 billion and telephone companies made a profit before taxes of over $4 billion. In both cases this was nearly a 25 per cent return on operating revenue.

TABLE 10-12
Growth of U.S. Foreign Private Investment, 1950–1969
41969

| Year | Value of Assets | | | Direct Capital Outflow | Direct Investment Income |
| | Total | Long-Term | Direct | | |
	(Billions of dollars at year-end)			(Billions of dollars during year)	
1950	19.0	17.5	11.8	0.6	1.3
1951	20.5	19.0	13.0	0.5	1.5
1952	22.1	20.6	14.7	0.9	1.4
1953	23.8	22.2	16.3	0.7	1.4
1954	26.6	24.4	17.6	0.8	1.7
1955	29.1	26.8	19.4	0.8	1.9
1956	33.0	30.1	22.5	1.8	2.2
1957	36.8	33.6	25.4	2.1	2.3
1958	40.8	37.3	27.4	1.1	2.2
1959	44.8	41.2	29.7	1.4	2.2
1960	49.4	44.4	31.9	1.7	2.4
1961	55.5	49.0	34.7	1.6	2.8
1962	60.0	52.7	37.3	1.7	3.0
1963	66.5	58.3	40.7	2.0	3.1
1964	75.8	64.9	44.5	2.3	3.7
1965	81.5	71.4	49.5	3.5	4.0
1966	86.3	75.7	54.8	3.7	4.0
1967	93.6	81.7	59.5	3.1	4.5
1968	102.5	89.5	65.0	3.2	5.0
1969	110.2	96.0	70.8	3.1	5.6

SOURCE: U.S. Department of Commerce, *Survey of Current Business* (monthly), annual articles on the international investment position of the U.S.
Reproduced from Richard C. Edwards, Michael Reich, and Thomas E. Weisskopf, *The Capitalist System* (Englewood Cliffs, N.J.: Prentice-Hall, 1972), p. 427.

Conclusion

The federal government is heavily involved in the economic institution. Gross economic inequalities persist despite limited ameliorative measures. Among the reasons are that those who control the economic resources have considerable political influence. Thus, legislation necessary for a more equitable distribution of income is not forthcoming. Furthermore, when the government acts during periods of inflation or recession to maintain the existing economic order, the steps taken typically help the rich and hurt the poor. During inflationary periods interest and/or tax rates are raised to reduce the amount of money in circulation. Those who have money to invest benefit from high interest rates. Those who need to borrow, for example, to build a home, suffer. During recession periods, corporation taxes are reduced so they will invest more to create jobs, which are usually low paying. They thus make more on their investments. During the 1972–1973 inflation, wages and prices were frozen, but profits were not. Corporation profits skyrocketed during the first two quarters of 1973 while consumer prices increased dramatically as price controls were lifted. Christopher Jencks points out:

> Americans now tend to assume that incomes are determined by private decisions in a largely unregulated economy and that there is no realistic way to alter the resulting distribution. Until they come to believe that the distribution of income is a political issue, subject to popular regulation and control, very little is likely to change. In this connection, it is worth noting that until a generation ago, Americans also believed that the rate of economic growth depended upon private decisions and that it could not be controlled by the government. Today, virtually everyone assumes that the federal government is responsible for the state of the economy. If private decisions are producing undesirable results, it is up to the government to find a remedy. The time may now be ripe for a similar change in attitudes toward income equality. We need to establish the idea that the federal government is responsible not only for the total amount of national income, but for its distribution. If private decisions make the distribution too unequal, the government must be held responsible for improving the situation.[30]

Despite this, our nation in general does have one of the highest standards of living in the world. A comparison of our poor with the poor of some other nations causes our poor to appear relatively well off. But, as Karl Marx wrote: "A house may be large or small. As long as the surrounding houses are equally small it satisfies all social demands for a dwelling. But if a palace arises beside the little house, the little house shrinks into a hut."[31] Inequalities within a nation are therefore often disturbing and degrading.

Social Consciousness and Inequality in America

The American sociologists William Form and Joan Huber Rytina suggest that it is not the conditions that actually exist but rather what people believe about the political underpinnings of a society and how they define the situation that determines their behavior. If people believe they can influence political policy that maintains an open society, they may feel they have an opportunity for improvement even though they are at the bottom in wealth and income.[32]

To test what Americans believe about the distribution of power, Form and Rytina studied a sample of people representing all segments of the industrial community of Muskegon, Michigan. They pre-

TABLE 10-13
**Selection of Societal Models of Power Distribution,
by Income and Race (Per Cents)**

		Models of Power Distribution			Total	
		Marx (Economic Dominance)	Mills (Elitist)	Riesman (Pluralistic)	%	(N)
Income	Race					
Poor	Negro	33	6	61	100	(36)
	White	23	22	55	100	(64)
Middle	Negro	40	16	44	100	(45)
	White	17	20	63	100	(143)
Rich	White	12	23	65	100	(43)
Total, analytic sample	%	22	19	59	100	
	(N)	(74)	(62)	(195)		(331)

SOURCE: William H. Form and Joan Huber Rytina, "Ideological Beliefs about the Distribution of Power in the United States," *ASR*, Vol. 34 (Feb. 1969), p. 21.

sented each of their respondents with three different descriptions of the distribution of political power currently held by different sociologists. The respondents were listed as espousing the *pluralist position* (which is the official American free-enterprise ideology) if they agreed that no one group really runs the government of this country. If they agreed that a small group of men at the top really run the government of this country, they were presumed to espouse the *power elite* theory of C. Wright Mills. If they said that big businessmen really run the government of this country, the respondents were assumed to believe in the Marxist view of *economic dominance*. The results are presented in Table 10-13.

Interestingly, almost two thirds of the total group supported the pluralist ideology. Most surprisingly, the differences among income groups were slight. Both those at the bottom, who are objectively most deprived under the existing arrangements, and those at the top, who benefit most, seemed to support the arrangement in roughly the same proportions. The social consciousness of most groups in America thus seems to accept the official free-enterprise ideology about the distribution of power in society, assuming that this limited study holds for the entire society. From the Marxist point of view, given the objective facts presented here, this indicates a considerable amount of false consciousness.

Lenski points out that much of the inequality that exists in economic areas can be traced to apathy among the people. If the large majority of people were seriously concerned about the distribution of wealth and power, they could do something about it through political

The Power Elite

C. Wright Mills's theory that at the national level American society is supported by a set of interlocking power elites that dominate the major areas of business, politics, and the military in the interests of the ruling classes receives some confirmation by the apparent ease with which those at the top of the pyramids of power in each of these bureaucracies change positions.

The game of musical chairs among the managers of the dominant American bureaucracies seems endless. Dean Rusk went from directing the Carnegie Foundation for International Peace (a philanthropic bureaucracy) to Secretary of State under President Lyndon Johnson, to eventually move to academic life. Johnson's Secretary of Defense, Robert McNamara, was president of the Ford Motor Company prior to his cabinet post and was subsequently named director of the World Bank.

At levels just below the top, the interchange is equally incessant and often lucrative for those involved. *The New York Times* noted that "hundreds of generals, high-level civil servants, commissioners, and congressmen each year switch from government jobs to closely related careers in private industry. Some of them live in two worlds, moving easily back and forth between government and industry—a pool of skilled professionals who alternate between sensitive political posts and high-salaried positions in business."[a] Illustrations cited by the *Times* include Bryce Harlow, who left the vice-presidency of Procter and Gamble to become counselor to President Nixon; Clarence Palmby, who was Assistant Secretary of Agriculture before he became vice-president of Continental Grain; and General James Ferguson, who was commander of the Air Force Systems Command before becoming a vice-president of the United Aircraft Corporation.

The interpenetration of the economic and political institutions that form our political economy is nowhere more clearly illustrated than in this interchange of personnel at the top of the pyramids of power. The super-rich also weave in and out of the top levels of the political, economic, and other bureaucracies. Averell Harriman, scion of one of the great nineteenth-century railroad fortunes, served intermittently for many years at high levels of the State Department and was a one-term governor of New York State, succeeded in that post by Nelson Rockefeller, who served almost four terms. The Rockefeller family, whose fortune was based on oil revenues but is now widely dispersed throughout the economy, dabbles in many institutional areas. One Rockefeller brother served as governor of Arkansas, another heads the Chase Manhattan Bank, and still others are influential in philanthropy and the arts.

FIGURE **10-2**
Power Elite and Upper Class

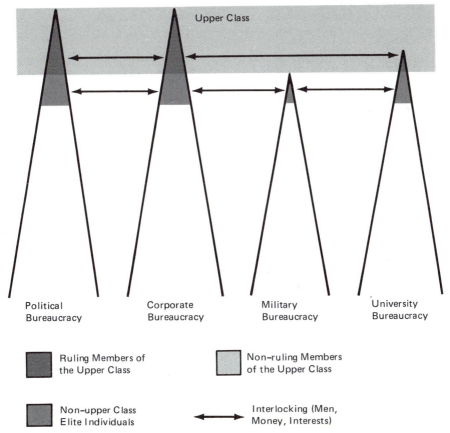

Power Elite and Upper Class

Upper Class

Political
Bureaucracy

Corporate
Bureaucracy

Military
Bureaucracy

University
Bureaucracy

Ruling Members of
the Upper Class

Non-ruling Members
of the Upper Class

Non-upper Class
Elite Individuals

Interlocking (Men,
Money, Interests)

SOURCE: Charles H. Anderson, *Toward A New Sociology* (Homewood, Ill: Dorsey, 1971), p. 208.

The sociologist Charles Anderson has diagramed the relationships among the upper class, the managerial elites in the various bureaucracies, and the distribution of power to illustrate their complex relations.

Even though the social consciousness of most Americans embodies the pluralist theory of the distribution of power as both factual and desirable, sociologists have discovered that a Millsian conception comes closer to the realities of our national political economy.

[a]*The New York Times* (Nov. 12, 1972), Sect. 3, pp. 1–2.

TABLE 10-14
Percentage Who Say They Have Attempted to Influence the Government (By Country)

Country	Local Government*	National Legislature†	N
U. S.	28%	16%	970
U. K.	15	6	963
Germany	14	3	955
Italy	8	2	995
Mexico	6	3	1295

SOURCE: Almond and Verba survey, unpublished data.
*Have you ever done anything to try to influence a local decision?"
†"Have you ever done anything to try to influence an act of the [national legislature]?"
Reproduced from Robert A. Dahl, *Modern Political Analysis* (Englewood Cliffs, N.J.: Prentice-Hall, 1963), p. 86.

action. Our nation is democratic and ideally abides by the will of the people. But this is not likely to happen given the degree of apathy shown in Table 10-14.

Furthermore, the increased standard of living for many people and the increased amount of leisure (see Figure 10-3) cause many not to care about how wealth is distributed so long as they get by and enjoy life. The relative lack of outrage among the general public about people who are living under conditions of poverty supports this view.

Rousseau was probably correct when he said:

Political distinctions necessarily produce civil distinctions. The growing equality between chiefs and the people is soon felt by individuals, and modified in a thousand ways according to passions, talents, and circumstances. The magistrate could not usurp any illegitimate power without giving distinction to the creatures with whom he must share it. Besides, individuals only allow themselves to be oppressed so far as they are hurried on by blind ambition, and looking rather below than above them, come to love authority more than independence, and submit to slavery, that they may in turn enslave others. It is no easy matter to reduce to obedience a man who has no ambition to command; nor could the most adroit politician find it possible to enslave a people whose only desire was to be independent.[33]

So long as people look below rather than above to draw comparisons inequalities will continue to exist.

A Brief Comparison with the USSR

The problem of political and economic inequality is not restricted to this country, as evidenced by data from the Soviet Union. The Marxist ideal stated that in a communist nation, the government, as a source of power and protector of differential privilege, would wither away eventually and that the production and distribution of goods and services would be based on the principle of "from each according to his

FIGURE 10-3
U.S. Time Budget and Time Division of Leisure, 1900, 1950, and 2000.

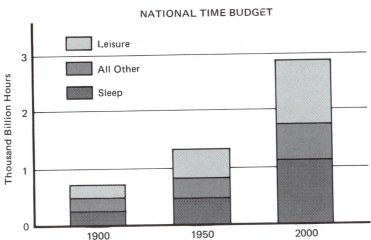

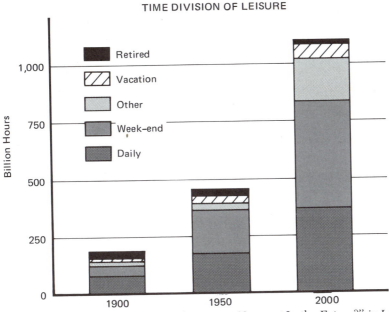

SOURCE: Marion Clawson, "How Much Leisure, Now and In the Future?" in *Leisure in America: Blessing or Curse?* ed. by James Charlesworth (Philadelphia: American Academy of Political and Social Science, 1964), Monograph No. 4, p. 11.

ability and to each according to his need." Although the Soviet revolution will be fifty years old in 1977, there is no indication that the "dictatorship of the proletariat" is ready to give up power. Indeed, just the opposite appears to be happening with an increasing centralization of political power in a small elite group.

TABLE 10-15
Income in Rubles per Month for Steel Workers in the USSR, 1959 and 1965

	1959	1965
Director of scientific research institute	600	600
Director of steel plant	400	400
Elevator operator, janitor, watchman	35	60
Typist, secretary	41	60

SOURCE: Murray Yanowitch, "The Soviet Income Revolution," *Slavic Review*, Vol. XXII, No. 4 (Dec. 1963). Reproduced from *Structured Social Inequality*, ed. by Celia S. Heller (New York: Macmillan, 1969), p. 144.

Furthermore, economic equality is a long way from becoming a reality in the Soviet Union, although minimal strides have been made in this direction since the Twenty-second Party Congress in 1961.[34] Table 10-15 shows the distribution of income in rubles per month for people at various levels in the steel industry in the USSR. The directors still make ten times more than the lower occupations and this does not include bonuses, which are more likely to go to directors than to the janitor or the clerk-typist.[35] The incomes of high-ranking members of the political elite are much higher. The classless society that Marx predicted and that the Soviet leaders hold out as the ideal is a long way from being realized.

REFERENCES

1. Lenski, Gerhard E. *Power and Privilege*. New York: McGraw-Hill, 1966, p. 44.
2. Ibid.
3. Ibid., p. 50.
4. Ibid., p. 46.
5. Ibid.
6. Weber, Max. *The Theory of Economic and Social Organization*. New York: Oxford U. P., 1947, pp. 328 ff.
7. Gerth, H. H., and C. Wright Mills. *From Max Weber: Essays in Sociology*. New York: Oxford U. P., 1958.
8. *Political Socialization*. Ed. by Edward Greenberg. New York: Atherton, 1970, p. 85.
9. Heilbroner, Robert L. "The Human Prospect." *The New York Review of Books* (Jan. 24, 1974), 30.
10. Polanyi, Karl. *The Great Transformation*. Boston: Beacon, 1957, p. 139.
11. Smith, Adam. *Inquiry into the Nature and Causes of the Wealth of Nations*, Book IV, Chapter II.
12. Polanyi, op. cit., p. 117.
13. Ibid., p. 131.

14. Hobbes, Thomas. *Leviathon*. Oxford: Clarendon, 1909.
15. Ibid., p. 97.
16. Rousseau, Jean Jacques. *The Social Contract and Discourses*. Trans. by G.D.H. Cole. New York: Dutton, 1950, pp. 234–235.
17. Ibid., p. 249.
18. Ibid., p. 251–252.
19. Ibid., p. 23.
20. Locke, John. *Two Treatises of Government*. Ed. with an introduction by Thomas I. Cook. New York: Haforer, 1947, pp. 122, 123.
21. Reich, Michael. "The Evolution of the United States Labor Force." In *The Capitalist Society*. Ed. by Richard C. Edwards, Michael Reich, and Thomas E. Weisskopf. Englewood Cliffs, N.J.: Prentice-Hall, 1972, p. 175.
22. Mills, C. Wright. *White Collar*. New York: Oxford U. P., 1956, pp. 8, 10.
23. Mesthene, Emmanuel G. *Technological Change: Its Impact on Man and Society*. Cambridge: Harvard U. P., 1970, p. 83.
24. See Sheppard, Harold L., and Neal Q. Herrick. *Where Have All the Robots Gone?* New York: Free Press, 1972; and Chinoy, Ely. *Automobile Workers and the American Dream*. Garden City, N.Y.: Doubleday, 1955.
25. Hughes, Everett C. *Men and Their Work*. New York: Free Press, 1958, p. 7.
26. Polanyi, op. cit., p. 68.
27. U.S. Bureau of the Census, *Statistical Abstracts of the United States*, 1972.
28. See Lundberg, Ferdinard. *The Rich and the Super Rich*. New York: L. Stuart, 1968.
29. For an excellent discussion of tax avoidance, see Stern, Philip M. *The Great Treasury Raid*. New York: Random, 1964.
30. Jencks, Christopher, *et al. Inequality*. New York: Basic Books, 1972, p. 264.
31. Marx, Karl. "Wage-Labor and Capital." *Selected Works*, Vol. 1. New York: International Publishers, 1933, pp. 268–69.
32. Form, William H., and Joan Huber Rytina. "Ideological Beliefs about the Distribution of Power in the United States." *American Sociological Review*, Vol. 34 (Feb. 1969), 19–30.
33. Rousseau, loc. cit.
34. Yanowitch, Murray. "The Soviet Income Revolution." *Slavic Review*, Vol. XXII, No. 4 (Dec. 1963), 683–697. Reprinted in *Structured Social Inequality*. Ed. by Celia S. Heller. New York: Macmillan 1969, p. 144.
35. Ibid., p. 151.

CHAPTER 11

Education

INTRODUCTION

In preindustrial societies learning was important for immediate survival. If young people did not learn to hunt or gather or how and when to plant and harvest in agricultural societies, they would not survive as adults. They also learned the myths, the rituals, the taboos, the games, kinship relations, folklore, and other cultural agreements of their society. People learned by doing and by participating with or listening to their elders. The knowledge acquired tended to be concrete and to be put to immediate use. The learning process itself was informal and occurred within the kinship institution and its extended family system.

Children became adults at an early age, typically at puberty, so that the age of dependency was greatly reduced from what it is today in industrial societies. Adolescence, the time between puberty and adulthood, as socially defined in industrial societies, did not exist. Ideally, children were anxious to learn what was necessary to become adults because being an adult increased one's prestige. Boys and girls were closely associated with adults in daily activities and learning occurred from these associations. Schools as places separate from real-life situations did not exist. Learning and living went hand in hand.

The child's needs were gratified in the process of living and learning. On the one hand, adults knew that their livelihood in old age depended on children learning what needed to be known for survival and for the perpetuation of the family or group. On the other hand, children knew learning from adults was necessary for their own future livelihood and the gratification of their needs and desires.

Life in preindustrial societies was not idyllic. If food was scarce

318

people went hungry. When sickness occurred, there were no modern medicines to produce cures. Life expectancy at birth was short. The intention here is not to portray some past educational Golden Age that never existed, but to present a contrast to the contemporary system of education that keeps children from real-life situations for a long period of time, within which they are expected to defer gratification of their basic needs.

Some form of education outside the kinship institution has been around for more than two thousand years in some societies. For example, the education of youth outside the family in ancient Athens and Sparta was quite elaborate and sophisticated. For the most part, however, history shows that until recently it was typically only the sons of the rich who had the opportunity to participate in formal schooling. It was not until after the founding of this nation that free formal public education became available to the masses. The practice spread rapidly, however, so that today most nations have a complex system of formal education. This is true even though in most nations differential chances for attaining various levels and kinds of education exist.

The discussion in this chapter will be limited to that of formal education in the United States and will concentrate on the social ordering of the school, what schools do in comparison with their idealized goals, and the consequences for students, particularly as these relate to racial and social class differences among students.

PUBLIC EDUCATION IN AMERICA

Discussing the history of public education in America, Michael B. Katz, a critic of public school education, points out that, "The structure of American urban education has not changed since late in the nineteenth century; by 1880, the basic features of public education in most major cities were the same as they are today."[1] Certain innovations and developments have taken place, such as "kindergartens, the junior high school, industrial education, testing, and the new math,"[2] but these have occurred *within* a given *structure* that has not altered. Katz sees this structure as being universal, tax-supported, free, compulsory, bureaucratically arranged, class-biased, and racist.[3] We will first examine the bureaucratic structure of public education in America.

Bureaucracy and American Education

The typical American school is a bureaucracy and, as such, tends *not* to allow the flexibility necessary for the gratification of the individual needs and desires of students. Furthermore, the classroom

FIGURE 11-1
Levels of School Bureaucracy and Types of Public Pressure.

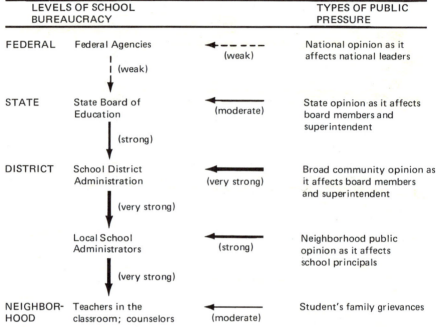

LEVELS OF SCHOOL BUREAUCRACY			TYPES OF PUBLIC PRESSURE
FEDERAL	Federal Agencies	◄ ─ ─ ─ ─ ─ (weak)	National opinion as it affects national leaders
	↓ (weak)		
STATE	State Board of Education	◄─────── (moderate)	State opinion as it affects board members and superintendent
	↓ (strong)		
DISTRICT	School District Administration	◄─────── (very strong)	Broad community opinion as it affects board members and superintendent
	↓ (very strong)		
	Local School Administrators	◄─────── (strong)	Neighborhood public opinion as it affects school principals
	↓ (very strong)		
NEIGHBOR-HOOD	Teachers in the classroom; counselors	◄─────── (moderate)	Student's family grievances

SOURCE: From *Patterns of Social Organization*, by Jonathan H. Turner. Copyright 1972, McGraw-Hill Book Company. Used with permission of McGraw-Hill Book Company.

teacher, who has the most contact with the student, is placed under a variety of constraints from those above him in bureaucratic positions of power, and directly or indirectly from powerful outside sources. Figure 11-1 shows these constraints. Neither the local school administrator nor the teacher in the classroom is in a position to do what he thinks is in the best interests of students.

The table also suggests that the student's family has only a moderate degree of control over teachers or school counselors and thus over the destiny of the child within the formal education framework. Given the control relationships among the parents of a student, teachers, and local school administrators, the teacher can be expected to be more responsive to the local school administrator than to a student's family. The administrator has the power to fire or withhold pay increases, a student's family does not. (The administrator's power is modified somewhat by the rules of tenure and by teachers' unions.)

Teachers as a professional group, are not always in agreement with the bureaucratic structure that tends to dominate their lives while they are at work. "In lower education, the teacher can exercise some professionalism in the classroom but there are many bureaucratic con-

TABLE 11-1
Demands in Bureaucracies and Professions

Bureaucracies	*Professions*
1 Standardization of role behavior	1 Flexibility in role behavior
2 Low degree of autonomous decision making	2 High degree of decision making
3 Role behavior is oriented to organization	3 Role behavior is oriented to client
4 Role behavior conforms to administrative practices of organization	4 Role behavior conforms to the standards of colleagues and professional associations

SOURCE: From *Patterns of Social Organization*, by Jonathan H. Turner. Copyright 1972, McGraw-Hill Book Company. Used with permission of McGraw-Hill Book Company.

straints, including (typically) a standardized curriculum, incessant evaluation by administrators, and the necessity for implementing administrative policies."[4] Many procedural demands made by the bureaucratic structure are inconsistent with professional ideals. Table 11-1 shows the potentially conflicting demands between professionals and the bureaucracies in which they work. Katz puts the matter bluntly:

> Bright, creative, and well-educated people want to function as professionals, to make decisions about how they will do their job. Education has not suffered from any freedom granted teachers to run schools as they see fit; it has suffered from the suffocating atmosphere in which teachers have had to work. The popular attitude, and even that of reformers, equates the aims of administrators with those of teachers; it blames teachers for bureaucracy. The important point is that a distinction must be made; teachers do not run the schools. They are, as they will tell you, harrassed by the administration, which, if they are any good, continually gets in their way.[5]

The complex web of constraint and control relationships in the total bureaucratic educational structure is such that no one is totally free to move in a direction that would more adequately meet the needs of students.

Numbers of Students and Funding Problems As Pressures Toward Educational Bureaucracy

Total enrollments in schools have nearly doubled since 1930. In 1970, the total educational system was processing 58,766,000 students. Of these, more than forty-three million were in public grade schools and high schools. Table 11-2 shows the increase in enrollment at various levels of education, both public and private, by decades since 1930.

TABLE 11-2
School Enrollment, by Type of School, 1930–1970

[In thousands. Prior to 1960, excludes Alaska and Hawaii. Beginning 1964, data as of fall of preceding year.]

Item	1930	1940	1950	1960	1964	1966	1970
Total	29,652	29,751	31,319	45,228	51,191	54,306	58,766
Kindergarten	786	661	1,175	2,293	2,555	2,493	2,821
Grades 1–8	22,953	20,466	21,032	30,119	32,117	33,266	34,290
Grades 9–12 and postgraduate	4,812	7,130	6,453	9,600	12,255	13,021	14,518
Higher education	1,101	1,494	2,659	3,216	4,234	5,526	7,136

SOURCE: U.S. Bureau of the Census, *Statistical Abstracts of the United States*, 1972.

Numbers alone create the necessity of control for the purpose of coordination. Without some complex system of organization, the schools would be in chaos. The sheer size of the student population places a constraint on communities to form a bureaucratic organization to control the education of students by some type of routinized process.

To complicate the problem of massive numbers, there are insufficient funds to do the kind of job that many professional teachers and administrators believe necessary. Table 11-3 shows the amount of money expended on all levels of education from 1930 to 1972. The amount spent has increased phenomenally. This increase is also reflected in the percentage of the GNP spent on education. Whereas in 1930 only 3.1 per cent of the GNP was being funneled into education, in 1972 this had risen to an estimated 8.2 per cent. Thus, a much higher percentage of the nation's wealth is going into formal education. Education is *big business* when spending is in excess of $86 billion per year at all levels, public and private!

Despite the large amount of money being spent, however, there is still not enough to provide the necessary kind and level of education. Many local schools are in debt and some have closed in recent years for short periods of time or have opened for only half a day because of a lack of funds. Some local school districts have refused to pass necessary tax levies to keep local schools operating at adequate levels.

Furthermore, the money spent on education is not equal across the nation. The differences in the amount of money spent per pupil in average daily attendance in the fifty states varies significantly. At the extremes, Alabama spent $590 in 1973 on each pupil, whereas New York spent nearly three times as much, $1,584 per student. This difference tends to reflect the average personal income in the state: in Alabama $3,050 per year and in New York $5,021 per year.

TABLE 11-3
School Expenditures—Public and Private, 1930–1972
[In millions of dollars, except per cent. Prior to 1960, excludes Alaska and Hawaii. Estimates for school years ending in year shown.]

	1930	1940	1950	1960	1965	1970	1971	1972 est.
Total	3,234	3,200	8,796	24,722	40,200	70,600	78,200	86,100
Per cent of GNP	3.1	3.5	3.4	5.1	6.4	7.2	7.5	8.2

SOURCE: U.S. Bureau of the Census, *Statistical Abstracts of the United States*, 1972.

There are also wide differences within states in per pupil expenditure by school districts. With some exceptions, school districts serving wealthy suburbs spend much more money per pupil than do school districts in less affluent areas, partly because the largest share of money for education comes from property taxes. The state and federal subsidies paid to local school districts reduce but do not eliminate this unequal support. Teachers' salaries also vary widely. Table 11-4 shows the 1973 distribution among the fifty states of expenditures per pupil, average teacher salaries, pupils per teacher, and changes in the first two categories since 1962–1963.

In the early 1970s, courts in some states, starting with California, declared the support of schools through the use of property taxes unconstitutional. In March 1973, however, the United States Supreme Court reversed these decisions. In the foreseeable future, the amount of money spent per pupil for education can be expected to remain unequal within as well as between states.

When money is short, higher levels of "efficiency" must be achieved. In education this usually means increasing the size of classes or cutting out some of the "frills" such as art, music, and other activities that are viewed as peripheral. This brings us to a basic question: What does the public want from the school system it supports with its taxes?

THE GOALS OF AMERICAN EDUCATION: PRODUCTS OR PEOPLE?

Robin M. Williams, Jr., tells us, in his discussion of American education, that "Emphasis is put upon the practical usefulness of formal education. Comtemplative or speculative thought, art, and highly abstract theoretic work are relatively little valued."[6] Formal education exists as a means to train students to take their place in other institu-

TABLE 11-4
States and Education: A Statistical Profile, 1973

	Expend-itures Per Pupil*	Change Since 1962–63	Average Teacher Salaries	Change Since 1962–63	Pupils Per Teacher*
Alabama	$ 590	139.8%	$ 8,262	101.5%	21.7
Alaska	1,473	140.6	15,176	101.9	19.4
Arizona	1,110	158.1	10,863	69.7	21.0
Arkansas	652	135.3	7,613	101.8	20.1
California	1,000	93.7	12,700	71.6	22.2
Colorado	955	117.0	10,280	78.8	21.6
Connecticut	1,241	132.8	11,200	65.8	18.2
Delaware	1,162	132.8	11,100	72.1	19.5
Washington, D.C.	1,327	173.0	NR	NR	19.3
Florida	902	154.0	9,740	72.5	21.0
Georgia	782	165.9	8,644	83.6	22.6
Hawaii	1,046	169.5	10,900a	79.6	20.4
Idaho	772	142.7	8,058	63.6	23.0
Illinois	1,144	150.3	11,564	77.0	19.1
Indiana	878	99.5	10,300	65.6	21.0
Iowa	1,058	138.8	10,564	98.9	18.9
Kansas	919	117.7	8,839	68.7	17.8
Kentucky	693	139.7	8,150	79.9	21.1
Louisiana	927	142.0	9,388	78.8	19.1
Maine	840	142.0	9,277	91.2	19.0
Maryland	1,188	153.3	11,787	83.1	20.0
Massachusetts	1,102	136.9	11,200	80.6	18.4
Michigan	1,183	164.6	12,400	92.4	22.4
Minnesota	1,146	139.7	11,115	86.0	20.3
Mississippi	689	202.1	7,145	94.5	21.1
Missouri	881	119.7	9,329	72.3	20.2
Montana	943	107.2	8,909	69.7	NR
Nebraska	735	96.0	9,080	86.1	18.5
Nevada	971	112.4	11,472	84.6	22.4
New Hampshire	892	121.3	9,313	82.9	18.1

tions in the society.[7] Americans do not believe that formal education should be fundamentally concerned with the emotional and intellectual development of students or the gratification of their immediate needs and desires.

The necessity for efficiency to educate large numbers of students with limited funds, plus the emphasis on producing a product for other institutions in the society creates an educational system antithetical to the present *needs* of students, and perhaps even to the possibility of their future happiness. People in the school bureaucracy come under heavy public constraints to produce products rather than people. The maverick in the typical public school is soon fired or feels pressured to leave.

The irony is that one of the original goals and ideals of public

TABLE **11-4**
States and Education: A Statistical Profile, 1973

	Expend-itures Per Pupil*	Change Since 1962–63	Average Teacher Salaries	Change Since 1962–63	Pupils Per Teacher*
New Jersey	$ 1,352	147.6%	$ 11,750	80.5%	NR
New Mexico	829	105.1	8,600	44.6	21.7
New York	1,584	132.9	13,450[b]	86.8	17.6
North Carolina	802	170.9	9,314	84.5	21.6
North Dakota	855	116.4	8,362	89.0	18.3
Ohio	945	124.4	9,800	64.7	21.6
Oklahoma	704	107.0	8,200	56.0	19.9
Oregon	1,004	93.8	9,949	60.3	19.7
Pennsylvania	1,177	160.9	11,000	88.4	20.0
Rhode Island	1,116	126.8	10,800	75.9	19.0
South Carolina	751	188.8	8,310	96.4	21.5
South Dakota	833	116.3	8,034	86.0	18.8
Tennessee	730	174.4	8,450	95.2	23.3
Texas	1,044	176.1	9,029	65.1	19.8
Utah	739	110.5	8,990	68.0	23.8
Vermont	1,211	219.5	9,110	82.2	16.3
Virginia	920	173.8	9,842	95.6	20.1
Washington	929	87.6	11,100	74.5	22.4
West Virginia	749	153.8	8,505	89.2	21.5
Wisconsin	1,134	135.7	10,812	82.0	18.7
Wyoming	960	82.5	9,900	69.5	17.2
Total U. S.	$1,034	138.7%	$10,643	79.8%	20.2

*Based on average daily attendance
NR — No report
[a]NEA estimate
[b]Median salary

SOURCE: *National Center for Educational Statistics and National Education Association*, p. 58. Reprinted from *The New York Times* (Jan. 6, 1974), p. 58.

schools was to educate people for participation as citizens in a democratic society. Thomas Jefferson pointed out that the maintenance of a democracy depends on an educated citizenry capable of thinking through public issues, voting with some degree of sophistication, and not easily taken in by a demagogue. Such goals are little valued and rarely realized in our schools. Harry L. Gracey sums it up:

> The educational institution is, then, one of the ways in which society is perpetuated through the systematic socialization of the young, while the nature of society which is being perpetuated—its organization and operation, its values, beliefs and ways of living—are determined by the primary institutions. The educational system, like other secondary institutions, *serves* the society which is created by the operation of the economy, the political system, and the military establishment.[8]

In schools, "Great attention is paid to the creed of democratic values."[9] But research studies show that political socialization emphasizing critical analysis of or democratic participation in society does not occur.[10] A stereotype civics course in "The Principles (or Problems) of Democracy" is usually required, but this does not offset the structural fact that the student stands at the bottom of an authoritarian hierarchy that tells him what to do and what to learn so that, upon graduation, the "product" can be successfully placed on the market.

> Schools have evolved in the United States not as a part of a pursuit of equality, but rather to meet the needs of capitalist employers for a disciplined and skilled labor force, and to provide a mechanism for social control in the interests of political stability.[11]

The best way to learn democracy is to continuously participate in a democratic process. Within the school system at all levels someone else always knows what is best for the student who has little say about the matter. "When students analyze issues objectively and are given the opportunity to generate and defend their own ideas about social events, they perform relatively high on all important political socialization measures."[12] But most textbooks and interaction in the classroom are not conducive to inquiry into social and political issues.[13] Instead, they foster apathy and a noncritical compliance with the existing system.[14] Thus, a product is produced that will fit into and support the existing economic and political system in an uncritical manner.

A public school teacher supports our argument very well from her own experience:

> Throughout all my years as a student and as a student teacher, this is the idea I was taught to accept—discipline means control. It exists for the convenience of the adults in the school. It consists of a set of rules imposed on the children by grown-ups; the children are expected to accept them and obey without question. The consensus is that only in this way can the school hope to preserve law and order. . . .
>
> And what do we teach the citizens of the future? Obedience is an important virtue; it is wrong to question higher authority; children who do not conform and obey are punished; and those who succeed best in accepting the system are put into positions of control in turn—they are charged with keeping their classmates in line.[15]

The Student Reaction

Robert J. Havighurst and Bernice L. Neugarten point out that: "The child grows up in two social worlds. One is the world of adults: his parents, teachers, club leaders, the store clerks, friends of the family, and the policeman. The second is the world of peers or age-mates: his

FIGURE **11-2**
The Two Worlds of the Child

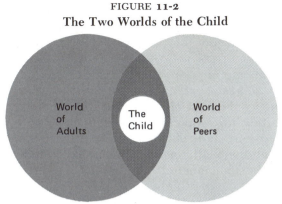

SOURCE: From Robert J. Havighurst and Bernice L. Neugarten, *Society and Education,* Third Edition, p. 170. © Copyright 1967 by Allyn and Bacon, Inc. Reprinted with permission.

friends, play groups, clubs and gangs, and school groups."[16] Figure 11-2 shows the child in the middle between the world of adults and the world of peers. In modern societies "being in the middle" may last until the age of eighteen or even longer, depending on how long a person stays in school. This contrasts with the child in preindustrial society who became a fully participating adult member of his society at puberty.

Being in the middle places children and adolescents in a position of potential strain if, as often happens, their peer group makes one set of demands and the adult world makes a contradictory set. Within the classroom, children are at the bottom of a power hierarchy that ignores many of their needs and desires. Typically they are not allowed to participate in the decision-making process that directly affects their lives. Willard Waller graphically described the school situation and the place of children within it:

> It is not enough to point out that the school is a despotism. It is a despotism in a state of perilous equilibrium. It is a despotism threatened from within and exposed to regulation and interference from without. It is a despotism capable of being overturned in a moment, exposed to the instant loss of its stability and its prestige. It is a despotism demanded by the community of parents, but specially limited by them as to the techniques which it may use for the maintenance of a stable social order. *It is a despotism resting upon children, at once the most tractable and the most unstable members of the community.*[17]

Student Subculture

This despotism and the consequent inability of students to actively participate in a meaningful way in the social ordering processes that affect their lives in schools leads to the creation of a variety of student subcultures and informal cliques within the school. In these subcultures and cliques, the students have more meaningful control over their own lives and are able to gratify their individual needs and desires.

Many students are more involved in these nonacademic activities that give them self-esteem than they are with the academic classroom activities. Among the best of many research studies providing evidence supporting the importance of student subcultures is James Coleman's year-long study of ten high schools in communities of various sizes in northern Illinois. Coleman asked students how they would like to be remembered. The results reported in Table 11-5 show that "the image of athletic star for boys, and the image of activities leader and most popular are more attractive to girls than [the image of] brilliant students."[18] For many students, the gratification of the need for self-esteem and other needs comes not from the formal academic system but from other informal sources over which at least some students have control. Coleman summarizes his data by noting that "Despite wide differences in parental background, type of community, and type of school, there is little difference in standards of prestige, the activities which confer status, and the values which focus attention and interest. In particular, good grades and academic achievement had relatively low status in all schools."[19]

Outside the classroom students have some control over their own lives and thus the possibility of finding individual meaning. A student who has little academic ability or interest goes unrecognized in the classroom but can hope to gain a sense of self-esteem by being an athletic star or a leader in extracurricular activities. Being an athletic star, a student leader, or popular among one's peers is immediately rewarding and need-gratifying. Some students do gain immediate gratification from being good students, but it is difficult to bring the world of adults and the world of student peers together for the achievement of a common purpose in the classroom because their reward systems are different.

C. Wayne Gordon, in his study of a suburban high school, found "that the dominant motivation of the adolescent was to achieve and maintain a generalized social status within the organization of the school."[20] Gordon's study also found "that student cliques provided security and protection for students and that the drop-out of 30 per cent appeared to be directly related to the least esteemed and disesteemed students."[21] In Gordon's study, the existence of students' cliques placed controls on classroom teachers that forced them to deviate from grading academic achievement. The more the teachers were involved with students in extracurricular activities, the greater was the tendency to deviate from grading by academic achievement alone. Even though students are at the bottom of the bureaucratic structure, they can exert considerable control over teachers.

TABLE 11-5
How Boys and Girls Want to Be Remembered in School—Fall and Spring

	Boys		Girls	
	Fall	Spring	Fall	Spring
Brilliant student	31.3%	31.5%	28.8%	27.9%
Athletic star (boys)	43.6	45.1		
Leader in activities (girls)			36.1	37.8
Most popular	25.0	23.4	35.2	34.2
Number of cases ("no" answers excluded)	(3,696)	(3,690)	(3,955)	(3,376)

SOURCE: James B. Coleman, *The Adolescent Society* (New York: The Free Press, 1962), p. 30.

Reciprocal Control by Students

As students exert control over teachers they participate in the social ordering of the classroom situation despite the bureaucratic structure in a variety of ways. First, many teachers use students for the gratification of their own needs. Teachers, like other people, have needs and desires and use favorable responses from students for their gratification. A teacher does not like to face a hostile class day after day and thus is often willing to "take it easy" with students in order to gain positive responses from them.

Secondly, teachers cannot completely ignore the subtle demands made by the strong informal cliques of students that exist in most schools. Some of these cliques, of course, have more potential power over teachers than others and exert pressure on the teacher to conform to at least some of their expectations. As Gordon points out, the basis of power that forms outside the classroom in informal cliques cannot be completely ignored in the classroom by the teacher.

Thirdly, the teacher is under constant surveillance by the local school administrator and must appear to be running an orderly classroom. If the teacher makes too many demands, the class may rebel, indicating to the administrator that the teacher cannot control students in the classroom—a sign of a "bad" teacher from the administrator's point of view. Many teachers, therefore, do not push students too hard because they might become hostile. Gordon found that sending students to the principal's office for misconduct came to be viewed by administrators as the sign of a bad teacher. After this, the number of students sent to the principal's office declined sharply.

Finally, the behavior of teachers in middle-and upper-class schools tends to be controlled by the pressure in the classroom of the sons and daughters of influential citizens. Teachers know that the parents of these students have power in the community. The behavior of teachers in predominantly lower-class schools tends to be controlled by the highly aggressive behavior of students in the classroom. Much of the class time is taken by control strategies used by the students and countercontrol strategies used by the teacher. Miriam Wagenschein reports some experiences of beginning teachers in lower-class schools:

> The reports which these teachers give of what *can* be done by a group of children are nothing short of amazing. A young white teacher walked into her new classroom and was greeted with the comment, "Another damn white one." Another was "rushed" at her desk by the entire class when she tried to be extremely strict with them. Teachers report having been bitten, tripped, and pushed on the stairs. Another gave an account of a second grader throwing a milk bottle at the teacher and of a first grader having such a temper tantrum that it took the principal and two policemen to get him out of the room. In another school following a fight on the playground, the principal took thirty-two razor blades from children in the first grade room. Some teachers indicated fear that they might be attacked by irate persons in the neighborhoods in which they teach. Other teachers report that their pupils carry long pieces of glass and have been known to threaten other pupils with them, while others jab each other with hypodermic needles. One boy got irate with his teacher and knocked in the fender of her car.[22]

Howard Becker points out that "In these schools a major part of the teacher's time must be devoted to discipline; as one teacher said: 'It's just a question of keeping them in line.' This emphasis on discipline detracts from the school's primary function, discriminating, in terms of available educational opportunity, against the children in these schools."[23]

Joan Roberts' study, aptly titled, *Scene of the Battle*, reports the following control strategies used by students:

> One boy lays his head on the desk while others begin the assigned work.
>   There is another student who is not paying attention or participating and he has placed his head on the desk as though he is sleeping.
>   One girl is sitting and looking out the window. There is construction going on across the street from the school and she seems to be observing it.
>   Two boys are out of it. One is gazing out the window. Another is reading comic books.
>   One boy and a girl are reading the newspaper.
>   One student begins marking something on the wall.
>   During this time, one girl is writing on the back of her neighbor's seat.
>   One student is tearing paper, another is doing homework, and still another is just looking out the window.
>   Two or three are chewing gum. Three others are engaged in making rather complicated necklaces out of chewing gum wrappers.
>   The general attitude of the class is such as to indicate an almost complete lack of interest in the information being given them. They go through the official motions of answering the teacher's questions but with remarks to each other or to the teacher.
>   The class is unresponsive and silent. The teacher provides his own answers to his questions.[24]

Apathy, passivity, and occasional anger are among the control strategies used by students, as they are by other relatively oppressed and powerless groups. The structure of the classroom is based on reciprocal control. Even though the bureaucratic system of the school gives the teacher considerable formal power, this is subverted by students with the use of a variety of control strategies that the teacher finds difficult to overcome.

Like many institutions that have become formalized, the educational institution tends to substitute means for ends. The intended purpose of the institution falls far short of realization. Schools do seem to fit within the over-all institutional framework of the society. Given the differential distribution of power and the control of decision-making process in local communities by those with more power the schools operate to maintain the status quo. If students were taught to question and to criticize this status quo the social order might change more rapidly.

Even though students do have some control over their teachers in the classroom situation and find some gratification in peer-group activities, they are relatively powerless to change the over-all formal structure of the school and the educational system.

Among the characteristics of the American educational institution are the extent to which it reflects the American class system and the system of dominant-minority relations and by so doing helps to perpetuate these systems of stratification. We now turn our attention to these problems.

The Educational Institution, the Social Class System, and Equal Opportunity

When discussing social stratification we found that formal education was the most important avenue of upward social mobility in our society. In discussing the political economy, we pointed out that the ideal of equality of opportunity is heavily stressed as one of our national ideals. The question becomes: Does the educational institution, as presently structured, provide the possibility of equal opportunities for all students in our democratic society?

Segregation by Class and Race

Persons in various social classes tend to be physically isolated from each other. They live in different neighborhoods and thus their children tend to attend different schools because most American elementary and secondary schools are located within neighborhoods. Because of this, there is a *tendency* for social class segregation to be present in many public schools. Children from different social classes attend different schools. (There are exceptions, as we will see later.)

Segregation also exists by race. Many black people are forced to live in the central city (whites move out) and thus the two groups attend separate schools. This *de facto* segregation separates blacks from white students in many school districts. This, along with the historical pattern of segregation in the South, has given rise to the issue of bussing, which has as its purpose the integration of public schools.

This segregation by class and race profoundly affects the school system at all levels. The school Socio-Economic Status Study (SES) collected data from 501 principals and 3,367 teachers in forty-one cities across the nation with populations of fifty thousand or more.*[25] The results show some of the consequences of segregation. For example, the lower the SES of the school, the greater the proportion of pupils with social and emotional problems, as shown in Figure 11-3. Only 9 per cent of the students in the highest SES schools suffer from social and emotional problems, whereas 27 per cent of the students in the lowest SES schools are defined as suffering from these problems.†

Furthermore the parents of children in the lowest SES schools were less interested in their children's schoolwork than the parents of children in higher SES schools: 86 per cent of the parents with children attending the highest SES schools reported an interest in their children's academic achievement, compared with 61 per cent of parents with children attending the lowest SES schools. Fifty-nine per cent of the parents of children in the highest SES schools compared with only 26 per cent of parents with children in the lowest SES schools showed an interest in their children's extracurricular activities. Only 15 per cent of the parents of children in the lowest SES schools, compared with 44 per cent of parents with children in the highest SES schools, reported having an interest in knowledge without practical value. These findings are consistent with the pessimism and apathy produced by living in the lowest class of our society, as we noted in analyzing social stratification.

The Public School As Gatekeeper

The schools serve a gatekeeper function by restricting entrance into jobs that require a high school degree and admission to college. Figure 11-4 shows that the lower the school SES, the smaller the propor-

---

*SES was a composite measure representing the income, occupation, and education of parents of students. As we saw in Chapter 7, in the American class system of stratification these characteristics correlate highly with each other.

†The definitions of social and emotional problems were made by middle-class researchers and their informants. This procedure exists for most research in the social sciences.

FIGURE 11-3

The Lower the School SES, the Greater the Proportion of Pupils with Social or Emotional Problems.

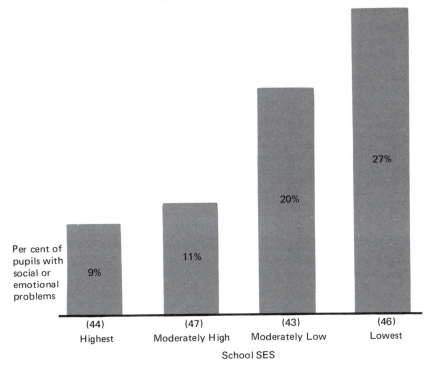

Per cent of pupils with social or emotional problems

| (44) | (47) | (43) | (46) |
| Highest | Moderately High | Moderately Low | Lowest |

School SES

SOURCE: Robert E. Herriott and Nancy Hoyt St. John, *Social Class and the Urban School* (New York: Wiley, 1966), p. 37. Reprinted with permission.

tion of pupils who will go to college and the greater the proportion who will drop out before finishing high school. Forty-four per cent of the students attending the lowest SES schools drop out before finishing high school and only 7 per cent go on to college, compared with only 7 per cent who drop out before finishing high school and 64 per cent who go to college in the highest SES schools.

That this is a result of the social class *composition* of the school and not just the social class background of the student was demonstrated in a study by A. B. Wilson that showed

not only, as we might expect, that the level of educational and occupational aspirations varied with the class composition of the school but that, within each social class, educational and occupational aspirations varied according to the social composition or social-class milieu of the school. For example, in the predominantly working-class schools, only a third of the sons of working-class parents wished to go to college, whereas in predominately middle-class schools half of the working-class boys had college aspirations. Moreover, the social-class milieu of the school also affected middle-class

FIGURE 11-4

The Lower the School SES, the Smaller the Proportion of Pupils Who "Will Go To College," and the Greater the Proportion Who "Will Drop Out."

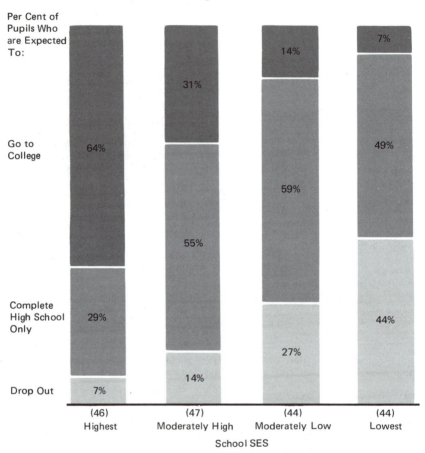

SOURCE: Robert E. Herriott and Nancy St. John, *Social Class and the Urban School* (New York: Wiley, 1966), p. 53. Reprinted with permission. Copyright 1966 by John Wily and Sons, Inc.

children. In predominately middle-class schools as many as 93 per cent of the sons of professional workers aspired to college, but this proportion dropped to below two thirds in predominately working-class schools.[26]

J. Michael, using a national sample of schools, found the same results.[27] The achievement scores of students from a high social class background attending a predominantly working-class school were actually lower than the achievement scores of students with a lower-class background attending predominantly middle-class schools. School milieu, then, appears to have some affect on achievement as well as aspirations.

FIGURE 11-5

Proportion of Pupils and of Teachers Who Are White or Nonwhite, by School SES.

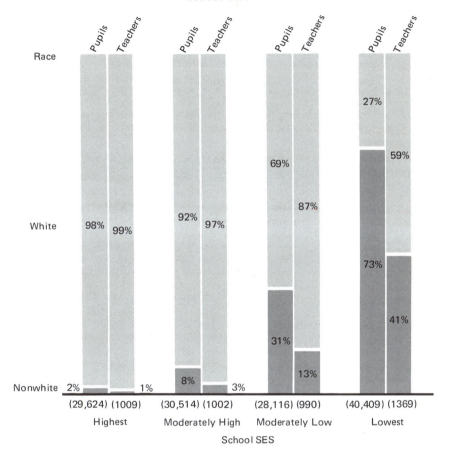

SOURCE: Robert E. Herriott and Nancy Hoyt St. John, *Social Class and the Urban School* (New York: Wiley, 1966), p. 78. Reprinted with permission. Copyright 1966 by John Wiley and Sons, Inc.

This may have implications for segregation by race, because the proportion of nonwhite students is much greater in the lower-class schools than in upper-class schools. Figure 11-5 shows the comparison. In the lowest-class schools 73 per cent of the pupils are nonwhite, whereas in the highest-class schools 98 per cent of the pupils are white. Segregation by social class, then, in cities of more than fifty thousand tends to mean segregation by race as well, so that the class influence in these cities is compounded by the race influence. Segregation by race can also be expected to affect aspiration as well as achievement, just as does social class.

THE COLEMAN STUDY

James Coleman and his associates have demonstrated in a massive study that segregation by race and class affects student achievement.[28] The study, sponsored by the U.S. Office of Education and commonly referred to as the Equal Educational Opportunity Study (EEOS) surveyed 570,000 students, 60,000 teachers, and nearly 4,000 schools across the nation. The researchers found that as the proportion of white students in schools increased, the scores on achievement tests of black students tended to be higher. Thus, there is some evidence that segregation of schools by both race and social class perpetuates unequal opportunity based on students' aspirations and affects their achievement.

Even though the mixing of individuals from different races does have some affect on achievement, the EEOS shows that achievement in all schools is closely related to social class backgrounds in the first grade and remains relatively unchanged as the child proceeds through school. This study concludes that:

> schools bring little influence to bear on a child's achievement that is independent of his background and general social context; and that this very lack of independent effect means that the inequalities imposed on children by their home, neighborhood, and peer evaluation are carried along to become the inequalities with which they confront adult life at the end of school. For equality of educational opportunity through the schools must imply a strong effect of schools that is independent of the child's immediate social environment, and that strong independent effect is not present in American schools.[29]

The EEOS also found that variations in school facilities, staff, or curriculum did not produce important differences in achievement.

THE JENCKS STUDY

A controversial study by Christopher Jencks and his associates, published in a book titled, *Inequality,* has received widespread attention. Jencks first considers cognitive skills (ability), by which he means "the ability to manipulate words and numbers, assimilate information, make logical inferences, and so forth"[30] as measured by IQ tests and shows that these correlate highly with achievement in school. He then shows that cognitive ability does not change dramatically once a child has entered school. He comes to the following conclusions:

1. If we could equalize everyone's genes, inequality in test scores would probably fall by 33 to 50 per cent.
2. If we could equalize everyone's total environment, test score inequality would fall between 25 to 40 per cent.
3. If we merely equalize everyone's economic status, test score inequality would fall by 6 per cent or less.
4. Equalizing the amount of schooling people get might reduce cognitive inequality among adults by 5 to 15 per cent, although this estimate is very rough.

5. Equalizing the quality of elementary schools would reduce cognitive inequality by 3 per cent or less.
6. Equalizing the quality of high schools would reduce cognitive inequality by 1 per cent or less.
7. Eliminating racial and socioeconomic segregation in schools might reduce the test score gap between black and white children and between rich and poor children by 10 to 20 per cent.
8. Additional school expenditures are unlikely to increase achievement, and redistributing resources will not reduce test score inequality.[31]

In essence, Jencks says that the major blame for inequality cannot, for the most part, be laid at the schoolroom door, but rather must be largely attributed to inheritance and the total environment of the child. Amount of schooling accounts for from 5 to 15 per cent and segregation by race and social classes within schools for 10 to 20 per cent of subsequent inequality. But these are small percentages compared with the 33 to 50 per cent attributed to genetic inheritance and the 25 to 40 per cent attributed to the total social environment of the child. For Jencks, then, little can be done *within* the school to improve the cognitive level of the students and, therefore, their achievement level. The only minor exception is to eliminate segregation by race and class, which would reduce the level of inequality somewhat.

Jencks's treatment has produced considerable controversy. First, his use of IQ test scores as a measure of ability and, therefore, of potential achievement has been questioned, especially when comparisons are made across social classes and races using the same test of intelligence. IQ tests, like most other tests, have a white middle-class bias. The tests are typically constructed by white middle-class scholars. The language patterns of white and of middle-class people tend to be different from the language patterns of lower-class and black people both in content and usage. Because language is used in the cognitive process, results may be biased. In addition, tests are typically administered by middle-class school personnel in a middle-class environment and may be intimidating or at least strange for the lower-class or black student. Middle-class children, because of their social backgrounds are more likely to be "test-ready" at any given age than are lower-class children. Motivation levels on an IQ test vary across race and class. The general apathy in the lowest class of the society suggests that children from this class would not care about doing well on a test even if they understood the language or other testing materials and were in a familiar situation.

Until recently middle- and upper-class children were much more likely to attend kindergarten and nursery schools than lower-class children. In the past few years government sponsored programs for lower-class children such as the Headstart Program have modified this situation. But the social background of these children still plays a large part in how they define themselves and how they are defined and treated by middle-class teachers.

Attempts to develop so-called culture-free measures of intelligence have been largely unsuccessful.[32] Given what we know about the differences in early childhood experiences across both class and race, a culture-free test can probably not be developed that could be validly used on a large scale. The fact that IQ test scores correlate highly with achievement as measured by school examinations may be partly because the same white middle-class bias is present in both, so the same social class and racial backgrounds influence performance on both.

The second major controversy arises because Jencks attributes 33 to 50 per cent of the cause of inequality to hereditary factors. There is literally no way at present to separate heredity from environmental influences. There is little doubt that genetic structure causes differences among people, but as even Jencks admits, the continuous interaction with social environment permeates and shapes what can be attributed to heredity. Red hair is inherited, and certain social definitions may be made of people with red hair that affect certain personal-

Policy Implications of Jencks's Study: Schools and Equal Opportunity

In an article summarizing their principal findings and clearly drawing what they believe to be the implications of their research for social policy, Jencks and one of his principal associates call the widespread American belief that schools can solve social problems (including the problem of inequality) a "recurrent fantasy," and go on to say the following:

Our research has led us to three general conclusions.

First, poverty is a condition of relative rather than absolute deprivation. People feel poor and are poor if they have a lot less money than their neighbors. This is true regardless of their absolute income. It follows that we cannot eliminate poverty unless we prevent people from falling too far below the national average. The problem is economic inequality rather than low incomes.

Second, the reforms of the 1960s were misdirected because they focused only on equalizing opportunity to "succeed" (or "fail") rather than on reducing the economic and social distance between those who succeeded and those who failed. The evidence we have reviewed suggests that equalizing opportunity will not do very much to equalize results, and hence that it will not do much to reduce poverty.

Third, even if we are interested solely in equalizing opportunities for economic success, making schools more equal will not help very much. Differences between schools have very little effect on what happens to students after they graduate. . . .

These findings imply that school reform is never likely to have any significant effect on the degree of inequality among adults. . . .

ity traits and perhaps even ability as measured by IQ tests and achievement. But, there is *no way* at present to isolate the effects of inheritance on ability for large numbers of people. There are too many contaminating factors that cannot be adequately controlled.

Because we cannot adequately test the effects of inheritance it is perhaps best in practice to act, in general, as though "all people are created equal" so far as intelligence is concerned. The educational as well as the political implications of designating certain individuals or groups as genetically inferior contradict our fundamental value that all people are created equal. Hitler's attempt to operate on the assumption that the Aryan race was genetically superior produced results of which we are all aware.

Effects of the Total Social Environment

Coleman, Jencks, and others agree that the total social environment has a considerable effect on the achievement of the child in school, whereas the school has relatively little ability to alter the results of a

---

Our research suggests ... that the character of a school's output depends largely on a single input, the characteristics of the entering children. Everything else—the school budget, its policies, the characteristics of the teachers—is either secondary or completely irrelevant, at least so long as the range of variation among schools is as narrow as it seems to be in America.

These findings have convinced us that the long-term effects of schooling are relatively uniform. The day-to-day internal life of the schools, in contrast, is highly variable. It follows that *the primary basis for evaluating a school should be whether the students and teachers find it a satisfying place to be.*

The main policy implication of these findings is that although school reform is important for improving the lives of children, schools cannot contribute significantly to adult equality. If we want economic equality in our society, we will have to get it by changing our economic institutions, not by changing the schools.

As is indicated in the text discussion, Jencks's methods, findings, and conclusions are controversial and hotly debated. Nonetheless, by drawing the issues and stating the problems in the starkest possible terms, he has forced us to come to grips with the relationship between such basic social institutions as education and the economic institution and to focus on critical social problems of equality and opportunity. Jencks's conclusion that the American educational intitutions may be a more important source of individual meaning than of upward social mobility throws an entirely new light on the significance of education.

[a]Mary Jo Bane and Christopher Jencks, "The Schools and Equal Opportunity," *The Saturday Review of Education* (Sept. 6, 1972), pp. 37–42.

deprived social background. From a sociological point of view, this is the major consideration and the most difficult to solve. Jencks says little can be done in schools to alter this. Coleman implies that something might be done, but not much. Other studies indicate that schools might make a difference if their basic structure were changed, but as Katz has pointed out, the basic structure of public schools has not changed since 1880. It is difficult to say what would result from basic structural changes. Most experiments with open classrooms, multimedia instruction, and programmed learning have had varying degrees of success within the existing over-all structure. Unless the basic structure and purpose of public education change radically, we can probably not expect schools to appreciably reduce inequality. They will continue to be the gatekeepers of the society as it is presently ordered.

Ability Grouping and Inequality in Schools

An additional factor that adds to the social class and racial bias of the public schools is ability grouping within school classes or among school classes. The National Education Association (NEA) found that in 1958–1959, 77.6 per cent of urban school districts practiced some form of between-class ability grouping in elementary schools. Mary Austin and Coleman Morrison found that more than 80 per cent of the schools across the nation either often or always use readiness tests for prereading evaluation in the first grade.[33] These tests are often used to place children in different ability groups. The practice of grouping by ability is widely practiced in American public schools.[34]

Standarized tests, with all their class and race biases, are used to place children into these ability groups. As H. R. White points out:

> The result is to sort children according to social class. The group with the "most" academic "ability"—the "gifted" group—will consist predominantely of upper- and middle-class children. The group with the least such ability—the "slow" group—will consist mostly of lower-class children. Perhaps a few from "the other side of the tracks" will wind up in the gifted group—and a few upper-class children in the slow group. In such cases, the lower-class child may feel "out of place"—and even be ridiculed by his lower-class peers. On the other hand, parents of the upper-class child may bring pressure on school authorities—pressure to disregard the child's low test score and put him in a group "with his friends."[35]

Figure 11-6 shows the IQ distribution of students attending schools at various class levels. Students attending the lowest SES schools have the lowest IQs and students attending the highest SES schools have the highest. Forty percent of those attending the lowest SES schools have IQs less than 90, as compared with only 7 per cent attending the highest SES schools. If these students from lower SES

FIGURE 11-6
The Lower the School SES, the Smaller the Proportion of Pupils with
IQs Greater than 100, and the Larger the Proportion of Pupils with
IQs Less Than 90.

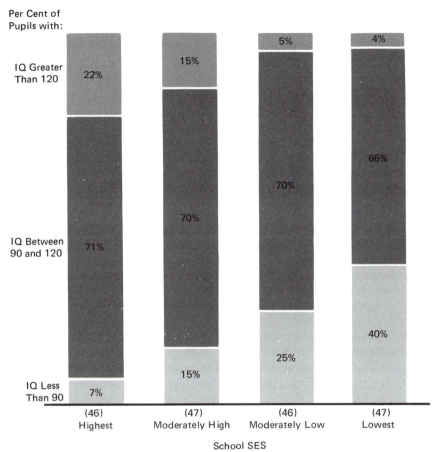

SOURCE: Robert E. Herriott and Nancy Hoyt St. John, *Social Class and the Urban School* (New York: Wiley, 1966), p. 43, reprinted with permission. Copyright 1966 by John Wiley and Sons, Inc.

schools were placed in schools where ability grouping is practiced, they would tend to end up in the lowest grouping. This would not be because they are necessarily less intelligent, but because the test used to measure IQ is biased against them.

Ability grouping defines a student as either "smart" or "dumb." Students in the bright sections are seen as smart and those in "slow" sections are seen as dumb. Students at all grade levels are very perceptive and soon identify the smart and the dumb students and treat them as such. Students in these groups, then, come to see themselves as smart or dumb, as do their teachers, and learning takes place or does not take place accordingly. "To define a situation as real makes it real in its consequences." W. B. Brookover and his associates have found that a student's self-concept is of critical importance in terms of achievement. If students are defined as dumb by significant others——parents, friends, teachers—there is a tendency for them not to achieve.[36] Placing students in a slow section causes their significant others to see them as dumb, and their achievement reflects this evaluation.

Jerome Kagan, reporting a three-year comparative project in other societies, comes to the same conclusions.[37] In Guatemala young children are much more deprived of intellectual stimulation than children in any of our slums. Until after they are one year old they do not leave their windowless huts, seldom talk with or play with parents, and have no toys. By the ages of four, five, and six these children are severely retarded by our criteria. But contrary to our experience and expectation, this early retardation makes no difference in later life. By the age of eleven, the Guatemalan children are bright, active, and alert. Kagan concludes that it is not early deprivation but *expectation* that is critical. If adults expect older children to be "normal," they turn out to be "normal."

He reasons from this that our "disadvantaged" children are different only by social definition. They are expected by significant others—parents, teachers and themselves—to fail and therefore they do fail. The definitions that are made of various students tend to put them not in their potential achievement place but to keep them in their socially defined place.

Table 11-6 shows the number of research studies reporting favorable, mixed, and unfavorable, or insignificant effects produced by ability grouping. This shows that over-all ability grouping favors the talented groups more than it does the slow groups. Eighteen studies found favorable effects for talented groups, whereas only twelve showed favorable effects for slow groups. Unfavorable or insignificant effects were equal for the talented and the slow groups. The number of studies showing mixed effects for the talented and slow are also about the same. On balance, the evidence is against ability grouping. That is, seventy-seven studies showed either mixed or unfavorable effects and only forty-one showed favorable effects, with the talented receiving more favorable affects than the slow. From this evidence, it would appear that ability grouping should be stopped.

Other Classroom Inequalities

To add to this already dismal picture, Herriott and St. John report that teachers in the lower SES schools are more inexperienced, stay in the school a briefer period of time, and are younger than teachers in

TABLE 11-6

Number of Studies Showing Various Effects of Ability Grouping on Achievement

Ability Level of Students	Favorable Effects	Mixed Effects	Unfavorable or Insignificant Effects
Talented	18	11	17
Average	11	12	10
Slow	12	10	17

SOURCE: *Ability Grouping*, Research Summary 1968-Se (Washington, D.C.: Natl. Education Assn., Research Division, 1968).

the higher SES schools.[38] In addition, in metropolitan schools (cities with populations of more than one million) teachers are paid less for teaching in the lower-class schools than they are for teaching in the higher-class schools. Furthermore, fewer teachers want to remain and more want to leave the lower-class schools than the upper-class schools. Teachers in lower-class schools are much less satisfied with student performance than are teachers in upper-class schools. In short, the morale of teachers in lower-class schools is poorer than that of teachers in upper-class schools.

Albert Yee, in a study of more than two hundred teachers in middle- and lower-class schools, found that "The factor of pupils' social class determines great and consistant differences in teachers' attitudes —warm, trustful, and sympathetic teachers instruct middle-class pupils and cold, blaming, and punitive teachers instruct lower-class pupils."[39] Because of these exclusionary practices and unequal treatment patterns, the lower-class student is more likely to become a "displinary case," eventually dropping out of school and perhaps joining a delinquent gang.[40] If lower-class students' needs are not gratified within the framework of a "middle-class" school, they may be gratified in delinquent gangs.

Brookover and Gottlieb sums up the work of Warner, Havighurst, and Loeb as follows:

1. Upper-class people ordinarily send their children to private schools, especially at the high school level.
2. For others in the community, the school may act as a means of social mobility by teaching skills essential for occupational advancement and the middle-class values and attitudes.
3. In high schools there is a relationship between the students socioeconomic status and the curriculum in which he is enrolled and, when intelligence is held constant, the proportion of high school graduates that go on to college decreases with socioeconomic status.
4. The type of school curriculum determines, in part, the quality of educa-

tion, for teachers and administrators give less prestige to vocational programs than they do to the college-oriented programs.

5. Children from the lower socioeconomic groups are penalized in the social life of the school because they do not conform to the school's middle-class standards.[41]

The American Educational System and Equal Opportunity

Our discussion of social stratification and political economy indicated that people with power create and maintain a system that is to their advantage. Teachers and school administrators usually compete for favored positions and salaries. As a result of such arrangements students are labeled on the basis of race and class and teachers act on these labels. The labeling in turn affects achievement.[42]

From all this, then, it appears that the structure of public schools in America is as Katz described it: bureaucratic, class-biased, and racist. Schools reflect rather than compensate for the inequalities that exist in the larger society.

Educational institutions in modern societies are at the periphery rather than the center of the society, which is dominated by the political economy. Secondary socialization, political socialization, and gate keeping, as performed within them, serve to perpetuate the status quo. It appears that the total social environment of the child determines his life-chances far more than the educational institution and that maximizing equal opportunity by tinkering with the school system is unlikely to produce substantial results.

This does *not* mean that humanizing the classroom environment, training for democratic values and participation, and helping students to find individual meaning and to satisfy their needs through their experiences in the educational institution are unimportant or unworthy of attention and effort. Nor does it imply that the present patterns of segregation by race and class are desirable or that they should be preserved.

REFERENCES

1. Katz, Michael B. *Class, Bureaucracy, and Schools: The Illusion of Educational Change in America.* New York: Praeger, 1971, p. 105.
2. Ibid.
3. Ibid., p. 106.
4. Turner, Jonathan H. *Patterns of Social Organization.* New York: McGraw-Hill, 1972, p. 166.
5. Katz, op. cit., p. 131.
6. Williams, Jr., Robin M. *American Society.* New York: Knopf, 1970, p. 319.
7. Green, Thomas F. "Schools and Communities: A Look Forward." *Harvard Educational Review,* Vol. 39 (Spring 1969).
8. Gracey, Harry L. "Learning the Student Role: Kindergarten As Academic

Boot Camp." in *Readings in Introductory Sociology*. Ed. by Dennis H. Wrong and Harry L. Gracey. New York: Macmillan 1967, pp. 288–289.

9. Williams, loc. cit.
10. See Langton, Kenneth P., and M. Kent Jennings. "Political Socialization and the High School Curriculum in the United States." *American Political Science Review,*Vol. 62 (Sept. 1968), 852–867; Ehman, Lee H. "An Analysis of the Relationships of Selected Educational Variables with the Political Socialization of High School Students." *American Educational Research Journal,* Vol. 6 (Nov. 1969), 559–589; Massialas, Byron G. *Political Youth, Traditional Schools*. Englewood Cliffs, N.J.: Prentice-Hall, 1972.
11. Wachtel, Howard M. "Capitalism and Poverty in America: Paradox or Contradiction?" *Monthly Review* (June 1972), p. 56.
12. Massialas, op. cit., p. 7.
13. Ibid., p. 8.
14. *Social Studies in the United States: A Critical Appraisal*. Ed. by C. Benjamin Cox and Byron G. Massialas. New York: Harcourt, 1967.
15. Schlesinger, Ina, and Michael D'Amore. *Children in the Balance*. New York: Citation, 1971, p. 60.
16. Havighurst, Robert J., and Bernice L. Neugarten. *Society and Education*. Boston: Allyn and Bacon, 1967, p. 169.
17. Waller, Willard. *The Sociology of Teaching*. New York: Wiley, 1967, p. 10.
18. Coleman, James S. *The Adolescent Society*. New York: Free Press, 1961.
19. Ibid., p. 338.
20. Gordon, C. Wayne. "The Role of the Teacher in the Social Structure of the High School." *The Journal of Educational Sociology*, Vol. 29, No. 1. (Sept. 1955), p. 22.
21. Ibid., p. 27.
22. Wagenschein, Miriam. "Reality Shock" (M.A. Thesis, University of Chicago, 1950), pp. 58–59. Reported in Becker, Howard S. "Social Class Variation in The Teacher-Pupil Relationship." *The Journal of Educational Sociology*, Vol. 25, No. 8, (April 1952), p. 458.
23. Ibid.
24. Roberts, Joan I. *Scene of the Battle*. Garden City, N.Y.: Doubleday, 1970 pp. 84–85.
25. Herriott, Robert E., and Nancy Hoyt St. John. *Social Class and the Urban School*. New York: Wiley, 1966. See also Gross, Neal, and Robert E. Herriott. *Staff Leadership in Public Schools*. New York: Wiley, 1965.
26. Wilson, A. B. "Residential Segregation of Social Classes and Aspirations of High School Boys." *American Sociological Review*, Vol. XXIV (1959).
27. Michael, J. "High School Climate and Plans for Entering College." *Public Opinion Quarterly (1961)*.
28. Coleman, James S. *Equality of Educational Opportunity. Washington, D.C.: U. S. Office of Education, 1966.*
29. Ibid., p. 325.
30. Jencks, Christopher *et al. Inequality*. New York: Basic Books, 1972, p. 53.
31. Ibid., p. 109.
32. See Charters, Jr., W. W. "Social Class and Intelligence Tests." In *Readings in the Social Psychology of Education*. Ed. by W. W. Charters, Jr. and N. L. Gage. New York: Allyn and Bacon, 1963.
33. Austin, Mary C. and Coleman Morrison. *The First R: The Harvard Report on Reading in Elementary Schools*. New York: Macmillan, 1963.
34. See Smith, M. "Equality of Educational Opportunity: The Basic Findings Reconsidered." In *On Equality of Educational Opportunity*. Ed. by Frederick Mosteller and Daniel P. Moynihan. New York: Random, 1972.

35. White, H. R. *Foundations of Education.* New York: McKay, 1968, p. 43.
36. See Brookover, Wilbur B. *et al. Second Report on the Continuing Study of the Relationship of Self-Concept and Achievement.* Michigan State Bureau of Educational Research Services, 1965.
37. From a paper presented at the annual meeting of the American Association for the Advancement of Science, 1972.
38. Harriott and St. John, loc. cit.
39. Yee, Albert H. "Social Interaction in Classrooms." *Urban Education,* Vol. IV (1969), p. 208.
40. See Cohen, Albert K. *Delinquent Boys: the Culture of the Gang.* New York: Free Press, 1955.
41. Warner, W. L., R. J. Havighurst, and M. B. Loeb. *Who Shall be Educated?* New York: Harper, 1944. See Brookover, E. W. B., and David Gottlieb. "Social Class and Education." In *Readings in the Social Psychology of Education.* Ed. by W. W. Charters, Jr., and N. L. Gage. Boston: Allyn and Bacon, 1963, p. 5.
42. Rist, Ray C. "Student Social Class and Teacher Expectations: The Self-Fulfilling Prophecy in Ghetto Education." *Harvard Educational Review,* Vol. 40 No. 3 (Aug. 1970).

C H A P T E R   1 2

The Family

INTRODUCTION

Even though the family is the oldest and most ubiquitous of social institutions, it is today perhaps the most powerless in the *direct* effects it has as a *unit* on the larger society. However, what happens in the family still affects what happens outside the family. Despite the vast changes that have occurred in the family (described in Chapter 9), there is still truth in the old saying that "The hand that rocks the cradle rules the world." Personalities and values are partly molded within the family. The family continues to influence some decisions throughout the life of a person. Family interaction patterns influence much that occurs in the larger society. These decisions and interaction patterns may be an extension of or a reaction to what occurs within the context of the family. The family is still an important social entity in modern society even though its power as a *unit* has been reduced.

We will first present and discuss types of family *structure*. Next, we will show the changes in the family institution that have been caused by outside constraints. We will then discuss the contraints and control strategies that structure the social order of families in our society and conclude with some remarks about the possible future of the family.

TYPES OF FAMILY STRUCTURE

Families have taken on many different structural forms throughout history. The structures of families differ from society to society as well as within societies. Family structures vary along five basic dimensisions: (1) marriage form, (2) family form, (3) type of residence pattern,

(4) distribution of power within the family, and (5) descent and inheritance. Table 12-1 shows the major types found under each dimension. The various types in each row of this table do not necessarily go together in structuring the family of a given society. This will become clear as we discuss each.

Marriage Forms

Marriage establishes the *nuclear family*, which consists of the parents and their children. The forms of marriage and the extensions of the nuclear family vary greatly from society to society.

Polygamy refers to marriages including at least two persons of one sex and one of the other. The two principal forms of polygamy are polygyny and polyandry. *Polygyny* is a form of marriage in which one husband has two or more wives. Even though this form of marriage has been *allowed* in many societies, it is not widely *practiced* because in any given society there are not enough women to permit every man to have more than one wife. In societies having this form of marriage, having more than one wife usually enhances the prestige of the male in the community in which he lives.

Under *polyandry*, a wife has two or more husbands; this form of marriage is infrequently practiced or allowed. It has been found only in Tibet and in three other known societies.[1] Female infanticide usually accompanies polyandry, thus ensuring that there will not be an excess number of females who are without males.

Monogamy is by far the most *widely practiced* form of marriage. In monogamy, there are only two partners, a husband and a wife. Given the relatively equal number of males and females in human societies, monogamy permits the *possibility* of each person having a mate. Table 12-2 shows the marriage forms permitted in 554 societies and their geographical distribution.

Family Forms

The family may take many different forms. In an *extended* family, more than two generations of the same kinship lineage live in a common residential setting. This may be the same dwelling or different dwellings closely grouped together. Extended families may be organized using any of the marriage forms discussed and, of course, the offspring of these marriages. Thus, an extended family may be quite large. If the form of marriage is polygynous and there are four living generations, the residential complex may be large. Polygamous families (polyandry or polygyny) or monogamous families may, of course, live in separate households, in which case the family unit is

TABLE **12-1**
Types of Family Structure°

Marriage Form	Family Form	Residence Pattern	Power	Descent and Inheritance
Polygyny	Extended	Patrilocal	Patriarchal	Patrilineal
Polyandry	(Consanguine)	Matrilocal	Matriarchal	Matrilineal
Monogamy	Conjugal	Neolocal	Democratic (Egalitarian)	Bilateral

*The various types in each row do not necessarily go together to structure a particular family or family system in a society.

equal to the *nuclear* family. These nuclear families are called *conjugal families* and include only two generations—the husband(s), wife (wives) and their unmarried children.

If blood ties are important in the structuring of the family, then the extended family tends to exist. Such family systems are referred to as *consanguine* systems. On the other hand, if marital ties take precedence over kinship ties, then the *conjugal* family is the prevailing type. In rural America, there were formerly some extended monogamous families in which at least one son and his wife and children lived with the son's father and mother to keep the farm going after the parents were too old to do the work alone. In our modern urban society, most families are monogamous and conjugal, living separately from their parents.

Patterns of Residence

Patterns of residence are closely related to consanguine and conjugal family forms. If there is patrilocal or matrilocal residence, the family is, by definition, consanguine. If it is *patrilocal*, the sons bring

TABLE **12-2**
Regional Variations in the Incidence of Plural Marriages

Form of Marriage	Africa	Circum-Mediter-ranean	East Eurasia	Insular Pacific	North America	South America	Total
Monogamy	8	43	34	23	19	12	135
Polyandry	0	0	3	1	0	0	4
Limited polygyny	16	17	36	43	40	32	184
General polygyny	92	17	21	29	50	21	231

SOURCE: George P. Murdock, "World Ethnographic Sample," *American Anthropologist*, Vol. 59 (Aug. 1957), p. 686. Used by permission.

their wives to live at the home of the son's father who, in turn, is living with his father if he is still alive. If it is *matrilocal*, the daughter brings her husband to live in her mother's home and the mother, in turn, is living with her mother. If the residence pattern is *neolocal*, the conjugal family establishes a new home, which is separate from that of the parents of both husband and wife.

Distribution of Power

Discussing who holds the power in the family requires extreme caution because all social relationships are based on reciprocal control. In the family situation either a husband or a wife can be pushed just so far before various control strategies are used to balance the situation. In less complex societies than ours how far a person with the most power can go is spelled out through cultural agreements so that the other mate(s) does not suffer unduly. In some societies the husband is permitted more power than the wife and has the final say in decision making. This is the *patriarchal* family. In other societies, the wife is permitted more power than the husband and has the final say in decision making. This is the *matriarchal* family.

In the third type, which is often said to prevail in American society, husband and wife are supposed to have about equal power. This is referred to as a *democratic* or an equalitarian family. We will examine later the problems the equalitarian family creates in decision making. If two people in a relationship disagree and neither is supposed to have the final say, an impasse is reached. Attempting to resolve this dilemma is often difficult and many control strategies are brought into play in the contemporary American family to maintain a balance of power.

Descent and Inheritance

Under *patrilineal* descent and *inheritance*, descent is traced through the male side of the family and the female side is essentially ignored. All of the *socially* relevant important kinship ties are traced through the male side of the family and males inherit the material goods of the family and have control over it.

If descent and inheritance are *matrilineal*, just the opposite occurs. The relatives on the male side tend to be ignored and the female side is the socially important basis for tracing family lineage. In addition, females inherit the material goods of the family and have control over it.

Under *bilateral* descent and inheritance both male and female sides are important in tracing family relationships. Inheritance and control of property are permitted to both males and females. This pattern prevails in our society. A child is likely to know both his father's relatives and his mother's relatives and to identify with them equally. The only exception is that the female takes the surname of the man upon marriage. This is compensated for in some middle and upper-class marriages by the new wife dropping her old middle name and using instead the surname of her family. Today, some couples use a hyphenated name, combining the surnames of both husband and wife, as in Smith-Jones.

The actual patterns of kinship are much more complex than this discussion indicates. Almost any combination of the major types discussed exists or has existed somewhere in the world. Cultural anthropologists study kinship systems intensively because in many primitive societies kinship structures tend to order the total structure of control relationships. Kinship patterns in such societies are extremely elaborate and important. In our society kinship is not of the utmost importance in how the society is structured. Indeed, many Americans do not know some of their living cousins on either the mother's or the father's side. The relative unimportance of lineage and kinship affects how the family is structured or destructured through divorce in American society.

As an ideal type, the American family is monogamous, conjugal, neolocal, egalitarian, and bilateral. Thus, the last line in Table 12-1 roughly characterizes the American family, although there are *many* important exceptions

THE HISTORICAL CHANGE IN THE AMERICAN FAMILY

The family as an institution was at one time almost totally responsible for all activities necessary for meeting the biological and psychological needs of its members. It took on as well the responsibility for the maintenance of order, the socialization of children, and provided a basis for individual meaning. As we discussed in detail in Chapter 9, primitive fusion no longer exists in urban industrial societies. They are much too complex to be maintained by independent or semi-independent family units. Thus, many of the activities that family members at one time performed *within* the context of the family have been taken over by more formalized institutions.

The Urban Family As a Source of Affection and Companionship

This transition occured gradually. The urban family became far different than the family in rural societies. Ernest W. Burgess and Paul Wallin[2] have developed an ideal typology of marriage and family life

TABLE 12-3
Marriage and Family Under Rural Life and Urban Life Conditions

Rural Life Conditions	Urban Life Conditions
1. Marriage a status of reciprocal rights and duties	Marriage an interpersonal relation of compatibility and of satisfaction of personality needs
2. Marriage arranged by parents (or by young people in accordance with parental standards of mate selection)	Freedom of young people in choosing a mate (ranging from predominance of romantic love to predominance of companionship as motives)
3. Separation of children and youth of the different sexes before marriage or only formal relations under strict chaperonage	Increasing freedom of social relations before marriage with decline of parental supervision and control
4. Love after marriage	Love and companionship before marriage
5. Emphasis upon the economic and legal aspects of marriage	Stress upon the primacy of personal relations
6. Evaluation of children as potential workers and economic assets	Appreciation of children as persons and interest in their personality development
7. Marriage relatively indissoluble	Divorce resorted to if marriage regarded as failure

SOURCE: From *Engagement and Marriage* by Ernest Burgess and Paul Wallin. Reprinted by permission of the publisher, J. B. Lippincott Company. Copyright 1953.

under rural life conditions and urban life conditions that is shown in Table 12-3.

The movement from rural to urban life conditions changed the structure of the family dramatically. In addition to the changes listed, the extended rural family structure gave way to a conjugal urban family structure.

Under the isolated conditions of rural life family members were highly dependent on one another to meet most needs. This high dependency placed family members under a heavy constraint to use cooperation as a means of economic, social, and psychological survival. The family was often the only meaningful reference group. Members of the rural family, bound to the toil of producing a livelihood, were bound to each other out of necessity.

As society became urbanized, individuals increasingly turned to other groups and institutions for the gratification of their needs. Many of the constraints that kept the family together as a natural unit began to disintegrate. If the family were to survive, a new foundation had to be constructed. Burgess sees the new core activities of the urban family as the provision of affection and companionship between husband and wife and between them and their children.[3] There is more individual freedom in choosing a mate because of the decline of parental supervision and control. Marriage can be based on romantic love.

Problems with the "Affection-Companionship" Model of the Urban Family

Most Americans probably would accept Burgess's affection-and-companionship family model as either "the way it is" or, perhaps better, "the way it should be." The problem, however, is that the changes that destroyed the rural family also destroyed the natural basis on which solid companionship might be built. Indeed, it will be argued here that more genuine affection and companionship was possible in the rural family type than in the urban family type under existing conditions.

The sheer dependence of members of the rural family on one another provided not only a basis for companionship but also a vehicle for the demonstration of affection. As the farm mother taught her daughter to cook, sew, and feed the chickens she could show affection. She was *concerned* that her daughter learn the necessary skills. As they did these things together a common bond of affection could possibly develop. The same bond could develop between father and son as the father taught the son the skills of farming and as they engaged in farming activities together.

There is a saying among certain religious groups that, "A family that prays together stays together." This can be generalized to suggest that "A family that does anything together stays together." As family members did things together they had the possibility of experiencing companionship and affection. Love could be *demonstrated* through the learning and sharing of necessary tasks.

In the urban family, even though companionship and affection are supposed to serve as its basis, there is little meaningful activity on which companionship and affection can be built. After breakfast, which may or may not be eaten together, depending on time schedules, family members go in their *separate* directions. The father and increasingly the mother go to work in *separate* places following different occupations that provide no *common* interest. The children go to school or a day care center at increasingly early ages. Under these conditions, there is little common basis for continued companionship and no vehicle through which affection can be demonstrated except in the pursuit of leisure. But even here as children reach adolescence, they tend to go in separate directions from their parents.

Because of this, we find the creation of artificial vehicles for the expression of affection and artificial bases for companionship. These include such activities as the father joining the Indian Guides with his son so that both can play Indian at the local YMCA, a process of reverse socialization. Or the family goes to watch the child play Little League baseball *with* other children, not with members of the immediate family or other relatives. Husbands and wives, especially in the middle classes, give each other and their children expensive gifts (many times bought on credit) to prove that affection is felt.

This should not be interpreted to mean that all farm families were tranquil and happy or that exploitation of children did not take place in some farm families. Furthermore, we are not saying that some urban families do not experience considerable companionship and affection. The point is that from an ideal type perspective the farm family had a higher possibility of *sharing* in mutually beneficial tasks than does the contemporary urban family. The historical farm family lived under a set of constraints that made sharing and doing things together necessary. This is not true of most urban families.

Industrialization and the Family Institution

An abiding interest among sociologists has been the reciprocal influences between industrialization and the family. The transformation from the rural extended family in the United States to the relatively isolated nuclear urban family (the conjugal family) described in the text has been attributed both to urbanization and to industrialization. Many studies of developing societies have traced the impact of these processes on traditional family forms.

William Goode has carefully assessed the evidence about the presumed "fit" between the conjugal family and urbanism-industrialism and has come to the following conclusions about how the process of industrialization influences the family in the direction of the relatively isolated conjugal unit typical of modern industrial societies:

1. Industrialism requires geographic mobility—a requirement that cannot be met if kin obligations involve frequent, intimate, and considerable interdependence among relatives.
2. Industrialism is associated with expansion of economic opportunities and facilitates the upward social mobility of people from lower strata. Here again, the weakening of extraconjugal kin ties is both a cause and effect of differential social mobility among kin.
3. Industrialism substitutes formal, nonkinship agencies and facilities for large kin groups in the handling of common problems of political protection, education, military defense, money leading, etc.
4. Industrialism emphasizes achievement over birth (ascription), reversing the traditional pattern, and thereby lessening the individual's dependence on his family (though by no means totally destroying this dependence).[a]

An Alternative Model of the Modern Urban Family: Permanent Availability As a Mate

Perhaps the chief activity of the urban family as a unit is as a *consumption* unit that buys things that are enjoyed together and that prepares for the "selling" of family members on many different "markets." Bernard Farber theorizes that some families have moved from being based on what he calls "orderly replacement of the family culture" to being based more on what he calls "permanent availability as a mate."[4] We will discuss each of these types of families in turn.

Orderly Replacement of Family Culture

Farber points out that "if orderly replacement of the family culture is to occur, each *family of orientation* (the family into which a person is born) must be organized to produce in its children's *families of*

We have earlier indicated that one of the possible reasons for the rise of industrial capitalism in Western societies (rather than in Asian societies or elsewhere) was the development of the Protestant ethic, which created an ideological basis for the formation of large reserves of capital and provided a motivational force facilitating the Industrial Revolution. An additional reason for the rapid development of industrialism in the West was that the family system was closer to the conjugal type than were the family systems in Asian societies or the other major non-Western societies. There is, thus, the possibility that the conjugal family is not only a consequence of industrialization but also that it was a contributory factor to industrialization's rapid spread in Western societies.[b]

If the historical and casual connections remain unclear, the reciprocal interaction between urban industrial economy on the one hand and the family institution on the other are evident. In modern industrial societies the family is a subordinate institution and the political economy is dominant. Whatever the historical processes were that produced this result, the person who wants to understand the over-all structuring of modern societies must recognize that the family institution is more determined than determining. The specific developments that constrain the modern family from without and the control strategies that order it from within are products of urban industrial society.

[a]William J. Goode, *World Revolution and Family Pattern* (New York: Free Press, 1963), pp. 369–370.

[b]Ibid., pp. 22–25.

procreation (the families which they begin upon marrying) patterns of norms and values identical to its own."[5] (Italics supplied.) When this is the case:

1. Values and norms relating to patterns of behavior in the family remain constant from one generation to the next.
2. Socialization of children is aimed at making children duplicates of their parents as their children achieve adulthood.
3. Because of this part in duplicating succeeding generations, the family and its auxiliary kinship system do not initiate change in society; the family is a force for conservatism in social arrangements.[6]

This type of family system can prevail only if certain controls are present. Among these are (1) the presence of an individual outside the particular nuclear family (example, a grandfather) who has responsibility and authority to judge and direct replacement in the family; (2) the restriction of marriage to individuals who come from families with identical norms and values and (3) a time-based system of authority—with older generations having authority over younger generations.[7]

If these conditions are present little change in the social ordering of the family is possible from generation to generation. The Amish family is an example of the orderly replacement of culture type still present in our society. However many families in modern societies are moving or have moved to Farber's second type.

Permanent Availability as Mate

In the permanent availability type there is little family control over who a child marries once adulthood has been reached. Indeed, "individuals become available for marriage with anyone and at any time during their adulthood."[8] Farber sees this type of family emerging where there is a bilateral kinship system. Given rapid social change and the social movement of people, it is difficult, if not impossible, to maintain the orderly replacement of family culture type because there is little control over mate selection. Family lineage is not considered important or cannot be maintained. Farber points out:

1. If patterns of intimate behavior are admitted between all persons who are potential mates, there will be a tendency for much intimate interaction to occur in cross-sex relationships in all parts of the society. . . . As a result, homogamy (the marriage of persons who have similar characteristics) with regard to social characteristics declines in importance in mate selection.[9]
2. The maintenance of marriage is personal rather than a kinship problem . . . and a marriage need not last beyond the desires of particular individuals. Thus we expect love marriages rather than arranged marriages. We also expect a high rate of divorce. Since the size of a domestic unit in the bilateral system is small, there is neither an immediate kinship au-

thority to control occurrence of divorce nor extra relatives in the home to be interested parties in the divorce.[10]

3. Since there are neither restrictions on patterns of intimate behavior nor imperative lineage considerations, each individual, at least theoretically, is permanently available as a potential mate to all other cross-sex individuals. An important point here is that being married does not restrict an individual with respect to his future potentiality as a mate in later marriages.[11]

Under this model (1) "The family takes the form of a voluntary association in which a person continues membership as long as his (her) personal commitments to the other family members exceed her (his) commitments elsewhere."[12] (2) Persons are "motivated to develop and maintain certain personal skills and attributes enhancing their ability to perform family activities and appeal to members of the opposite sex. (3) The child is socialized to be a perennially marketable product. Thus "the child is required to develop a pleasing personality, competence in interpersonal relations, a pleasant appearance and occupational career skill regardless of sex (not only to facilitate a good marriage but also to facilitate disengagement from an 'unsatisfactory' marriage."[13] (4) "Having children is a voluntary pledge by the parents to maintain their marital relationship."[14] But this pledge can be broken if it becomes detrimental to family members. (5) "Without temporal (time) or marital-status restrictions on availability, neither premarital chastity nor marital fidelity have bearing on availability as a potential mate."[15] (6) "Since neither time nor prior marriage (including current married status) reduces the availability of the individual as a potential mate, there is no incentive to delay marriage." On the contrary, to fulfill personal needs and maintain intimate relationships, persons are under pressure for both early marriage and remarriage later in life if divorce or death of the mate occurs. Remarriage, moreover, provides the children of an earlier marriage with a full complement of relatives. Both early marriage and a pressure to remarry are expected in society characterized by bilateral kinship.[16]

Farber's model of permanent availability fits well within the framework of a *market society*, even though Farber does not attribute its emergence to the development of the market society. We believe that the bilateral kinship system, to which Farber attributes the permanent-availability type, tended to emerge with or perhaps as a result of the development of a market society. The market society forced the breakdown of the orderly replacement type of family. Orderly replacement is difficult to maintain in such a society.[17]

Marx and Engels, in 1848, suggested that "The bourgeoisie has torn away from the family its sentimental veil, and has reduced it to a mere money relation."[18] There is now considerable agreement about the affect of the creation of a market society on the family.[19]

The market society has implications for family life patterns and what is emphasized within the family. In a market society, the idea of *worth* based on a set of traditional values (Farber's orderly replacement of culture type) changes to worth on a variety of different markets, depending on the assets of an individual. When self-esteem cannot be gained by the use of traditional values, people search in other places for this self-esteem. We find persons attempting to sell themselves on a variety of different markets to validate their worth as people and to find meaning.

The markets include (1) a sex market, based on physical appearance; (2) a personality market, based on an outgoing personality; (3) an occupational market, based on a marketable skill or profession; (4) an acceptability market, based on skill in interpersonal relationships; and (5) an educational market, based on demonstrated intelligence and creativity. Parents are aware of these markets and attempt to socialize their children so they will be saleable in one or more of them—the more the better, especially for parents following the permanent availability model.

THE SEX MARKET

Many people, both females and males, attempt to keep themselves physically attractive so they can sell themselves on the sex market. Billions of dollars are spent annually on cosmetics, cosmetic surgery, hair transplants, silicone treatments to increase the size of female breasts, and clothing that is not needed for protection against the environment but to keep one sexually attractive. *Playboy Magazine,* and others like it, sell by the millions portraying "throwaway" models of women. Many TV commercials cash in on the sex market by displaying current models of "sexy" men and women. Sex sells and people who want to be available on the sex market attempt to be sexy.

THE PERSONALITY MARKET

Many parents attempt to develop in their children an outgoing personality, the saleable model in American society. To be shy is to be left out and to have one's self-esteem shattered. If parents fail, Dale Carnegie courses help. So do the sensitivity groups that have sprung up all over the nation to help people get over their hang-ups so they too can be outgoing and available. Psychiatrists do a thriving business in helping to create saleable personalities for people who can afford the price of this specialized service.

THE ACCEPTABILITY MARKET

This is related to both the personality market and the fad market. A person lacking skill in interpersonal relations can always tag along in one of the movements that periodically sweep the country, be it civil rights, the fight against pollution, the anti-Vietnam War movement, or the Jesus people. Some people are very serious about these issues, but there is a tendency on the part of many to jump from issue to issue. This makes them acceptables as they see it and may help increase their esteem.

THE OCCUPATIONAL MARKET
In a market society the occupational maket is important. The better the job one has, the higher the prestige that may produce self-esteem and even a sense of meaning if the job is creative and enjoyable. This market is highly competitive. Many parents are aware of this and do their best to keep their children in school as an an avenue to a better position in this market.

THE EDUCATIONAL MARKET
Many parents, especially in the middle class, begin preparing their children for the educational market at a very early age. The earlier a child can read, the better. Some parents are anxious about their children's measured IQ and their graded section in school. This also is a highly competitive market and many do not make the grade(s). Middle-class parents love to brag about grades Susie or Johnny earned in school if they are high. If they are not, there is shamed silence.

THE SOCIAL ORDERING OF THE MODERN AMERICAN FAMILY

The popular American myth is that the relationship between husband and wife is based on romantic love and that the process of social ordering in the total family unit is based on the mutual love of all family members. If this were fact, everyone in the family would typically do what pleased others in the family and a generally peaceful atmosphere would persist without feelings of oppression. Many families attempt to control their image in the community by presenting a public front as if the myth were fact.

Even though affection is present in the family, its social ordering is based also on outside constraints and on the use of control strategies by family members in their interaction with each other. We will show how outside constraints and internal control strategies affect the social ordering of the family as a unit in modern society.

Outside Constraints

There are many constraints outside the family that affect its social ordering. Among the most important are (1) the organization of work and how the use of time by husband and/or wife fit into this; (2) laws governing school attendance; (3) the general social value of the economic worth of the family unit, which tends to be the basis for prestige evaluation; and (4) the large number of voluntary associations and activities that exert a variety of constraints on family members.

The Organization of Work Time Outside the Home

How the work force is organized in terms of time and how the husband or wife fits into these time sequences determines when each will be at home if both work, the patterns of sleeping, and other activities within the home. For example, if both husband and wife work the same hours outside the home, they will see each other more often than if both work at different times. But if they work at the same time this requires someone outside the family to take care of any young children present in the home. How this problem is handled depends on the age of the children and, in particular cases, the income of the family and the availability of relatives. If the children are of preschool age, day care centers or nursery schools may be utilized, a baby sitter may be hired to stay home with them, or they may be left with relatives. If the husband and wife work at different times, they see each other less but one parent may be at home with the children.

If one parent works a night shift, the household must be kept quiet so that the person can sleep during the day. The scheduling of working hours affects meal times, who eats together at each meal, and so forth. Thirty per cent of the mothers with children under six and 50 per cent of all mothers with children six to seventeen years of age are now in the labor force.[20] Many families have only one parent, which produces additional problems if that parent works outside the home. How the work force is organized and how one or both parents fit into it places a variety of constraints on the organization of the everyday activities of the family.

School Attendance

Most states require that a child begin school at the age of five or six and remain there until the age of sixteen or eighteen. The school year typically lasts at least nine months. There is also pressure on middle-class families to send their children to nursery school at an even earlier age because attending nursery school presumably gives a child a competitive advantage on the educational market. Lower-class children may attend government sponsored early childhood education programs or be placed in day care centers. In general, children are outside the home at an earlier age and remain outside the home during the day until they are adults or nearly adult. This places constraints on the family to organize itself around school activities.

Family Prestige (Economic Worth)

When discussing the social class system we noted that the family as a unit tends to be judged by the quantity and quality of its visible economic assets as portrayed in a certain style of life. Thorstein Veblen points out in his *The Theory of the Leisure Class* that people below the upper class attempt to emulate (copy) the life-styles of those above, which takes money.[21] Additional evidence from a study by Lenski found people ranking the social position of the families with whom they were not familiar solely by their displayed wealth.[22]

This evaluative process places constraints on both husband and wife to attempt to display wealth in as many ways as possible to "keep up with the Joneses." To display wealth, one must have access to money. Thus, there is pressure for both mates to work outside the home even though they might not need to just to "keep food on the table." Some people work at two jobs, not to survive but to enhance their ability to display wealth in the community. All this places various constraints on how the family is organized.

Being a housewife (the word *homemaker* has come into use in an attempt to enhance the prestige value of the role) is not valued as highly as it once was. Being "only" a housewife in some social circles is devalued and carries a negative value for self-esteem. Being a good housewife used to carry high social esteem in the community. One's abilities as a housewife could be displayed at the County Fair, at church suppers, or by how well a woman "kept house." In the urbanized setting the family has tended to become very private. Few other people see what goes on inside it.[23] Hidden from public view, the family cannot be evaluated. Being a housewife has been made easier, even if less creative, by modern appliances.

If the wife is to have a sense of self-esteem, she must often go outside the family to find it. She may pursue a career or attempt to find self-esteem and meaning by involving herself in a variety of voluntary associations or social service projects. The latter is common among women in the middle and upper classes. Or the mother may *use* her children as a source of self-esteem. Some parents gain a sense of self-esteem and meaning by helping their children "make it" in the market society. Children as commodities are used not for their cash value but for their *use* value in gratifying the esteem needs of parents.

The preceding observations should not be construed to mean that the woman's place is necessarily in the home. The woman's place in modern society depends increasingly on where she wants it to be, keeping in mind that the available alternatives are still heavily restricted by a male-dominated society.

Voluntary Associations and Leisure-Time Activities Outside the Family

A variety of voluntary associations and leisure-time activities place constraints on some parents and children to spend time outside the home. Many of these separate family members from each other. Outside the home, parents and children tend to go in different directions. However, if husband and wife participate *together* in voluntary association and other leisure pursuits, the marital bond is strengthened.[24] The numerous activities available outside tend to shift the basis of primary need gratification from the family to groups of individuals or voluntary associations outside the family. This constrains the family to adjust its social ordering to accommodate all these activities, which are most numerous among the middle class.

Given these constraints on the family, its social ordering as a unit becomes relatively fixed. Some families have more alternatives than others to structure the social order of the family from within, depending on the type and intensity of constraints from without. Yet, it is often difficult to clearly specify the number and types of alternatives. For example, families on welfare with neither the father nor the mother working are relieved of the time constraints placed on families with both parents working. Families on welfare, however, are placed under different constraints by the *absence* of a decent income. The middle-class mother who is not working outside the home might feel constrained to engage in more community services. Few, if any, families are completely free to structure their social order from within.[25] We now turn to a discussion of some of the internal control strategies used to structure the social order of the family, operating within the framework set by the outside constraints.

Control Strategies Used to Structure the Family Unit

Historically, cultural strategies were far more important in structuring the social order of the family than they are in modern family types. Certain roles were ascribed to the wife, husband, and children. Each family member was rewarded by the use of positive sanctions if the ascribed roles were performed as prescribed or punished by the use of negative sanctions if they were not. If the cultural agreement specified that the wife was to care for the children and the home while the husband was to work and furnish the necessities of life and make the ultimate decisions, the division of labor and distribution of power in the family and thus its social order were relatively fixed. Even under these conditions, however, many family members used manipulative, exchange, and coercive strategies that modified the social order of the family. Occasionally, withdrawal strategies such as divorce, desertion, or a child running away were used.

If the mother received esteem, felt secure, had a sense of meaning and so forth by being a "good" wife and mother, as defined by the cultural agreement, there was no reason to use other strategies. On the other hand, if her husband refused to work and provide a living although able to do so, the same woman might be expected to resort to the use of threats. If conditions became bad enough she might leave the husband to his own misery. Cultural strategies are used when they work or if there are no alternatives.

As the society became more urbanized, old cultural strategies lost their usefulness in the social ordering of the family. The family became increasingly based on what some sociologists call a negotiated order. This change is coming to characterize the American family. The historical family, of course, was not devoid of negotiation any more than the modern family is completely devoid of some cultural agreements. Furthermore, a process of negotiation may result in time in cultural agreements. The major difference between the historical family and the modern family is that in the latter agreements are negotiated over a broader range of behaviors and the agreements reached are not as lasting as formerly. There are reasons for this. For example, in many communities in earlier periods, women were frowned on if they engaged in "male" occupations or if they worked outside the home when they still had young children. This being the case, the wife was negotiating from a weak position. Her alternatives were severely limited.

The basis for the social ordering of the family is changing from a heavy reliance on cultural strategies toward a greater use of other control strategies. The basis for the social ordering of the American family is the extensive use of a variety of control strategies; this produces a negotiated order that may change rapidly. Therefore, we must look at the distribution of power in the family, what produces a basis for power for various family members, and the control strategies family members are likely to use.

Forming the Negotiated Family: The Courtship Process

In modern societies negotiation begins during the process of dating and courtship, which, if successful, leads to marriage.[26] William J. Goode, a leading family sociologist, makes the following points.

> All courtship systems are "marriage markets," but the American version differs from others in the extent to which each individual tries to sell his own wares and carry out his or her own negotiations. In many traditional societies, by contrast, elder kinsmen made these arrangements for younger people.[27]

In dating and courtship, the persons in the relationship want to achieve the best for themselves, as each defines best. Each party negotiates using available resources. A person with the most resources is in th most advantageous negotiating position. In our society, important resources, at least initially, in the dating and courtship process are physical beauty, a pleasing personality, skills in interpersonal relations, a variety of talents and interests, career potential, and such other resources as may be seen by members of the opposite sex as valuable. The value of a specific resource may change over time and be different for different persons. The value of a resource may also differ among communities and among social classes. Goode describes one social process in the American "free courtship" system:

> One is the ordinary market process of supply and demand. Some people ask for more than they can get on the market, and others ask less, but in general brides and grooms are likely to be roughly similar in their traits and assets. A girl who is physically attractive can marry a young man who is less handsome but upwardly mobile. A young man in a higher social class is most likely to marry a woman from his own class, but he may go outside his class to choose someone who has money or beauty. An older man is most likely to marry a younger woman than himself (but still in an older age bracket); but if he is rich or influential, he has a good chance of marrying a much younger woman who is very attractive. In general, marital choices are homogamous: like marry like, and discrepancies are likely to be balanced off.[28]

A person "displays" his or her resources on the "dating market" and bids are taken. Bids among males take the form of asking a female for a date. Females for the most part, still bid by flirting. It is still "improper" in many communities for a female to openly ask a male for a date, so she must make her bid for the male's resources by either flirting or asking a friend to let him know she is interested in exploring a relationship with him. There is a tendency for a relationship to begin with the person who, on the surface, is the highest bidder—the person of the opposite sex with the most valued resources.

The typical person plays the dating market for a while by having several or even many casual dates with different people with no intention of becoming serious. How early in life a person becomes serious or even wants to become serious depends on career plans, escape from a bad home life, and a variety of idiosyncratic factors. Casual dating may go on for years or it may not go on at all. A person may marry the first person dated if the valued resources are the best that can be expected given the resources that he or she has to offer.*

*When a person is trying to escape from something, such as insecurity or a bad home life, he or she may take the first person who comes along, although his or her resources are not the most valued. If the person could wait, he might be able to do "better."

DATING AND THE COURTSHIP PROCESS

Casual dates may lead to serious courtship. Casual dating provides the resources of experience in interacting with members of the opposite sex.

As dates are accepted, evaluation occurs between the two parties. If one or the other is serious, they begin to sell themselves to each other. This situation is always delicate because, in the beginning, neither person is sure of the degree of seriousness, or potential seriousness, of the other and neither yet knows the full resources the other possesses. Physical beauty, which may have first attracted two people to each other, may be the only resource that one or the other person possesses.

Sexual Exploitation During the Courtship Process

Exploitation may occur during the casual dating period, especially in the area of sex. The table shows that when the boy has a higher social position than the girl sexual intercourse is much more likely to occur than when the boy and girl are of equal social status or when the social status of the girl is higher than the boy's. The lower-class girl "trades" sex for a chance to be upwardly socially mobile through marriage. However, the boy is not likely to marry the girl because most marriages are among people in the same social class.

Maximum Premarital Intimacy, by Comparative Social Class of Partners

Maximum Premarital Intimacy	Comparative Social Class			Girl/Boy Direction
	Boy Higher	Equal	Girl Higher	
Holding hands	6%	6%	20%	+
Necking, light petting	13	39	47	+
Heavy petting	16	26	16	=
Sexual intercourse	66	30	18	−
Total	101%	101%	101%	
Number of relationships	154	531	107	

Adapted from Winston W. Ehrmann, *Premarital Dating Behavior* (New York: Holt, 1959). Reprinted with permission of Macmillan Publishing Co., Inc. from *The Family* by Robert O. Blood, Jr. Copyright © 1972 by The Free Press, a Division of Macmillan Publishing Co., Inc. Source: 531 male students at the University of Florida (Gainesville) enrolled in a course on preparation for marriage, reporting their experience in dating various partners. Of the 531 men in the study, 338 had dated only at their own class level; 86 dated both equals and lower girls; 39, both equals and superior girls; and 68, at all three levels. Necking and light petting included kissing, hugging, and fondling the girl's clothed breasts. Social class was measured in terms of father's occupation.

Each party in the relationship continues to explore the degree of seriousness and the depth of resources and commitment of the other as the courtship process continues.

As they get to know each other better, each may find that the other is serious and that the resources that the other has are those that each values highly. As this occurs, mutual affection begins to develop. Each is negotiating from his (her) position of strength in an attempt to convince the other that he (she) has what the other values or will come to value.

As affection, built initially on the basis of mutually valued resources, develops, being together comes to be mutually rewarding and superficial fronts[29] start to be dropped. As these fronts are dropped, if each still values the genuine resources of the other, a match has been made and each makes a commitment to the other. They become engaged, thereby announcing to themselves and others that they intend to marry. If during the engagement period mutual affection continues to replace evaluation, a marriage will probably ensue. Each enjoys the company of the other. Being together is intrinsically rewarding, as each gratifies the needs of the other.

MARRIAGE AS AN INTERIM STAGE

Marriage may not be the final stage, however, when permanent availability is the accepted family pattern. Each partner continues to maintain, and, if possible, enhance his (her) resources to be permanently available. If Farber is correct, in our market society it is essential for continuous self-esteem that people be able to convince themselves that they continue to be worth something on the sex market. Furthermore, there is the possibility that one or both mates may not have been completely honest about the resources they actually possess. All fronts may not have been dropped, or expectations that were created during courtship cannot be met in the marriage. Living together may then come to be a disappointment to one or both parties. It is difficult to hide what one really is over a long period of time in intimate company with another. There is still some truth in the old saying, "Love is blind but marriage is an eye-opener."

Among *some* dating couples older conventions have been dropped. Couples take up residence together before a formal marriage occurs and explore each other's depth of commitment and resources *before* the formal marriage vows. Many marriages also occur because of premarital pregnancy. Different people get married for different reasons, depending on the strength of their needs. One person may have a strong need for self-esteem; another for security. The gratification of one may be traded for the gratification of the other and so forth. Courtship is a complicated and involved process involving controls and countercontrols, exchanges and counterexchanges. The net result of the process is to set up a negotiated family. We now turn to the control strategies used *within* the family system.

Control Strategies Used Within the Family

The social ordering of the family is based on a variety of control strategies used by each of the family members. Affection will neither wash the dishes nor provide income for the family. These are tasks that must be done. *The resources that produce a marriage may not be the same resources that sustain a marriage.* This is one of the major problems of the American dating market. For example, a man may be attracted to a woman because she is beautiful and eventually marry her only to find that she has a violent temper. Or, a woman may be attracted to a man because he is a popular football player and finds after marriage that he has no qualities that make for a good companion in marriage. Parsons points out that those qualities that are emphasized as a basis for romantic love may not be the same qualities that make a happy or enduring marriage.[30] To get the necessary jobs done by each mate and achieve a sense of distributive justice, control strategies are used by husband and wife. These control strategies, used over time and operating within the outside constraints, are what structure the social order of the family.

If both husband and wife work outside the home, someone must still cook the meals and clean the home. If the husband expects the wife to do this on the basis of traditional role definitions, she might well declare such definitions inoperative. Exchange strategies, including accommodation, can be used to work out an equitable division of labor within the home so that both partners can feel that distributive justice has been achieved.

Distribution of Power by Education and Employment

As the wife's resources increase, the power of the husband, as measured by who makes the basic decisions, tends to decrease. Table 12-4 shows the husband's power by comparative education of husband and wife in several nations. With two exceptions, the partner with the most education was the dominant decision maker in the family. Those couples with equal education fall in between. The power of the wife also increases if she works outside the home. Table 12-5 shows the husband's power by comparative employment status of husband and wife in various nations.

TABLE 12-4
Husband's Power by Comparative Education of Husband and Wife

Husband's Power by		Comparative Education			Wife/ Husband Direction
Country	Location	Husband More	Equal	Wife More	
France	Paris–Bordeaux	2.07	1.99	1.85	—
Germany	Urban	5.27	4.75	4.81	—
	Farm	6.01	5.42	5.05	—
Greece	Athens	2.67	2.80	2.67	—
Japan	Tokyo, middle-class	5.25	5.07	4.88	—
USA	Detroit	5.45	5.22	4.91	—
Yugoslavia	Kragujevac, auto workers	2.37	2.05	1.90	—

SOURCE: Reprinted with permission of Macmillan Publishing Co., Inc. from *The Family* by Robert O. Blood, Jr. Copyright © 1972 by The Free Press, a Division of Macmillan Publishing Co., Inc.

TABLE 12-5
Husband's Power by Comparative Employment Status of Husband and Wife

Country	Employment Status		
	Husband Only Employed	Both Employed	Wife Only Employed
France	2.03	1.90	
Germany (urban)	5.40	4.52	
Greece	2.78	2.33	
Japan	5.40	4.92	
USA	5.44	4.48	2.67
Yugoslavia	2.79	1.94	

SOURCE: Reprinted with permission of Macmillan Publishing Co., Inc. from *The Family* by Robert O. Blood, Jr. Copyright © 1972 by The Free Press, a Division of Macmillan Publishing Co., Inc.

As the woman's resources increase, by bringing money into the home, her degree of power in the home also increases. This relationship held in all six nations studied.[31]

Furthermore, when the wife works outside the home the husband's task performance in the home increases. However, Robert O. Blood, Jr., points out that

> If marriage were really a 50-50 proposition, we might expect the division of housework to become 50-50 when both partners hold outside jobs. Husbands are not generally that helpful, however. In one American study, the number of hours devoted to household tasks by husbands increased only

from 15 per cent to 25 per cent of the total.[31] Thus, the main burden of responsibility for housework continued to rest on the wives' shoulders even when they had full-time jobs elsewhere. Husbands carried an increased share of that burden but rarely an equal share.[31]

Blood notes, however, that husbands of working wives are more likely to do all the outside work, such as lawn mowing and snow shoveling, so that the total work load does tend to be somewhat equalized within and around the house when the wife is working.

In the early years of marriage we typically find a variety of control strategies being used as both mates attempt to work out a marital arrangement which they can "live with." If things are unsatisfactory to the husband, for example, he may stay out late, spend all his off-work time watching T.V. (a withdrawal strategy) or resort to coercive strategies by using threats or at times even beating his wife. The dissatisfied wife, on the other hand, may refuse to do agreed upon housework, quite her job if she has one, use threats and manipulative strategies or also coercive strategies.

COERCIVE STRATEGIES

It is a myth that coercive strategies are seldom used by husbands and wives in the structuring of their relationships. William Goode goes so far as to suggest that the basic strategy that structures the family is either the use or threatened use of force and violence both by family members or outsiders who want to maintain the structure of the family.[33] In an explanatory study of intrafamily violence, Richard J. Gelles found that about 54 per cent of the couples he studied had used physical force of one kind or another on each other.[34] Raymond I. Parnes estimates the police are called on more often to solve conflict between spouses than any other category of crime.[35] The use of coercive strategies, thus, appears to be quite common between husbands and wives.[36]

DIVORCE AS A TERMINAL WITHDRAWAL STRATEGY

If after a period of time a mutually satisfactory arrangement based on the use of various control strategies fails, a divorce may ensue as one or both mates decide to withdraw from the situation. This is happening at an increasing rate in our society. At the current rate, four out of every ten new marriages will end in divorce.[37] Table 12-6 shows how divorce has increased since 1940.

If divorce occurs, both parties are likely to once again go back on the market in an attempt to find another mate. They are typically successful. Having been married and divorced does not hamper one's chances for remarriage in our society as it did when our family form was more traditional and based primarily on cultural strategies.

TABLE 12-6
Divorces 1940–1971 [Prior to 1960, excludes Alaska and Hawaii]

		1940	1950	1955	1960	1965	1968	1969	1970	1971
Total	1,000	264	385	377	303	479	384	639	713	768
Rate per 1,000										
population		2.0	2.6	2.3	2.2	2.5	2.9	3.2	3.5	3.7
Percent divorced of population 18 years old and over*										
Male		1.4	1.8	1.9	2.0	2.5	2.6	2.6	2.5	2.9
Female		1.8	2.3	2.4	2.9	3.3	3.6	3.7	3.9	4.0

*SOURCE: U.S. Bureau of the Census, *Current Population Reports*, series P-20.
SOURCE: Except as noted, U.S. Public Health Service, *Vital Statistics of the United States*, annual.
Reproduced from U.S. Bureau of the Census, *Statistical Abstracts of the United States*, 1972.

If children are present in the home, the nature of the control strategies used tends to change because more than two parties are involved. We have already discussed the control strategies used by

A Modern Marriage Contract: Bride Duties and Groom Duties Among the Americans

In Chapter 2 we discussed the bride price as an exchange control strategy that is common in some primitive societies. The American marriage system appears to be developing a variant of this in the form of a negotiated contract between the partners to the marriage relationship in which formal rules and procedures for carrying out the duties of each partner are set down. The general principles of one such contract were stated as follows:

I. Principles
1. We reject the notion that the work which brings in more money is the more valuable. The ability to earn more money is already a privilege which must not be compounded by enabling the larger earner to buy out of his/her duties.
2. We believe that each member of the family has an equal right to his/her time, work, value, choices. If he/she wants to use it making money, fine. If he/she want to spend it with spouse, fine. If not, fine.
3. As parents we believe that we must share all responsibility for taking care of the children and home—not only the work, but the *responsibility*.
4. In principle, jobs should be shared equally, 50–50, but deals may be made by mutual agreement. Any deviation from 50–50 must be made for the convenience of both parties. The schedule should be flexible, but for the time being, changes must be formally agreed upon. The terms of this agreement are *rights* and *duties*, not *privileges* and *favors*![a]

After this broad statement of agreements, the contract goes on to specify in great detail the rights and duties of the various parties. For example,

young children to get their way in the chapter on socialization. We will restrict our discussion here to older children and parents.

FAMILY STRATEGIES AND CHILDREN

When there are more than two parties involved in a relationship, as Simmel pointed out,[38] coalitional strategies may be used. A coalition may form among children against parents or a coalition may form between a child and one parent against the other parent in an attempt to balance the control relationships in the family and to gratify needs. A child, for example, may act as though he loves only one parent to force the other parent to make concessions. Parents may, and often do, form a coalition against children and use a variety of control strategies to make them do what the parents want done. They may use such strategies as withholding allowances, threats, keeping children from going out with friends, and a variety of others until the children finally comply so they can get what they want or need. The child becomes "good" to get what he wants.[39]

Parents have considerable power over younger children because

---

under the category of "Housework—laundry" the agreement is that "the wife does home laundry, husband picks up cleaning. She strips beds, he remakes them." Under the "Job Breakdown" that is provided for each aspect of family living, precise prescriptions are provided:

A. *Children:* Mornings. Waking children, getting out clothes, notes, homework, money, bus passes, books, brushing their hair, giving them breakfast. Every other week, each parent does all.
B. *Children:* Weekends. All usual child care, plus special activities. Split equally: Husband free all Saturday, wife free all Sunday.
C. *Housework:*
   1. Cooking: Whoever invites guests does shopping, cooking, and dishes.
   2. Shopping: Generally wife does daily food shopping, husband does special shopping.[b]

While suspecting that item C-1 here might substantially reduce the number of invited guests, we recognize in this contract one outcome of the negotiated courtship and marriage process in which the bargaining power of the participants is roughly equal.

Even if marriage partners do not explicitly and formally spell out the details of their agreements, implicit negotiated understandings about such aspects of the relationship are an increasing part of many modern marriages.

[a]Alix Kates Shulman, "Work Agreement for Marriage," *Life* (April 28, 1972), p. 45.
[b]Ibid., pp. 45–46.

such children have fewer resources. On the other hand, children are not powerless. They can refuse to study; embarrass parents; and throw temper tantrums to get what they want. Many parents follow Dr. Spock or other child-rearing specialists who have set down strategies for child rearing. Parents are often very anxious to avoid ruining children not only because of their affection for them but also because their own self-esteem is at stake. The self-esteem of many parents is based on producing a marketable child. If children become aware of this (and most do) their control advantage is increased. Some children play this advantage for all it is worth. Some parents are reluctant to allow their children freedom as they grow older because they continue to be viewed as the product of the parent being displayed in the community, thus putting the parents' self-esteem at stake.

Just as spouses use coercive strategies to structure their relationship with each other, they also use coercive strategies to structure the relationship with their children. There is also much violent sibling rivalry. Straus, Gelles, and Steinmetz report from an exploratory study that 62 per cent of siblings at age seventeen and eighteen had hit each other during a twelve-month period. Younger children fight even more often. In addition, they point out that physical punishment by parents is nearly universal.[40]

In modern society much time is spent outside the home either at work, at school, or in leisure-time activities. Even when family members are at home, watching TV often takes up a considerable amount of time, so that a great deal of meaningful interaction may not occur. All this removes much pressure.

Affection is also present among members of many, and perhaps most, families, which helps to relieve some of the pressure. Each person has needs and desires that require gratification. *If this were not the case, control would neither be necessary nor possible. If people did not have needs they would not be motivated to participate in social life* and if they wanted nothing from a relationship, their behavior could not be controlled. It is only when we need something from others that we must allow our behavior to be controlled. If we needed nothing from a relationship, we could remove ourselves from it and therefore move away from the control of others over our lives.

The Family of the Future and the Future of the Family

Some scholars have argued that the family institution may disappear in the not too distant future. One scholar says:

Yet one fine day human society may realize that the part-time family, already a prominent part of our social landscape, has undergone a qualitative transformation into a system of mechanized and bureaucratized child rearing, cleansed of the standardized overtones these words now imply. As already pointed out, an institutional environment can be warm and support-ing, often warmer than a family torn by obligations its members resent.[41]

Another scholar argues the opposite position, seeing the family as having made great gains in personal freedom and remaining necessary in the future. He says:

> the making of the family must be within the remaking of society as a whole, and the making of community must be such as to preserve the great gains and improvements which have been so painstakingly achieved.[42]

The sources of these scholarly differences probably lie more in the realm of ideology and wishful thinking than in empirical evidence.

Current trends in family patterns in modern societies are moving in two directions. On one hand, more mothers are working outside the home and leaving children in day care centers or with baby sitters at earlier ages. Furthermore, the family has lost many of its former reasons for existence. There appears to be more sexual permissive-ness outside of marriage or at least it is more openly talked about and condoned. Marriage is no longer a necessary prerequisite for legiti-mate sex in the eyes of at least a sizeable minority of people.

On the other hand, the work week will probably be much shorter in the future, permitting parents to spend more time with their children. What will be done *with* this time is yet to be determined, but it could be used constructively. The new baby does need a very close physical and psychological attachment to a particular individual if it is going to develop into a healthy person. It is difficult to imagine anyone but parents having enough concern to give the new baby the kind of loving care and attachment it needs. Formal bureaucracies tend to be mechanical and sterile. Babies are extremely sensitive to actual feel-ing states. To do something because you care is different from doing it because you are paid to. Most parents care even though they may at times care for the wrong reasons. Furthermore, the family does pro-vide a refuge for people of all ages in a highly impersonal society. There is much more interaction among kin groups than might be ex-pected in an urban society.[43] Most families will accept and support a family member despite what is done, even though certain demands may be made. These demands are typically more limited than the demands made in the larger society. The family also provides people a place for some privacy and a place to let off steam. A person might be able to "kick" his/her spouse occasionally and get by with it, but if he/she were to kick the boss a job would be lost. The family provides a place of refuge and security.

A recent study at a large state university found a random sample of freshmen placing the family far above all other institutions in impor-tance. This indicates considerable support for and commitment to the family institution, the so-called generation gap notwithstanding.[44]

It appears that the family in one form or another will be around for some time to come unless a more effective institutional arrangement can be discovered to more adequately provide for the gratification of human needs and desires.

REFERENCES

1. Murdock, George P. "World Ethnographic Sample." *American Anthropologist,* Vol. 59 (Aug. 1957).
2. Burgess, Ernest, and Paul Wallin. *Engagement and Marriage.* New York: Lippincott, 1953.
3. Burgess, Ernest W., Harvey J. Locke, and Mary Margaret Thomas. *The Family from Institution to Companionship.* New York: Am. Bk. Co., 1963.
4. Farber, Bernard. *Family: Its Organization and Interaction.* San Francisco: Chandler, 1964.
5. Ibid., p. 105.
6. Ibid.
7. Ibid., pp. 105–106.
8. Ibid., p. 106.
9. Ibid., p. 108.
10. Ibid., pp. 108–109.
11. Ibid., p. 109.
12. Ibid., p. 110.
13. Ibid., p. 111.
14. Ibid.
15. Ibid., p. 112.
16. Ibid.
17. See, for a similar view, Parsons, Talcott, and Robert Bales. *Family, Socialization and Interaction Process.* New York: Free Press, 1955.
18. Marx, Karl, and Friedrich Engels. *The Communist Manifesto.*
19. Farber, op. cit., p. 132.
20. U.S. Bureau of the Census, *General Social and Economic Characteristics:* United States Summary, 1970.
21. Veblen, Thorstein. *The Theory of the Leisure Class.* New York: Macmillan, 1912.
22. Lenski's study is reported in Cuber, John F., and William Kenkel. *Social Stratification in the United States.* New York: Appleton, 1954, Chap. 5.
23. On the privatization of the family, see Halmos, Paul. *Solitude and Privacy.* New York: Philosophical Library, 1953.
24. This is a point made by Burgess, Locke, and Thomas, loc. cit.
25. For a discussion of institutional forces affecting the family, see Bott, Elizabeth. *Family and Social Network.* London: Travistock, 1957.
26. The following is based, in part, on ideas generated by Blau, Peter M. *Exchange and Power in Social Life.* New York: Wiley, 1964, pp. 76–87; and Waller, Willard, and Reuben Hill. *The Family.* New York: Dryden, 1961.
27. *The Contemporary American Family.* Ed. by William J. Goode. Chicago: Quadrangle, 1971, p. 20.
28. Ibid., p. 21.
29. The sociologist Goffman discusses the idea of fronts. See the bibliography at the end of Chapter 1.

30. Parsons, Talcott. *Essays in Sociological Theory.* New York: Free Press, 1954, Chap. 5.
31. For further discussion, see Blood, Jr., Robert O., and Robert Hamblin. "The Effect of the Wife's Employment on the Family Power Structure." *Social Forces*, **36** (1958), 347–352.
32. Blood, Jr., Robert O. *The Family.* New York: Free Press, 1972, p. 533.
33. Goode, William J. "Force and Violence in the Family." *Journal of Marriage and Family*, **33** (Nov. 1971), 624–636.
34. Gelles, Richard J. "An Exploratory Study of Intra-Family Violence." (Ph.D. diss. University of New Hampshire, Durham, 1973).
35. Parnes, Raymond I. "The Police Response to the Domestic Disturbance." *Wisconsin Law Review*, **914** (Fall 1967), 914–960.
36. For a more complete discussion of this, see Straus, Murray A., Richard J. Gelles, and Suzanne K. Steinmetz. "Themes, Methods, and Controversies in the Study of Violence Between Family Members," a paper presented at the 68th annual meeting of the American Sociological Association (Aug. 1973). I have drawn on this paper in the text discussion. Also, see *Violence in the Family.* Ed. by Suzanne K. Steinmetz, and Murray A. Straus. New York: Dodd, 1974.
37. *Newsweek* (March 12, 1973).
38. *The Sociology of Georg Simmel.* Ed. and trans. by Kurt H. Wolff. New York: Free Press, 1950.
39. For a discussion of coalitions in the family, see Blood, op. cit., pp. 558–574.
40. Straus, Gelles, and Steinmetz, op. cit., p. 8.
41. Moore, Jr., Barrington. *Political Power and Social Theory.* New York: Harper, 1962, p. 177.
42. Fletcher, Ronald. "The Making of the Modern Family." In *The Family and Its Future.* Ed. by Katherine Elliott. London: J. and A. Churchill, 1970, p. 191.
43. See Sussman, Marvin B., and L. Burchinard. "Kin Family Network: Unheralded Structure in Current Conceptualizations of Family Functioning." *Journal of Marriage and Family Living*, Vol. 24 (1962), 231–240.
44. Based on a longitudinal study being conducted by this writer and Don Shilling.

CHAPTER 13

Religion

INTRODUCTION: DEFINITIONS OF RELIGION

This chapter perhaps more than any other develops many of the fundamental ideas of the text. These include the problem of social order, the problem of individual meaning, the presence of individual needs, and the necessity of using a variety of control strategies in an attempt to order one's world so that needs can be gratified.

If we lived in a "perfect" world in which (1) there were no discrepancies, so that everything we attempted would be accomplished according to our expectations; and (2) all of our needs and desires were gratified because we had complete control over the conditions for their gratification; and (3) there was no human suffering, or death, or accidents, or natural catastrophes; and (4) we completely understood our social, biological, and physical worlds, then there would perhaps be no need for a religious institution.

This may seem ridiculous since it seems to say that religion would not be necessary if men had the powers of a god. But it is not so ridiculous because what it does say is that, under certain conditions, individuals need a god *because* they are not gods. This brings us to the core problems of religion: *meaning* and *control.*

Most sociologists and anthropologists define religion by emphasizing meaning or control or both. Charles Y. Glock and Rodney Stark, drawing on the work of many sociologists,[1] define it as follows: *"Religion, or what societies hold to be sacred, comprises an institutionalized system of symbols, beliefs, values, and practices focused on questions of ultimate meaning."*[2] Anthony F. C. Wallace, an anthropologist, says that *"Religion is a set of rituals, rationalized by myth, which mobilizes supernatural powers for the purpose of achieving or preventing transformations of state in man and nature.*"[3] The first definition emphasizes ultimate meaning. The second emphasizes control in the sense of mobilizing supernatural powers for human purposes. Both definitions see religion as being used for human purposes either to achieve meaning or control.

Science, Magic, and Religion As Control Strategies

There are similarities among religion, science, and magic in their emphasis on control. All three can be considered as control strategies. We have already considered the control component in religion. Science attempts to understand the "laws" of the phenomenon being studied so that control becomes possible by human manipulation of these laws. Magic attempts control by the use of certain rituals that supposedly coerce supernatural laws for human purposes.

Early anthropologists and sociologists recognized the similarity of the control focus in science, magic, and religion. Lucien Levy-Bruhl (1857–1939), for example, interpreted magic among primitive peoples as prescientific thought.[4] He implicitly assumed that when science develops, magic would no longer be necessary for the purposes of control.* James B. Frazier (1854–1941), another anthropologist, saw an evolutionary development in human societies, from magic through religion to science.[5] Auguste Comte (1798–1857), sometimes referred to as the "father" of sociology, agreed with Frazier describing thought as moving from what he called the theological stage through a metaphysical to a final positivistic scientific stage. At this stage sociologists could specify the conditions for both order and meaning and thus control social processes.[6]

Bronislaw Malinowski (1884–1942), also an anthropologist, suggested that people *use* religious ritual in situations in which rational control is not possible. Malinowski studied the Trobriand Islanders, who were highly dependent on fishing for food, and found that when these people fished on the lagoons, which were quiet and peaceful and thus "under control," no religious ritual was practiced. When they fished in the ocean, however, where there was great danger, the Trobrianders practiced elaborate religious rituals hoping to control the winds and the waves.[7]

Some scholars believe that once science is established and people thereby understand and can control the forces that impinge on them, magic and religion will no longer be necessary. If these scholars are in error, it is not in their assumption about the control component common to magic, science, and religion but in their belief that science,

*He was later shown to be wrong in his interpretation.

once fully established, can provide the necessary understanding to *satisfactorily* meet all needs and explain all discrepancies. Science cannot answer the important question "Why?" or, as Parsons puts it, "What of it?"[8] in a satisfactory or completely meaningful manner. People are self-aware and ask questions that go beyond those that can be *meaningfully* answered by the methods of science. Because we live in an imperfect world with discrepancies between expectations and accomplishments; with suffering, death, accidents, and catastrophes; and with an incomplete understanding of our experiences even through science—for all these reasons—religion, magic, and science exist and coexist.

RELIGION AS SOCIALLY INTEGRATIVE

Sociologists such as Durkheim focus on the problem of religion and social integration.[9] They emphasize only that aspect of religion oriented to making sense of the social order and thus supposedly giving meaning to life within it. These scholars see religion as a force that integrates a society and prevents conflict. Durkheim, for example, saw God as a projection of what we have called cultural agreements. Religious leaders reinforce these cultural agreements and order is maintained.

There is evidence that supports this integrative view of religion. Even in our complex secularized society, we find the American Legion sponsoring a "Back to God Hour" on national television, the Boy Scouts giving a "God and Country Award," the American Flag being displayed alongside the Cross in some churches, and "In God We Trust" printed on our coins.

In Herberg's hypothesis, cited earlier, the "American Way of Life" *is* the American religion that God supports. Protestants, Catholics, and Jews now tolerate each other's religion because all have internalized the basic value system of the society.[10] National leaders and others who have a vested interest in existing cultural agreements accept and publicly proclaim this point of view. Most politicians believe that wrapping themselves with symbols of God and Country (often blended together) will win votes from those who believe in the cultural agreements that these symbols evoke.

Civil Religion: The American Way of Life

In modern societies, a socially integrative type of religion is called civil religion.[11] N. J. Demerath and Phillip E. Hammond say that

In the United States, such civil religion has been called the religion of democracy, the common American faith, the American way of life, and, pejoratively, syncretism or American Shinto. Building upon the Judeo-Christian heritage (a cliché whose prominence reflects its impact on virtually all ideologies in the West), this civil religion has its own saints, sacred literature, symbols, places of worship, and social structures for handling moral questions. In America, the bulk of these institutions may be said to be located in the apparatus of government, and probably this transfer from religion to political institutions of civil religions is characteristic of modern societies.[12]

Civil religion is *used* by government as a control strategy. Political leaders and others who *use* civil religion do so to convince members of the society that they have the *moral* right to make and enforce certain decisions, thus legitimatizing their power and converting it to authority based on cultural agreements. However, the interpretation of religion (civil or otherwise) as a primary integrative force in a society is more applicable to primitive than to modern societies. The distinction between churches and sects makes this apparent.

Dimensions of Religion: Church and Sect

The concepts of church and sect are ideal types, polar opposites that define a continuum along which most religious groups in the real world are placed. A *church* is a well-established and highly institutionalized religious group that is integrated into the society of which it is a part. A *sect* tends to be smaller, less-well established, and often in opposition to the basic values or practices of the society of which it is a part.

Ernest Troeltsch (1866–1923), a German sociologist who expanded the work of Max Weber, saw the church as a basic part of "The Establishment."[13] The church supports the established institutions in a society, helping the elite in other formalized institutions to maintain their power. They in turn reciprocate and support the established church. Thus, the established church tends to support the idea of combining "God and Country," even though many of the historical values of the church may be violated in doing so.

The established church *tends* to draw its membership from people who are relatively well off financially or who have their basic needs met within the framework of the existing society. They have a vested interest in supporting the established church, which in turn supports the existing structure of control relationships in a society.

Sect groups, on the other hand, *tend* to draw their members from the lower classes of a society. In forming sect groups, people reject the established church and make the claim that the church has sold out to worldly interests. This claim, of course, is often correct. Troeltsch points out that

> The fully developed Church, however, utilizes the State and the ruling classes, and weaves these elements into her own life; she then becomes an integral part of the existing social order; from this standpoint, then, the Church both stabilizes and determines the social order; in so doing, however, she becomes dependent upon the upper classes, and upon their development. The sects, on the other hand, are connected with the lower classes, or at least to those elements in Society which are opposed to the State and Society; they work upward from below and not downward from above.[14]

A favorite passage of scripture for a sect group would be "Blessed are the poor for they shall inherit the earth." Poverty is a virtue and wealth a sin in many sects. People in Christian sects are likely to maintain that Jesus told the rich young ruler that he had to sell all that he had and to give the money to the poor before he could enter the Kingdom of Heaven.

H. Richard Niebuhr, the theologian, discussing sects within Protestantism, says:

> In Protestant history the sect has ever been the child of an outcast minority, taking its rise in the religious revolt of the poor, of those who were without effective representation in church and state and who formed their conventicles of dissent in the only way open to them, on the democratic, associational pattern.[15]

In many sect groups, however, as members become richer and more accepted, the sect tends to become a church and thus part of the establishment it once rejected. Neibuhr is again insightful here:

> As generation succeeds generation, the isolation of the community from the world becomes more difficult. Furthermore, wealth frequently increases when the sect subjects itself to the discipline of asceticism in work and expenditure; with the increase of wealth the possibilities for culture also become more numerous and involvement in the economic life of the nation as a whole can less easily be limited. Compromise begins and the ethics of the sect approach the churchly type of morals.[16]

Members of both church and sect use religion as a control strategy both to meet individuals needs through group worship and fellowship and to help them control their social worlds. Table 13-1 shows some of the specific differences between church and sect.

Sects tend to be small in size, reject other religious groups, have limited wealth and church property, have expressive religious services, an unspecialized clergy, make a literal interpretation of scriptures, emphasize other-world rewards, require religious conversion, be at war with the secular world, and draw mainly lower-class members. The church or denomination, on the other hand, has many mem-

TABLE 13-1
Characteristics of Sect Groups and Denominations (Church)

Characteristic	Sect	Denomination (Church)
Size	Small	Large
Relationship with other religious groups	Rejects—feels that the sect alone has the "truth"	Accepts other denominations and is able to work in harmony with them
Wealth (church property, buildings, salary of clergy, income of members)	Limited	Extensive
Religious services	Emotional emphasis—try to recapture conversion thrill; informal; extensive congregational participation	Intellectual emphasis; concern with teaching; formal; limited congregational participation
Clergy	Unspecialized; little if any professional training; frequently part-time	Specialized; professionally trained; full-time
Doctrines	Literal interpretation of scriptures; emphasis upon other-worldly rewards	Liberal interpretations of scriptures; emphasis upon this-worldly rewards
Membership requirements	Conversion experience; emotional commitment	Born into group or ritualistic requirements; intellectual commitment
Relationship with secular world	"At war" with the secular world which is defined as being "evil"	Endorses prevailing culture and social organization
Social class of members	Mainly lower class	Mainly middle class

SOURCE: From *Sociology of Religion* by Glenn M. Vernon. Copyright 1962 by McGraw Hill Book Company Inc., p. 174. Used with permission of McGraw-Hill Book Company.

bers, accepts other denominations, has extensive wealth in church property, has a professionally trained clergy, interprets the scriptures liberally, emphasizes this-world rewards, has its members born into the group, endorses the prevailing culture, and draws mainly from the middle and upper class.

RELIGION IN AMERICA

In 1970, 63 per cent of all Americans belonged to some religious body. Protestants, Catholics, and Jews remain the dominant religious groups. The Eastern Orthodox churches are fourth in membership. Table 13-2 shows that both Catholics and Protestants gained about twenty million members each between 1950 and 1970. Proportionately, Catholic membership grew much more rapidly than did Protestant membership. Jewish congregations added 870,000 members in

TABLE 13-2
TABLE 13-2
Religious Bodies—Church Membership, 1950–1971, and Number of Churches, 1971
(Membership in thousands, except as indicated.)

Item	Membership						Number of churches, 1971
	1950	*1960*	*1965*	*1969*	*1970*	*1971*	*1971*
Total	86,830	114,449	124,682	128,505	131,046	131,390	329,672
Members as percent of population[1]	57	64	64	62	63	62	(X)
Average members per local church	304	359	382	399	399	399	(X)
Buddhist Churches of America	73	20	92	100	100	100	60
Eastern Churches	1,650	2,699	3,172	3,745	3,850	3,848	1,545
Jewish Congregations[2]	5,000	5,367	5,600	5,780	5,870	5,870	5,000
Old Catholic, Polish National Catholic and Armenian Churches	250	590	484	818	848	867	657
The Roman Catholic Church	28,635	42,105	46,246	47,872	48,215	48,391	23,796
Protestants[3]	51,080	63,669	69,088	69,740	71,713	71,865	297,032
Miscellaneous[4]	142			449	449	449	1,582

(X) Not applicable.   [1]Based on Bureau of the Census estimated total population as of July 1.   [2]Includes Orthodox, Conservative, and Reformed Congregations.   [3]Includes nonprotestant bodies such as "Latter Day Saints" and "Jehovah's Witnesses."   [4]Includes nonchristian bodies such as "Spiritualists," "Ethical Culture Movement," and "Unitarian-Universalists."
SOURCE: National Council of the Churches of Christ in the United States of America, New York, N.Y., *Yearbook of American and Canadian Churches*, annual. (Copyright.)

this twenty-year period. This gives a brief over-all view of the distribution of the various religious faiths. Protestants are divided into more than two hundred thirty different formerly organized denominations and sects. This does not include the many store front churches, and those that are formed in people's home, and so forth.

Class, Income, and Religion

American religion tends to be class and income linked, as shown in Tables 13-3 and 13-4. The data for Table 13-3 were collected in 1952, and those for Table 13-4 in 1962. Those religious groups most represented in upper-class positions are Christian Science, Episcopal, Congregational, Presbyterian, and Jewish. Groups least represented in upper-class positions are Protestant (small bodies), Roman Catholic,

TABLE 13-3
Social Class Profiles of American Religious Groups

Denomination	Upper	Class Middle	Lower	N
Christian Scientist	24.8%	36.5%	38.7%	(137)
Episcopal	24.1	33.7	42.2	(590)
Congregational	23.9	42.6	33.5	(376)
Presbyterian	21.9	40.0	38.1	(961)
Jewish	21.8	32.0	46.2	(537)
Reformed	19.1	31.3	49.6	(131)
Methodist	12.7	35.6	51.7	(2100)
Lutheran	10.9	36.1	53.0	(723)
Christian	10.0	35.4	54.6	(370)
Protestant (small bodies)	10.0	27.3	62.7	(888)
Roman Catholic	8.7	24.7	66.6	(2390)
Baptist	8.0	24.0	68.0	(1381)
Mormon	5.1	28.6	66.3	(175)
No preference	13.3	26.0	60.7	(466)
Protestant (undesignated)	12.4	24.1	63.5	(460)
Atheist, Agnostic	33.3	46.7	20.0	(15)
No Answer or Don't Know	11.0	29.5	59.5	(319)

SOURCE: Herbert Schneider, *Religion in 20th Century America* (Cambridge, Mass.: Harvard U.P., 1952), Appendix, p. 228. Copyright 1936 by the President and Fellows of Harvard College. Used by permission.

Baptist, and Mormon. All religious groups have upper-, middle-, and lower-class members, but there is a definite correlation between social class position and religious affiliation.* Thus, as shown in Table 13-4, the various religious bodies can be rank-ordered by average family income, occupational socioeconomic status, and amount of education.

Among Protestants, with the exception of the Christian Science group, the older denominations, such as the Episcopalians, Presbyterians, and Congregationalists, have a higher class rank than do the newer churches or sects. This conforms with the differences between churches and sects.

Religious Beliefs

There is considerable difference in beliefs among the various religious bodies. Table 13-5 shows what members of different Christian groups definitely believe. The older established denominations tend to be much more liberal in their beliefs than the newer denominations

*Catholics as a total group now have a higher average social position than do Protestants as a total group with Jews being higher than both Catholics and Protestants.

TABLE 13-4

Mean Values of Family Income, Occupational Socioeconomic Status, and Education within 13 Religious Groups (Male, Fully Employed Heads of Households in 1962 National Sample)

Religious Group*	N	Family Income	Occupational SES	Education
Entire sample:	7,518	$6,941	36.1	11.2
Jewish	242	9,839	53.4	13.3
Episcopalian	199	9,173	50.0	13.5
Congregationalist	127	9,067	44.7	12.9
Presbyterian	435	8,013	43.2	12.5
All other religions	101	7,847	43.3	12.6
Mormon	101	7,188	41.0	12.0
Methodist	1,031	7,185	37.3	11.6
Catholic	1,936	7,132	35.9	11.1
Lutheran	680	7,120	35.6	11.1
Protestant, unspecified	333	7,038	34.2	11.2
No religion	253	6,579	33.8	10.5
Protestant, other	367	5,831	30.2	10.1
Baptist	1,713	5,612	30.5	10.1

*Definitions of some of the groups identified in this paper are as follows:

"Congregationalist" includes Evangelical and Reformed, plus those respondents who gave the postmerger name of these denominations, i.e., United Church of Christ.

"All other religions" includes Christian Science, Unitarian-Universalist, plus all other responses which could not be included in one of the other twelve categories. Preliminary tabulations revealed that about one-sixth of this group had been coded "Oriental" in race; presumably they reported an affiliation with one of the Eastern religions.

"Protestant, other" includes specific Protestant denominations or sects which could not be included in one of the other Protestant categories.

"Protestant, unspecified" includes respondents who answered "Protestant" to the question, but either failed to elaborate or were not asked their specific denomination by the interviewer.

SOURCE: Galen Gockel, "Income and Religious Affiliation: A Regression Analysis," *American Journal of Sociology*, Vol. 74 (May 1969), p. 637. Used by permission. Copyright 1969 by The University of Chicago.

and sect groups. Among Southern Baptists and sect groups, more than 89 per cent definitely hold all the historical beliefs listed. Among Congregationalists, Methodists, and Episcopalians fewer than one half definitely believe in most of the historical Christian doctrines, with the exception of a definite belief in God. Even for this belief, the percentages are relatively low. These findings are also consistent with the church-sect ideal typology.

Economic Support of Religion

A good measure in our market society of peoples' values and commitments is how they spend their money. Table 13-6 reports consumer spending in the United States for the years 1957 and 1969. With

TABLE 13-5
Religious Beliefs of People Belonging to Different Christian Churches and Sects*

	Congregational (151)	Methodist (415)	Episcopalian (416)	Disciples of Christ (50)	Presbyterian (495)	American Lutheran (208)	American Baptist (141)	Missouri Lutheran (116)	Southern Baptist (79)	Sects (255)	Total Protestant (2,326)	Roman Catholic (545)
I know God really exists and I have no doubts about it.	41%	60%	63%	76%	75%	73%	78%	81%	99%	96%	71%	81%
Jesus is the Divine Son of God and I have no doubts about it.	40%	54%	59%	74%	72%	74%	76%	93%	99%	97%	69%	86%
Jesus was born of a virgin. Percentage who said "completely true."	21	34	39	62	57	66	69	92	99	96	57	81
Miracles actually happened just as the Bible says they did.	28	37	41	62	58	69	62	89	92	92	57	74
There is a life beyond death. Percentage who answered "completely true."	36	49	53	64	69	70	72	84	97	94	65	75
The Devil actually exists. Percentage who answered "completely true."	6	13	17	18	31	49	49	77	92	90	38	66

*Based on a sample of 3,000 persons randomly selected from the church member population of four northern California counties.
SOURCE: Rodney Stark and Charles Y. Glock, *American Piety: The Nature of Religious Commitment* (Berkeley: University of California Press, 1968), Chap. 2. Originally published by the University of California Press; reprinted by permission of the Regents of the University of California.

TABLE 13-6

U.S. Consumer Spending 1957–1969
(In Billions of Dollars)

	1957	1969	% Rise
Food and tobacco	$ 79.2	$131.9	66.6%
Housing	38.5	84.0	118.1
Household operation	41.2	81.5	97.8
Transportation	37.9	78.0	105.8
Clothes and accessories	29.5	59.4	101.4
Medical care	15.2	42.6	180.3
Recreation	15.3	36.3	137.3
Personal business	11.9	31.9	168.1
Private education and research	2.9	9.7	234.5
Personal care	4.3	9.7	125.6
Religious and welfare	3.7	8.1	118.9
Foreign travel	1.7	4.3	152.9
Total	281.4	577.4	105.2

SOURCE: U.S. Department of Commerce, Office of Business Economics. *Survey of Current Business* (July 1970).

the exception of foreign travel, Americans spend less money for religious activities and welfare than any other category of spending listed. In 1969, Americans spent four and one-half times more money on recreation than they did on religion and welfare.

Because giving is a measure of commitment, we would expect sect groups and the newer groups to give proportionately more than the established denominations. Table 13-7 shows this to be true. Those who belong to the newer groups have a significantly lower annual income but give significantly more to the financing of religious activities. For example, 64 per cent of the Congregationalists make more than $10,000 per year, yet only one per cent give $15 or more to the church per week. On the other hand, only 22 per cent of those in sect groups make more than $10,000 per year, yet 28 per cent of these people give $15 or more per week to their religious group.

Attendance at Religious Services

By inference from the church-sect ideal type, we would expect that sect group members would attend religious services more often than members of the older denominations. Table 13-8 shows this relationship to hold. For example, only 15 per cent of the Congregationalists attend church every week, compared with 80 per cent of the members belonging to sect groups.

Conclusion

American sect groups are more committed to their religion in adopting its beliefs, giving financial support, and attending religious services than are members of older established churches. Sect group members, who tend to be poorer, take their religion much more seriously than do members of the established church, who tend to be richer, and thus have a greater vested interest in this world and the good things of life with which it provides them. Members of the established church take an integrative position protecting the existing society, whereas members of sects assume an other-worldly orientation. Both are using religious control strategies. We now discuss these control strategies and how they developed.

RELIGIOUS CONTROL STRATEGIES

Marx on Religion As an Opiate

Karl Marx's famous characterization of religion as "the opiate of the people" identifies religion as a double-edged control strategy. On the one hand, the other-worldly orientation of the proletariat's religion kept workers from engaging in revolutionary activity. The proletariat used religion as a control strategy (opiate) to compensate for their miserable existence in this world. On the other hand, the bourgeoisie encouraged this other-worldly orientation to control the proletariat by keeping them from engaging in revolutionary struggle to improve their condition in this life.[17]

Lower-class people are more other-worldly in their approach to religion. In a classic study of the relationship between mill officials and established churches in Gaston County, North Carolina, in the 1920s and 1930s,[18] Liston Pope found that the mill officials almost completely controlled the churches. They built many of them, paid part of the ministers' salaries, and held important lay offices. Any minister (and these were few) who challenged the authority of the mill officials or criticized their labor policies was soon relieved of his pulpit. Pope sums up the conditions:

> Structural relations between churches and mills in Gaston County mill villages render control of churches and ministers by mill officials almost inevitable, provided the latter wish to exercise that control. Control is seldom made explicit; it simply inheres in accepted relations. Its manifestation is almost always disguised in terms of the general welfare of the community, over which mill officials have final supervision. Positive and direct coercion appears very infrequently, because opposition does not demand it.

TABLE 13-7

Church Contributions and Annual Income (Church-member sample)

"What is the range of your family's weekly contribution to your church?"

	Congregational (151)	Methodist (415)	Episcopalian (416)	Disciples of Christ (50)	Presbyterian (495)	American Lutheran (208)	American Baptist (141)	Missouri Lutheran (116)	Southern Baptist (79)	Sects (255)	Total Protestant (2,326)	Roman Catholic (545)
Number:												
$15 or more	1%	6%	7%	12%	6%	8%	15%	8%	32%	28%	10%	2%
$7.50–$14.99	14	12	11	26	14	16	24	18	27	28	16	4
$4.00–$7.49	33	27	22	24	22	24	33	23	8	16	23	16
$1.00–$3.99	42	41	46	32	49	39	19	46	20	18	40	63
Less than $1	5	8	9	4	5	5	4	4	6	4	6	11
No answer	5	7	5	2	4	6	5	1	6	6	6	5
Percentage who give at least $7.50:	15	18	18	38	20	24	39	26	59	56	26	6
Members' Annual Income												
$10,000 or more	64%	52%	47%	46%	48%	44%	39%	41%	26%	22%	43%	34%
$7,000–$9,000	15	26	23	26	24	24	28	29	33	30	25	28
$5,000–$6,000	10	10	13	10	11	19	16	16	17	23	15	23
$4,000 or less	6	5	10	14	12	9	10	7	14	20	11	9
No answer	5	7	7	4	5	4	7	7	10	5	6	6

SOURCE: Rodney Stark and Charles Y. Glock, *The Nature of Religious Commitment* (Berkeley: University of California Press, 1968), p. 97. Originally published by the University of California Press; reprinted by permission of The Regents of the University of California.

TABLE 13-8
Church Attendance (Church-member Sample)
"How often do you attend Sunday worship services?"

	Congregational (151)	Methodist (415)	Episcopalian (50)	Disciples of Christ (495)	Presbyterian (205)	American Lutheran (141)	American Baptist (116)	Missouri Lutheran (79)	Southern Baptist (255)	Sects (2,326)	Total Protestant (545)	Roman Catholic
Number:												
Percentage who answered:												
Every week	15	23	31	34	29	34	39	43	59	80	36	70
Nearly every week	30	28	25	34	29	31	36	30	25	13	27	10
Total nearly weekly or better	45	51	56	68	58	65	75	73	84	93	63	80

SOURCE: Rodney Stark and Charles Y. Glock, *American Piety: The Nature of Religious Commitment* (Berkeley: University of California Press, 1968), p. 84. Originally published by the University of California Press; reprinted by permission of The Regents of the University of California.

389

When it does appear, the mill management has no difficulty in ridding itself of the troublemaker—for the good of the community.[19]

The sect groups in the community were somewhat less controllable than were the established churches. Some of their members were more accessible to union organizers but, on the whole, they too were against any kind of agitation by labor groups. Pope evaluates the position of most of the sects as follows:

> Being relatively less integrated into the larger community, they are the more easily enlisted for campaigns that challenge prevailing conditions. They offered almost the only religious sanction accorded to strikers in Gastonia in 1929. *For the most part, however, they favor organization to await the Second Coming of Christ rather than to secure immediate economic cures.*[20] (Italics supplied.)

On the one hand, as Marx would have predicted, the mill officials supported and controlled the more wealthy established churches, which, in turn, supported them. On the other hand, the sect groups serving the poor of the community, even though giving some support to labor organizers and strikers, were more concerned with the afterlife and the return of Jesus. They thus served as an opiate, blinding and dulling their members to their deprived conditions in the here-and-now.

Nietzsche on Resentment

Friedrich Nietzsche (1844–1900), the nineteenth-century philosopher, makes a similar argument. In his discussion of resentment, he interprets religion as a control strategy used by the weak against the powerful.

> The revolt of the slaves in morals begins in the very principle of resentment becoming creative and giving birth to values—a resentment experienced by creatures who, deprived as they are of the proper outlet of action, are forced to find their compensation in an imaginary revenge.[21]

Thus, the "slave" who suffers turns suffering into virtue and weakness into strength. He attempts to gain control by making "righteous" the characteristics that define his social existence and "evil" that which defines the social existence of his powerful and, for Nietzsche, rightful master. As Nietzsche puts it:

> Who is really evil according to the meaning of the morality of ressentiment? In all sternness, let it be answered thus:—*just* the good man of the other morality, just the aristocrat, the powerful one, the one who rules, but who is distorted by the venomous eye of resentfulness, into a new color, a new significance, a new appearance.[22]

Nietzsche sees religion as a control strategy used by the downtrodden against the powerful, with good results according to Nietzsche's interpretation of Western civilization. Many of the teachings of the New Testament are control strategies from Nietzsche's point of view. Humility, meekness, forgiving, going the second mile, and so forth were made virtues in the teachings of Jesus. If people have no power, prestige, or financial (or other) assets, then making *virtues* of what one has makes sense. People who lack "the good things of life" in this world can gain a sense of self-esteem by emphasizing those characteristics such as humility and meekness that are available to anyone while preparing themselves for a beautiful life after death.

Poor people who form sect groups emphasize such teachings. For example, black people in this nation who were reduced to slavery believed these Christian teachings because they had few alternatives. They also emphasized the next life as a place of tranquility and joy.[23] As alternatives presented themselves, however, black people did revolt against their masters. In the 1950s and 1960s, Martin Luther King, an ordained minister, and his followers used religion as a strategy to gain more in this world. They stressed that the Bible also teaches brotherhood and equality.[24] Depending on the circumstances, different types of religious control strategies will be used.

Weber on Mysticism and Asceticism

Weber, discussing the plight of the lower castes in India, suggested that they did not engage in revolutionary activity because of the limits set by the available alternatives. These were, at the extremes, either being reborn into a higher caste or as a worm in the intestines of a dog. If a person follows ritual rules, he can control the destiny of his rebirth into a higher caste. He who revolts, on the other hand, and breaks ritual rules such as maintaining physical distance thereby places his future abode at a lower level of existence.[25] Brahmans, of course, must also follow ritual rules, but their lives are much more gratifying psychologically and socially, as we saw earlier in our discussion of caste.

Weber's theoretical work also supports the interpretation of religion as a control strategy. Among the solutions to the problem of meaning Weber identifies are the use of such withdrawal control strategies as inner-worldly and other-worldly mysticism.[26]

Other-worldly mystics attempt to escape almost literally from the social world by taking up residence in monasteries or hiding themselves away in contemplation to achieve "oneness" with the "Universe." The other-worldly mystic must keep alive by what can be found in nature or by begging from others. He sees participation in the institutions of this world as a temptation that must be guarded against to maintain his state of grace. The practices of a Buddhist monk are an example of this type of religious control strategy. His life is spent in contemplation.

Inner-worldly mystics also contemplate but do so "after work." Inner-worldly mystics remain in the world and within its institutions to the extent necessary to maintain their livelihood, although their main goal remains contemplation. They attempt to rid themselves of all worldly desires in order to achieve "oneness." Many Hindus in India use this strategy.

Both types of mystic, in the final analysis, attempt to transcend self. Their goal is to join the self with the "oneness" of the "All." When and if this occurs, control strategies are no longer necessary because a distinct self no longer exists as a separate identity. Thus, individual needs do not cry out for gratification. When Nirvana is accomplished, the journey of the distinct self is at an end from the mystical point of view and control strategies are no longer necessary. As Weber puts it:

> It entails inactivity, and in its most consistent form it entails the cessation of thought, the nemesis of everything that in any way reminds one of the world, and of course the absolute minimization of all outer and inner activity. By these paths the mystic achieves that subjective condition which may be enjoyed as the possession of, or mystical union with, the divine.[27]

Evelyn Underhill defines the union that is the goal of the mystic and that results in the annihilation of self:

> Union: the true goal of the mystic quest. In this state the Absolute Life is not merely perceived and enjoyed by the Self, as in Illumination: but it is one with it.
> It is right, however, to state here that Oriental Mysticism insists upon a further stage beyond that of union, which stage it regards as the real goal of the spiritual life. This is the total annihilation or reabsorption of the individual soul in the Infinite.[28]

Weber's two types of religious asceticism, world-rejecting and inner-worldly, are also control strategies. In the use of these religious strategies, the individual "feels himself to be a warrior in behalf of God, regardless of whom the enemy is and what the means of doing battle are." The individual is an "instrument of God" rather than a "vessel," as in mysticism. Even though the world-rejecting ascetic gives up all "creaturely interests," his goal is not to "join" but to find and do the will of God. This is a rational, instrumental path to God. The sacramental path of the Catholic is an example of this type of religious control strategy. Salvation is the ultimate goal. The inner-worldly ascetic operates "within the institutions of the world but in opposition to them." In the use of this religious strategy "the distinctive goal always remains the alert, methodical control of one's own pattern of life and behavior." The Protestant ethic, discussed earlier, is an example of this type of control orientation. In discussing the possible activities of the person using this strategy, Weber says:

> He may have the obligation to transform the world in accordance with his ascetic ideals, in which case the ascetic will become a rational reformer or revolutionary on the basis of the theory of natural rights. Examples of this were seen in the "Parliament of Saints" under Cromwell, in the Quaker State of Pennsylvania, and in other types of radically pietistic conventicle communism.[29]

Contemporary Religious Strategies

During the 1960s, many students used coercive strategies in an attempt to change the world in which they lived. They used nonviolent coercive strategies such as sit-ins, demonstrations, and marches and violent coercive strategies such as burning and bombing buildings. Concurrently, and as these failed, the use of drugs came into existence in an attempt to escape the realities of this world through what might be called an artificial mysticism. A drug cult developed with Timothy Leary as its high priest. Finally, the Jesus People movement emerged and some students gave up the use of drugs and attempted to lose the self in Jesus. The Jesus People movement is not a strategy to change the world but a strategy to change self through mystical salvation in the body of Christ. A person gives his self to God. Eastern religions also became popular on university campuses as students sought a source of meaning or escape from a world from which they felt alienated. Students who were unable to find meaning through the use of other control strategies turned either to "revolution" in an attempt to change the world or to the use of a variety of religious strategies.

This discussion may seem to imply that new religious control strategies originate only in the lower classes or among other socially disadvantaged people. This is incorrect, as demonstrated by the Christian Science movement, which has been relatively successful not only in this country but abroad, and which began and has remained an essentially middle-class phenomenon.[30] When various needs are not being gratified, a change in religious strategy can be expected if a person seeks gratification in a religious direction.

A study of popular inspirational religious literature by Louis Schneider and Sanford M. Dornbush lends insight into this phenomenon.[31] They studied the contents of a random sample of the best-selling inspirational religious literature from 1875 to 1955. They found changes occurred in the conceptions of God during this interval. In the latter period, there was much less emphasis on sin, guilt, and punishment than there was in earlier periods. More emphasis was being placed on religion as giving peace of mind and power to live by. Involvement in religion was believed to yield correct decision making, success, mastery of life, and salvation in this life rather than the next.

They point out that "The quality of magic is stamped upon a good portion of the literature precisely because of its unreserved promise of results."[32] The authors refer to the religious practices suggested in this literature as "spiritual technology." There is also a striking emphasis on *power* in this literature. We find such book titles as: *Power Through Constructive Thinking, The Power to See It Through, Find*

New Religious Forms in America: How Many People Are Involved?

Accurate estimates of the numbers involved in the new religious forms and control strategies that developed in the late 1960s and early 1970s are hard to arrive at. In his survey, *New Gods in America*, Peter Rowley suggests that

> In 1970 about two and a half million people belonged to the new religions of America—Indian, Sino-Japanese, avant-garde Christian and others even more unusual. Ten, twenty, or thirty years ago the total was less than one hundred thousand, based on information given me by their disciples, as well as my own observations. . . .[a]

Unfortunately, Rowley does not describe in sufficient detail the basis for his estimate of two and a half million Americans involved in new religious forms for us to assess its reliability.

The various forms of the encounter movement, which include group techniques such as T groups, sensitivity training, psychodrama, Synanon, and Gestalt therapy have also affected millions of Americans who have walked, touched, and talked their way through group experiences designed to increase their personal awareness and achieve individual growth. The encounter movement has been sharply criticized for excesses and inanities, but even its severest critics do not deny its impact. Schoolteachers, industrial managers and foremen, Strategic Air Command pilots, social workers, and others have participated in encounter groups as part of their occupational roles.[b]

We can reasonably conclude that the new religious forms are widespread control strategies in our society. Their variety is ranging from ascetic sect groups through secularized encounter groups, but they share a search for new paths to individual meaning.

[a]Peter Rowley, *New Gods in America* (New York: McKay, 1971), p. 3.
[b]*The New York Times* (Jan. 13, 1974), p. 50.

and Use Your Inner Power, Quiet Talks on Power, and *The Power of Positive Thinking.* E. Stanley Jones prays, "Power-power, we need."[33] Religious strategies change over time and religion is used as a source of power to live by in the gratification of psychological needs as well as in helping one to be successful in and adjusted to this world.

In contrast to these people, who use the spiritual technology strategies discussed by Schneider and Dornbusch, during the 1960s there emerged a group of people who created what was called the Underground Church. These people had two major concerns, to make changes in the social order and at the same time to establish a meaningful commuity in this world.[34]

The use of religion as a control strategy is not limited to the United States and the Christian world. In a study of modern messianic cults* in various parts of the world, Vittorio Lanternari found two general strategies used: religious escapism and determined opposition, at times to the point of militant opposition.[35] The former he found being used in those situations in which there is internal conflict. He calls to these endogenous movements† and says:

> In the final analysis, all the endogenous messianic movements, regardless of their cultural level, are impelled by their nature to escape from society and from the world in order to establish a society and a world of their own beyond history, beyond reality, and beyond the necessity of fighting to bring about change and improvement. These movements only engage in social and political struggle when they can do so as a force, having become external to their own society and to the hostile powers within that society from which they had originally sought to escape. In these particular conditions, the endogenous movements take on the characteristics of the messianic movements of external origin, as well as their purpose, which is to defeat the enemy rather than escape from him.[36]

Movements motivated by intersocietal conflict use determined opposition and fight within this world in an attempt to throw off the oppressor. People living in less complex societies who have been influenced by Christian teachings used these to good advantage against those who brought them the "faith." As Lanternari points out, the Judeo-Christian tradition was founded, in part, as a religious response to political oppression.

As another example, Ivan Vallier found the power elite of the traditional Catholic church in South America, which tended to ignore the misery of the masses, coming under attack from a variety of fronts.[37] The most damaging of the attackers is a group of Catholics he calls the pluralists who are concerned with the ending of human suffering *in this world* rather than seeing suffering as inherent in the human con-

---

*A messianic cult is a group of people concerned with the deliverance from oppression by the use of religion.

†An endogenous movement is a movement *within* a society.

dition. This latter viewpoint is held by the religious elite, which is predictably in coalition with the political power elite.

Religion is, thus, used as a control strategy in a variety of different ways by people and groups seeking to overcome varying degrees of powerlessness and meaninglessness in their lives or to maintain an existing order of control relationships.

Religious Rituals As Control Strategies

Religious rituals can also be interpreted as control strategies. F. C. Wallace, whose definition of religion as "a set of rituals, rationalized by myth, which mobilizes supernatural powers for the purpose of

---

Witchcraft in Tanzania: An Example of a Ritual of Antitherapy

Many anthropologists have studied witchcraft in a wide variety of human societies. Norman N. Miller has published several detailed reports of witchcraft practices among the native peoples of Tanzania that provide a clear picture of the contents of one manifestation of this ritual of antitherapy:

Witches are believed able to do miraculous, supernatural, and evil deeds. They can directly cause death, sickness, loss of cattle and property, or they can place curses that will be activated in the future.

Witches are often believed to be predominantly women and common male attitudes toward women support this distrust. Suspicion that women are evil is confirmed when excessive drinking, barrenness, poor farming techniques, "European ways," or general laziness are perceived. In patrilineal societies, furthermore, it is expedient to suggest that witchcraft is passed on through women in order to keep male descent lines unblemished.

Accused witches, male or female, are usually social misfits who live alone and are unpopular for their miserly ways, or for their refusal to treat neighbors with the traditional etiquette. In many cases envy of a close neighbor is a primary motive behind witchcraft accusations. Indeed, witches themselves are thought to lust after those commodities in the society that are in short supply, such as meat, milk, cloth, or tangible wealth. Others might be accused if they are proud or arrogant, have retiring personalities, or are solemn by nature. Nervous looks, sidewise glances, or piercing eyes can also lead to suspicion.

Because witchcraft beliefs vary markedly between tribes, and even between chiefdoms or clans within tribes, they can be fully understood only within their social context. The Nyakyusa of southwestern Tanzania illustrate the complex nature of such beliefs. Here, witches are traditionally thought to have pythons in their stomachs and thus to have the power to choke and wound men, to throttle cattle, and to kill when necessary. A witch's spirit is believed able to leave the body and fly through the night in search of victims. Witches may also ride baboons to attack a victim, beat him with invisible sticks, or send flies into his nose while he sleeps. They may draw lines with poison on the ground where a man

achieving or preventing transformations of state in man and nature," was cited earlier,[38] has identified five different types of religious ritual, each of which can be viewed as a control strategy.[38]

Ritual As Technology

"Technological rituals are rituals intended to control various aspects of nature, other than man itself, for the purpose of human exploitation."[39] Wallace divides technological rituals into three major types: (1) *Divination rituals* are used to obtain useful information from nature. An example of this still found in the United States is water witching. This is a ritual in which a person called a dowser, using a forked stick, finds a place to dig a well for water. Divination

---

walks, eat or otherwise destroy his entrails, and cause the untimely deaths of his children. Witches can cause envy between neighbors, insanity, impotence, and, in short, any form of behavior that is considered evil, immoral, or unwanted within Nyakyusa society.[a]

Miller's general conclusions support our interpretation that witchcraft is most likely to occur in societies where there is a lack of other control strategies to resolve conflict and where there are many unlegitimated or uncontrolled relationships. He suggests that "modern forms of witchcraft practices are emerging as rapid economic and political changes occur."[b] Assessing the implications of witchcraft practices for Tanzanian society as a whole, he locates them "in the area of political and social control," and goes on to state:

> Witchcraft beliefs safeguard the local morality and provide rules of behavior. They force compliance with tribal etiquette, and effectively punish those who break social rules. Politically, such beliefs are a method of maintaining order and resolving local conflicts. In a micropolitical sense, the system is strongly authoritarian and may dictate a large portion of a man's behavior during periods of stress. For individuals living in face-to-face proximity, therefore, witchcraft serves as a control for competitive relations that are not otherwise shielded by age or sex differences, kinship sentiments, or status and prestige differences.[c]

Tanzanian witchcraft thus facilitates the process of adaptation to the transformation from folk community to urban society that is occurring in that developing nation. The relations accompanying economic and political changes that are uncontrolled or are structured by unfamiliar competitive control strategies are controlled and given meaning by the traditional rituals of witchcraft strategies.

[a]Norman N. Miller, *Witchcraft and Sorcery in Tanzania, Part I: The General Dimensions* (Hanover, N.H.: East Africa Series, American Universities' Field Staff Reports, 1969), Vol. VIII, No. 1, pp. 8–9.
[b]Ibid., p. 14.
[c]Ibid., p. 17.

was also used in many hunting societies in an attempt to find game. (2) *Rituals of intensification* are "intended to control those physical processes of nature that are relevant to success in the hunt, in herding, or in the fields."[40] These rituals are used to insure the fertility of the soil, the presence of game that can be killed for food, or to bring rain to water crops among agricultural peoples. The rituals that the Trobriand Islanders use before going fishing on the ocean, mentioned earlier, are rituals of intensification as well as protective rituals. (3) *Protective rituals* are used, as the name implies, to protect persons and property from natural catastrophes such as storms at sea as well as to bless working tools and thus prevent them from breaking.

Ritual As Therapy and Antitherapy

Rituals of therapy and antitherapy are "those rituals that aim to control human health, principally for therapeutic purposes, but also for antitherapeutic purposes."[41] In many less complex societies a shaman (priest) is available for a fee of some kind to attempt to make sick people well. In our society, we still find the clergy visiting the sick to pray for their return to health in a ritual of therapy.

Antitherapy is witchcraft, which Wallace defines "as an individual's use of religious ritual to control, exploit, or injure unsuspecting, or at least uncooperating, other persons."[42] Witchcraft sometimes works because people believe it works, following the familiar sociological precept that to define a situation as real makes it real in its consequences. There have been many reports of people dying because they believed they were bewitched.

Witchcraft tends to be present in those societies in which there is a lack of other control strategies to resolve conflict. Two important studies, which Wallace cites, support this. A study by Beatrice Whiting[43] of twenty-six societies found that where there was no superordinate punishment present,* witchcraft tended to be practiced. In those societies where superordinate punishment was present it tended not to be practiced. The results of her study are shown in Table 13-9.

The second study, by Guy Swanson,[44] of twenty-eight societies, found that when there was unlegitimated or uncontrolled relationships† the prevalence of witchcraft tended to be high. Table 13-10 shows the results of his study. Both of these studies show that if other control strategies were not used in a society, witchcraft tended to be used as a type of control strategy.

---

*Superordinate punishment is punishment by people who are in positions of recognized power. Police in our society would be an example.

†Unlegitimated or uncontrolled relationships occur where there is no recognized authority, thus leaving control relationships relatively unstructured.

TABLE 13-9
Witchcraft and Authority

Witchcraft	Authority		
	No Super-ordinate Punishment	Super-ordinate Punishment	Total
Witchcraft important	15	1	16
Witchcraft not important	2	8	10
Total	17	9	26

SOURCE: Adapted from Beatrice Whiting, *Paiute Sorcery* (New York: Viking Fund Publications in Anthropology, 1950), No. 15, p. 90.
Reprinted from Anthony F. C. Wallace, *Religion: An Anthropological View* (New York: Random, 1966), p. 182. Reprinted with permission.

TABLE 13-10
Witchcraft and Unlegitimated or Uncontrolled Relationships

Witchcraft	Unlegitimated or Uncontrolled Relationships		
	Absent	Present	Total
High prevalence	1	17	18
Low prevalence	9	1	10
Total	10	18	28

SOURCE: Adapted from Guy E. Swanson, *The Birth of the Gods: The Origin of Primitive Beliefs* (Ann Arbor: University of Michigan Press, 1960), pp. 137–152 by permission of The University of Michigan Press. Copyright © by The University of Michigan Press 1960.
Reprinted from Anthony F. C. Wallace, *Religion: An Anthropological View* (New York: Random, 1966), p. 183. Reprinted with permission.

Ritual As Ideology

"Ideological rituals are rituals intended to control, in a conservative way, the behavior, the mood, the sentiments, and values of groups for the sake of the community as a whole."[45] We disagree slightly with Wallace because there is evidence that ideological rituals are used, at least in complex societies such as ours, by those with more power to control those with little power. The established church, as well as the state, is more likely to use ideological rituals to conserve the status quo of control relationships for the benefit of those in power rather than for the sake of the community. In less complex societies in which high scarcity creates the need for cooperation, ideological rituals would more likely be used for the sake of the community.

Wallace also recognizes rituals of rebellion, which are mechanisms to relieve frustrations caused by the structure of control relationships in a society. However, these are rigidly controlled by those with the power to do so. An example of a secularized ritual of rebellion is the Mardi Gras in New Orleans where many forbidden things are temporarily permitted by those in power. People need or desire to do these things, but a variety of controls and constraints prevent them from doing so under everyday conditions.[46]

Ritual As Salvation

The use of ritual as salvation is necessary from a religious point of view "when identity is seriously impaired, therefore, we can expect that the experience will call for strenuous efforts to understand and repair damage to self-esteem; the deeper the impairment, the more desperate the efforts for salvation."[47]
Salvation rituals are useful as control strategies for individuals when their self-identity has been damaged or destroyed and their need for self-esteem goes unrecognized. Under these conditions, salvation can provide the individual with a new identity by transforming him into a new and "better" kind of person. In our society better is usually defined by the Bible or by the clergy, who have a vested interest in causing persons to seek salvation and a new identity.

Ritual As Revitalization

When the order of control relationships in a society has broken down, or when individual life in a society has lost meaning for a large number of people, rituals of revitalization are used. Such rituals are "aimed at the dual goal of providing new and more effective rituals of salvation and of creating a new and more satisfying culture."[48]
Wallace also lists what he calls the "elementary particles of ritual," which include "prayer, song, physiological exercises, exhortation (as in preaching), recitation of texts (reading from the Bible), simulation, *mana* (touching things), taboos (not touching things), feasts, sacrifice, congregation, inspiration, and symbolism."[49] All of these are types of religious control strategies that are used under specified conditions.

An Example: American Rituals of Salvation

Rituals of salvation have been an important strategy for many Americans. Salvation rituals are seen as necessary when the identity of the individual is seriously damaged. Therefore, we can expect that the experience will call for strenuous efforts to understand and repair damage to self-esteem, a basic human need. The deeper the impairment, the more desperate the efforts to find a solution.

The individual's control orientation is based on his identity as a person. If an individual cannot control his world in a way that will produce gratification of the need for self-esteem, we expect him either to move to a situation that can be controlled using his present identity, to attempt to change his present situation, or to attempt a change of self-identity.* Religious salvation permits the last-named control possibility.

The salvation strategy most explicitly familiar to the American is the mystic experience. Discussing this, Wallace says:

> The ritual techniques for achieving the mystical experience of salvation are various, depending upon individual temperament and cultural repertoire. In our society today, Zen Buddhism may provide a path that satisfies some; for others, the revivalist enthusiasm of the Protestant camp meeting or the quiet discipline of the Catholic nunnery or monastery is the way.[50]

Within Protestantism today the strategy of the mystic experience is found primarily among lower-class sect groups in temporary storefront churches or camp meetings. In these situations, the individual may experience a violent emotional release from a "sinful and worldly" self and be reborn with a new identity and a self-esteem within the fold of the Good Shepherd. Middle-class people, historically, have tended not to need this rebirth because, by definition, they can more easily accept their worldly selves. Their social and economic position in this world is higher and they feel a higher sense of worth.

Once lower-class persons have been reborn, they too can feel a sense of self-worth because they have a new and "better" identity. Even though lower-class people have low prestige in this world, by doing what they see as the right thing, they enhance their self-esteem and this is usually validated by other persons in the church or sect with which they are associated. The religious ritual of salvation is used as a control strategy to gratify basic needs and to find individual meaning.

Why Gods Are Born

Gods are born (conceptualized) because people need to understand and control their worlds. The natural equipment they have or the order of control relationships does not always permit this. They are, therefore, forced to create a supernatural source of power and control outside themselves. This external source of power and control can be

*Other possibilities include the use of psychological control strategies such as rationalization, projection, or even mental illness. Where mental illness is "chosen," a change of identity may be produced by the psychotherapist.

used either individually (for example, in salvation rituals) or collectively (for example, in revitalization rituals).

To limit God conceptions as Durkheim and some others do to the support of the existing order of control relationships is to leave unresolved the dilemmas of meaninglessness and powerlessness that have their origins *within* the existing structure of control relationships. If social order were as perfect as some believe, we would not find the perpetual tension between society and some types of religion, and so many mystics, including some students, would not desire to withdraw from society so completely.

The American sociologist of religion J. Milton Yinger sums up his theory about religion (and therefore about why gods are born) in traditional sociological concepts in a manner that clearly complements and supports our interpretation of religion as a control strategy to resolve basic human dilemmas:

> The human individual, blessed (and sometimes cursed) with the power of language, capable, therefore, of anticipating the future, including a foreknowledge of his own death, able to verbalize ideal states, to create standards, is continually threatened with failure, with frustration, with his conception of justice unfulfilled. These problems tend to loom up as overwhelming or "absolute evils." Religion is man's attempt to "relativize" them by interpreting them as part of some larger good, some conception of the absolute that puts the individual's problems into new perspective, thus to remove or reduce their crushing impact. At the same time, man's social relations, his societies, are threatened by these same problems. Fear and frustration can lead to disrupting hostilities, unless they can be reinterpreted as part of a shared experience. In addition to that, there is the tendency of each individual to think only of himself, to make his joys, his desires into "absolute goods," threatening the patterns of mutual adjustment that social life requires. Religion [at times] is the attempt to "revitalize" the individual's desires, as well as his fears, by subordinating them to a conception of absolute good more in harmony with the shared and often mutually contradictory needs and desires of human groups.[51]

THE FUTURE OF RELIGION

Some scholars have argued that as science progresses, supernatural religion will gradually fade away. This is the position of Anthony F. C. Wallace:

> Thus, in starkest form, the question about the evolutionary fate of religion is a question about the fate of supernaturalism.
> To the question put this way, the answer must be that the evolutionary future of religion is extinction. Belief in supernatural beings and in supernatural forces that affect nature without obeying nature's laws will erode and become only an interesting historical memory. To be sure, this event is not likely to occur in the next generation; the process will very likely take several hundred years, and there will probably always remain individuals,

FIGURE 13-1

Churchgoing Since '55

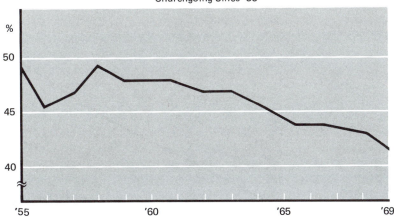

SOURCE: *Yearbook of American Churches* (New York: Council Press, 1971), p. 221. Used by permission.

or even occasional small cult groups, who respond to hallucination, trance, and obsession with a supernatural interpretation. But as a cultural trait, belief in supernatural power is doomed to die out, all over the world, as a result of the increasing adequacy and diffusion of scientific knowledge and of the realization by secular faiths that supernatural belief is not necessary to the effective use of ritual. The question of whether such a denouncement will be good or bad for humanity is irrelevant to the prediction; the process is inevitable.[52]

Recent trends do indicate that church going is declining. Figure 13-1, based on Gallup polls covering the years from 1955 to 1969, shows that church attendance reached its peak in 1958 at 49 per cent of all adults attending church in a typical week. The decline continued to a low of 42 per cent in 1969.

Gallup states that the drop in Catholic attendance over the past eleven years has been about twice that for Protestants. Catholic attendance has declined eleven points since 1958, from 74 per cent to 63 per cent, while Protestant attendance dropped from 43 per cent to 37 per cent. Jewish attendance placed at 30 per cent in 1958, declined to 22 per cent in 1969. The drop in attendance over the last eleven years has come principally among young adults of all faiths. The percentage of adults twenty-one to twenty-nine who attended church in a typical week of the current year (1969) is fifteen points lower than the percentage recorded for this age group in 1958. Attendance over the same period of time is down six points among adults thirty to forty-nine and four points among fifty and older.[53]

Another index of the decreasing importance of religion during the last few years is the number of people who say that religion is losing its influence on American life. In 1970, three adults in every four thought religion was losing its influence on American life. This trend

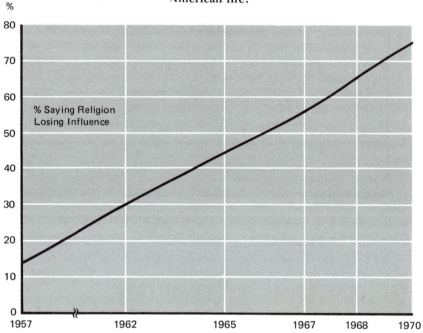

FIGURE 13-2
At the present time do you think religion is increasing or losing its influence on American life?

SOURCE: *Yearbook of American Churches* (New York: Council Press, 1971), p. 224. Used by permission.

is shown in Figure 13-2. Those adults saying religion is losing its influence increased from 13 per cent in 1957 to 75 per cent in 1970. "Respondents to the Gallup survey mentioned the following reasons for the decline in influence of religion, among others: (1) the church is 'outdated,' (2) 'it is not relevant to today's world,' (3) 'morals are breaking down,' (4) 'people are becoming more materialistic.' "[54]

Making a concrete prediction about the future of religion is impossible at this time. We cannot agree with Wallace that religion will go out of existence. On the contrary, we argue that such a development is unlikely because of the existence of the various needs and desires that have their source in the socialization process: self-esteem, security, response, meaning, and distributive justice. The order of control relationships *within* a society makes it impossible for many people to gratify these needs and desires because of their lack of individual control over situations they encounter. There *is* human suffering, uncertainty, the fact of death, and natural catastrophies over which we have little control. Furthermore, even with modern science and, at times, because of scientific findings we do not completely understand, to the point of meaning, many of the phenomena which occur in our social, physical, and biological worlds. Distributive justice is not achieved in many social interaction processes, creating a sense of frustration and meaninglessness.

As long as these conditions exist, people will create gods as a source of power outside themselves and their social world. These gods will help them meet their needs, make sense of their existence, compensate for the lack of distributive justice in this life, and in some cases help them to remake their social world or use the mystic strategy to escape it.

REFERENCES

1. Durkheim, Emile. *The Elementary Forms of the Religious Life*. London: G. Allen, 1915. Parsons, Talcott. *The Social System*. New York: Free Press, 1951, Chap. VIII. Yinger, J. Milton. *Religion Society and the Individual*. New York: Macmillan, 1957, Chap. 1. Nottingham, Elizabeth K. *Religion and Society*. New York: Random, 1954, Chap. 1. Williams, J. Paul. "The Nature of Religion." *Journal for the Scientific Study of Religion*, Vol. II (Fall 1962), 3–14. On the definition of religion, see also, Berger, Peter L. *The Sacred Canopy*. Garden City, N.Y.: Doubleday, 1969.
2. Glock, Charles Y., and Rodney Stark. *Religion and Society in Tension*. Chicago: Rand McNally, 1965, p. 4.
3. Wallace, Anthony F. C. *Religion: An Anthropological View*. New York: Random, 1966, p. 107.
4. Bruhl, Lucien Levy. *How Natives Think*. Trans. by Lillian A. Clare. London: G. Allen, 1929. *Primitive Mentality*. Trans. by Lillian A. Clare. New York: Macmillan, 1923.
5. Frazer, James George. *The Golden Bough*. New York: Macmillan, 1941.
6. Comte, Auguste. *Positive Philosophy*. Trans. by Harriet Martineau. London: G. Bell, 1896.
7. Malinowski, Bronislaw. *Magic, Science and Religion*. Garden City, N.Y.: Doubleday, 1948.
8. Parsons, Talcott. *The Social System*. New York: Free Press, 1951. See his discussion in Chap. 8.
9. Durkheim, loc. cit.
10. Herberg, Will. *Protestant, Catholic, Jew*. Garden City, N.Y.: Doubleday, 1955.
11. See Bellah, Robert N. "Civil Religion in America." *Daedalus*, Vol. 96 (Winter 1967), 1–21.
12. Demerath, N. J., III, and Phillip Hammond. *Religion in Social Context*. New York: Random, 1969, pp. 205–205.
13. Troeltsch, Ernst. *The Social Teachings of the Christian Churches*. New York: Macmillan, 1931.
14. Ibid., p. 331.
15. Niebuhr, H. Richard. *The Social Sources of Denominationalism*. New York: World, 1957, p. 19.
16. Ibid., p. 20.
17. For the views of Marx and Engels, see Marx, Karl, and Freidrick Engels. *On Religion*. London: Lawrence and Wishart, 1957.
18. Pope, Liston. *Millhands and Preachers*. New Haven, Conn.: Yale, 1942.
19. Ibid., p. 159.
20. Ibid., p. 165.

21. Nietzsche, Friedrick. *The Genealogy of Morals.* Trans. by Horace B. Samuel. New York: Russel, 1964, p. 34.
22. Ibid., p. 39.
23. For sources dealing with the religion of black people, see Frazier, E. Franklin. *The Negro Church in America.* New York: Schocken, 1964; Arthur H. Fauset, *Black Gods of the Metropolis.* Philadelphia: U. of Pa., 1944. For a summary view, see Glenn, Norval. "Negro Religion and Negro Status." In *Religion, Culture and Society.* Ed. by Louis Schneider. New York: Wiley, 1964.
24. Washington, Jr., Joseph R. *Black Religion.* Boston: Beacon, 1966.
25. Weber, Max. *The Religion of India.* Trans. by H. H. Gerth and Don Martindale. New York: Free Press, 1958.
26. See Weber, Max. *The Sociology of Religion.* Trans. by Ephraim Fischoff. Boston: Beacon, 1963.
27. Ibid., p. 169.
28. Underhill, Evelyn. *Mysticism: A Study in the Nature and Development of Man's Spiritual Consciousness.* New York: Noonday, 1955, p. 170.
29. Weber, *The Sociology of Religion,* op. cit., p. 166.
30. For a brief history of the Christian Science movement as well as a discussion of other types of *sect* groups, see Wilson, Bryan. *Religious Sects.* New York: McGraw-Hill, 1970.
31. Schneider, Louis, and Sanford M. Dornbusch. *Popular Religion.* Chicago: U. of Chicago, 1958.
32. Ibid.
33. Ibid.
34. For a discussion of these groups, see *The Underground Church.* Ed. by Malcolm Boyd. New York: Sheed, 1968.
35. Lanternari, Vittorio. *The Religions of the Oppressed.* New York: Knopf, 1963.
36. Ibid., pp. 248–249.
37. Vallier, Ivan. "Challenge to Catholicism in Latin America." *Trans-action* (June 1967).
38. Wallace, op. cit., p. 107.
39. Ibid.
40. Ibid., p. 110.
41. Ibid., p. 113.
42. Ibid., p. 114.
43. Whiting, Beatrice. *Paiute Sorcery.* New York: Viking Fund Publications in Anthropology, 1950.
44. Swanson, Guy M. *The Birth of the Gods: The Origin of Primitive Beliefs.* Ann Arbor: University Press of Michigan, 1960.
45. Wallace, op. cit., p. 126.
46. For a discussion of rituals of rebellion, see Gluckman, Max. *Custom and Conflict in Africa.* New York: Blackwell, 1955. *Rituals of Rebellion in Southeast Africa.* Manchester, 1954. Norbeck, Edward. "African Rituals of Conflict." In *Gods and Rituals.* Ed. by John Middleton. Garden City, N.Y.: Natural Press, 1967.
47. Wallace, op. cit., p. 140.
48. Ibid., p. 158.
49. Ibid., p. 83.
50. Ibid., p. 153.
51. Yinger, op. cit., pp. 15–16.
52. Wallace, op. cit., pp. 264–265.
53. *Yearbook of American Churches.* New York: Council Press, 1971, p. 221.
54. Ibid., p. 224.

PART IV

Deviance and Social Change

In Part IV deviant behavior, collective behavior, and social change are explored. Deviant behavior is behavior that some members of a society or group define as conduct about which something should be done. Collective behavior includes a wide variety of relatively un-structured behaviors engaged in by large numbers of people, such as panics, crazes, crowds, mobs, and riots. Social change is the pervasive and continuous process whereby control relationships change over time. Sometimes these changes are dramatic and sharp (as in a revolu-tion), at other times they are slow and long term. Sometimes they are deliberately intended and caused by individuals who have joined together for purposive social action, as in a social movement. At other times dramatic and far-reaching changes occur as unintended conse-quences of seemingly minor innovations. The intricate relationships among these factors will occupy us in Chapters 14 and 15.

In *any* existing order of control relationships some opposition is present and various strains are continuously generated. Our analysis has shown, for example, how the existing systems of stratification and dominant-minority relations in American society incorporate strategies that reward some groups and deprive others. In discussing the social institution of religion, we explored the consequences of the imperfections, inequities, problems in finding individual meaning, and failure to gratify needs that exist to some degree in every society. The oppositions and strains that are part of every system of control relationships cause individuals and groups to adopt and use control

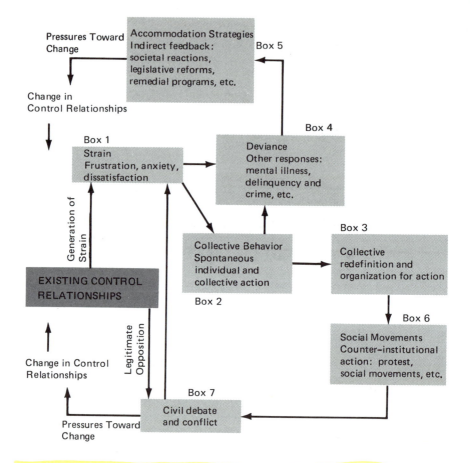

strategies that, in turn, continuously change society and the individuals and groups within it.

The above figure, adopted and modified from the work of Walter Buckley,* provides a point of departure for our discussion of these dynamics.

Taking as its starting point the existing order of control relationships, the figure suggests a number of directions that opposition and strain may take to produce group and individual changes and ultimately changes in the existing order of control relationships. Legitimate opposition arises where the promises based on cultural agreements have not been met. A common result of such a failure to meet these promises is civil debate or conflict (box 7), which in turn can provide substantial pressures for changes in the existing system of

*Walter Buckley, *Sociology and Modern Systems Theory* (Englewood Cliffs, N.J.: Prentice-Hall, 1967), p. 138. Used by permission (modified by Sites).

control relationships. A prime example is the failure of the American political ideology to fulfill its promise of equal opportunity for all. The civil debate over equal opportunities for minorities inherent in "The American Dream" has generated substantial changes in legal and economic control relationships that have increased (although by no means fully equalized) opportunities for minority groups. The civil debate and conflict may also lead to frustration, anxiety, or dissatisfaction (box 1), especially if there is little progress in achieving goals.

Frustrations, anxiety, and dissatisfaction are present in various degrees in all societies. To alleviate these strains, people may engage in spontaneous individual and collective action (box 2). These may lead, in turn, either to some kind of individual behavior labeled as deviant, such as mental illness, delinquency, or crime (box 4), or to collective redefinition and organization for action (box 3).

If the latter occurs, counterinstitutional action in the form of protest or social movements for change may result (box 6). Such collective action leads to civil debate and conflict (box 7) and produces pressure for change. Whether or not far-reaching changes occur depends on the relative power held by the parties involved. If change does not occur as a result of civil debate and conflict, frustration, anxiety, and dissatisfaction continue.

If frustration, anxiety, and dissatisfaction lead to individual responses labeled as deviant (box 4), then societal reaction may occur (box 5), such as a crackdown on crime or drug usage. There may also be legislative reforms so that laws permit what was previously illegal behavior. A third possibility is remedial programs to relieve the source of frustration. Any of these actions may produce change in the existing control relationships.

Pressures toward change are an integral part of the process of social ordering. These pressures are continuous, particularly in complex societies. The sociologist attempts to understand the existing order of control relationships and the generation of strains and legitimate opposition as they structure and change the existing order. Through research, the sociologist explores the behaviors present in each of the boxes contained in the figure.

CHAPTER 14

Deviance

INTRODUCTION

We will use the definition of deviance set forth by Kai T. Erikson: "Deviance can be defined as conduct which is generally thought to require the attention of social control agencies, that is, conduct about which 'something should be done.' Deviance is not a property *inherent in* certain forms of behavior; it is a property *conferred upon* these forms by the audience which directly or indirectly witnesses them."[1] A social control agency may be an individual, a group, or many people in a society who have more power than do those who are labeled as deviant.

Because no act is inherently deviant, whether or not an act is labeled deviant depends partly on who is doing the defining. J. L. Simmons asked 180 respondents with various social backgrounds to list those acts or persons they regarded as deviant. They listed 252 distinct acts and persons as deviant.

> The sheer range of responses predictably included homosexuals, prostitutes, drug addicts, radicals, and criminals. But it also included liars, career women, Democrats, reckless drivers, atheists, Christians, suburbanites, the retired, young folks, card players, bearded men, artists, pacifists, priests, prudes, hippies, straights, girls who wear makeup, the President, conservatives, integrationists, executives, divorcees, perverts, motorcycle gangs, smart-alec students, know-it-all professors, modern people, and Americans.[2]

Almost any act or person can be viewed as deviant in some regard by somebody. "Sociologically, then, the critical variable in the study of deviance is the social *audience* rather than the individual *person*, since it is the audience which eventually decides whether or not any given action or actions will become a visible case of deviation."[3]

411

Deviance, like other human behavior, is based on the dynamics of reciprocal control. In an attempt to control his world, a person engages in a certain type of behavior. His audience—those with whom he interacts or who observe or judge his behavior—is also attempting to exert control and may label his behavior deviant. If this occurs, and if the label can be made to stick *because the audience doing the labeling has more power* than the person engaging in the behavior, a deviant is created.

Before elaborating on our labeling-and-power theory of deviance, we want to consider other points of view. Because some deviance is highly visible and is a matter of public concern to many in society, there may be, especially in simpler societies, a cultural agreement about what is or is not deviant behavior. The absolutist or dichotomous view of deviant behavior takes this situation as the model for all forms of deviance. Other sociologists locate the sources of deviant behavior in the social and cultural structure, ignoring the significance of labeling and power relationships in defining and maintaining deviance.

THE NORMAL-DEVIANT DICHOTOMY

The Absolutist Position

This viewpoint argues that all behavior can be classified either as normal or deviant. Behavior is either good or bad, moral or immoral. Little consideration is given to the part the audience or the differential distribution of power play in defining deviance. Jack D. Douglas, discussing the absolutist view of deviance says:

> A crucial element of the traditional absolutist world view dominant in Western societies has been the taken-for-granted assumption that morals (right and wrong, morality and immorality) are not only necessary and external to man but also obvious to individuals in any situation: what is morally right and wrong in any situation has been assumed to be completely nonproblematic. As a result, moral decision making has been seen as almost entirely automatic. It was seen as simply the result of applying the given morals to the given situation. . . . There was no choice concerning what was right or wrong and no choice concerning right or wrong in what ways or to what degrees. All of this was given by the iron necessity of God's will, or Being, or nature, or some other absolute.[4]

A research study adopting this point of view, for example, presented the types of sexual behavior seen as immoral or deviant in various societies. Table 14-1 shows the number of societies in which the researcher found people punishing specific types of sexual behavior because of their implied immorality.

TABLE 14-1
Number of Societies Punishing Specific Types of Sexual Behavior

Number of Societies Measured	Percentage Punishing	Type of Behavior and Person Punished
54	100	Incest
82	100	Abduction of married woman
84	99	Rape of married woman
55	95	Rape of unmarried woman
43	95	Sexual relations during post-partum period
15	93	Bestiality by adult
73	92	Sexual relations during menstruation
		Adultery
88	89	(paramour punished)
93	87	(wife punished)
22	86	Sexual relations during lactation period
57	86	Infidelity of fiancee
52	85	Seduction of another man's fiancee
		Illegitimate impregnation
74	85	(woman punished)
62	84	(man punished)
30	77	Seduction of prenubile girl (man punished)
44	68	Male homosexuality
49	67	Sexual relations during pregnancy
16	44	Masturbation
		Premarital relations
97	44	(woman punished)
93	41	(man punished)
12	33	Female homosexuality
67	10	Sexual relations with own betrothed

SOURCE: Julia S. Brown, "A Comparative Study of Deviations from Sexual Mores," *ASR*, (April 1952), p. 138.

Incest and the abduction of married women were seen as deviant and were punished in all the societies studied, whereas masturbation was seen as deviant and punished in only 44 per cent of the societies. Male homosexuality was punished in 68 per cent of the societies studied, whereas female homosexuality was punished in 33 per cent.

Such a study implies that most people in the societies studied were willing to define certain types of behavior as deviant when asked. A cultural agreement *seemed* to exist among people in these societies that allowed the researcher to establish what types of behavior were seen as deviant and were punished and which were not. The absolutist view suggests that there are limits of tolerance agreed to by most members of a community or society. Deviance can therefore be defined in these terms. "Only those situations in which behavior is in a disapproved direction, and of sufficient degree to exceed the tolerance level of the community, constitute deviant behavior."[5]

FIGURE 14-1
Normal Curve of Conformity and Deviance

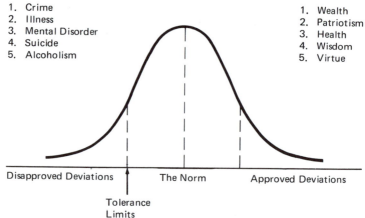

1. Crime	1. Wealth
2. Illness	2. Patriotism
3. Mental Disorder	3. Health
4. Suicide	4. Wisdom
5. Alcoholism	5. Virtue

Disapproved Deviations   The Norm   Approved Deviations

Tolerance
Limits

SOURCE: Reprinted with permission of Macmillan Publishing Co., Inc. from *Society in Transition: A Social Approach to Deviancy* by Robert W. Winslow. Copyright © 1970 by The Free Press, a Division of Macmillan Publishing Co., Inc.

This viewpoint is diagramed in Figure 14-1, which suggests that there is a range of normal behavior, a range of approved deviations, and a range of disapproved deviations, with the tolerance limits drawn only by the range of disapproved deviations. Crime, illness, mental disorder, suicide, and alcoholism are seen as examples of disapproved deviations, whereas wealth, patriotism, health, wisdom, and virtue are seen as examples of approved deviations from the statistical norm.

We would argue that these approved and disapproved deviations depend on the *audience* doing the defining. The normal range, if it exists at all, constantly fluctuates. For example, there are people in our society who see those with great wealth as evil and perceive those who vigorously embrace patriotism as undesirable. All people do not see mental illness or alcoholism as deviant. Many people disagree with laws that define certain behaviors as criminal, and some have organized to try to change these laws. The laws concerning the use of marijuana are perhaps the best current example.

Robert K. Merton and the Normal-Deviant Dichotomy

Perhaps the most well-known and widely quoted sociologist espousing the normal-deviant dichotomy is Robert K. Merton.

In an influential paper published in 1938 and widely reprinted since, Merton argues that social structures themselves generate pressures toward deviance when there is a disjunction between widespread culturally shared goals and access to the socially sanctioned means for achieving these goals. Merton set up the following table of individuals' adaptations to cultural goals and institutionalized means for achieving those goals. In this table (+) stands for acceptance, (−) for rejection, and (±) for the rejection of prevailing means or goals and the substitution of new ones in their place.[6]

Modes of Adaption	Cultural Goals	Institutionalized Means
I. Conformity	+	+
II. Innovation	+	−
III. Ritualism	−	+
IV. Retreatism	−	−
V. Rebellion	±	±

Merton notes, for example, that the cultural goal of success as measured by monetary income is a widely shared value in American society. The *conformist* is the individual who shares the cultural goal and adopts the institutionalized means that are provided to achieve (or try to achieve) the goal, such as hard work, thrift, and education. The *innovator* accepts the goal, but rejects the institutionalized means. The white-collar criminal, for example, wants to get rich, but does so by theft or fraud, adopting means that are not accepted as culturally legitimate. The *ritualist* loses sight of the goal (while not overtly rejecting it) and gratifies his needs by mindlessly repeating the same meaningless activity. The *retreatist* rejects both goal and means, and withdraws from the society, perhaps to a monastery or to a skid row existence as an alcoholic. The *rebel* rejects both the culturally prescribed goals and the approved means and tries to substitute new values and means. In our terms, he seeks to change the order of control relationships.

Rather than seeing society structured by reciprocal control, Merton sees the *structure* of society as based primarily on the use of what we have called cultural strategies. Any departure from the agreements contained in these strategies is deviant and therefore a threat to social order. A high degree of conformity in following both cultural goals and institutionalized means is required. Merton argues that the structure of society exerts pressure on individuals to reject either cultural goals or institutionalized means or both. Such rejection is seen as deviant rather than as a control strategy that structures the society. Every minus sign in the table represents an act of deviance. Every person who does not conform to what is defined culturally as normal is deviant, returning us to the normal-deviant dichotomy view of deviance.

TABLE **14-2**
The Nature of Deviance

Type of Deviant	Example of Deviation	Nature of Normative Order	Nature of Deviation
Freak	Midget, dwarf, or giant; Ugly, fat, or disfigured person; Mentally retarded person	Physical, physiological, and intellectual ideals	Aberrant in being
Sinful	Sinner, apostate, heretic, traitor	Religious or secular ideologies	Rejects orthodoxy
Criminal	Murderer, burglar, embezzler, addict	Legal codes	Unlawful in action
Sick	Psychotic, psychoneurotic	Cultural definitions of mental health	Aberrant in action
Alienated	Bum, tramp, suicide, hippie, bohemian	Cultural ends and/or means	Rejects dominant cultural values

SOURCE: *Deviance: Studies in the Process of Stigmatization and Societal Reaction*, ed. by Simon Dinitz, Russel R. Dynes and Alfred C. Clark (New York: Oxford U.P., 1969), p. 13. Used by permission.

Types of Deviance, Labeling, and Stigmatization

Recognizing the difficulty of precisely defining deviance, Simon Dinitz, Russel R. Dynes, and Alfred C. Clarke suggest that "Deviance can be considered as behavior that represents some form of *undesirable behavior*" and that "This difference can be viewed in various ways, depending on the nature of the normative referent."[7] They classify deviation from five different normative vantage points: (1) the deviant as freak; (2) the deviant as sinful; (3) the deviant as criminal; (4) the deviant as sick; and (5) the deviant as alienated.[8] These types are shown in Table 14-2, along with an example of each, the nature of the normative order that defines the deviant, and the nature of the deviation. Dinitz and his colleagues come closer to our point of view because they recognize the importance of labeling. However, they continue to assume a relatively fixed normative order that defines the deviant.

Labeling usually leads to stigmatization. The person who is successfully labeled as deviant is publicly stigmatized and thereby devalued and degraded. This is an act of control by the person applying the label. Table 14-3 shows the ideal-typical process of stigmatization for each of the five types of deviant listed in Table 14-2. In interpersonal relationships with each type of deviant (column 1) certain reactions occur, such as fear, anxiety, tension, and so forth (column 2). These cause interpersonal sanctions such as withdrawal of affection, shunning, rejection, and gossip (column 3).

TABLE 14-3
The Process of Stigmatization

1 *Type of Deviant*	2 *Interpersonal Reactions*	3 *Interpersonal Sanctions*	4 *Societal Definition of Individual's Responsibility*	5 *Institutionalized Forms of Reaction*	6 *Resultant Self-definitions*
Freak	Fear Anxiety Tension Pity Sympathy	Withdrawal of affection Shunning Rejection	Minimal	Protection, rehabilitation	Acceptance of low self-esteem
Sinful man			Total	Punishment, excommunication, banishment	Variable, ranging from acceptance of low self-esteem to appeal to higher values
Criminal man	Anger Hostility	Isolation Ostracism	Total	Punishment, imprisonment	Variable acceptance of low self-esteem
Sick man	Revulsion Feelings of aggression Etc.	Ridicule Laughter Gossip Etc.	None	Protection institutionalization, therapy	Acceptance of low self-esteem
Alienated man			Partial to Total	None, usual integrative mechanisms	Variable, ranging from acceptance of low self-esteem to appeal to higher values

SOURCE: *Deviance: Studies in the Process of Stigmatization and Societal Reaction*, ed. by Simon Dinitz, Russell R. Dynes, and Alfred C. Clarke (New York: Oxford U.P., 1969), p. 20. Used by permission. (Column numbers added by Sites.)

Others define the deviant by assigning him a degree of responsibility for his behavior, ranging from none for the sick person to total for the criminal (column 4). An institutionalized form of reaction then occurs such as protection or rehabilitation for the freak and punishment or imprisonment for the criminal (column 5). These activities in turn may cause certain self-definitions (types of stigma) by the deviant, such as acceptance of low self-esteem by the freak or appeal to higher values by the sinful or alienated (column 6).

Once a person is labeled as deviant and the label is accepted by the deviant, stigma is likely to result.[9] Erving Goffman refers to stigma as "spoiled identity."[10] People having the power to label and make the label stick can spoil the identity of others by degrading and devaluing them in the eyes of significant others and ultimately also in their own eyes.

The approach of Dinitz and those who share his views represents an advance over the static Mertonian conceptions that locate the source of deviance in the social structure but ignore the processes of deviance making. Recognizing the significance of labeling and stigmatization and the importance of differential power and definitions of deviance makes the control aspect apparent.

DEVIANCE STRUCTURED BY NEEDS, CONTROL STRATEGIES, LABELING, AND DIFFERENTIAL POWER

People use a variety of control strategies in an attempt to gratify their needs and desires. Many commonly used control strategies may, under certain conditions, be labeled as deviant. Howard S. Becker suggests that

> Social groups create deviance by making the rules whose infraction constitutes deviance, and by applying those rules to particular people and labeling them as outsiders. From this point of view deviance is *not* a quality of the act a person commits, but rather a consequence of the application by others of rules and sanctions to an "offender."[11]

If an act is labeled as deviant and the deviant is stigmatized, "treated," or punished, the persons or groups doing the labeling and other activities have more control in the situation than does the individual or group being labeled as deviant. If homosexuals, who are now labeled by some as deviant, had more power than heterosexuals, then being heterosexual might be labeled as deviant.

Many practices that are now labeled by many in our society as deviant have been, or are now in other societies, accepted as normal. Prostitution as part of religious rituals, the use of many kinds of drugs,

TABLE 14-4
Most Frequent Responses to the Question "What Is Deviant?"

Response	Per cent
Homosexuals	49
Drug addicts	47
Alcoholics	46
Prostitutes	27
Murderers	22
Criminals	18
Lesbians	13
Juvenile delinquents	13
Beatniks	12
Mentally ill	12
Perverts	12
Communists	10
Atheists	10
Political extremists	10

SOURCE: Adapted from J. L. Simmons, "Public Stereotypes of Deviants," *Social Problem,* **13** (Fall 1965), p. 224.

polygamy, and ritual murder are but a few of the behaviors that have been accepted in some societies. We must conclude, then, that deviant control strategies exist only because some people or groups have more power than others and thereby can effectively use the control strategy of labeling to gratify their own needs and serve their own interests.

In another study J. L. Simmons[12] asked people to respond to the question: "What is deviant?" The responses in rank order of frequency are shown in Table 14-4. Homosexuals head the list with drug addicts and alcoholics running a close second and third.

This rank ordering may reflect the degree of perceived threat to the values and identities and therefore to the meaning systems of those labeling these various acts as deviant. A person who labels an act as deviant has something to maintain or gain by doing so. Labeling is a control strategy used by some persons against others. Simmons's study was reported in 1965. Subsequently more people have begun to use and to accept the use of drugs. Homosexuals have become organized and have increased their degree of power and acceptance. Under these circumstances, we would expect that today fewer people would label drug users and homosexuals as deviant.

In a simple society where there is widespread and continuous acceptance of cultural agreements over time, the normal-deviant dichotomous view of deviance probably comes close to describing the real world. But in a society such as ours, in which change occurs rapidly and in which people are increasingly willing to try out new types of behavior in an attempt to gratify their needs, the line between normal and deviant is increasingly vague in many areas.

A *particular* audience may be important in attempting to apply the deviant label. For example, in the 1960s, some adults in the larger community attempted to label many college students as radicals or hippies because some of the men wore their hair long or because some of the women wore jeans rather than dresses. Today these hair and dress styles are accepted by many people and few are willing to attach a deviant label to those who adopt them. If people do not have the power to change a behavior they want to label as deviant, and if this behavior continues over time, they may ultimately be labeled as deviant for *not* accepting the behavior.[13]

Assessing Deviance: The Case of the Jazz Musician

It is sometimes difficult to distinguish between a tolerated subculture that exists within the framework of a pluralistic society and a deviant subgroup that is labeled and stigmatized. Furthermore, as indicated in our example of homosexual persons, these evaluations may change over time partly as a result of the actions of the persons labeled as deviant who may organize to change their social evaluation.

Howard S. Becker, who advanced the labeling-stigmatization theory of deviance, identified jazz musicians as a prominent deviant subgroup in our society. Himself a jazz pianist, Becker wrote:

> Every interest of this group emphasized their isolation from the standards and interests of the conventional society. They associated almost exclusively with other musicians and girls who sang and danced in night clubs in the North Clark Street area of Chicago and had little or no contact with the conventional world. They were described politically thus: "They hate this form of government anyway and think it's real bad." They were unremittingly critical of both business and labor, disillusioned with the economic structure, and completely cynical about the political process and contemporary political parties. Religion and marriage were rejected completely, as were American popular and serious culture, and their reading was confined solely to the more esoteric *avant-garde* writers and philosophers. In art and symbolic music they were interested also in only the most esoteric developments. In every case they were quick to point out that their interests were not those of the conventional society and that they were thereby differentiated from it.[a]

However, a recent study of the history of the New Orleans black jazz performers by a sociologist and a jazz performer questions the validity of Becker's thesis.[b] The authors, Jack Buerkle and Danny Barker, suggest that Becker may have drawn his general conclusions from a narrow and restricted group, and that the image of jazz musicians as "wild, irresponsible, antisocial" reflects stereotyped thinking rather than empirical realities.[c]

The problem of who labels (and therefore controls) whom and in whose interest brings us to a consideration of the process of rule making, most clearly exemplified in the legal system.

Law and Rule Making

Rule making includes both the laws enacted by the political institution of the state and the formal rules that exist within formal groups. In a brief discussion of the history of law, Richard Quinney points out that

> Criminal law, as an aspect of public policy, is established to govern the lives and affairs of the inhabitants of a politically organized society. The

Buerkle and Barker argue that the jazz musicians in the New Orleans tradition are devoted to and deeply involved emotionally with pleasing their audience. Much of their self-esteem and need gratification comes through this relationship. The authors quote jazzmen as saying, "I like to see that I'm gettin' across to people, and makin' 'em happy," and go on to conclude that

> This approach to the audience is in decided contradiction to what some of the sociologists have said; that is, that there exists a conflict between the jazzman desiring to be a creative artist and the audience insisting that he follow their dictates. The musicians of Bourbon Street Black don't see it this way. They feel they have considerable latitude in which to be creative and that this is what their audience expects of them.[d]

The authors go on to demonstrate that beliefs about the heavy use of hard drugs and alcohol among jazz musicians are also erroneous and violate the norm of devotion to musical tradition and the goal of becoming a jazz hero that motivate youngsters to become and remain members of the jazz musicians' subculture. The picture they present is of persons integrated into a subculture that in turn has deep reciprocal relations with the rest of society.

These differences in views about the position of the jazz musician in American society are presented not only because they are intrinsically interesting but because they highlight the difficulties in measuring deviance, separating stereotypes from empirical realities, deciding who is doing the labeling and who is being labeled, recognizing changing patterns of deviance over time, and avoiding the pitfalls of generalizing from limited samples.

[a]Howard Becker, "The Professional Dance Musician and His Audience," *American Journal of Sociology*, **LVII** (Sept. 1951), p. 143.
[b]Jack Buerkle and Danny Barker, *Bourbon Street Black: The New Orleans Black Jazzman* (New York: Oxford U. P., 1973).
[c]Ibid., p. 201.
[d]Ibid., pp. 202–203.

concept of criminal law emerged only when the custom of private vengeance was replaced by the principle that the community as a whole is injured when one of its members is harmed. Thus, the right to act against wrongdoing was taken out of the hands of the immediate victim and his family and was, instead, granted to the state as the representative of the people.[14]

Most people agree that the state acts wisely when it passes laws against violence within a society because these laws provide a basis for security. Laws of this type represent the interests of *most* people in a society.

On the other hand, the state does not represent all people equally. Some people in a society have more power than others and thus can influence the creation of laws to serve their special interests. An example provided in William J. Chambliss's analysis of the English vagrancy laws shows how law changed to meet the needs of powerful interests. Chambliss presents a detailed survey of changes in the statutory provisions of English laws effecting vagrants beginning in 1349, when it was a crime "to give alms to any who were unemployed while being of sound mind and body," through the eighteenth century:

These laws were a legislative innovation which reflected the socially perceived necessity of providing an abundance of cheap labor to landowners during a period when serfdom was breaking down and when the pool of available labor was depleted. With the eventual breakup of feudalism the need for such laws eventually disappeared and the increased dependence of the economy upon industry and commerce rendered the former use of the vagrancy statutes unnecessary. As a result, for a substantial period the vagrancy statutes were dormant, undergoing only minor changes and, presumably, being applied infrequently. Finally, the vagrancy laws were subjected to considerable alteration through a shift in the focal concern of the statutes. Whereas in their inception the laws focused upon the "idle" and "those refusing to labor" after the turn of the sixteenth century, emphasis came to be upon "rogues," "vagabonds," and others who were suspected of being engaged in criminal activities. During this period the focus was particularly upon "roadmen" who preyed upon citizens who transported goods from one place to another. The increased importance of commerce to England during this period made it necessary that some protection be given persons engaged in this enterprise and the vagrancy statutes provided one source for such protection by refocusing the acts to be included under these statutes.[15]

Chambliss concludes that "laws change as ... institutions change" and that most laws clearly reflect the needs and interests of those who control the dominant social institutions.[16]

Moral Entrepreneurs and Rule Making

Becker points out that

> Whenever rules are created and applied, we should be alive to the possible presence of an enterprising individual or group. Their activities can properly be called *moral enterprise*, for what they are enterprising about is the creation of a new fragment of the moral constitution of society, its code of right and wrong.[17]

Moral enterprise is led by what Becker calls moral entrepreneurs, who take it on themselves to press for the passage of a rule or law, based on their own moral code, that will regulate the behavior of others. At times the general public or disadvantaged groups may benefit from the activities of these people. Few would disagree, for example, that the abolitionists or those who labored for the passage of child labor laws made a contribution to humanity.

However, as Becker points out:

> Moral crusaders typically want to help those below them to achieve a better status. That those beneath them do not always like the means proposed for their salvation is another matter. But this fact—that moral crusaders are typically dominated by those in the upper levels of the social structure —means that they add to the power they derive from the legitimacy of their moral position, the power they derive from their superior position in society.[18]

People in the lower social classes may desire certain laws that would benefit them, but they have little power or money to influence legislation unless strong coalitional or coercive strategies are used. Laws protecting the rights of working people to organize unions resulted from the efforts of a strong coalition of working people even though they were opposed by powerful economic groups.

Some people have a vested interest in *not* having certain laws enacted. People who make a living manufacturing and selling pornography do not want censorship laws passed that would put them out of business. Most medical doctors do not want a law passed enacting a national health program, nor do most lawyers want a federal no-fault automobile insurance law. The latter two laws would probably be best for the *general* public, but they might also reduce the fees or the freedom of doctors and lawyers.

Powerful people with vested interests and moral entrepreneurs are typically those who create rules or laws or have them created. Some laws benefit most people in a society and some rules benefit most members of a group, but others benefit only a few. Laws that benefit many may also be harmful to a few and cause that few to be labeled as deviant. At times these "few" are such sizeable minorities as homosexuals and people who use marijuana. If laws and rules did not *help or harm* someone, there would be no reason for their enactment. Procedural strategies, which include rules and laws, are useful control strategies.

Law Enforcement and Nonenforcement

Many people who engage in behavior that breaks a law are never apprehended. Using illegal control strategies many times pays off in our society.

Table 14-5 shows that in 1970 there were 2,925,235 serious crimes reported in the United States. Of these, only 579,389, or 19.8 per cent, were cleared. Total arrests amounted to only 561,768, or 19.2 per cent, and the number of people actually charged was 489,471, or 16.7 per cent. Being charged, of course, does not mean being found guilty. Only 4.8 per 100 offenses were found guilty as charged, with 0.8 per 100 offenses being found guilty of lesser offenses with 2.2 per 100 offenses being acquitted or dismissed. Nearly 170,000 were referred to juvenile court in 1970. Reported crimes involving violence are more likely to result in arrests than are reported property crimes. Arrests for violent crimes in 1970 were 42.7 per 100 offenses, whereas arrests for property crimes were only 17.4 per 100 reported offenses. Reported offenses of various types ("offenses known" in Table 14-5) vastly outnumber arrests, which in turn outnumber convictions.

The Nonuse of Law Enforcement Agencies

Many crimes are committed but are never reported to the police for investigation. In 1966–1967, the National Opinion Research Center of the University of Chicago conducted a nationwide survey of ten thousand households. Persons were asked if they or any member of their household had been a victim of crime during the past year, if the crime had been reported, and if not, the reason why it was not.[19] Table 14-6 shows the percentage of cases for various crimes committed that were not reported to the police. The percentages of cases not reported was extremely high, ranging from 11 per cent for auto theft to 90 per cent for consumer fraud. Various reasons were given by respondents for not reporting crimes. "The reason most frequently mentioned for all offenses was that police could not do anything. The next most frequent reason was that the offense was a private matter or that the victim did not want to harm the offender. Fear of reprisals was least often cited, but was highest in cases of assaults and family crimes."[20]

Robert W. Winslow draws several conclusions from this study:

First, crimes of a relatively serious nature are quite widespread in American society. Roughly 1.5 per cent of Americans are victimized by serious crime each year, as indicated by official records [see Table 14-5]; unoffi-

TABLE 14-5
Serious Offenses and Arrests, by Type of Crime: 1970
(Covers crimes constituting "FBI Crime Index." Excludes pending cases. Represents 2,221 cities with a total 1970 population of 59,932,000 as estimated by FBI.)

Type	Total, serious crimes	Violent Crime					Property Crime			
		Total	Murder and nonnegligent manslaughter	Forcible rape	Robbery	Aggravated assault	Total	Burglary-breaking or entering	Larceny-theft	Auto theft
Offenses known	2,925,235	200,384	4,400	11,861	97,558	95,466	2,715,851	728,805	1,642,095	344,951
Offenses cleared	579,389	100,868	3,853	6,667	27,012	63,336	478,521	135,266	286,373	56,882
Per cent cleared	19.8	48.2	85.6	56.2	27.7	66.3	17.6	18.6	17.4	16.5
Total arrests	561,768	89,378	4,588	6,081	31,337	47,372	472,890	116,565	299,450	56,375
Per 100 offenses	19.2	42.7	102.0	51.3	32.1	49.6	17.4	16.0	18.2	16.3
Persons charged	489,471	83,167	4,302	5,738	28,286	44,841	406,304	103,138	253,616	49,550
Per 100 offenses	16.7	39.7	95.6	48.4	29.0	47.0	15.0	14.2	15.4	14.4
Persons guilty as charged	139,170	20,050	1,164	1,232	5,550	12,104	119,120	19,259	92,057	7,804
Per 100 offenses	4.8	9.6	25.9	10.4	5.7	12.7	4.4	2.6	5.6	2.3
Persons guilty of lesser offenses	22,641	7,116	405	626	1,570	4,515	15,525	6,310	7,254	1,952
Per 100 offenses	0.8	3.4	9.0	5.3	1.6	4.7	0.6	0.9	0.4	0.6
Persons acquitted or dismissed	65,295	18,208	1,076	4,550	4,736	10,846	47,087	10,959	30,138	5,990
Per 100 offenses	2.2	8.7	23.9	13.1	4.9	11.4	1.7	1.5	1.8	1.7
Juveniles referred to juvenile court	169,342	15,792	355	980	8,262	6,195	153,550	48,248	78,459	26,843
Per 100 offenses	5.8	7.5	7.9	8.3	8.5	6.5	5.7	6.6	4.8	7.8

SOURCE: U.S. Federal Bureau of Investigation, *Uniform Crime Reports for the United States, 1970.*

TABLE 14-6
Percentage of Cases in Which Police Are Not Notified

1. Auto theft	11%
2. Robbery	35%
3. Aggravated assault	35%
4. Larceny ($50 and over)	40%
5. Burglary	42%
6. Sex offenses (other than rape)	49%
7. Family crimes (desertion, nonsupport, etc.)	50%
8. Simple assault	54%
9. Larceny (under $50)	63%
10. Other fraud (bad checks, swindling, etc.)	74%
11. Consumer fraud	90%

SOURCE: NORC Survey. Reprinted with permission of Macmillan Publishing Co., Inc. from *Society in Transition: A Social Approach to Deviancy* by Robert W. Winslow. Copyright © 1970 by The Free Press, a Division of Macmillan Publishing Co., Inc.

Crime As an American Way of Life

The preceding title was chosen by the sociologist Daniel Bell for an influential article he published in 1953. He showed the intricate interweaving patterns of American crime and the historical development of the social structure of American cities.[a] Bell suggested that "Crime, in many ways, is a Coney Island mirror, caricaturing the morals and manners of a society. The jungle quality of the American business community, particularly at the turn of the century, was reflected in the mode of 'business' practiced by the coarse gangster elements, most of them from new immigrant families, who were 'getting ahead,' just as Horatio Alger had urged."[b] Bell provided a detailed description of the relations between organized crime, urban political machines, and crime as an avenue to upward social mobility.

A similar argument was expressed in less academic terms by the detective story writer Raymond Chandler in one of his best pieces of fiction, *The Long Goodbye*:

Crime isn't a disease, it's a symptom. Cops are like a doctor that gives you aspirin for a brain tumor, except that the cop would rather cure it with a blackjack. We're a big, rough, rich, wild people and crime is the price we pay for it, and organized crime is the price we pay for organization. We'll have it with us for a long time. Organized crime is just the dirty side of the sharp dollar.

Americans do seem obsessed with crime. Newspapers and television stations devote extensive coverage to "crime news." Periodic crime waves are discovered to brighten up doldrums in the media and a sensational crime or a crime with a new twist is assured of immediate and intense

cially, ten times that figure. It is doubtful that all or even a sizeable majority of these crimes are committed by lower-class offenders, as the deviancy theories assume. Second, a minority of crimes of violence (excepting robbery) are committed by strangers to the victim. Since crimes of violence occur in every social class, it is doubtful that the offender (who is quite likely a friend or relative) is invariably a lower-class person.... Last, studies of public tolerance of crime indicate that crimes are often not reported because the victim does not want to harm the offender, indicating the strong possibility that offenders are of the same or higher social class as their victims, and as such a number of crimes are committed by upper- and middle-class offenders but never reported.[21]

Apparently middle- and upper-class people use as many control strategies that *could be* labeled as criminal or deviant as do people in the lower classes, but the crimes by those in the upper strata are less often reported than crimes by lower-strata people. A study in New York of roughly 1,700 people who were mostly middle class found that

---

coverage. An endless flow of crime novels, crime television dramas, and crime movies emerge to entertain the public. Outstanding criminals are both reviled and admired, often simultaneously. The Chicago gang leader Al Capone was a combination folk hero and devil during the 1930s, and the 1960s nostalgia craze revived bank robbers Bonnie and Clyde as sources for popular titillation.

Crime, of course, is also a reality, as the statistics in the text demonstrate. Crime and the fear of crime are important elements affecting the control strategies that many Americans use to organize their lives. Law and order themes rank with support of the flag and motherhood as constituents in the campaigns of most American politicians. Many Americans choose where they will live and work partly by their perceptions of crime rates.

Bell's approach (and Raymond Chandler's) follows the Mertonian theory by locating the sources of crime in the social structure and suggesting that many of the aspects we like and admire about our society are also the causes for what we label as deviant and undesirable, such as crime. Our theoretical perspective points to how powerful persons and groups are able to define acts that oppose their interests as criminal, while preventing the labeling and stigmatization of their own behavior. For example, the economic costs to the general public of a large price increase in a vital product or service may be far greater than the total cost of thousands of burglaries and robberies. Yet one is a justified business practice whereas the other is a criminal offense.

[a]Daniel Bell, "Crime As an American Way of Life," *Antioch Review*, **XIII** (Summer 1953), pp. 131–154.
[b]Ibid., p. 132.

nonreported crimes were common among people thought to be respectable members of the community. A full 99 per cent of these
people reported they had committed one or more of forty-nine crimes
that were punishable under the penal code of New York state and that
were serious enough to draw a prison sentence of more than one year.
The men studied had committed an average of eighteen crimes and
the women an average of eleven crimes. All had gone unpunished.
Sixty-four per cent of the men and 29 per cent of the women studied
had committed one or more felonies, which are serious crimes
punishable by substantial jail terms and fines.[22]

Such evidence suggests that the important question is not who uses
control strategies that could be labeled as deviant but rather, as Austin
T. Turk puts it: "Why is one person who engages in certain behavior
given the status of criminal while another who engages in the same
behavior is not?"[23] In other words: Who is most likely to be labeled as
deviant?

Who Is Labeled As Deviant?

In looking at *official* crime rates, Turk points out that *"For most
offense categories the rates are relatively high for lower status,
minority groups, young, males, transient, urban populations."*[24] He
goes on to say that "The common attribute of all the categories except
that of male appears to be their vulnerability when confronted by
authorities; the attributes defining the categories are associated with
relative powerlessness."[25] Quinney makes the same point when he
says, *"Persons in the segments of society whose behavior patterns are
not represented in formulating and applying criminal definitions are
more likely to act in ways that will be defined as criminal than those
in the segments that formulate and apply criminal definitions."*[26]
Those with power can define who is deviant and see to it that the
labels are applied and stick, with their accompanying stigmatization.

Edwin M. Schur[27] suggests that people with high resources and
thus more power have (1) a higher ability to resist imputations of
deviant identity so that they are not labeled or so that the label cannot
be made to stick; (2) a high resistance to processing efforts, such as
being arrested, being brought to trial, and being convicted; (3) a
higher probability of being seen as "conformist"; and (4) a higher
ability to *impose* rules. The opposite is true for people with low resources. These relations are set forth in Table 14-7.

Empirical evidence that this is the case is reported in Table 14-8,
which shows that white-Spanish and black youths, both males and
females, are consistently more likely to be brought into juvenile court
than are whites. In addition, the higher the income of the juvenile's

family, the less the likelihood of his being brought to juvenile court. Quinney sums much of this up when he says, *"The probability that criminal definitions will be applied varies according to the extent to which behaviors of the powerless conflict with the interests of the power segments."*[28]

CASE STUDIES IN THE USE OF DEVIANT CONTROL STRATEGIES AMONG THOSE WITH LIMITED ALTERNATIVES

People have needs and desires. In attempting to gratify them, they use control strategies in their interactions with other people. When working- and lower-class people and others with little power use control strategies that *could* be labeled as deviant, they are more likely to be so labeled and punished than are people in the middle (white-collar) and upper classes using the same or similar control strategies. Why do people in the working and lower classes use control strategies knowing that there is a risk of being labeled deviant and punished? Some people in these classes *see few, if any, alternative ways of gratifying needs* for food, shelter, and the other basic needs. The following three classic studies in sociology demonstrate this.

Life, Liberty, and Property[29]

Alfred Jones studied attitudes toward corporate property in Akron, Ohio, a city famous for its rubber industry, in 1938 when there was considerable labor strife and feelings were running high. To measure attitudes toward corporate property indirectly, Jones constructed a series of stories to which his subjects were asked to respond. One story described coal mines that had been shut down because of the low price of coal and the consequent plight of the miners thrown out of work who were without money to buy food and other necessities for their families. These miners resorted to stealing coal from the closed mines, which were private property, and burning it to keep warm or selling it to buy food for their families. The respondents were asked if they approved or disapproved of this theft of coal.[30]

The respondents from the business sector of the community disapproved of the behavior of the miners. On the other hand, members of the CIO Rubber Workers Union tended to approve highly the miners' stealing coal. Some of the responses of these workers were, "I hold right with the miners. They were forced to do it." "They were hungry. I'd do the same." "They had to keep warm. I would have done the same thing."[31]

TABLE 14-7
Relation Between Salient Resources and Deviance Outcomes

	Interpersonal Reactions	Organizational Processing	Collective Rule Making
High resources (of individual or group)	High ability to resist imputations of deviant identity or to "manage" desired deviant roles successfully	High resistance to processing efforts Low rates of "official" deviance	Dominant social perception of individual or group norms as "conformist" High ability to impose rules
Low resources (of individual or group)	Low ability to resist imputations of deviant identity or to manage desired deviant roles successfully	Low resistance to processing efforts High rates of "official" deviance	Dominant social perception of individual or group norms as "deviant" Low ability to impose rules

SOURCE: Table "Relation between salient resources and deviance outcomes" in *Labeling Deviant Behavior* by Edwin M. Schur (New York: Harper & Row, 1971).

TABLE 14-8
Area-Adjusted Juvenile Court Delinquency Rates by Age, Income, and Number of Parents in Home

Individuals	Age				Income				Parents in Home		
	8–10	11–13	14–16	17	0–$2,500	$2,500–$5,000	$5,000–$10,000	Over $10,000	2	1	0
Males											
White	13	45	91	108	27	80	15	3	21	74	25
White-Spanish	11	27	80	165	22	50	8	3	15	55	27
Negro	38	111	267	315	77	111	35	4	47	110	46
Females											
White	2	8	28	20	7	25	2	0	4	26	10
White-Spanish	2	10	31	25	7	13	3	0	4	18	6
Negro	5	30	78	36	27	20	9	0	9	29	14

SOURCE: Victor Eisner, The Delinquency Label: The Epidemiology of Juvenile Delinquency (New York: Random, 1969), p. 49. Used by permission.

These two groups of people had contrasting attitudes associated with their differential power. The business group had a vested interest in corporate property and the laws that protect it. They had good incomes and, thus, available alternatives within the law to meet their basic needs. On the other hand, the rubber workers were paid relatively low wages and had little vested interest in corporate property and the laws that protect it. These people would have few alternatives if they had lost their jobs and thus were willing to approve stealing to feed their families and keep them warm. They approved the use of control strategies that would meet basic needs even if the use of these strategies would cause those who used them to be labeled as deviant and to be punished if apprehended. Some might attribute this willingness by workers to approve stealing to the labor strife or the low wages being paid in the 1930s. However, a replication of this study in the late 1960s produced essentially the same results.[32]

The Unadjusted Girl[33]

W. I. Thomas, writing in the early part of this century, was among the first to approach deviance from the modern point of view. He was not interested in deviant behavior as such. "One of his goals was to erase the line between 'normal' and 'abnormal' behavior, for he considered both forms to be varying manifestations of the same human phenomena."[34] For him, as for us, all behavior (and therefore all control strategies) results from the effort expended by human beings attempting to come to terms with their physical and social environment.[35]

In *The Unadjusted Girl*, Thomas's major concern was the behavior of the prostitute. Through a number of life histories, he attempted to show that when girls are brought up in a deprived home situation where there is little opportunity for the gratification of what Thomas calls the four wishes or desires* (the desire for new experience, the desire for security, the desire for response, and the desire for recognition),[36] they may attempt to gratify these desires by becoming prostitutes. Many of these young women had severely restricted alternatives. They had little opportunity for education or economic security. Nearly one half had never finished the primary grades and an additional 40 per cent had finished only grammar school. Only four had completed high school.[37]

Coming from impoverished backgrounds and with few alternatives these young women entered prostitution in an attempt to gratify their basic "desires." They could make much more money by prostitution

---

*These are essentially what we have been calling basic needs.

than by pursuing any other available occupation, assuming they could get a job at all. Prostitution enabled them to buy beautiful clothing and to live lavishly. These girls entered prostitution to gratify needs even though they would be labeled as deviant and be punished. Thomas emphasizes that their behavior was motivated by the *same* needs that motivate the behavior of all of us.

Delinquent Boys: The Culture of the Gang[38]

Albert K. Cohen, one of the foremost contemporary authorities in the study of deviance, begins his study of delinquent boys with the same assumption as that made by Thomas. Cohen says:

> Our point of departure, we have said, is the psychogenic assumption that innovations, whether on the level of action or the underlying frame of reference, arise out of problems of adjustment.[39]

For him, as for us, "status problems are problems of achieving respect in the eyes of one's fellows,"[40] and "the continued serviceability and therefore the viability of a subculture solution entails the emergence of a certain amount of group solidarity (providing security) and heightened interaction among the participants in the subculture."[41]
Cohen discusses what it is like to grow up in a class-stratified society, pointing out that children from middle-class families have more advantages, not only in their home lives but also in their future alternatives. The child in the working-class family is left much more on his own and does not receive the constant psychological backing from his parents that the middle-class child receives. Furthermore, children learn very early to which social class they belong. Middle-class parents encourage their children to associate with the "right kind of friends."
When working-class children enter school, they are at times thrown in with not only middle-class students but also middle-class teachers who may reject them. Their needs for esteem and security are not gratified. They are often excluded from those activities within the school that would give them a sense of pride and achievement. Partly as a reaction to this, the potential delinquent boys may join together and form gangs, thus embracing a delinquent subculture. Joining such a delinquent gang is a way to meet basic needs by making an adjustment not possible within the middle-class school where the lower-class boy cannot successfully control the behavior of others to receive positive responses.
Cohen points out that

> As long as the working-class corner-boy clings to a version, however attenuated and adulterated, of the middle-class culture, he must recognize

his inferiority to working-class and middle-class college boys. The delinquent subculture, on the other hand, permits no ambiguity of the status of the delinquent relative to that of anybody else. In terms of the norms of the delinquent subculture, defined by its negative polarity to the respectable status system, the delinquent's very nonconformity to middle-class standards sets him above the most exemplary college boy.[42]

His prestige and self-esteem come to have a different basis than the respectability demanded by middle-class standards. "It expresses contempt for a way of life, making its opposite a criterion of status."[43] A new system of norms is created. The lower-class boy can gratify his needs by conforming to these and by rejecting the middle class that has put him down.

Many delinquent activities are against the law. This places the lower-class delinquent in a position to be labeled as a delinquent by those who have the power to do so. This, of course, does not mean that there is no illegal activities among middle-class youth. However, they are much less likely to be apprehended, and, if apprehended, punished to the same degree as lower-class youths.

MENTAL ILLNESS AS DEVIANT BEHAVIOR

Thomas J. Scheff places mental illness within the framework of deviance and labeling by introducing the concept of residual rule breaking:

> [the] diverse kinds of rulebreaking for which our society provides no explicit label, and which, therefore, sometimes leads to the labeling of the violator as mentally ill, will be considered to be technically residual rule breaking.[44]

Even where no formal codified law exists that would allow those with power to label someone as criminal whose behavior they want to control, they have the alternative of identifying the behavior as residual rule breaking, thus labeling the person as mentally ill and controlling his behavior.

Scheff points out that "relative to the rate of treated mental illness, the rate of unrecorded residual rule breaking is extremely high."[45] Thus, "most residual rule breaking is 'denied' and is of transitory significance."[46] Where residual rule breaking is "denied," one of two things has happened: the rule breaking was completely unnoticed or, if noticed, it was ignored. Both noticing or not noticing and ignoring or not ignoring (and therefore labeling) depend on certain factors. If one person wants to do damage to another who is a residual rule breaker, or if he has something to gain by labeling the residual rule breaker as mentally ill, the person might be expected to look for and notice a minimum amount of residual rule breaking in the other person's behavior and to label it as mental illness. Some older people are labeled as mentally ill and "put away" to get their money or just to "get them out of the way."

On the other hand, noticing residual rule breaking can be bother-some, because if noticed "something should be done about it," which will take time and effort. Furthermore, if it is noticed and there is nothing to be gained by labeling it mental illness, it may be easier to call it eccentricity or even genius, as Scheff points out. Or if noticed and a person has something to lose by labeling it mental illness, he may ignore it. A worker is not likely to label his boss mentally ill, at least publicly, whereas a schoolteacher is likely to suggest that a troublesome child in her classroom "needs help."[47]

There are also individuals who want to be labeled as mentally ill. Becoming mentally ill may be a useful control strategy if there is no other way out of a confused situation. One can break the residual rules hoping to be labeled mentally ill and to secure help from others or at least be relieved from one's obnoxious daily tasks and from immediate stress. Scheff argues that such help seeking commonly occurs.[48] In his discussion of the stereotypes of mental illness and the labeling pro-cess, Scheff concludes that

1. Labeled deviants may be rewarded for playing the stereotyped deviant role.[49]
2. Labeled deviants are punished when they attempt the return to conven-tional roles.[50]
3. In the crises occurring when a residual rule breaker is publicly labeled, the deviant is highly suggestible, and may accept the proffered role of the insane as the only alternative.[51]
4. Among residual rule breakers, labeling is the single most important cause of careers of residual deviance.[52]

Although there are a wide variety of contingencies which lead to labeling they can be simply classified in terms of the nature of the rule breaking, the person who breaks the rules, and the community in which the rule breaking occurs. Other things being equal, the severity of the societal reaction is a function of, first, the degree, amount, and visibility of the rule breaking; second, the power of the rule breaker and the social distance between him and the agents of social control; and finally, the tolerance level of the community, and the availability in the culture of the community of alterna-tive nondeviant roles.[53]

Scheff thus finds the same dynamics at work in the interpersonal relations that label mental illness that we found in other areas of deviant behavior.

DEVIANCE AND THE SOCIOLOGIST: A WALK ON THE BIASED SIDE

Deviance is a difficult area to study objectively. Alexander Liazos points out that we tend to see as deviants *only* "those who have been successfully labeled as 'deviants!' "[54] These include some of the types mentioned throughout the chapter, such as the mentally ill, homosexuals, prostitutes, and juvenile delinquents, or as Liazos graphically puts it, "nuts, sluts, and perverts." He points out that, "Little attention has been paid to the unethical, illegal, and destructive actions of powerful individuals, groups, and institutions in our society."[55] We focus on the acts of violence that occur in the slums but give little or no attention to the violence that occurs in illegal wars, or that is directed against those incarcerated in the nation's prisons and mental hospitals. In all these cases "a person is violated—there is harm done to his person, his psyche, his body, his dignity, his ability to govern himself."[56]

The lives of many people are violated by the everyday workings of social institutions, but we tend to dwell on the dramatic and the predatory. Liazos provides an excellent example from the writing of Stokely Carmichael and Charles V. Hamilton, who distinguish between *individual* racism and *institutional* racism:

> When white terrorists bomb a black church and kill five black children, that is an individual act of individual racism, widely deplored by most segments of the society. But when in the same city—Birmingham, Alabama—five hundred black babies die each year because of lack of proper food, shelter, and medical facilities, and thousands more are destroyed and maimed physically, emotionally, and intellectually because of conditions of poverty and discrimination in the black community, that is a function of institutional racism.[57]

Liazos goes on to say:

> Surely this is violence; it is caused by the normal, quiet workings of institutions run by respectable members of the community. Many whites also suffer from the institutional workings of a profit-oriented society and economy; poor health, dead-end jobs, slum housing, hunger in rural areas, and so on, are daily realities in their lives. This is surely much worse violence than any committed by the Hell's Angels or street gangs. Only these groups get stigmatized and analyzed by sociologists of deviance, however, while those good people who live in luxurious homes (fixing tax laws for their benefit) off profits derived from an exploitative economic system—they are the pillars of their community.[58]

All this helps us put the concepts of "deviant" and "normal" in their proper perspectives. Quantitatively and perhaps qualitatively more harm may be done to human beings by the "normal" than by those labeled as deviant. The irony is that the "deviant" suffer initially because they are poor or powerless. They are caused to suffer even more when they engage in behavior that is labeled as deviant and stigmatized by those with power. The powerful who do this labeling often create the conditions that restrict the alternatives of people with less power. Those with less power are, therefore, more likely to engage in behavior that leads to their being labeled deviant, stigmatized, and punished. Those who are "normal" may engage in the same behavior, even though they have a broader range of alternatives, but escape unlabeled and unstigmatized because of their greater power. Given the unequal distribution of power, we can expect in any society that those who have more will get more and those who have less will not only get less but also will be caused to suffer more. This is another irony of the human condition.

REFERENCES

1. Erikson, Kai T. "Notes on the Sociology of Deviance." *Social Problems*, Vol. IX (Spring 1962), 308.
2. Simmons, J. L. *Deviants*. Berkeley, Calif.: Glendessary Press, 1969, p. 1.
3. Erikson, loc. cit.
4. *Deviance and Respectability*. Ed. by Jack D. Douglas. New York: Basic Books, 1970, pp. 14–15.
5. Clinard, Marshall. *The Sociology of Deviant Behavior*. New York: Holt, 1962, p. 22.
6. Merton, Robert K. *Social Theory and Social Structure*. New York: Free Press, 1957, Chap. IV. The diagram appears on p. 140.
7. *Deviance: Studies in the Process of Stigmatization and Societal Reaction*. Ed. by Simon Dinitz, Russel R. Dynes, and Alfred C. Clarke. New York: Oxford U. P., 1969, p. 12.
8. Ibid.
9. Goffman, Erving. *Stigma: Notes on the Management of Spoiled Identity*. Englewood Cliffs, N.J.: Prentice-Hall, 1965. This is an excellent treatment of stigma.
10. Ibid.
11. Becker, Howard S. *Outsiders*. New York: Macmillan, Inc., 1963, p. 9.
12. Simmons, J. L. "Public Stereotypes of Deviants." *Social Problems*, Vol. 13 (Fall 1965).
13. For a discussion of the dynamics involved in this process, see Cory, Donald Webster, and John P. Leroy. "The Homosexual in His Own Behalf." In *The Homosexual and His Society*. New York: Citadel, 1963, pp. 240–250.
14. *Crime and Justice in Society*. Ed. by Richard Quinney. Boston: Little, Brown, 1969, p. 5.
15. Chambliss, William J. "Elites and the Creation of Criminal Law." In *Sociological Readings in the Conflict Perspective*. Ed. by William J. Chambliss. Reading, Mass.: Addison-Wesley, 1973, p. 442.
16. Ibid., p. 442.
17. Becker, op. cit., p. 145.
18. Ibid., p. 149.
19. Winslow, Robert W. *Society in Transition: A Social Approach to Deviancy*. New York: Free Press, 1970, p. 180.
20. Ibid.
21. Ibid., pp. 181–182.
22. Wallerstein, James S., and Clement J. Wyle. "Our Law-Abiding Law Breakers." *Probation* (April 1947). For other discussions of middle- and upper-class crime, see *Middle-Class Delinquency*. Ed. by Edmund W.

Vaz. New York: Harper, 1967. Ferdinand, Theodore N. *Typologies of Delinquency.* New York: Random, 1966. Sutherland, Edwin H. *White Collar Crime.* New York: Dryden, 1949.

23. Turk, Austin T. *Criminality and Legal Order.* Chicago: Rand McNally, 1969, p. 17.
24. Ibid.
25. Ibid.
26. Quinney, Richard. *The Social Reality of Crime.* Boston: Little, Brown, 1970, p. 21.
27. Schur, Edwin M. *Labeling Deviant Behavior.* New York: Harper, 1971.
28. Quinney, loc. cit.
29. Jones, Alfred W. *Life, Liberty and Prosperity.* Philadelphia: Lippincott, 1941.
30. Ibid., pp. 144–145.
31. Ibid., p. 172.
32. Maxey, Amy. "Life, Liberty, and Property: Thirty Years Later." (M.A. thesis, Kent State University, 1968).
33. Thomas, W. I. *The Unadjusted Girl.* New York: Harper, 1963. Originally published in 1923 by Little, Brown.
34. Ibid., p. x in the Introduction, written by Michael Parenti.
35. Ibid.
36. Ibid., p. 4.
37. Ibid., p. 116.
38. Cohen, Albert K. *Delinquent Boys: The Culture of the Gang.* New York: Free Press, 1953.
39. Ibid., p. 69.
40. Ibid., p. 65.
41. Ibid., p. 67.
42. Ibid., pp. 130–131.
43. Ibid., p. 134.
44. Scheff, Thomas J. *Being Mentally Ill.* Chicago: Aldine, 1966, p. 34.
45. Ibid., p. 47.
46. Ibid., p. 51.
47. See Erikson, Kai T. Op. cit., 307–314.
48. See Scheff, op. cit., Chap. 3. Also, see Szasz, T. S. "The Myth of Mental Illness." *American Psychologist,* Vol. 15 (Feb. 1960), 113–118.
49. Ibid., p. 84.
50. Ibid., p. 87
51. Ibid., p. 88.
52. Ibid., pp. 92–93.
53. Ibid., pp. 96–97.
54. Liazos, Alexander. "The Poverty of the Sociology of Deviance: Nuts, Sluts, and Perverts." *Social Problems,* Vol. 2, No. 1 (Summer 1972), 109.
55. Ibid., p. 111.
56. Ibid.
57. Carmichael, Stokely, and Charles V. Hamilton. *Black Power.* New York: Random, 1967, p. 4.
58. Liazos, op. cit., p. 112.

Social Change
and Collective Behavior

INTRODUCTION

Social ordering is a process based on constraints and the reciprocal use of control strategies by individuals and groups. Social change is always occurring. As the types of control strategies used and the constraints encountered shift and change, social ordering changes. Usually these changes are slow and difficult to detect, but at times, as after violent revolutions, they become obvious.

The structure and content of the control strategies and the structure and intensity of the constraints also change over time. For example, cultural agreements may change and thereby change the content of cultural control strategies. At one point in a society's history procedural strategies may be used in its political institution that allow laws to be created by one person—for example, in an absolute monarchy. Subsequent social changes may cause changes in control strategies so that laws are enacted democratically. The instruments of force available to those who use violent coercive strategies also change. There is a difference, for example, in an international order in which only clubs are available and one in which atomic weapons are available for use.

To understand the processes of social ordering, the changing nature and the differential use of each of the control strategies must be considered. At one period of time the use of cultural strategies may predominate, whereas at another time the use of procedural or coercive strategies will predominate. As the structuring components change, social ordering changes. This process is continuous over time.

To elaborate the complex processes of social change, we will (1) review some of the constraints discussed earlier and show how these and others produce changes in social ordering; (2) show how changes in control strategies and their differential use change the social order; (3) discuss social change and individual meaning; and (4) develop the relationship between social change and social movements and collective behavior.

CONSTRAINTS AND CHANGE

In Chapters 5 and 6 we showed how the growth of population was facilitated by better agricultural methods, medical technology, and industrialization. In turn, these new constraints moved modern societies toward increased urbanization, a greater division of labor, and mass society. Two ideal types, the folk community and the urban society, were developed to show the changes produced by the new constraints. These constraints changed the order of control relationships within modern societies, social groups, and social institutions from a heavy reliance on the use of cultural strategies toward a greater use of procedural, manipulative, and exchange strategies. In effect, the social order was thereby changed producing what we called the Great Transformation from premodern to modern social forms.

Similarly, poverty and the need for employment place constraints on people to migrate to urban areas. Movements of population cause changes to occur in the places people leave as well as in the places they enter. If too many people leave a place, the potential development of that place may be restricted. When people enter a new place, they may be reduced to minority group status or reduce the price of labor. Ecological and time constraints cause people to locate in specific places, producing a high density of population that causes additional changes in the social ordering. The invasion of an area within the city by a different group or by industry or business may, at times, lead to conflict and a change in control relationships.

In contemporary societies, the constraints caused by pollution and the scarcity of natural resources have already produced changes in social ordering and we can expect these constraints to produce even more changes. As examples: (1) the increase in pollution placed constraints on all levels of government to pass laws for pollution control; (2) the shortage of wheat and the poor 1972 harvest in the USSR were among the constraints influencing the leaders of the USSR to meet with President Nixon in 1973 to work out trade agreements and an international detente; (3) the shortage of oil in this country in the winters of 1972–1973 and 1973–1974 placed a constraint on the United States government to drop its restrictions on oil imports and to allocate fuels. The scarcity of natural resources in various parts of the world will continue to place increasing constraints on the ordering of international relations and produce shifts in the economic orders within nations and among international coalitions.

Increased automation will produce constraints that will affect the order of control relationships in the work place and, in turn, as workers work fewer hours, affect the order of control relationships in the family and in other sectors of the society. These examples illustrate how the presence of one or more constraints act on one area of society to produce changes that in turn will have ramifications throughout the total society and in the patterns of social relationships. A seemingly innocuous or isolated constraint can by this ramifying process of interacting changes produce major alterations in social ordering.

Invention

Invention is the creation of new ideas or things. Although our tendency is to think of inventions as technical developments, such as a laser beam or an integrated electronic circuit, the concepts and theories (the ideas) in physics and chemistry that produced these technical developments as a by-product are also inventions (based at times, on discoveries), as are the social forms within which such ideas develop and are exploited. The wheel surely was a major technical invention that profoundly affected human societies. An equally important social invention was the idea of the corporation as a legal entity endowed with property rights, continuity in ownership, and limited legal liability.

Technological as well as social invention can produce influential constraints on people to change their behaviors and thus alter the social order. In their classic study of a community in Indiana, the Lynds[1] showed how the introduction of the automobile broke up old patterns of interaction in neighborhoods as people accepted the new alternative of driving into the country rather than talking with their neighbors. The story of the automobile and its effects on visiting, working patterns, travel, the building of shopping centers, and the total economy would take thousands of pages to tell, so profound and pervasive has been its influence on modern societies.

Any new invention or idea that is accepted can be expected to constrain a group or society toward change in living patterns. Many changes in the social order of the family are attributable either directly or indirectly to technological inventions.

As the technological base of a society grows the rate of invention increases. Invention is a process of combining elements that are already known. As the number of these elements increases because of the larger technological base, more inventions become possible. The Industrial Revolution shows how rapidly a technological base can grow and how this growth can produce changes in many areas of social life, summed up in the Great Transformation from the folk community to the urban society.

Culture Lag

William Ogburn coined the term *cultural lag* to refer to his belief that the technological sphere changes much more rapidly than does the social sphere of values, ideologies, and social organization. This lag constrains the social sphere to adapt to changes in the technological sphere.[2] Ogburn's idea has been criticized because of the difficulty of measuring progress in values and other social forms. Despite these limitations the notion of "cultural lag" is suggestive. We have invented highly destructive weapons, but our social ability to control their use lags behind their destructive capabilities. The use of modern technology and its products pollutes the air we breathe, contaminates our water, and destroys our environment. Yet, the control relation-

---

Are We Americans?[a]

Our solid American citizen awakens in a bed built on a pattern which originated in the near East but which was modified in Northern Europe before it was transmitted to America. He throws back covers made from cotton, domesticated in India, or linen, domesticated in the Near East, or wool from sheep, also domesticated in the Near East, or silk, the use of which was discovered in China. All of these materials have been spun and woven by processes invented in the Near East. He slips into his moccasins, invented by the Indians of the Eastern woodlands, and goes to the bathroom, whose fixtures are a mixture of European and American inventions, both of recent date. He takes off his pajamas, a garment invented in India, and washes with soap invented by the ancient Gauls. He then shaves, a masochistic rite which seems to have been derived from either Sumer or ancient Egypt.

Returning to the bedroom, he removes his clothes from a chair of southern European type and proceeds to dress. He puts on garments whose form originally derived from the skin clothing of the nomads of the Asiatic steppes, puts on shoes made from skins tanned by a process invented in ancient Egypt and cut to a pattern derived from the classical civilizations of the Mediterranean, and ties around his neck a strip of bright-colored cloth which is a vestigial survival of the shoulder shawls worn by the seventeenth-century Croatians. Before going out for breakfast he glances through the window, made of glass invented in Egypt, and if it is raining puts on overshoes made of rubber discovered by the Central American Indians and takes an umbrella, invented in southeastern Asia. Upon his head he puts a hat made of felt, a material invented in the Asiatic steppes.

ships in our society and some of our values have prevented us from adequately dealing with these problems.

Diffusion

Diffusion is another broad category of constraint that produces social change. It is the process by which a way of life, a tool, or any other aspect of culture such as beliefs, values, and fashions, is transferred from one society to another or from person to person or group to group in the same society. Typically no single society or group is completely responsible for its own construction. It has borrowed much from others. In the modern world new inventions, ways of doing, and beliefs spread rapidly. Much of our technology and way of life is the result of diffusion. The insert "Are We Americans?" describes how the process of diffusion has affected our way of life.

Diffusion, however, is a selective process. Not every invention of one society will be borrowed by another, nor will an invention within a society necessarily spread throughout that society. Americans did not

On his way to breakfast he stops to buy a paper, paying for it with coins, an ancient Lydian invention. At the restaurant a whole new series of borrowed elements confronts him. His plate is made of a form of pottery invented in China. His knife is of steel, an alloy first made in southern India, his fork a medieval Italian invention, and his spoon a derivative of a Roman original. He begins breakfast with an orange, from the eastern Mediterranean, a canteloupe from Persia, or perhaps a piece of African watermelon. With this he has coffee, an Abyssinian plant, with cream and sugar. Both the domestication of cows and the idea of milking them originated in the Near East, while sugar was first made in India. After his fruit and first coffee he goes on to waffles, cakes made by a Scandinavian technique from wheat domesticated in Asia Minor. Over these he pours maple syrup, invented by the Indians of the Eastern woodlands. As a side dish he may have the egg of a species of bird domesticated in Indo-China, or thin strips of the flesh of an animal domesticated in Eastern Asia which have been salted and smoked by a process developed in Northern Europe.

When our friend has finished eating he settles back to smoke, an American Indian habit, consuming a plant domesticated in Brazil in either a pipe, derived from the Indians of Virginia, or a cigarette, derived from Mexico. If he is hardy enough he may even attempt a cigar, transmitted to us from the Antilles by way of Spain. While smoking he reads the news of the day, imprinted in characters invented by the ancient Semites upon a material invented in China by a process invented in Germany. As he absorbs the accounts of foreign troubles he will, if he is a good conservative citizen, thank a Hebrew deity in an Indo-European language that he is 100 per cent American.

[a]Ralph Linton, *The Study of Man: An Introduction* (New York: Appleton, 1936), pp. 326–327. Used by permission. Copyright, 1936 by D. Appleton-Century Co. Inc.

borrow monarchy from England nor do we borrow communism from the Soviet Union. The Amish are not willing to borrow many technological advances from the larger society. Many people refuse to smoke marijuana. In general, people will tend not to accept an invention or to borrow an item from another group or society if it violates their basic system of values or is seen as destructive of their way of life unless they are forced to do so. However, people may at times accept something that is new without being aware of its potential consequences, including the possible destruction of their way of life or values. Any type of change may result in unanticipated consequences.[3]

CONTROL STRATEGIES AND CHANGE

Constraints of various kinds produce changes in control relationships. Changes in specific control strategies and in the differential use of control strategies change social ordering. For example, the increased use of manipulative strategies made possible by the mass media of radio, television, magazine, and newspapers makes it possible for one segment of the population, that can afford to buy time or space in these media, to exert a potentially controlling influence on the lives of many people. The control of the mass media is, therefore, of critical importance in large societies because it permits the widespread use of manipulative strategies that break down the effective use of older cultural agreements. Fidel Castro, for example, made effective use of television after the Cuban revolution. Dictators use the mass media to control the lives and minds of people as they attempt to change the structuring of social order. In our society the mass media are used by corporations to attempt to manipulate the buying patterns of people and by political candidates in an attempt to win votes or, if in political office, to sell their programs and themselves to the public. Only people and groups with money or power have access to these media. Every voice does not have an equal chance of being heard. Thus, the direction of change is affected by some more than others.

The increased use of procedural strategies by organizations within the more formalized institutions also makes it possible to reduce the degree or control by the use of cultural strategies. The procedural strategies used by corporations and businesses affect family life as well as education, religion, and other areas of living. The procedural strategies of governments are increasingly important in changing the social order in democratic as well as in totalitarian states.

Arthur Vidich and Joseph Bensman, in *Small Town in Mass Society,* show how the procedural strategies used by experts who entered a community from the "outside," produced significant changes in the daily habits and lives of people in a small rural town.[4] Teachers and ministers "professionalized" in outside universities or seminaries brought new values into the community. Agricultural agents trained in "rational" methods of farming introduced changes in farming techniques. These, in turn, produced changes in family life-styles and changed the living patterns in the community. Even the small, relatively isolated town cannot escape changes produced by the increased use of procedural strategies.

All over the world, the procedural strategies used by technological and social experts are producing changes at a rapid rate by breaking down old cultural agreements that formerly were very important in structuring social order. This process of change will continue as underdeveloped societies expend their technological base as the tendency toward a mass society spreads in developed societies.

CHANGE AND INDIVIDUAL MEANING

Any basis for individual meaning must be validated within the framework of some social context. For some persons individual meaning may come from following institutional practices. The basis for individual meaning for many, however, is found within cultural agreements, which provide the necessary social validation. Cultural agreements may also validate some institutional practices. Furthermore, following procedural rules can also provide meaning if these have been in existence for a long period of time. In sum, for most people, *any* existing order of control relationships may provide a basis for individual meaning if that order has existed for a reasonable period of time and if accepting one's place within it "makes sense" to the individual. Meaning is possible when people can make sense of their social worlds in relationship to their own personal lives.

Under conditions of rapid social change, either in the content of control strategies or their differential usage, the world may be rendered meaningless for many individuals. For example, when experts come into a situation and tell the old-timers that they are doing everything all wrong and proceed to change things the meaning system of the old-timers may be shattered. When there is no way to depend on what tomorrow will bring, life may lose meaning.

Meaning springs from values or what persons place value on. This may be contained in a cultural agreement, a procedure, or existing control relationships. When these values or things that are valued are shattered, life is rendered meaningless. C. Wright Mills put this succinctly when he wrote:

> When people cherish some set of values and do not feel a threat to them, they experience *well-being*. When they cherish values but *do* feel them to be threatened, they experience a crisis—either as a personal trouble or as a

public issue. And if all their values seem involved, they feel the total threat of panic.

But suppose people are neither aware of any cherished values nor experience any threat? That is the experience of indifference, which, if it seems to involve all their values, becomes apathy. Suppose, finally, they are unaware of any cherished values, but still are very much aware of a threat? That is the experience of *uneasiness*, of anxiety, which, if it is total enough, becomes a deadly unspecified malaise.[5]

In Mills's terms rapid social change may produce individual feeling states and behavior patterns ranging from panic through indifference and apathy to uneasiness, anxiety, and malaise.

People respond in a variety of ways to this loss of individual meaning and the accompanying emotional states. For the balance of this chapter we will examine some of these varied responses, which we group under the broad rubrics of social movements, in which people get organized to produce or resist changes, and collective behavior, which includes such diverse strategies as mobs, riots, and panics.

SOCIAL MOVEMENTS

Social movements are organized attempts by a group of people to produce or prevent change in the existing control relationships in a community or society. The many types of social movements range from relatively minor and uninfluential religious movements, such as the Jesus People, to political and social movements aimed at totally changing the existing political order and radically altering the control relationships in a society. There are also social movements that attempt to prevent threatened changes. The Ku Klux Klan and the John Birch Society are examples of this type.

Types of Social Movements

Drawing from the work of several scholars, Bruce Ryan has developed a useful classification of four different types of social movements.[6] Each will be discussed briefly.

Expressive Movements

Expressive movements are primarily concerned with gratifying the needs of individuals rather than with changing the existing order of control relationships in a society. People who join these movements cannot find gratification for their needs within the existing order but do not see themselves as having the power to change that order.

Therefore, they escape into the movement in an attempt to find meaning and to gratify their needs. The best examples of expressive movements are the religious sect groups whose major goal is preparing individuals for eternal salvation. Ryan points out that even though these movements usually do not intend to change the existing order of control relationships, they may produce such changes—if for example they contribute to a religious revival that sweeps through the society.[7]

Revitalistic Movements

Revitalistic movements have as their major goal to reassert traditions, "creating group solidarities and creating or reaffirming unfulfilled group destinies."[8] These movements usually encompass only relatively small groups in large, complex societies. Examples are the Black Muslim movement and the Pentecostal Church in Christianity. The John Birch Society and the Ku Klux Klan are also classified under this type.[9]

Reform Movements

Reform movements seek to change the existing order of control relationships without destroying the over-all political structure. People who join these movements typically want reforms that will allow them more control over their own lives or some other type of gain that they feel they deserve. They feel cheated by the reward system of the society (and many times are) and form movements to gain these rewards. Examples here are the Civil Rights movement and the Women's Liberation movement.

Revolutionary Movements

Revolutionary movements have as their goal the complete reorganization of the existing control relationships in one or more of the institutions in a society. To accomplish this in modern societies requires access to political power, usually through the use of violent coercive strategies. Modern examples include the Russian, Chinese, and Cuban revolutions. Once people in revolutionary movements gain access to the political power structure, they may move to change the control relationships in other institutions if they have enough support to do so. Typically, revolutions do not produce as much change as their leaders would like because many people resist change in the existing structure, especially if they have much to lose from the changes. Once revolutions have occurred, counterrevolutions are always possible. Terror strategies and purges usually follow a revolution in an attempt to prevent this possibility.

The Internal Development of Social Movements

Social movements have a history. Many emerge and disappear rapidly. Others persist for many years, sometimes changing their original purposes. C. Wendell King divides the internal development of social movements into three phases: incipient, organizational, and stable.[10] Each will be discussed briefly to provide an understanding of *how* social movements come into existence and develop.

Incipient Phase

The incipient phase of a social movement begins with a group of people who are discontented by some aspect of the existing control relationships or by a threat to change them. There may be many people who are discontented about the same issue or problem, but in the incipient phase they are not organized into a cohesive group. Typically a leader brings a small group of people together to discuss the possibility of achieving the desired change or preventing an undesired change. King points out that:

> During the first phase, goals are likely to be general and regarded by at least some members as immediately attainable; other ideological elements remain nebulous and tactics crude or unformulated. Loyalty is usually intense and group cohesion strong, reinforced by personal contacts between founder and disciples and by the emotional momentum generated through participation in a new undertaking.[11]

The first phase is relatively unorganized, with the people involved held together more by emotional ties and commitment than by a carefully planned organization.

These incipient groups may meet secretly if the proposed movement is likely to encounter violent public reaction. The secrecy heightens the emotional attachment and tension, as Simmel pointed out in his classic essay on the secret society:

> The secret gives one a position of exception; it operates as a purely socially determined attraction. It is basically independent of the content it guards but, of course, is increasingly effective in the measure in which the exclusive possession is vast and significant.[12]

Many people who join social movements perceive them as possessing vast significance. If the movement is kept secret in its incipient phase, a dimension of real attraction is added.

In a large, complex society there are literally hundreds of small groups that form from time to time to discuss the possibility of doing something to change some aspect of the control relationships or to keep changes from occurring. Sometimes these groups form spontaneously. For example, a group of like-minded people may get together for an evening of fun during which someone suggests that something should be done. Hours may be spent discussing possibilities. That may be the end of it, or additional meetings may be held and the discussion continued.

Relatively few "movements" get past the incipient stage and thus never emerge as full-fledged social movements. Interest may be lost by the organizers, enough followers may not be recruited, or the incipient group is seen as such a threat to the existing order of control relationships that it is put to death by those in power before it has a chance to develop.

The incipient phase may also begin in a local disorder, such as a riot or mob action. A leader may have initiated this disorder or may emerge from it. When the disorder occurs police are likely to disperse the people participating. This may be the end of it. Or, the leader may regroup those who remain interested in doing something about the issue that precipitated the disorder and so proceed into the organizational phase.

The Organizational Phase

The organizational phase tends to evolve gradually out of the incipient phase. New members are added, the group begins to develop an internal structure, and specific duties are assigned to different people. A formal organization emerges from the earlier informal group.

Discussing the adding of new members, William Bruce Cameron points out that:

> At least two processes operate in the selection of members. First, people of different ages and in different walks of life have different opportunities and encounter different problems; they develop different abilities and techniques; they evolve different attitudes. Consequently, they will appraise the social scene differently and assign different values to the purposes and promises of a social movement. Thus, a social movement which appeals strongly to young rural males may seem insignificant or even abhorrent to old urban females.
>
> Secondly, a social movement appeals to a particular category of people not only because of their similar purposes, but also because its membership already includes their kind of people.[13]

In the assignment of duties in the organizational phase, petty jealousies and dissatisfactions may weaken the movement and eventually cause it to go out of existence. Splinter groups may break off with ideas of their own about what should be done. This is more likely to happen if there are several strong potential leaders in the group, each of whom wants a larger piece of the action than a well-organized movement will permit.

If the group stays together, the organization grows and a division of labor develops. Cell groups in different parts of the society may be organized that grow and develop so that a societywide organization can be put together. An ideology is developed and the general strategies to be used are set down. As King points out:

> Rapid growth at this stage carries inherent dangers as new members bring into the movement new points of view; the reservoir of potential func- tionaries swells and competition for status achievement is intensified; local units may seek greater autonomy and local leaders greater recognition; the apostate becomes an increasing possibility and with him a major internal cleavage. Then, too, many who join under impulse, in a flush of en- thusiasm, may easily become disenchanted—especially if immediate satis- factions are not strong or if there is scant evidence of progress toward the attainment of goals.[14]

THE TRUE BELIEVERS

There are many people in nearly every community or society who will join almost any movement, whatever the cause it espouses, be- cause sheer involvement helps to gratify needs of theirs that are not being met. Eric Hoffer called these people true believers.[15] They give themselves to the movement emotionally rather than rationally. Lee Harvey Oswald, the man who killed President John F. Kennedy, was a classic example of such a person. At one time he joined the anti-Castro movement in New Orleans, professing that he hated communism. Later, when the opportunity presented itself, he went to Russia and became a Communist. Evidence indicates that he even liked Kennedy as a person and agreed with his policies. Oswald was a rebel without a cause who appeared willing to accept any cause that came along that might gratify his overwhelming need for the self-esteem and security constantly denied him throughout his life.[16] These true believers, always ready to join any movement, may be dangerous to its success because they are overzealous and want movement goals reached im- mediately so that their psychological needs can be gratified. If they do not receive sufficient gratifications they may betray the movement and join in attempts to suppress it.

SOCIAL MOVEMENTS AND INDIVIDUAL MEANING

For some people joining a social movement adds a dimension of meaning to their lives. People who have been alienated from the larger society or from groups within it find limited meaning within the context of the existing social order. A social movement offers them the possibility of involvement and gives them something for which they can live—and, occasionally, even something for which they can die.

Most social movements begin because some aspect of the existing social order does not make sense to a number of people. Those people who join social movements to protect the existing order feel that all meaning would be lost if the existing social order were to be changed.

Thus, the desire for individual meaning and often the desire for distributive justice are important to understand how social movements develop and why certain people become members.

The Stable Phase

The dynamics of the stable phase of a social movement depend on the type of movement, its ideology, and the type of strategies worked out during the organizational phase. In all three phases, the amount of resistance and the relative power of parties involved in the movement must be considered. We will briefly specify the types of control strategies and organizational arrangements that can be expected for each of the four types of social movements discussed above. All social movements adopt coalitional strategies and use other control strategies as circumstances warrant.

Expressive movements typically use withdrawal strategies, asking only to be left alone. People in this type of social movement set up separate and usually relatively simple organizations outside the arena of existing control relationships and attempt to maintain these over time. Their primary concern is the gratification of individual needs and desires. A highly complex organization would tend to defeat this purpose.

Revitalization movements typically use manipulative strategies such as propaganda but, at times, may use both nonviolent and violent coercive strategies, depending on their goal and the amount of opposition. For example, the Ku Klux Klan used many terror tactics, including lynchings, in an attempt to achieve its goals. Such movements often set up elaborate organizations with a complex system of offices and rigid rules. In addition, these movements often have elaborate systems of ritual to help produce and maintain group solidarity.

People in reform movements also use manipulative strategies, usually propaganda, and may also use coercive strategies such as strikes, boycotts, demonstrations, marches, and acts of civil disobedience. Many of these movements also set up highly organized structures to accomplish their goals during the stable phase. Local chapters may be formed in many communities with regional offices and a national coordinating office. The Women's Liberation movement, for example, already has a fairly elaborate system of organization.

Revolutionary movements take many forms. So-called palace revolutions are relatively simple and involve little organization if the leaders have a sizeable portion of the military on their side. These revolutions usually accomplish little more than a change of names on the office doors of the ruler's palace and are often short-lived. More far-reaching revolutionary movements involve considerable planning and organization, culminating in the use of violent coercive strategies to overthrow the existing regime. Once in power, the new leaders typically use terror strategies, including purges, until the threat of a counterrevolution is extinguished.

Social movements typically die when they are either completely suppressed by those with more power or when they are completely successful in achieving their objectives. However, some people heavily involved with a movement build up a great vested interest in the organization. When the movement's goal is reached, their vested interest in the organization remains. These people may seek other goals to keep the organization alive. This is particularly true of reform and some revitalistic movements. In successful revolutions those who hold power become the new "establishment," embodied in a highly complex organization that continues to exist.

An example of a social movement that maintained its organization after its original goal had been reached was the movement initiated to

---

Case Study of a Social Movement: Students for a Democratic Society (SDS)

SDS was a reform movement that emerged and gained substantial influence on college and university campuses during the 1960s, suffered several divisive splits, and has now splintered into several relatively ineffective, small revolutionary groups. Kirkpatrick Sale has written a lengthy history of these developments, and we will draw on his study in presenting our material.[a]

SDS grew from a long tradition of small socialist youth groups that had existed in American society since the turn of this century. Its immediate predecessor was the Student League for Industrial Democracy (SLID), the youth wing of the reform-minded, trade-union supported socialist League for Industrial Democracy. During the early 1960s a group of activist graduate students and young people gained control of the SLID and eventually split off from the parent organization.

Renamed SDS, the group grew from an organization of a few hundred and a budget of a few thousand dollars in its earliest days to a "national membership of 6,400, a total membership of perhaps thirty thousand, an annual budget of at least $87,000, a formal presence on two hundred and fifty campuses (and influence on many more), eight regional travelers, off-campus projects in six major cities, and an established national office with a dozen or so full-time workers" by its high point in 1967.[b]

Sale attributes the rise and rapid growth of SDS to a number of factors. First and foremost, he identifies a crisis of confidence in existing social institutions and an inability of many young people to find individual mean-

fight infantile paralysis. This organization became highly complex with chapters in major cities and many smaller towns. When Jonas Salk discovered a vaccine to provide immunity against this disease, the organization was no longer needed for its original purpose. To stay alive, it merely expanded its goal to include other crippling diseases and remains today a strong organization providing a service to the society.

More About Revolutions

Revolutions are social movements and have, therefore, been discussed here along with other types of social movements. However, revolutions also differ from other social movements because they are "violent civil disturbances that cause displacement of one ruling

ing in them and in their supporting values that culminated during the early 1960s:

> families were no longer the places where the young learned their values or the old sought their solace; marriages collapsed at a greater and greater rate, or were artificially sustained after the life had left them; sexuality was seen, and used, as a commodity; organized religion had lost its purpose and many of its followers; alcohol was accepted as the necessary basis for much social and economic converse and many familial arrangements, to which drugs ran a close second and were to increase; crime was abnormally high and on the verge of a threefold jump; cities were choked with an excess population they could not cope with, becoming behavioral sinks in which neither air nor relationships could be cleansed. The *economic* structure that had begun to crack in the thirties and had since been sustained by artificial means (government intervention, a permanent military economy, aerospace boondoggles, colonial investment, overseas monopolies, racial and sexual subjugation, waste, pollution, advertising, planned obsolescence, and inefficiency) began to show new signs of deterioration: high and unstoppable unemployment (especially among the young and the blacks), permanent poverty for a third of the nation, runaway inflation, recurrent dollar crises leading to devaluation, and minority control of much of the economy through vast new conglomerates, monopolies, and investment funds. The *political* life of the nation as it sank in its postwar doldrums was increasingly seen to be characterized by corruption, inefficiency, giant federal bureaucracies, identically rigidified parties, favors for the rich, apathy among the voters, power among the special interests and lobbies, and general unresponsiveness and remoteness—ultimately moving toward a profound swapping process in which the populace passively agreed to sacrifice certain individual rights and freedoms (privacy, speech, political belief, social mobility) for government promises of personal security, material comfort, and national quietude. And the *international* position of the nation, tied to a cold war ideology, involved an acknowledged practice of foreign intervention (covertly through a massive secret "intelligence"

group by another that has a broader popular basis for support."[17]

Karl Marx predicted that revolutions would occur in capitalist societies when the proletariat was inevitably reduced to a position of absolute degradation and despair. James C. Davies reminds us, however, that Marx also predicted that revolutions might occur after the welfare of the proletariat had improved:

> A noticeable increase in wages presupposes a rapid growth of productive capital. The rapid growth of productive capital brings about an equally rapid growth of wealth, luxury, social wants, social enjoyments. Thus, although the enjoyments of the workers have risen, the social satisfaction that they give has fallen in comparison with the increased enjoyments of the capitalist, which are inaccessible to the worker, in comparison with the

system assuring regimes bought, coerced, or overthrown to our liking, overtly through economic penetration and military occupation) and the production of a vast system of planet-destroying armaments, rattled from crisis to crisis with an effect especially debilitating for the young. Taken together, all of this evidence argued persuasively that the nation's systems were severely strained and distended—and this was felt by many people, but particularly the young, as the decade opened.[c]

If we accept Sale's statement about the crisis of confidence and meaning in traditional American institutions we can understand how young people, who are acutely sensitive to the gap between promise and performance, became susceptible to an organization that promised to secure needed reforms.

Sale notes that demographic factors also increased the likelihood of success for SDS. Not only were there more people below the age of twenty-five than ever before in 1960, both in absolute numbers and in proportion to other age groups in the population, but they were better educated than any preceding group of youth, and more conscious of themselves as a group.[d] Sale also suggests that "adolescents of college age in the sixties were inclined to protest not just out of the blue, but rather because they were likely to be the products of a psychological upbringing predisposing them to distrust and resist authority and to emphasize moral values, especially those lacking in the parental generation."[e]

Protest movements by blacks and other minorities and against the war in Vietnam were also occurring during the 1960s, and the student activists incorporated these causes as part of their own reformist goals. SDS members were active in campus protests against the Vietnam war, against racism, and against many of the traditional authoritarian practices of university and college administrations. The SDS leaders drew up policy statements critical of American economic, political, and educational institutions and demanded basic reforms that involved restructuring the control strategies these institutions embodied.

state of development of society in general. Our desires and pleasures spring from society; we measure them, therefore, by society and not by the objects which serve for their satisfaction. Because they are of a social nature, they are of a relative nature.[18]

In his discussion of the French Revolution, Alexis de Tocqueville comes to the same conclusion as Marx. Reviewing the economic and social decline in France during the seventeenth century, followed by rapid growth in the eighteenth century, de Tocqueville says:

> So it would appear that the French found their condition the more unsupportable in proportion to its improvement. . . . Revolutions are not always brought about by a gradual decline from bad to worse. Nations that have

---

Other sectarian groups, such as the small revolutionary Progressive Labor Party, envied SDS's success on the campus, and sought to infiltrate it and seize organizational power, a process that culminated in a fatal split into sectarian factions by the end of the 1960s. Powerful groups in the society also organized to oppose SDS and to fight against its programs and policies. Newspapers and congressmen, the traditional "viewers with alarm" of attempts to change the established order with its prerogatives for the powerful, condemned SDS and all its works. As SDS became more militant and shifted from reformist goals and strategies to revolutionary goals and strategies under the stress of repeated failures to achieve reformist goals and infiltration by revolutionary groups, outside condemnation became increasingly shrill. Senator John McClellan of the Senate Subcommittee on Investigations, for example, lumped SDS with revolutionary organizations that "advocate the use of violence and disruption as a means of attaining their goals and that . . . are dedicated to callous and cynical exploitation of issues and grievances in urban areas and on campuses. . . ."[f]
Internal ideological disputes sundered SDS. Membership and funds dropped drastically as small groups within the organization turned to violence, including bombing and burning campus buildings and physical assaults on those with whom they disagreed. Some SDS factions, such as the Weathermen, went underground and proclaimed themselves professional revolutionaries. As severe repressive control strategies were undertaken by powerful individuals and groups, SDS lost its former influence and it has apparently disappeared as a stable, broad-based social movement.

[a]Kirkpatrick Sale, *SDS* (New York: Random, 1973).
[b]Ibid., p. 351.
[c]Ibid., pp. 18–19.
[d]Ibid., p. 21.
[e]Ibid.
[f]Ibid., p. 546.

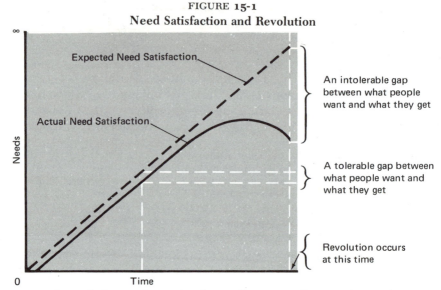

FIGURE 15-1
Need Satisfaction and Revolution

SOURCE: James C. Davies, "Toward a Theory of Revolution," *ASR*, Vol. 27 (Feb. 1962), p. 6. Used by permission.

endured patiently and almost unconsciously the most overwhelming oppression often burst into rebellion against the yoke the moment it begins to grow lighter. The regime which is destroyed by a revolution is almost always an improvement on its immediate predecessor. . . . Evils which are patiently endured when they seem inevitable become intolerable when once the idea of escape from them is suggested.[19]

Drawing on Marx and de Tocqueville, Davies argues that "Revolutions are most likely to occur when a prolonged period of economic and social development is followed by a short period of sharp reversal."[20] This short period of sharp reversal produces an intolerable gap between what people expect and what they get, illustrated in Figure 15-1. As long as *actual* need satisfaction is close to *expected* need satisfaction, revolution will not occur, even though people may be severely deprived. When the gap between *actual* need satisfaction and *expected* need satisfaction widens intolerably, revolution is likely to occur.

We can, therefore, expect that more revolutions will occur in developing nations than in highly developed nations with a large middle class, such as in the United States. The majority of American people tend to be satisfied basically, mostly because they fear change might reduce rather than enhance their level of living. In some nations in South America and in Africa, however, revolutions can be expected until a large middle class develops through industrialization. In the

Union of South Africa and in Southern Rhodesia, class is subordinate to race as whites attempt to keep all blacks powerless. Blacks can be expected to revolt against their oppressors unless they are granted full citizenship, equal power, and the opportunity for mobility.

People who are extremely impoverished think little about political activity. They are more concerned with gratifying their immediate needs for food, warmth, and shelter. That is, their focus is on immediate survival. When people see the opportunity for more, however, but are denied it, they are likely to engage in revolutionary activity.

COLLECTIVE BEHAVIOR

Kurt and Gladys Lang define collective behavior as "those patterns of social action that are spontaneous and unstructured, inasmuch as they are not organized and are not reducible to social structure."[21] They see collective behavior as a "transitory social phenomenon."[22] Even though collective behavior is spontaneous, unstructured, and transitory it does affect, directly or indirectly, the existing order of control relationships in a society. People not engaged in collective behavior typically respond to collective behavior by others. Neil J. Smelser, views "collective behavior as purposive behavior, in which people are trying to reconstitute their social environments."[23]

Collective behavior, then, includes a variety of control strategies that are used when the participants believe that other alternatives have been exhausted or are not immediately available. When people with little power use certain types of collective behavior control strategies, they are seen by others as being out of control. From the viewpoint of those with great power, they *are* out of control, as defined by the existing order of control relationships in the society.

The concept of collective behavior has been used to cover a variety of behaviors. Robert R. Evans points out that

> The area thus encompassed is very broad; it would take an uncomfortably fat book to carry uncut papers covering all its facets. Its focus has been on riot, revolution, insurrection, rebellion, disorder, protest, strike, disaster, panic flight, hysteria, fads, crazes, fashion, rumor, contagion, communication; mob, crowd, audience, public, mass; social, political, religious patterns of destruction, and other movements or cults; of preconditions, of motivations, of effects; characteristics of leaders, of followers; means of control and causes of loss of control.[24]

Social movements have already been discussed in this book. We will now discuss panics, crazes, mobs, and riots. These are among the most important and widely studied forms of collective behavior.

Panics

Smelser defines panic as "a *collective flight based on a hysterical belief*. Having accepted a belief about some generalized threat, people flee from established patterns of social intercourse in order to preserve life, property, or power from threat."[25] Panic is based on fear, which, under certain conditions, causes flight. Smelser sees panic as a possible response when fearful people *believe* there is a way out of a threatening situation or condition that is limited and possibly closing. If people *know* there is a way out that will definitely remain available, or if they know there is absolutely no way out, panic is not likely to occur. E. L. Quarantelli sums this up:

> The important aspect is the belief or feeling of possible entrapment. This is reiterated again and again in the remarks of panic participants. It is not that affected individuals believe or feel they are definitely trapped. In such instances panic does not follow.... The flight of panic arises only when being trapped is sensed or thought of as a possibility rather than an actuality.[26]

Panics have occurred under many conditions: fires in crowded theaters, or nightclubs; natural catastrophes; enemy troops marching on a town in wartime; shortages of food, and epidemics. Under conditions of threat and limited and narrowing alternatives people may panic in an attempt to save their lives, their property, their power, or whatever else they value.

Crazes (Fads and Fashions)

Whereas panics involve flight from a *threatening* situation or event, *crazes* are produced by the *attraction* of an object or event. Smelser defines "the craze as mobilization for action based upon a positive wish-fulfillment belief."[27]

Crazes may occur in almost any area of social life, especially in modern societies with large numbers of people and mass communications. The recurrent fads and fashions in music, dance, and dress that sweep the country from time to time are crazes. Many people accept these fads and fashions in an attempt to bolster their self-identity or for the gratification of various needs and desires.

Crazes and fads appear in all sectors of our society. The California and Alaskan gold rushes were crazes, as are the common get-rich-quick schemes involving land speculation and certain Wall Street stocks. Even the "rational" world of economics is not free of crazes. The pass-fail system of grading nearly reached craze proportions in the late 1960s as many colleges and universities rushed to incorporate this method of grading to avoid appearing backward. Other educational "reforms" at times have swept the country equally rapidly. The craze of religious revivalism has affected this nation many times in its history.

Indeed, most of us have, at one time or another, participated in some type of craze behavior. Crazes tend to be relatively short-lived as one replaces another. However, some may have a lasting effect by changing the control relationships in a society as people use them to gain something or to gratify basic needs.

Mobs

Mobs typically develop from what Park and Burgess have called the "milling crowd."[28] "Out of this milling process a collective impulse is formed which dominates all members of the crowd."[29] When this collective impulse emerges, the crowd becomes a mob. Many people become "lost" in the mob and participate in activities that they would not participate in alone. The dense crowd and the mob give the individual a sense of security and belonging and a high degree of anonymity; he feels hidden from others. Being members of a mob tends to remove people from the everyday control relationships. They feel free to do what in their minds at that time must be done.

Both those with little power and those with more power can be expected to engage in mob behavior under conditions of real or perceived threat to their aspirations. White racists in the South engaged in mob actions by lynching blacks whom they saw as a threat to their positions. Blacks, in more recent years, have formed mobs against whites whom they see as oppressing them and denying their aspirations for higher positions. People are likely to use violent coercive strategies when their positions are threatened or when they are denied what they feel is rightfully theirs.

Riots

Riots also may emerge from milling crowds. Riots differ from mobs because behavior in riots tends to be random and more individualized. There is no single object or person on which people using riotous strategies focus. Rather, people in riots tend to destroy everything in their path, often engaging in looting and killing.

Riots emerge in situations in which people have reached a high point of frustration. Unfulfilled promises to improve conditions may have been repeatedly made by those with power. People may be hungry when food is known to be available. People may be embittered over a political event or decision. People who feel powerless to do anything about unjust conditions may use riots because no other alternatives seem to be available. Procedural strategies are too slow and the rules and laws often are stacked against those who want to produce rapid changes.

Many riots occurred in America during the 1960s and early 1970s, mostly in black ghettos and on college and university campuses. Black people living in inner-city ghettos suffered under various kinds of frustration. Much had been promised by a variety of federal, state, and local programs but little had been delivered. Many black people had tried nonviolently for years to do something about the deprived conditions under which they lived, but few changes had occurred. In the late 1960s, some people turned to what seemed the only control strategy available: rioting. Property in several American cities worth millions of dollars was destroyed and hundreds of people were killed or wounded as black people rioted from a sense of frustration and powerlessness. On university campuses, students opposing the Vietnam war and other practices they defined as social evils also felt a sense of powerlessness and frustration. Many nonviolent strategies such as sit-ins and demonstrations seemed to have little effect on those in power. Riots ensued on many campuses.

Sometimes military or police units provoke riots. The agents of those in power want to be sure that the existing control relationships are not changed. Thus, they resort to inciting riots to maintain the existing order. People who are peacefully gathered to protest something may be perceived by the powerful as a threat to the existing social order. To break up this peaceful protest, military or police units are brought in, provoke a riot, and thus bring things under *their* control. The agents of the state maintain a monopoly on the legal use of tear gas, guns, and other instruments of coercion, and usually gain the ascendancy in such encounters.

Riots are sporadic and short-lived. People with power will not permit continuous rioting by the powerless. Riots and the threat of riots may produce limited change in control relationships. The riots in the ghettos brought some limited relief and riots on campuses *may* have helped to bring pressure to stop the Vietnam war. There may be reciprocal adjustments and accommodations made by the powerful under conditions of riot and the threat of riot by the powerless.

We thus see how both social movements (the organized purposive behavior of people to effect or prevent change) and the forms of collective behavior (which include such diverse phenomena as panics, crazes, mobs, and riots) can alter the control relationships in a society.

Collective behavior and social movements may also interact to provide changes. Riots, for example, may be the prelude and lay the groundwork for revolution. The chaos and disruption produced by recurrent rioting may enable tightly organized revolutionary social movements to seize the centers of political power and thus begin a process of change that will affect every social institution.

Still a third broad factor is important in producing social change: forms of communication.

COMMUNICATION AND SOCIAL CHANGE

Propaganda and rumor were identified in Chapter 2 as manipulative control strategies that are used to influence the attitudes and behavior of persons and groups. These manipulative strategies often are used most effectively in efforts to produce or prevent various forms of social change.

Propaganda

The understanding of propaganda is especially important in the study of social movements. People engaged in social movements attempt to influence others to join their cause through the use of propaganda. Those opposed to the movement may also use propaganda in an attempt to keep the movement from being successful. Propaganda is used in an attempt to influence public opinion either for or against various changes.

There are many types of propaganda. Alfred McClung Lee and Elizabeth Briant Lee[30] have delineated the following commonly used types. (1) *Name calling*: this places a bad label on an idea or issue; (2) *glittering generalities*: this strategy associates an idea or activity with something that is virtuous; (3) *transfer*: this strategy attempts to attach or transfer the authority or prestige of something accepted to something that the propagandist wants the public to accept; (4) *testimonial*: this strategy has a respected person say that what the propagandist is trying to sell is good. Hated persons may also be used to produce the desired results; (5) *card stacking*: this strategy selects certain favorable or unfavorable facts or even falsehoods for presentation to the public while it withholds other information that might negatively affect the issue or idea the propagandist is trying to sell; (6) *band wagon*: this strategy is an attempt to give the idea to the public that everyone is doing what the propagandist desires so that others will want to go along with it.

Rumor

Rumor is especially important in certain types of collective behavior. Under conditions of high instability in control relationships, people are often at a loss to know what to do or in what direction to turn. The use of rumor then becomes especially important. Tamotsu Shibutani sees rumor as a substitute for news.[31] When normal channels of news have been disrupted or are not available because of the rapid movement of events, rumor becomes a substitute. Shibutani calls rumors improvised news.

Rumors, of course, are often false and may even cause panics or riots to occur. For example, if a rumor spreads that a threat is present, people may panic and flee a situation even though in fact, no threat is present. Under conditions of riot, literally hundreds of rumors emerge and spread. Rumors may quell or intensify a riot. In addition, a rumor may cause a crowd to form and develop into a mob whose destructive actions are based on it.

This substitute news is not seen by Shibutani as pathological.[32] People must attempt to use some type of control to come to terms with what is true or what might be true. When the more normal channels of news are unavailable or defined as unbelievable, people must use some method of defining a situation to come to grips with it. Rumor provides one possibility, even though a specific rumor may be false.

Many cities and university campuses set up rumor control centers in the late 1960s in an attempt to sort true from false rumors and to communicate these findings to people. The use of these was an attempt to normalize the communication of news.

Summary and Conclusion: Social Change and Control Strategies As Continuous Interacting Social Processes

Social change is a complex area of study. Change is constantly occurring even though, at times, its rate may be slow. It is, therefore, often difficult if not impossible to state specifically *when* change can be said to *have occurred*. It is probably better to think in terms of *process,* because the word change has a connotation that something *has* happened rather than that something *is* happening. (We have used the word *change,* rather than *process,* because in contemporary sociology change is a specific area of study and, thus, to use process might create unnecessary confusion for the student who takes additional courses in sociology.)

The use of language often places obstacles in the path of understanding. In sociology, this is apparent in the study of how social ordering *occurs*. In Chapter 1 we discussed the *process* of social ordering, indicating that it was continuous over time. Yet, in this chapter and in others we talked about an *existing* order of control relationships, indicating a *static* formation. This semantic confusion is present in contemporary sociology and is difficult to correct within the framework of an introductory text.

It is important to recognize that like social change, social ordering is a continuous process. In this chapter, we have discussed a variety of events "as if" they had a *definite* beginning and a *definite* ending, although we know they do not. The use of language is restrictive. Revolution, for example, only *appears* on the surface to have a *definite* beginning and a *definite* ending. Before the first shot is fired in a revolution there is always some dissatisfaction among many people in a society that affects social ordering. *After* the last shot is fired and the revolution is "over," feelings and actions continue that affect the process of social ordering. The use of violent coercive strategies that we called revolution is only a *phase* of a continuous process.

In short, as various people and groups use a variety of control strategies, change is constantly occurring. Because of this, it is better to think in terms of the process of social ordering. The various phenomena we have discussed in this chapter are instances of a continuous process.

In addition to the constraints discussed in earlier chapters, we have examined invention and diffusion as major constraints producing social change. Social movements, including revolutions and the various types of collective behavior, were identified as important control strategies producing change. Constraints and control strategies cannot be separated in the real world as they are for analysis. For example, a person or corporation with great power and a vested interest in the status quo can keep a major invention from being placed on the market.

In Chapter 1, we quoted C. Wright Mills' description of the sociological imagination. It is the task of the sociologist to make it possible for every citizen to achieve this. As Mills points out:

> The first fruit of this imagination—and the first lesson of the social science that embodies it—is the idea that the individual can understand his own experience and gauge his own fate only by locating himself within his period, that he can know his own chances in life only by becoming aware of those of all individuals in his circumstances. In many ways it is a terrible lesson; in many ways a magnificent one. We do not know the limits of man's capacities for supreme effort or willing degradation, for agony or glee, for pleasurable brutality or the sweetness of reason. But in our time we have come to know that the limits of "human nature" are frighteningly broad. We have come to know that every individual lives, from one generation to the next, in some society; that he lives out a biography, and that he lives it out within some historical sequence. By the fact of his living he contributes,

however minutely, to the shaping of this society and to the course of its history, even as he is made by society and by its historical push and shove.[34]

The achieving of the sociological imagination, then, will not only help individuals to *know* their place and *why* they are in it but to *make* their place within a society—a place that will hopefully gratify the basic needs and desires that have been produced in the process of their becoming self-conscious human beings. This place can be known and made only if individuals realize that the process of social ordering is based on the use of a variety of control strategies by themselves and others. Far too many still believe that society simply exists and that there is nothing they can do to change it. To believe this not only reduces the individual's control potential but also reduces the possibility of individual meaning. Meaning is born as individuals make choices based on values and carry these choices into action.

REFERENCES

1. See Lynd, Robert S., and Helen Merrell Lynd. *Middletown in Transition: A Study in Cultural Conflicts.* New York: Harcourt, 1937.
2. See Ogburn, William. *Social Change.* New York: Viking, 1st ed., 1927; new edition, 1950, pp. 200–213.
3. For a discussion of unanticipated consequences of social behavior see Merton, Robert K. *Social Structure and Social Theory.* New York: Free Press, 1957. For a book summarizing and integrating many studies of diffusion, see Rogers, Everett M. *Diffusion of Innovation.* New York: Free Press, 1962.
4. Vidich, Arthur J., and Joseph Bensman. *Small Town in Mass Society: Class, Power and Religion in a Rural Community.* Princeton, N.J.: Princeton University Press, 1958.
5. Mills, C. Wright. *The Sociological Imagination.* New York: Oxford U.P., 1961, p. 11.
6. Ryan, Bryce F. *Social and Cultural Change.* New York: Ronald, 1969, p. 184.
7. Ibid., p. 185.
8. Ibid.
9. For a case study of a revitalistic movement, see Wallace, Anthony F. C. *The Death and Rebirth of the Seneca.* New York: Random, 1969.
10. King, C. Wendell. *Social Movements in the United States.* New York: Random, 1956.
11. Ibid., p. 43.
12. *The Sociology of Georg Simmel.* Trans. and ed. by Kurt H. Wolff. New York: Free Press, 1950, pp. 332–334.
13. Cameron, William Bruce. *Modern Social Movements.* New York: Random, 1966, p. 37.
14. King, op. cit., p. 46.
15. Hoffer, Eric. *The True Believer.* New York: New American Library, 1958.
16. For a case study and interpretation of Oswald's life, see Sites, Paul. *Lee Harvey Oswald and the American Dream.* New York: Pageant Press, 1967.

17. Davies, James C. "Toward a Theory of Revolution." *American Sociological Review*, Vol. 27 (Feb. 1962), 6.
18. Marx, Karl, and Frederick Engels. "Wage Labour and Capital." *Selected Works in Two Volumes*. Moscow: Foreign Language Publishing House, 1955, Vol. 1., p. 94. Quoted in ibid. p. 5.
19. de Tocqueville, Alexis. *The Old Regime and the French Revolution*. Trans. by John Bonner. New York: Harper, 1856, p. 214. Quoted in Davies op. cit, pp. 5–6.
20. Davies, op. cit., p. 6.
21. Lang, Kurt, and Gladys Engel Lang. *Collective Dynamics*. New York: Crowell, 1961, p. 4.
22. Ibid., p. 3.
23. Smelser, Neil J. "Theoretical Issues of Scope and Method." *Sociological Quarterly*, (April 1964), 116.
24. *Readings in Collective Behavior*. Ed. by Robert R. Evans. Chicago: Rand McNally, 1969, p. 1.
25. Smelser, Neil J. *Theory of Collective Behavior*. New York: Free Press, 1963, p. 131.
26. Quarantelli, E. L. "The Nature and Condition of Panic." *American Journal of Sociology*, Vol. 60, (1954–55) 273. Quoted in ibid., p. 136.
27. Ibid., p. 171.
28. Park, Robert E., and Ernest W. Burgess. *Introduction to the Science of Sociology*. Chicago: U. of Chicago, 1921.
29. Ibid., p. 869.
30. Lee, Alfred McClung, and Elizabeth Briant Lee. *The Fine Art of Propaganda*. New York: Harcourt, 1939.
31. Shibutani, Tamotsu. *Improvised News*. Indianapolis, Ind.: Bobbs, 1966.
32. Ibid., p. 62.
33. Mills, C. Wright. *The Sociological Imagination*. New York: Oxford U.P., 1959, pp. 5–6.

INDEX

Wagenschein, Miriam, 330
Wallace, Anthony F. C., 377,
　396, 401, 402
Wallen, Paul, 351, 352
Waller, Willard, 327
Walton, John, 143, 145, 146
Warman, Henry J., 127
Warner, W. Lloyd, 204, 206, 207,
　210, 238, 252, 343
Warren, Roland L., 138, 139,
　145
Washington, Booker T., 251
Wattenberg, Benjamin, 240
Wealth, ownership of, 304–305
Weber, Max, 98, 99, 100, 101,
　108, 185, 186, 187, 188,
　194, 195, 196, 282, 283,
　379, 391, 392, 393

Weil, Robert, 30, 31
Weisskopf, Thomas, 293
Welfare, 276–277, 305
White, H. R., 340
White, Langdon, 127
Whiting, Beatrice, 398, 399
Williams, Robin M., Jr., 240,
　242, 323
Wilson, A. B., 333
Winslow, Robert, 414, 424
Wirth, Louis, 136, 137, 237
Witchcraft, 396–397, 398–399
Withdrawal
　physical, 64
　ritual, 64
Withdrawal strategies, 64, 94,
　109, 251, 266, 363, 369,
　391, 451

Withholding
　information, 57, 58–59
　rewards, 60
　services, 60–61
　use of facilities, 61
Wordsworth, William, 16
Woytinsky, Emma S., 172
Woytinsky, Wladimir, 172
Wright, Charles, 97

Yanowitch, Murray, 31
Yee, Albert, 343
Yinger, J. Milton, 402

Zinkin, Taya, 190